AF705878

Labour Law in Hungary

Labour Law in Hungary

József Hajdú

This book was originally published as a monograph in the International Encyclopaedia of Laws/Labour Law and Industrial Relations.

Founding Editor: Roger Blanpain
General Editor: Frank Hendrickx
Volume Editor: Frank Hendrickx

Wolters Kluwer

Published by:
Kluwer Law International B.V.
PO Box 316
2400 AH Alphen aan den Rijn
The Netherlands
E-mail: lrs-sales@wolterskluwer.com
Website: www.wolterskluwer.com/en/solutions/kluwerlawinternational

Sold and distributed by:
Wolters Kluwer Legal & Regulatory U.S.
920 Links Avenue
Landisville, PA 17538
United States of America
E-mail: customer.service@wolterskluwer.com

DISCLAIMER: The material in this volume is in the nature of general comment only. It is not offered as advice on any particular matter and should not be taken as such. The editor and the contributing authors expressly disclaim all liability to any person with regard to anything done or omitted to be done, and with respect to the consequences of anything done or omitted to be done wholly or partly in reliance upon the whole or any part of the contents of this volume. No reader should act or refrain from acting on the basis of any matter contained in this volume without first obtaining professional advice regarding the particular facts and circumstances at issue. Any and all opinions expressed herein are those of the particular author and are not necessarily those of the editor or publisher of this volume.

ISBN 978-94-035-2328-6

e-Book: ISBN 978-94-035-2338-5
web-PDF: ISBN 978-94-035-2348-4

This title is available on www.kluwerlawonline.com

© 2024 Kluwer Law International BV, The Netherlands

All rights reserved. No part of this publication may be reproduced, stored in a retrieval system, or transmitted in any form or by any means, electronic, mechanical, photocopying, recording, or otherwise, without the prior written permission of the publisher.

Permission to use this content must be obtained from the copyright owner. More information can be found at: www.wolterskluwer.com/en/solutions/legal-regulatory/permissions-reprints-and-licensing

The Author

Professor József Hajdú was born on 17 July 1965; after graduating, he practised law for a short time. In 1990, he was appointed assistant professor of the Department of Labour Law and Social Security at 'József Attila' University, later the Szeged University. In 1998, the Szeged University conferred upon him the title of Doctor of Philosophy (Ph.D.) in Political and Jurisprudential Sciences. In 2004, he committed his habilitation and the Szeged University conferred upon him the habilitation title in Jurisprudential Sciences. He was a member of the Executive Committee of the International Society for Labour Law and Social Security. He is a member of the European Committee of Social Rights of the Council of Europe, in Strasbourg. He is the author of books and articles in the field of Labour Law and Social Security. He was a former Vice-President of the International Society for Labour Law and Social Security. He was President of the Hungarian Society for Industrial Relations and Hungarian Society for Data Protection. He has lectured in many countries. He has been involved in many international research projects. He was secretary of the International Seminar for Comparative Labour Law, Industrial Relations and Social Security in Szeged, Hungary. At present, he is the Head of the Department of Labour Law and Social Security in the Faculty of Law at the Szeged University, Szeged. He is the Director of the Institute of Industrial Relations and Social Security Education, at the Szeged University, Szeged, Hungary.

The Author

Table of Contents

Table of Contents

Acknowledgements

The author gratefully acknowledges the help and support received from Ms Mengxuan Chen PhD candidate from the Faculty of Law of Szeged University.

Acknowledgements

Part I. Introduction to Hungarian Social and Legal System

§1. General Background

I. Geography, Location, Size and Boundaries

1. Hungary is situated in the Carpathian Basin. It occupies an area of 93,032 square kilometres – three times bigger than Belgium – and has 2,242 kilometres of frontier, bordering Ukraine, Slovakia, Austria, Slovenia, Croatia, Serbia and Romania. The country had a population of 9.6 million persons in 2023.[1]

2. The Hungarians (Magyars) lived eastwards of the Ural Mountains as members of Finno-Ugric tribes around 1000 BC. In the course of their migrations, they settled in the Carpathian Basin in 896 BC. Soon the tribal-clan society began to transform itself into a feudal socio-economic system, similar to that of neighbouring countries. The centralized state was founded by the first Hungarian king, who was crowned in 1001 BC. The succeeding centuries were characterized by a constant struggle between the central power and the discordant forces of the feudal aristocracy. The first character, determining the order of the state and the relationship between the nobility and the king, was the Golden Bull, issued in 1222 BC. In 1241, the Tatar hordes reached Hungary and devastated the country. After their departure, the king tried to restore and strengthen the central power but in the second half of the 13th century, the feudal disintegration of the country increased. In the course of the 14th century the Anjou dynasty, which ascended the throne, managed to curb the oligarchy and to establish a strong monarchy. However, after it died out, feudal anarchy again prevailed. From the beginning of the 15th century, Hungarian history was characterized by the constant encroachment of the expanding Turkish empire. In the second half of the 15th century, the strengthened and centralized royal power halted the advance of the Turkish army for a short period. However, the growing despotism of the landlords and the deterioration of the situation of the serfs aggravated internal conflicts. In 1514, a crusade was organized against the Turks but the tens of thousands of assembled serfs turned against the landlords. The revolt was defeated and it was followed closely by cruel landlord reprisals and a vigorous increase in the oppression of the serfs. Meanwhile, the Turkish menace again intensified and the Turks gained a decisive victory over the Hungarians at the battle

1. Population and Vital Events (2023), https://www.ksh.hu/population-and-vital-events (26 Jul. 2023).

of Mohács in 1526. In later years the country was split into three parts. The western and northern part came under the rule of the Habsburgs; the central and southern part was occupied by the Turks; and in the east the independent principality of Transylvania took shape.

3. At the end of the 17th century Turkish domination ceased and the whole country came under the rule of the Habsburg dynasty. During the following years, there were several national revolutions against Austrian oppression. However, owing to the numerical superiority of the Austrians and also to certain internal conflicts, the struggle for national independence was finally defeated. In the first half of the 19th century – as a consequence of the bourgeois transformation of society in Western Europe – the battle against political and economic dependence on Austria was renewed. This 'Reform Period' started with the 1825 diet and ended with the 1848–1849 bourgeois revolution and the war of national independence.

4. One of the main aims of the revolution, starting on 15 March 1848, was national independence. In the Declaration of Independence adopted in 1849, the dethronement of the Habsburgs was pronounced. However, the struggle for national independence was defeated by the forces of reaction – the joint armies of imperial Austria and tsarist Russia. The war was followed by years of terrorism and oppression. This period ended with the 1867 compromise and the formation of the Austro-Hungarian monarchy. This secured economic and political hegemony for Austria and preserved the feudal social system. In subsequent decades, as a result of manufacturing activities and railway construction, there were possibilities for bourgeois development. The organizations of industrial workers became stronger. The working class organized its own political party. Among the rapidly growing agrarian proletariat agitation was steadily increasing.

5. As a result of its defeat in the First World War, the monarchy disintegrated. The international socio-economic conflicts, aggravated by the war, led to the bourgeois-democratic revolution of October 1918, and the Hungarian Republic was proclaimed. In the spring of 1919, a Soviet Republic was created. After its downfall – in the summer of 1919 – the former Hungarian monarchy was restored. The country lost about two-thirds of its territory in accordance with the Treaty of Versailles of 1920. In the inter-war period, Hungary was still an agrarian country. 50% of the population lived on the land; 36% of agricultural workers were landless labourers and day workers. About one thousand large-scale landlords owned 30% of the land. The technology of agricultural production was not advanced. Industrial production was characterized not only by its relatively small size but also by the fact that about 40%–50% of industrial manpower worked in small-scale industry. Economic growth was slow. There were considerable differences in income distribution. The industrial and agrarian proletariat – around 43% of the population – shared 24% of all personal income.

6. In the summer of 1942 Hungary was going to war against the Soviet Union. In 1944–1945 the country became an area of war and was occupied by the Soviet army. On 21 December 1944, a Provisional National Government was elected. The following week, the Government declared war against Nazi Germany and in January 1945, it concluded an armistice with the Allied Powers. In the same year, a Republic was proclaimed. In 1949 the constitution declared the establishment of the Hungarian People's Republic as a socialist state. This situation was changed in 1990 when democratic elections took place. The Parliament, elected in the spring of 1990, announced a modification of the Constitution and Hungary was proclaimed a Republic. According to the Fundamental Law (Constitution) in 2011 the official name of the state is: Hungary.

7. Owing to the war, the situation in the country was desperate. Industry and transport were paralysed. About 90% of industrial plants suffered damage, about half of their capacity was destroyed or transported abroad. About 85% of railway stock and nearly 90% of road transport were destroyed. The productive capacity of agriculture diminished. The total amount of war losses came to four to five times the 1938 national income.

8. During the first year after the war, the major task, on the one hand, was to repair the immense material damage caused by the war and, on the other hand, to begin the development of a socio-economic state. In March 1945 the Law on Land Reform was enacted. Altogether 1.9 million hectares of land were distributed among 642,000 landless agrarian proletarians and smallholders and 1.3 million hectares were taken over by the state. In the shortest possible time nationalization of industry, banks, commerce and transport took place. This process was completed with the nationalization of plants employing more than 10 workers in 1949. During the following years, a planned economy was introduced starting with the Five Year Plan which provided for industrialization and a socialist transformation of agriculture. Based on the experiences of the following years, it would become obvious that the actual economic system could not promote the development of the national economy. In 1968, an economic reform was introduced. It provided for the application of some elements of a market economy. Realization of the reform was very slow within the actual political and public structure of the country. The situation was changed towards the end of the 1980s. Instead of a planned economy the transition to a market economy and privatization of a part of state ownership began.

II. The Socio-political System

9. The basic features of the social system of the country, the structure of the state and the rights and duties of citizens are laid down in the Fundamental Law (Constitution) of 2011, which defines Hungary as an independent democratic constitutional state.

10. All power resides in the people who exercise their popular sovereignty through their elected representatives as well as directly. No individual organization, no element of government, nor an individual citizen shall act in any manner or entertain in any activity designed to obtain power by force or to obtain exclusive power. Every person has the right and, at the same time, the duty to initiate legal proceedings against the aforementioned activities. Political parties may be formed and function freely in conformity with the Fundamental Law and its provisions. They take part in the shaping and the expression of the will of the people.[2]

11. The supreme organ of state power and popular representation of Hungary is Parliament. It exercises all rights deriving from the sovereignty of the people, guarantees the constitutional order of society and determines the organization, direction and conditions of government. It elects the President, the Prime Minister, the members of the Constitutional Court, the President and Vice President of the State Audit Office, the President of Supreme Court (Curia), the Parliamentary Commissioner for Citizens' Rights (Ombudsman) and the Chief Prosecutor. Parliament is elected for a term of four years on the basis of universal, equal and direct suffrage by secret ballot. The franchise extends to every adult citizen over the age of 18.

12. The President is also the Head of State representing the unity of the nation and protecting the democratic operation of the state-organization. He serves as the Commander-in-Chief of the Armed Forces. The President is elected by Parliament for a term of four years. Any person who is a citizen of Hungary, qualified to vote, and at least 35 years old on the day of election is eligible to hold the office of President.

13. The Government is elected and dismissed by Parliament on a motion of the President. Members of the Government take part in and may address parliamentary sessions. The Government is the supreme executive body of state administration. Within its own sphere of functions, the Government issues decrees and passes resolutions. The Government is responsible to Parliament for its activities. It is bound to render regular account of its work to Parliament.

14. The Constitutional Court supervises the constitutionality of laws and regulations and performs the duties as conferred upon it by law. In the case of it establishing something unconstitutional, it annuls laws and other statutory provisions. Only the Members of the Parliament and the Parliamentary Commissioner for Citizens' Rights (Ombudsman) shall have the right to initiate the proceedings before the Constitutional Court in the cases as provided by law. The Constitutional Court is composed of fifteen members who are elected by Parliament. The members of the Constitutional Court are elected by a majority of at least two-thirds of the votes of the members of Parliament. Members of the Constitutional Court must not be members of any political party, and must not be involved in political activities besides those arising from the activities within the competence of the Constitutional Court.[3] They are elected for twelve years.[4]

---

2. Árva Zsuzsanna, *Nagykommentár Magyarország Alaptörvényéhez*, Budapest, Wolters Kluwer, 2022.
3. https://alkotmanybirosag.hu/ (26 Jul. 2023).
4. TRÓCSÁNYI László – SCHANDA Balázs: *Bevezetés az alkotmányjogba*, Budapest: HVG-ORAC, 2012. pp. 356–373.

15. The government in 2010 restricted the competence of the Constitutional Court to review certain fiscal matters, therefore the Hungarian Constitutional Court does not examine the constitutionality of financial, budgetary and tax laws – as long as the state debt exceeds half of the gross domestic product (GDP).[5]

16. The limitations of the Hungarian Constitutional Court's powers have been a subject of strong criticism: 'Although it is undoubtedly the constitution-making power's competence to amend the competences of the Constitutional Court, their curtailing is hardly in line with the rule of law. It is definitely not acceptable if an entire sector (finances and taxation) is exempted from the requirement of compliance with the constitution.'[6]

17. The Parliamentary Commissioner for Citizens' Rights has the duty to investigate or to make investigations. Everyone has the right to initiate proceedings before the Parliamentary Commissioner for Citizen's Rights. The Parliamentary Commissioner is elected by Parliament upon the recommendation of the President.[7]

18. The State Audit Office is the organ of financial-economic control of Parliament. Within its scope of authority, it checks the economy of public revenue, whether proposals for the State Budget are sound and well founded, the necessity and efficiency of the appropriations and expenditure and it countersigns contracts affecting credits raised by the State Budget; it carries out preliminary inspections on the legality of appropriations/expenditure made by the State Budget; it controls the management of state property, the activities of publicly owned enterprises and undertakings in respect of maintaining and increments of assets; it discharges other duties as referred to by law and within its scope of authority. The State Audit Office performs its audits on the basis of legality, efficiency and efficiency/effectiveness. The State Audit Office reports to Parliament on the audits performed by it. The reports shall be made public.[8]

19. The territory of the country is divided into the capital (Budapest), nineteen counties, local territorial districts, townships, towns and communities. The capital

5. *See* in Art. 37(4) of the Fundamental Law: 'As long as the state debt exceeds half of the Gross Domestic Product, the Constitutional Court may, within its powers set out in Article 24(2)b) to e), review the Acts on the central budget, the implementation of the central budget, central taxes, duties and contributions, customs duties and the central conditions for local taxes for conformity with the Fundamental Law exclusively in connection with the rights to life and human dignity, to the protection of personal data, to freedom of thought, conscience and religion, or the rights related to Hungarian citizenship, and it may annul these Acts only for the violation of these rights. The Constitutional Court shall have the unrestricted right to annul also Acts having the above subject matters, if the procedural requirements laid down in the Fundamental Law for the making and promulgation of those Acts have not been met.'
6. Opinion of the President of the Constitutional Court, *see* Péter Paczolay: International Conference on Jurisdiction of the Constitutional Court 'Limits and Possibilities of Expansion', 26 Sep. 2013, Riga.
7. Alapvető Jogok Biztosának Hivatala http://www.ajbh.hu/ (26 Jul. 2023).
8. POZSÁR-SZENTMIKLÓSY Zoltán – SOMODY Bernadette, *Alkotmányos alapok*, Budapest: HVG-ORAC, 2012. pp. 21–26.

and larger towns may be divided into urban districts. Local governments are active in the capital, counties, towns, urban districts and communities. The members of local government – elected by adults for a term of four years – are bound to regularly render account of the work of the local government and their own activities to the constituents. Local governments represent the interests of people within the given sphere of operations. They ensure the realization of central state and local objectives, the independent discharge of functions assigned to them, and the enforcement of the rule of law. They draw up their plans and budgets, direct and supervise the execution of the plans and the appropriation of budgetary means, and manage their own material resources. They are responsible for regional and local development and for organizing the provisions for the needs of the population. Within their sphere of operation, governments may pass decrees or resolutions.[9]

20. Based on the Fundamental Law of 2011 of Hungary and on Act CLXI of 2011 on the Organisation and Administration of the Courts, in Hungary the justice is administered in a four-level court system: (1) by the Curia (former name was Supreme Court), (2) the regional courts of appeal [Táblabíróság], (3) the county courts (including the Municipal Court of Budapest) [törvényszék] and (4) the local courts. First instance, jurisdiction in most matters rests with the local courts, effecting the principle that the overwhelming part of the cases shall be settled at the local level, within the easiest reach of the parties. The courts of first instance administer justice in divisions formed of professional judges and, in some cases, lay assessors. Professional judges are appointed by the President for an indefinite period. Judges are independent and are subordinate only to Acts of Parliament. Lay assessors are elected by the county council. Appeals against the decisions of the local courts may be submitted to the county courts (and the Municipal Court), which thus function mainly as appellate courts, however, in cases specified by law (e.g., in criminal cases with a sentence up to life imprisonment) they have first instance jurisdiction. The territorial competence of the local and country courts is determined by and identical with the areas of public administration. The regional courts of appeal hear the appeals lodged against the decisions of the local and county courts. There are five courts of appeal throughout the country in Budapest, Szeged, Pécs, Debrecen and Győr. Taking over the task of examining appeals, the regional courts of appeal significantly contributed to the reduction of the backlog of cases before the Curia and as a result, the Curia is now able to concentrate on its main function of ensuring the uniform application of law and examining applications for the review of final judgements as extraordinary remedy. Directives and decisions on issues of principle by the Curia are binding upon all courts. The President of the Curia is elected by Parliament.[10]

21. As from 1 January 2018, labour lawsuits may include labour claims arising from employment (established in accordance with Act I of 2012 on the labour code

---

9. Digitalcity Magyarország http://magyarorszag.digitalcity.hu/digitalcity/entity/entityHomePage.jsp?efm=AAAAOEYI&dom=AAAABIOO&prt=AAAALJJW&egd=AAAAFOZQ (26 Jul. 2023).
10. TRÓCSÁNYI László – SCHANDA Balázs: *Bevezetés az alkotmányjogba*, Budapest: HVG-ORAC, 2012. pp. 307–342.

(Labour Code), or from public servants' service status, or from public service status with the exceptions laid down in law, or from public works relations, or from employment relations established under the Sports Act, or from study contracts entered into in vocational training, or from study contracts entered into under the National Higher Education Act, or from work contracts made with a member of a social cooperative and employment cooperative.

22. These lawsuits may include those related to wages or other benefits related to work, or to termination of employment (lawsuits for sanctions due to unlawful termination of employment, etc.), lawsuits for damages against employers or employees, or lawsuits related to collective bargaining or factory agreements.

23. Labour lawsuits are initiated by filing of a petition. In labour disputes – when the plaintiff proceeds without the involvement of a legal representative – the petition may be filed by completing a relevant form, leaving no room for individual drafting or editing of the petition. In labour disputes, the litigants are not under any obligation to resort to legal representatives.

24. There was a fundamental change in labour court system in 2020. The former Administrative and Labour Courts were abolished as of 31 March 2020. In administrative court cases the Budapest-Capital, Budapest Environs, Debrecen, Győr, Miskolc, Pécs, Szeged and Veszprém Regional Courts proceed with regional competence on first instance.

25. The Budapest-Capital Regional Court has exclusive competence in cases that previously had been in the exclusive competence of the Budapest-Capital Administrative and Labour Court until 31 March 2020, as well as in most of the cases that had been in the exclusive competence of the Budapest-Capital Regional Court.

26. In administrative court cases, the Curia acts on second instance and in review procedures and has exclusive competence in certain types of cases.

27. In labour court cases, on the first instance the competent Regional Civil Law Courts, on the second instance the Regional Courts of Appeal, on review procedure the Curia proceeds.[11]

28. The new administration model of the court system was introduced in 2011 (*see* details later). The administrative and professional governance of the judiciary system was separated. The task of administrative governance belongs to the newly established National Office for the Judiciary (hereinafter referred to as NOJ). The professional governance of judiciary belongs to the President of the Curia (formerly

11. Change in administrative and labour procedures' judicial system (2020) https://birosag.hu/en/news/category/about-courts/change-administrative-and-labour-procedures-judicial-system-information (26 Jul. 2023).

Supreme Court). From 1 January 2012 on, the president of the Curia can concentrate all attention on the operation of the Curia. This could be facilitated significantly by the changing rules of the harmonization procedure and the setting up of the so-called teams for analysing the judicial practice.

29. The aim of the new administrative system is to operate the judicial organization effectively, along with providing for the maximum independence of judges: the courts should implement the procedures on a high professional level, and they should complete them within a reasonable timeframe.[12]

30. Hungary's economy is a market economy. Public and private property enjoy equal rights and protection. Based on the principle of impartial competition, Hungary recognizes and promotes the right of entrepreneurship and the freedom of competition, which can be restricted only by the Fundamental Law.

31. The Hungarian Fundamental Law declares that Hungary respects human rights. Civic rights must be exercised in harmony with the interests of society. The exercise of rights is inseparable from the performance of civic duties. The Fundamental Law guarantees liberty of conscience and freedom of worship to all citizens, freedom of speech, freedom of the press and freedom of association and assembly. The Fundamental Law ensures the personal freedom and inviolability of citizens, the privacy of correspondence and of the home. In Hungary, no one is persecuted for his/her political beliefs. Every citizen has the right to take part in the management of public affairs. The Fundamental Law protects the institution of marriage and the family. The State pays special attention to the development and education of youth.[13]

32. Accession to European Union. Being the first to pull down the 'iron curtain' and to sign the Hungary-EC Association Treaty, which placed economic and commercial co-operation onto a new basis, Hungary, together with Poland and the then Czechoslovakia provided an example to the other Central and Eastern European countries. At the beginning of the transition, a complex system of relations, similar to those existing between the members of the Union, was established, with Western participation in foreign direct investments, privatization, and production co-operation. In this process, a significant role was played by the already mentioned Association Agreement – in everyday usage: European Agreement – signed in December 1991, which ensured further assets for the development of financial, legal and political co-operation. Hungary gained a possibility to begin and accelerate the process of closing up to its Western European partners, in the context of settled conditions, and utilising more and more complex forms and means of cooperation.

33. In the spirit of the above, Hungary submitted its application for EU membership on 1 April 1994. While the preparations and the negotiations for NATO membership were ongoing, the Hungarian government took extraordinary measures

12. Magyarország Bíróságai http://www.birosag.hu/birosagi-szervezetek (26 Jul. 2023).
13. KISS Barnabás, *Alkotmányjogi alapismeretek*, Szeged: Polay Elemér Alapítvány, 2012. pp. 26–29.

in order to accelerate the closing up to the European Union. The direction and development strategies of national economic policy were defined in keeping with this objective. Therefore, the dominant elements of the 1990s were the approximation, the adaptation to Hungary's future European partners, as well as gradual political, legal harmonization and economic closing up. The aim was to prepare the Hungarian society and economy to meet the membership requirements of the European Union, and to make the country actually ready for membership in the European Union.

34. The adoption of the new members in 2004 had its own characteristic features just like any earlier enlargement. This time, the large number of the candidates was exceptional, and their economies were relatively poor compared to the majority of the Member States. With the enlargement, the EU's population increased by about 80 million people.[14]

35. Joining the European Union is seemingly a unilateral process: the candidate countries have to accept the contents of the community's legal order and provide the basis for applying the community's rules, the acquis communautaire. It has never been the integration itself which was adjusted to the new members, but rather the latter ones have had to adapt to the community. This is exactly what happened this time as well. Hungary and the other candidates, in harmony with their national interests, have gradually adjusted to community practices and to the acquis communautaire, and have developed their economy and political system in keeping with the expectations of the future membership.[15]

36. After the legal harmonization process of the past years, the main EU directives on individual and collective labour law have been transposed to the Hungarian labour law legislation. The Labour Code is practically in line with the EU legislation.[16]

III. Vital Statistics

37. The population of the country is 9.6 million on 1 July 2023. On the present territory of Hungary, the population number was the highest in 1980 (10 million 709 thousand), a number continuously decreasing since that time.

38. Hungary's UNDP Human Development Index (HDI) is at a very high level of human development (2019: 0.854) but the fourth lowest in the EU. Average life expectancy at birth is currently 76.9 years. The inequality adjustment of the Hungarian HDI (7.4%) is one of the highest in Central and Eastern Europe, demonstrating the high impact of poverty and inequality on human development.

---

14. http://www.parlament.hu/biz/eib/link1/jogharm.htm (26 Jul. 2023).
15. KISS György, *Az Európai Unió munkajoga*, Budapest: Osiris Kiadó, 2003. pp. 23–31.
16. HANTI Erzsébet, *Az Európai Uniós munkaügyi irányelvek és érvényesítésük a hazai kollektív tárgyalásos gyakorlatban Kézikönyv*, Budapest: Vasas-Köz Nyomda, 2003. pp. 9–14.

39. Inequalities increased since the Orbán government took office in 2010, in line with a redistribution policy that generally favours the upper-middle class. According to Eurostat, the Gini coefficient increased from 24.1 to 28.6 between 2010 and 2014 and has since hovered around 28. Although lower than the EU average, this figure suggests significantly higher inequality compared to neighbouring countries. Since 2010, the GDP share of the two highest income deciles has increased, underlining the bottom-up redistribution flow in Hungary.

40. According to the Hungarian Statistical Office (KSH), the percentage of people at risk of income poverty was 17.7% in 2019, following a constant decrease since 2012, with 12.2% suffering from relative income poverty. Vulnerable groups, such as pensioners, children, the unemployed and Roma are particularly exposed to poverty. Poverty risk among pensioners rose to 19.1% from 4.4% in 2010. Among the unemployed, 61.8% faced the risk of poverty or social exclusion as Hungary offers one of the least generous unemployment benefit schemes in the EU. Based on OECD data and methodology, in 2019, relative income poverty among children was 16.9%, which is significantly higher than Hungary's Central and Eastern European neighbours. The risk of poverty among the Roma is more than three times the national average (52.9% in 2019) but has significantly decreased (89.9% in 2013).[17]

IV. Market, Economy and Competition

41. According to the IMF's 2018 shadow economy report, the informal economy amounted to 22.2% of Hungary's GDP in 2017, over five percentage points above the European average. This is mainly the result of the still relatively high tax burden on work, although the government implemented a series of tax cuts in 2017 and 2018: the social contribution tax was cut from 27% to 19.5%. According to OECD, the overall tax burden decreased from 39.5% of GDP in 2008 to 36.6% in 2018.

42. Hungarian VAT is the highest in the EU at 27%; the consumption tax disproportionately affects low-income groups. The tax system is highly complicated – in 2020 the National Tax and Customs Administration collected 54 different taxes. While the number of taxes has slightly decreased in recent years, special taxes introduced during the COVID-19 pandemic reversed that trend. The government used the pandemic as a pretext to funnel local business taxes into the state budget, depriving municipalities of crucial income sources while prohibiting the introduction of new local taxes by municipalities.

43. The Hungarian Competition Authority (GVH) is responsible for enforcing competition rules, but its independence is questionable. Although it generally operates fairly and evaluates cases according to professional considerations, it is liable

17. Hungary Country Report 2022; https://bti-project.org/en/reports/country-report/HUN (26 Jul. 2023).

to government interference and self-censorship when pro-government businesspeople or strategically important sectors are involved. For media mergers and acquisitions, the GVH must request a preliminary resolution from the media council that is binding on the competition authority.

44. Hungary has one of the highest numbers of public procurement processes with a single bidder in the EU. In January 2021, the European Commission asked Hungary to systematically reform its public procurement legislation and practices as they serve as vehicles for organized political corruption. Hence, public procurement can be considered a channel for politically redistributed subsidies, which undermines fair competition in various sectors.[18]

45. Weaknesses in institutional performance weigh on the business climate and reduce the growth potential of the economy. The unstable regulatory environment is one of the biggest barriers to doing business in Hungary, with insufficient stakeholder engagement and evidence-based policymaking. The transparency and predictability of the budget process remain limited. Public procurement is still characterized by limited competition and transparency. Corruption risks remain high and there are notable gaps in the measures taken to address the issue.[19]

46. In November 2016, the government agreed with the social partners to increase substantially the minimum wage and to decrease employers' social security contributions. The corporate income tax was cut from the former two-tier rate of 19% for large companies and 10% for SMEs to a single rate of 9% for all companies.[20]

47. It is important to note that Hungary was a major beneficiary of the European Structural and Investment Funds (ESI Funds) with an allocation of EUR 25 billion for the period 2014–2020. This was equivalent to 3.1% of GDP annually (over 2014–2017) and 39% of the expected national public investment. Out of the EU financing, EUR 2.3 billion is planned for delivery via financial instruments (a substantially higher amount than in the 2007–2013 period). By 31 December 2016, EUR 13.1 billion, which represents about 52% of the total allocation for ESI Funds, had already been allocated to concrete projects.[21]

---

18. Hungary Country Report 2022; https://bti-project.org/en/reports/country-report/HUN (26 Jul. 2023).
19. Communication from The Commission to The European Parliament, The Council, The European Central Bank and The Eurogroup 2017 European Semester: Assessment of progress on structural reforms, prevention and correction of macroeconomic imbalances, and results of in-depth reviews under Regulation (EU) No. 1176/2011 {COM(2017) 90 final}{SWD(2017) 67 final to SWD(2017) 93 final}, Brussels, 2017.
20. Communication from The Commission to The European Parliament, The Council, The European Central Bank and The Eurogroup 2017 European Semester: Assessment of progress on structural reforms, prevention and correction of macroeconomic imbalances, and results of in-depth reviews under Regulation (EU) No. 1176/2011 {COM(2017) 90 final}{SWD(2017) 67 final to SWD(2017) 93 final}, Brussels, 2017.
21. Communication from The Commission to The European Parliament, The Council, The European Central Bank and The Eurogroup 2017 European Semester: Assessment of progress on structural

V. Employment and Unemployment Policies and Statistics

A. *Labour Market and Unemployment*

48. The recent government has fundamentally reshaped the Hungarian social welfare regime and redistribution policies according to its workfare society agenda. Redistributive policies are also actively used to promote the government's conservative social agenda and favour support for married couples over single parents. While the welfare system was restructured to favour the well-off over those at risk of poverty and exclusion, social expenditures were also cut significantly. Since 2010, Hungary's social expenditures have continuously fallen and dropped from 23% of GDP in 2010 to 18.1% in 2019; health expenditures also dropped, from 7.5% in 2010 to 6.4% in 2019.

49. Access to disability benefits and early pensions was significantly curbed, and vocational early pensions were abolished. As a result, approximately 600,000 individuals (21.5% of those formerly eligible for pensions) were excluded from the pension scheme by 2012. While the pension ceiling was abolished, the minimum pension remained at EUR 90 for more than 10 years. The share of pensioners at risk of poverty and exclusion was 19.1% in 2019 – practically quadrupling since 2010 (4.4%) and nearly doubling since 2017 (11.1%).

50. School enrollment rates for boys and girls are 99.9% and 100% in primary, and 99.2% and 99.7% in lower-secondary schools, respectively. Male students are overrepresented in early school drop-out. School segregation and structural discrimination of Roma remain endemic; segregation is allowed by law in church-run schools if it serves the purpose of 'the pastoral care of Roma.'

51. The gender pay gap is below the European average (11.8% in 2018 *v.* 14.8%), while the employment gap significantly exceeds the EU average (15.3% *v.* 11.5%). Research suggests that women face significant barriers returning to the labour market after giving birth. Childbearing is also responsible for a significant part of the gender wage gap. According to the European Institute for Gender Equality (EIGE), the share of women in leading business positions is only 18.2% in Hungary.

52. According to Hungarian Central Statistical Office (KSH) data, GDP expanded by 4.6% in 2019, following robust growth in the previous years. In contrast, the economy contracted by 5–6% in 2020 as a result of the COVID-19 pandemic, according to the Hungarian Ministry of Finance. According to Eurostat, Hungary's GDP per capita in purchasing power parity (PPP) terms was 73% of the EU27 average in 2019, the eighth lowest among Member States. Although the

---

reforms, prevention and correction of macroeconomic imbalances, and results of in-depth reviews under Regulation (EU) No. 1176/2011 {COM(2017) 90 final}{SWD(2017) 67 final to SWD(2017) 93 final}, Brussels, 2017.

increase (68% in 2017) is partially due to a lower EU level due to Brexit, Hungary has outperformed Poland and Slovakia since 2018.

53. In 2019, the debt-to-GDP ratio totalled up to 66.3% after years of moderate but constant decreases. In 2020, due to the fiscal implications of the COVID-19 pandemic and the government's crisis management measures, it jumped to 81.2%. This value is not only higher than in the aftermath of the 2008/2009 global economic crisis but also negated the results of debt reduction efforts over the past decade. The annual budget deficit was 2% of GDP in 2019, while in 2020 the Ministry of Finance expected a deficit between 7% and 9% of GDP. Regarding the labour market, in December 2020, the unemployment rate rose to 4.3% from 3.5% year-on-year.

54. The length of unemployment benefits is three months, the shortest in the EU. A large-scale public works scheme dominates active labour market policy measures such as training, mentoring or wage subsidies. The risk of poverty and exclusion for unemployed persons increased from 44.8% in 2018 to 61.8% in 2019. Social assistance is coupled with compulsory participation in public work schemes.

55. In 2020, the government launched an Economy Protection Strategy to cushion the economic and social implications of the COVID-19 pandemic-induced economic downturn. At the end of 2020, measures that were part of the strategy amounted to 28% of GDP, including subsidies of up to 70% of wages for non-active employees to preserve employment and a payment moratorium on household loans.

56. Equal opportunity legislation protecting vulnerable groups from discrimination formally exists in line with EU laws, but the government increasingly attempts to hamper the law's implementation. The National Assembly disbanded the Equal Opportunity Authority (EBH) in January 2021, passing its competencies on to Hungary's ombudsperson for fundamental rights. The EBH has acted as an independent and professional safeguard since its establishment by Hungary's first comprehensive equal opportunity act in 2003. Since the former and recent ombudspersons since 2013 maintained an uncritical, often-biased attitude toward the executive, the EBH's dissolution may seriously hamper the enforcement of non-discrimination legislation. As a sign of concern about the independence of the ombudsperson, the Global Alliance for National Human Rights Institutions (GANHRI) suspended the accreditation of the Hungarian ombudsman in 2019, which has been under review since.[22]

57. Unemployment in Hungary has grown considerably since accession to the EU. In 2012 it peaked at 506,520, compared to 252,000 in 2004. The bulk of this rise derived from the crisis that began in 2008. The unemployment level remained

22. Hungary Country Report 2022; https://bti-project.org/en/reports/country-report/HUN (26 Jul. 2023).

high until 2012 when it began to drop – as a direct result of the government's workfare programmes. The number of jobless who have taken part in these programmes (so-called fostered workers) has risen substantially recently.

58. Hungary – unemployment rate was 3.90% in December of 2022, according to the Eurostat. Trading Economics provides the current actual value, a historical data chart and related indicators for Hungary – unemployment rate – last updated from the Eurostat in July of 2023. Historically, Hungary – unemployment rate reached a record high of 10.90% in March of 2012 and a record low of 3.30% in June of 2022. Hungary – unemployment rate dropped to 4.00% in April 2023, from the previously reported figure of 4.10% in March 2023.[23]

59. There are, however, growing indications that the labour market is tightening. Employment growth is expected to slow in the coming years as labour supply becomes more limited. There are skill shortages in numerous sectors and it is increasingly difficult to match both the skilled and unskilled labour force with vacancies. Consequently, there is a significant pressure on wage growth, which is another indicator of tightening labour market.[24]

B. Public Work Programme, as a Special Tool for Fight Against Unemployment

60. The most important task of the public employment system is to activate long-term unemployed people and to prevent permanent job seekers from getting out of working life. However, serious consultation on an alternative active labour market policy is lacking. There are the people of working age, with low education and no professional skills that are the most difficult to involve in employment. Public employment offers work primarily for these people.

61. It offers temporary employment to individuals, durably excluded from the primary labour market, generally living in disadvantaged districts and settlements and putting in place conditions and opportunities for value-adding work by financing the direct expenses on employment.

62. It is another important objective to include the development and learning of a working culture required for finding a job on the primary labour market, the acquisition of the required qualifications and laying down the foundation of actual producing, self-sustaining 'social enterprises', social cooperatives based on public employment. The public employment system provides an income for hundreds of

23. Hungary-Unemployment rate (2023); https://tradingeconomics.com/hungary/unemployment-rate-eurostat-data.html (26 Jul. 2023).
24. Communication from The Commission to The European Parliament, The Council, The European Central Bank and The Eurogroup 2017 European Semester: Assessment of progress on structural reforms, prevention and correction of macroeconomic imbalances, and results of in-depth reviews under Regulation (EU) No 1176/2011 {COM(2017) 90 final}{SWD(2017) 67 final to SWD(2017) 93 final}, Brussels, 2017.

thousands of citizens and their families each year, also contributing to the development of settlements, and the creation of a more orderly attractive and cleaner residential and natural environment. The Government's aim with public employment system was to provide temporary employment and income to job seekers instead of benefits in the most disadvantaged regions of the country, where this type of employment is mainly the only option to earn money.

63. In the future, in line with the long-term goals of the Hungarian employment policy, the national expenditures for active labour market policy are planned to be gradually increased, whereas expenditures of the public work schemes will be decreased in the upcoming years. According to Government Decision No. 1139/ 2017. (III. 20.), significant changes will be introduced in the next years in order to encourage that public workers find employment in the primary labour market. The most important new regulations are the following:

(a) ensure that people who are expected to be able to find employment in the labour market on their own – including also people with qualifications – are not involved in the public work schemes, only in case if (a) the placement attempt of the district office had been unsuccessful three times – for any reason occurring on the employer's side, or (b) the district office had been unable to offer an appropriate job for such person for three months;
(b) ensure that people who have any qualification are involved in the public work schemes only if (a) the placement attempt of the district office had been unsuccessful three times for any reason occurring on the employer's side, or (b) the district office had been unable to offer an appropriate job for the job-seeker for three months;
(c) ensure that the periodically recurring involvement of people employed in the framework of public employment relationships in public work schemes is excluded, in the manner that in a phasing-out system as of 1 June 2018 and within a period of three years the maximum duration of employment in the framework of public employment relationship shall be one year, except if the private sector offers no actual job opportunity to the individual, and therefore the individual concerned cannot find employment due to no fault of his/her own.[25]

64. The Government's plan is to continuously decrease the monthly average maximum number of participants in the public work schemes to 150,000 people by 2020.

65. The public work policy has been criticized by many observers for its low efficiency in reintegrating people into the primary labour market, its poor targeting (involving not only those in the most disadvantaged positions, from disadvantaged regions), and for the fact that it absorbed funds from other more efficient labour

25. Lajos Tamás SZABÓ (2020) The Effect Of Public Work Programme In Hungary on Private Sector Wages, MNB Working Papers No. 7; https://www.mnb.hu/letoltes/mnb-wp-2020-7-final.pdf (26 Jul. 2023).

market tools and provided a lower income than the minimum wage. The massive extension of public works took place at the expense of other, more efficient active labour market policies such as training and mentoring. The European Commission repeatedly urged the government to reconsider the scheme, warning that it did not improve prospects for the jobless.

66. According to the latest data, the number of people involved in public works decreased from 202,500 in 2016 (highest number in the history of modern public work in Hungary) to 72.100 in 2022. The number of public workers has been reduced mostly in the least economically and socially advanced eastern parts of the country. Latest statistics indicate that the number is still on the decrease. The government planned to transfer public workers from the PWS into local social cooperatives. While statistically cooperative members are considered employees in the private sector, there is no change in their pay and working conditions. Their wages do not increase, since social cooperatives have been removed from the application of the labour code that guarantees a minimum wage. Finally, this plan has not been completed.[26]

C. Migration and Its Influence on Labour Market

67. In EU comparison, Hungary has been among the countries with low but positive international net migration since the 1990s. In recent years, the rate of emigration accelerated; however, we encounter difficulties in its accurate measurement.

68. By now every sector is affected by the shortage of workforce in the Hungarian labour market. Although KSH (Central Statistical Office) measured the gap to be 80,000 people, in reality, the number of unfilled jobs can be much more depending on the sector. The absence of skilled workforce represents an increasing problem in every sector of the Hungarian economy. Sectors such as the construction industry, catering industry and tourism are in the worst situation where finding and retaining skilled employees means a daily problem.

69. Single male skilled workers aged between 20 and 39 represent the largest group of Hungarians who work abroad. Officially 99,000 people, or 2.5% of the workforce worked abroad in January 2023. The majority of workers abroad were men aged between 25 and 44 with vocational diplomas and 85% worked in Austria, Germany and the UK.

70. According to OECD estimates, the number of Hungarian EU internal plus UK migrants who left the country in the past decade in order to live somewhere else either permanently or temporarily is closing in on 1 million. Nevertheless, it seems

26. Hungary: shrinking Public Work Scheme after reform (2020) https://www.etui.org/covid-social-impact/hungary/hungary-shrinking-public-work-scheme-after-reform (26 Jul. 2023).

like there are now at least 600,000 Hungarians living in Europe. The main target countries with number of registered employees: 115,000 in Austria, 190,00 in Germany, and 170,000 in UK.[27]

71. Even though, the number of those working abroad was down, Hungary struggles hard with labour shortage which affects almost every sector of the economy. The situation is getting worse in construction and industry, but there are considerable problems in transport, as well – reported the Hungarian Central Statistical Office (HCSO). Furthermore, the situation worsened in the info-communication and the service sector. The government is continuing to work on increasing the number of pensioners and women with children in employment, both through funding and by expanding possibilities of part-time employment.

72. Mainly due to the after COVID-19 effect an increasing number of foreign employers are recruiting, including in Hungary, by offering teleworking, even without moving abroad, in exchange for much more substantial financial compensation. Another piece of information is that Facebook groups specialising in working abroad and relocating are almost like think tanks, offering both job opportunities and information based on experience.[28]

VI. Underlying Social and Cultural Values of the Society and Basic Principles of Labour Law

A. Effectiveness of the Right to Work

73. According to the Hungarian Fundamental Law every citizen has the right to work, and it was also urged that this right is not solely assured by legal means. At the same time, the role of labour law cannot be neglected either. First, a legal framework must be developed within which every citizen can utilize his/her potential. That is why many different measures are necessary:

(a) First of all, the possibility of employment must be ensured. Practically, this is a prerequisite for the fulfilment of the ideas of the Fundamental Law. Positive measures are needed in order to assure the success of the citizen's decision, i.e., regulation concerning the freedom to accept a job. On the other hand, this kind of regulation must contain prohibitions as well, in order to eliminate groundless differentiation among workers, employees etc.
(b) Creating jobs and making choices possible does not automatically mean that everyone is able to take the job he/she wants. For personal, family, or other reasons certain people or groups cannot easily find suitable employment (e.g.,

27. Hat éve nem hagyta el annyi ember Magyarországot, mint 2022-ben (2023); https://index.hu/gazdasag/2023/04/09/kivandorlas-europai-unio-magyarorszag-nemetorszag-ausztria-brexit-gazdasag/ (26 Jul. 2023).
28. Labour market outlook (2022); https://www.hrportal.hu/hr/labour-market-outlook-20230227.html (26 Jul. 2023).

mothers with small children, persons with reduced capacity to work, people living far from large settlements). They can use their ability fully only if they receive assistance. This is realized by setting up institutions to this end (e.g., job centres) or when an employer is forced to give a candidate certain advantages.[29]

(c) To assure the right to work, further regulations are needed which realize the intentions of the parties – especially those of the workers – in regard to employment. At the same time, these should set out unambiguously the conditions ensuring the security of the worker's position. Within this category fall the rules concerning the legal capacity, as well as the rules referring to the contract of employment.[30]

(d) In addition, such security must be provided to eliminate the possibility of groundless dismissal. Consequently, labour law must provide guarantees to assure job security. This is done partly by those regulations which prescribe the circumstances and means of termination of employment. On the other hand, it defines those cases where employment cannot be terminated or where termination depends on certain conditions.[31]

B. The Freedom to Enter into Employment

1. The Subjective Right to Enter into Employment

74. It was noted previously that merely declaring the right to work does not suffice; legal regulation is needed to realize this idea. Therefore, the Hungarian Fundamental Law basically grants every citizen the right to enter into employment relationship.

75. Reducing joblessness the compulsory workfare system was introduced. Since 2012 all jobs that labour offices offer to unemployed persons have to be accepted, even if they require far lower qualifications than those possessed by the applicant. Those who reject the job lose the social assistance benefit – approximately EUR 75 per month since 2012. The public works programme and the compulsory workfare regime have involved more and more unemployed people since 2010.[32]

---

29. HAJDÚ, József *Right to Work and Partial Unemployment Based on the Reflection of the ECSR on COVID-19* In: Ristivojević, Branislav (szerk.) Harmonizacija srpskog i mađarskog prava sa pravom Evropske unije = A szerb és a magyar jog harmonizációja az Európai Unió jogával = Harmonisation of Serbian and Hungarian Law with the European Union Law Újvidék, Szerbia: Újvidéki Jogtudományi Kar, Kiadói Központ (2022) 466 p. pp. 305–318., 14 p.
30. HAJDÚ József: *Az Alaptörvény munkajogi tartalmú cikkeiről* In: Balogh Elemér (szerk.) Számadás az Alaptörvényről: Tanulmányok a Szegedi Tudományegyetem Állam- és Jogtudományi Kara oktatóinak tollából. Budapest: Magyar Közlöny Lap- és Könyvkiadó, 2016. pp. 64–79.
31. HAJDÚ József, *IEL Labour Law, Hungary*, Wolters Kluwer, Kluwer Law Online, 2019. https://kluwerlawonline.com/Manuals/Corporate+Acquisitions+and+Mergers/705 (26 Jul. 2023).
32. Annamaria Artner (2016) https://www.socialeurope.eu/inside-hungarys-work-based-society (26 Jul. 2023).

2. The Prohibition of Discrimination

76. In addition to positive regulations, measures which eliminate groundless discrimination are also needed. In this respect section 12 of the Labour Code states that in connection with employment relations the principle of equal treatment must be strictly observed. Any consequences of the breach of the principle of equal treatment must be properly remedied; the remedy shall not result in any violation of or harm to the rights of another worker.

77. It must be noted that previous Labour Code (1992) contained quite a wide range of provisions relating to equal treatment. However, the enactment of the Act CXXV of 2003 on Equal Treatment and the Promotion of Equal Opportunities (hereinafter referred to as Equal Treatment Act) mainly took over the task of the Hungarian Labour Code. The Equal Treatment Act consists of two parts: (1) regulations on equal treatment and (2) the promotion of equal opportunities.[33] Although the violation of equal treatment may not only arise in the context of employment, in recent years a number of decisions appeared finding and sanctioning discrimination against employees.[34]

78. The Equal Treatment Authority (ETA) was established to safeguard the implementation of the legislation. The establishment of the ETA with national competence was based on EU law. Its main task was to investigate complaints about discrimination and to enforce equal treatment. An application for a discrimination investigation can be made by the injured party if they have been disadvantaged by one of their protected characteristics. Protected characteristics are listed by law, including gender, skin colour, nationality, health status, religious or ideological beliefs, political or other opinion, marital status, sexual orientation, gender identity, age, sexual orientation and financial situation.[35]

79. On 1 December 2020 the Hungarian Parliament decided that as of 1 January 2021, one of the most effective bodies in the fight against discrimination, the Equal Treatment Authority (ETA) will be abolished. Its duties, including the legal protection against racial, gender and other discrimination, will be taken over by the Commissioner for Fundamental Rights. The proceedings ongoing on 1 January 2021 will be suspended until 31 January 2021. Likewise, ongoing administrative lawsuits appealing against decisions of ETA on 1 January 2021 will be suspended until 31 January 2021.[36]

33. CSÉFFÁN József, *A munka törvénykönyve és magyarázata*, Szeged: Szegedi Rendezvényszervező Kft., 2023.
34. József HAJDÚ: *The basic principles of the Hungarian labour law* In: TÓTH Judit (szerk.) Ünnepi kötet Dr TÓTH Károly címzetes egyetemi tanár 70. születésnapjára. 646 p., Szeged: Szegedi Tudományegyetem Állam- és Jogtudományi Kar, 2015. pp. 394–404. (Acta Universitatis Szegediensis. Acta juridica et politica; 77.).
35. Equal treatment Authority – Hungary; https://adsdatabase.ohchr.org/IssueLibrary/EQUAL%20TREATMENT%20AUTHORITY%20(Hungary).pdf (26 Jul. 2023).
36. Levente CSENGERY (2020) The Equal Treatment Authority Will Be Abolished from 1 Jan. 2021; https://ceelegalmatters.com/hungary/15413-the-equal-treatment-authority-will-be-abolished-from-1-january-2021 (26 Jul. 2023).

3. Guaranteed Minimum Income

80. Until 2011 in the framework of tripartite Interest Reconciliation Council the national-level social partners agreed on the volume of next year's minimum wage increase. After that, the amount of the minimum wage has been legally fixed. In July 2011 the National Interest Reconciliation Council was ended, and the new body – the National Economic and Social Council – has only the right to make proposals. The government usually in every year fixes the amount of the minimum wage and guaranteed minimum income which is valid for the coming calendar year. The Government's decree fixes minimum wages and guaranteed minimum wage for hourly, daily, weekly and monthly basis.

81. There are two types of minimum wages: (1) National Minimum Wage is for employees without any profession (it is paid to unskilled workers or employees who are skilled but work in a position which does not require their certificate or skill) and (2) Guaranteed Wage Minimum is set for professional workers. It is established in accordance with the level of education/vocational training required for a particular job or position. Both minimum wages are national-level minimum wages, however only the so-called guaranteed minimum wage should be earned by workers who are at least professional workers and has a job which is professional. For example, if a professional worker performs work which is auxiliary work, then he is entitled to receive only the 'minimum wage' which is lower than the 'guaranteed wage minimum'.[37]

82. The legal effect of the minimum wage is that every employee, if working full time, must receive at least the minimum wage or guaranteed wage minimum.

C. *Fundamental Principles of Hungarian Labour Law*

83. Before dealing with the system regulating labour law and with its detailed rules, it is necessary to refer briefly to the principles underlying the law. First, the relevant constitutional principles are being dealt with. Subsequently, some general legal principles which govern the whole of labour law will be discussed. In the course of this discussion, there will, however, be no explanation of how these principles and institutions are put into practice, leaving this to the next two sections of this book.[38]

---

37. Hungary National Minimum Wage – NMW (2023); https://countryeconomy.com/national-minimum-wage/hungary (26 Jul. 2023).
38. FERENCZ Jácint – GÖNDÖR Éva – GYULAVÁRI Tamás – KÁRTYÁS Gábor, *Munkajogi alapismeretek*, Budapest: ELTE Kiadó, 2013. pp. 35.

1. Basic Principles of the Fundamental Law (Constitution)

84. The Fundamental Law of Hungary (in Hungarian: *Magyarország Alaptörvénye*), the country's constitution, was adopted on 18 April 2011, promulgated a week later and went into force on 1 January 2012. Hungary's first constitution to be adopted within a democratic framework and following free elections, it succeeded the 1949 Constitution, adopted on 20 August 1949 and heavily amended on 23 October 1989. That document was Hungary's first permanent written constitution, and until its replacement, the country was the only former Eastern Bloc nation that did not adopt an entirely new constitution after the fall of Communism.

85. The Fundamental Law[39] has restructured the location of fundamental freedoms and slightly diminished the employment-related fundamental rights. There is a chapter in the Fundamental Law on fundamental rights related to work. It is also mentioned in the National Avowal that the power of the community and the honour of human beings is based upon work, the product of human intellect. It is mentioned among the general principles that the economy of Hungary is based upon value-producing work and the freedom of enterprise. The role of the State to take measures for the opening of employment options is then stipulated as an objective of the State in the chapter on fundamental freedoms. The State should present the opportunity for everyone to work. The Fundamental Law also affirms that every person must be obliged to contribute to the community's enrichment with his/her work to the best of his/her abilities and potential.[40] A value content is thus attached to the possibility of physical and intellectual work and enterprise in the Fundamental Law.

86. In contrast to the Constitution, the Fundamental Law sets out an objective regarding the provision of human habitat and access to public services.[41] It must also be noted that the Fundamental Law's chapter on fundamental rights also relies on the European Charter of Human Rights.[42]

87. The labour law-related basic rights in the Fundamental Law are as follows:

(1) Freedom of association and organization.
(2) The right to free choice of employment.
(3) Non-discrimination.
(4) Social rights.[43]

39. Formerly it was called Constitution.
40. *See* Article XII.
41. *See* Article XXII.
42. András PATYI-Balázs SCHANDA-András Zs. VARGA (eds) *The Basic (Fundamental) Law of Hungary, A Commentary of the New Hungarian Constitution* Clarus Press, 2015 http://www.eui.eu/Documents/General/DebatingtheHungarianConstitution/TheBasicLawofHungary.pdf (26 Jul. 2023).
43. HALMAI, Gábor – TÓTH Gábor Attila, *Emberi jogok*, Budapest: Osiris Kiadó, 2008. pp. 837–847.

a. Freedom of Association and Organization

88. Paragraphs 2–5 of Article VIII practically rearrange and unify the rules that have been set out in various provisions of the former Constitution regarding the freedom of association and organization. The Fundamental Law names two sub-rights of the freedom of assembly, (1) to establish and (2) to join organizations. Contrary to the former regulation, it does not mention the objectives of the organization.

89. The rule of the Fundamental Law on the free establishment and operation of the parties poses the unconditional requirement that state organs must not hamper the establishment and operation of the parties functioning according to constitutional standards. The right to establish and operate a party is behoved for all and for all parties, and the ground, therefore, is the Constitution itself.[44]

90. It must also be noted that this clause also covers the contents of Article 12 of the Charter of Fundamental Rights of the European Union[45] and Article 11 of the Convention for the Protection of Human Rights and Fundamental Freedoms of the Council of Europe.[46] This regulation also fits in the terminology and regulatory models used in European constitutions.

b. The Right to Free Choice of Employment

91. Paragraph 1 of Article XII of the Fundamental Law – besides breaking from a clause of the Constitution that was a remnant from the era of state socialism, the strict understanding of the right to work, which can only be enforced among full employment conditions – practically implements Article 70/B of the Constitution.[47] This means no real modification because the persistent practice of the Constitutional Court identified the right to work as the freedom of choice of profession and employment.[48]

92. The second phrase of paragraph 1 of Article XII of the Fundamental Law formulates the right to establish enterprise as a fundamental right. It sets out that the right to enterprise is an aspect of the free choice of employment, which means that there is no hierarchical relation among the right to work, freedom of choice of employment and the freedom of enterprise, consequently, they are not different from each other as fundamental rights.[49]

44. Decision 2179/B/1991 CC.
45. 'Everyone has the right [...] to freedom of association at all levels, in particular in political, trade union and civic matters, which implies the right of everyone to form and to join trade unions for the protection of his or her interests.'
46. 'Everyone has the right [...] to freedom of association with others, including the right to form and to join trade unions for the protection of his interests.'
47. TRÓCSÁNYI László (ed.), *A mi alkotmányunk*, Budapest: Osiris Kiadó, 2006. pp. 461, 464.
48. Decision 21/1994 CC.
49. Decision 21/1994 CC.

93. The second sentence of paragraph 1 of Article XII is completely novel. 'Every person shall have the obligation to contribute to the enrichment of the community through his or her work, in accordance with his or her abilities and possibilities.' It can refer to an obligation to work for the benefit of the community according to one's abilities and potential, but also to the general and proportionate sharing in taxation in connection with work. However, it definitely cannot refer to any coerced work, as that would be contrary to international instruments binding to Hungary.

94. Paragraph 2 reflects the social side of the right to work according to the practice of the Constitutional Court, which pointed out that there must be a distinction made between the fundamental right to work and the social right to work, particularly the institutional side thereof, the obligation of the State to present employment policy and to create jobs, etc.[50]

c. Non-discrimination

95. Equality before the law, legal capacity, the prohibition of discrimination and tasks related to equal opportunities are all regulated in the same part of the Fundamental Law.[51] Equality before the law, legal capacity borne by all, and the prohibition of discrimination are different aspects of the same equality principle; these could also be derived from the human dignity provisions.[52] The Fundamental Law follows the tradition set out by the Constitution (which is an unusual solution in constitutions) and grants every person legal capacity in Hungary, according to the text of Article 6 of the Universal Declaration of Human Rights and Article 16 of the Covenant on Civil and Political Rights.[53]

d. Social Rights

96. One of the cornerstones of the chapter on freedoms is the regulation of the right to social security. The previous Constitution set forth that citizens have the right to social security[54] and they are entitled to the support required to live.[55] The

50. Decision 21/1994 CC.
51. LEHOCZKYNÉ KOLLONAY, Csilla, 'Kezdeti lépések a foglalkoztatási diszkrimináció bírósági gyakorlatában' *Fundamentum*, Vol 2 No 4, p. 94, 1998.
52. TRÓCSÁNYI László, 'Magyarország alaptörvényének létrejötte és az alaptörvény vitatott rendelkezései' *Kommentár* Vol 6 No 4, 2011. http://kommentar.info.hu/iras/2011_4/magyarorszag_alaptorvenyenek_letrejotte_es_az_alaptorveny_vitatott_rendelkezesei (26 Jul. 2023).
53. András PATYI-Balázs SCHANDA-András Zs. VARGA (eds) *The Basic (Fundamental) Law of Hungary, A Commentary of the New Hungarian Constitution* Clarus Press, 2015, http://www.eui.eu/Documents/General/DebatingtheHungarianConstitution/TheBasicLawofHungary.pdf (26 Jul. 2023).
54. TRÓCSÁNYI László szerk.: A mi alkotmányunk, Complex Kiadó, Budapest, 2006 p. pp. 483–484.
55. However, for the sake of accuracy it must be mentioned that the provisions of the 1989 Constitution relating to social rights were the subject of debate in the practice of the Constitutional Court, too. [*See* Constitutional Court Order No. 24/1991 (V. 18.)] The issue under debate was whether these were rights or were formulated only as a state objective. Finally, the practice of the Constitutional Court reinforced the latter position, i.e., that the Constitution's rules on social rights served only as

Fundamental Law, however, identifies social security as a state goal instead of right: "Hungary shall (only) strive to provide social security to all of its citizens, and the level of assistance is determined not as the extent necessary for subsistence but 'statutory subsidies' are provided for" (*See* Article XIX).[56]

97. At the same time, in connection with the Fundamental Law it must be noted that it adds to the state goals within the scope of social rights. The state aims to provide every person with decent housing[57] and access to public services, which were not included in the previous Constitution (Article XXII).[58] Here the institutional guarantees of social security must be mentioned by all means. The 1989 Constitution mentioned the social insurance system and the system of social institutions in relation to implementing social security, while the Fundamental Law talks about a general state pension system and a system of social institutions. Besides the state pension system, the Fundamental Law allows for the 'operation of voluntarily established social institutions'[59] – which also promotes the livelihood of the elderly. Thus, the two-pillar pension system (1st pillar: statutory state pension and 2nd pillar: voluntary pension funds) is stabilized by the Fundamental Law,[60] however, the text of the Fundamental Law rules out the reinstatement of the previously eliminated compulsory private pension fund (which was originally the second pillar under the World Bank concept) and there is absolutely no mention of social insurance.[61]

98. In summary, pursuant to the provisions of the Fundamental Law, the state has increased freedom in providing social rights. One might venture to say that the prohibition set up by Constitutional Court Decision 43/1995 (VI. 30), according to

---

guidance for the state and no right derived from the Constitution (in spite of being worded as a right), and at best they can be secondary, subjective rights created by legislation. The consideration underlying this opinion was that they shall not be fundamental rights because they depend on the economic performance of the state. If the economic performance declines, there are two options to choose from: 1. either the state does not observe the provisions of the Constitution and thus the Constitution will be devalued, or 2. it observes them and impending state bankruptcy will follow.

56. József HAJDÚ *The right to Social Security in the Hungarian Fundamental Law in. The right to Social Security in the Constitutions of the World: Broadening the moral and legal space for social justice*; Alexandre Egorov and Marcin Wujczyk (eds), International Labour Organization (2016) pp. 89–106.
57. The Constitutional Court examined the issue within the framework of constitutional interpretation whether the right to housing can be deduced from the Constitution and reached a negative answer, at the same time maintaining that in the case of imminent danger to life the state shall provide dwelling (Constitutional Court Decision No. 42/2000 (XI. 8.).
58. JUHÁSZ Gábor: A gazdasági és szociális jogok védelme az Alkotmányban és az Alaptörvényben, Fundamentum 2012. évi 1. szám. http://www.fundamentum.hu/sites/default/files/12-1-02.pdf (26 Jul. 2023).
59. These are the voluntary and supplementary pension funds.
60. However, the two-pillar pension system implied by the Fundamental Law is not the same as the two-pillar – statutory social insurance pension and compulsory private pension – model proposed earlier by the World Bank.
61. József HAJDÚ *The right to Social Security in the Hungarian Fundamental Law in. The right to Social Security in the Constitutions of the World: Broadening the moral and legal space for social justice*; Alexandre Egorov and Marcin Wujczyk (eds), International Labour Organization (2016) pp. 89–106.

which the abrupt change of a social insurance service or its downgrading from insurance to assistance qualifies as interference with a fundamental right, no longer exists in this form. The provisions of the Fundamental Law on social rights clearly show that it is possible to interfere with existing rights, to rearrange them and ultimately to transform the social security system. According to the Fundamental Law, the state enjoys a great degree of freedom in the field of social rights, and this may result in social and economic policies which are more flexible and better suited to the requirements. Accordingly, the provisions of the Fundamental Law do not constrain the state in a worse economic situation, and the rules on social security alone will not bankrupt the state merely because they shall be observed under all circumstances. However, the ultimate limit lies not in the regulations on social rights but in realizing human dignity.[62]

2. General Legal Principles of the Labour Code

99. According to the legislators' concept, it is also necessary to consider certain general legal principles within the Labour Code which affect labour law. A system of guarantees based on the basic principles permeates the whole of the regulation which protects both the employer and the employee, such as the principles of mutual cooperation, good faith and fairness, the obligation of the parties to provide information on a mutual basis, the right to representation of interest and self-organization, the ban on discrimination, the protection of the weaker party, positive discrimination based on social grounds, the requirement of proper legal practice etc. If legal assurances are violated, the injured party has the right to seek remedy in a court of law.[63]

100. Several new legal principles have appeared in the Labour Code, some of which are entirely new. However, the majority have been developed by judicial practice in the past and have only now been turned into written law by the Code. For example, the Code has general rules governing when declarations have legal effect in employment. These are significant, particularly when determining the legal status of employers' policies which have been issued unilaterally.

101. Moreover, the Labour Code changed the basic approach to labour law: as compared to the earlier regulation, individual and collective agreements are given a

62. József HAJDÚ *The right to Social Security in the Hungarian Fundamental Law in. The right to Social Security in the Constitutions of the World: Broadening the moral and legal space for social justice*; Alexandre Egorov and Marcin Wujczyk (eds), International Labour Organization (2016) pp. 89–106.
63. KOZMA Anna – LŐRINCZ György – PÁL Lajos, A Munka Törvénykönyvének magyarázata, Budapest: HVG-Orac, 2020.

much broader scope, thereby shifting the parties' relationship towards juxtaposition; in addition, the general requirements of conduct are also formed according to the rules of civil law. In this way, employment risks are for the most part placed from the employer onto the employee.[64]

102. Above the basic principles of the Hungarian Fundamental Law (Constitution) which determine the content of labour law are outlined. Furthermore, according to Chapter I of the new HLC, the principles of labour law can be divided into two groups: A. general principles (compliance principle) and B. behavioural principles.

103. A. The general (compliance) principles of Hungarian Labour Code are as follows:

(a) conformity with EU law;
(b) limitation of the interpretation of agreements.

104. B. The behavioural principles of the HLC are as follows:

(a) principle of expected conduct;
(b) principle of equitable assessment;
(c) obligation to provide information on a mutual basis;
(d) proper exercise of rights;
(e) protection of the legitimate economic interests of the employer;
(f) requirement of maintaining confidentiality;
(g) protection of personal rights;
(h) restriction of the employer's right of control;
(i) equal treatment.

a. General (Compliance) Principles of the HLC

105. The general provisions of the HLC are of decisive importance in respect of the application of law because these rules include the fundamental principles which determine labour law and the general provisions which are applied universally to all (most) of the legal institutions which are incorporated in the other parts of the HLC:

(a) Conformity with EU law. Pursuant to the basic interpretation principle of the HLC, the provisions of the labour code must be interpreted in accordance with the legislation of Hungary and the European Union. The practical importance of the fundamental principle lies mainly in the fact that, in the course of the application of law, the labour law directives of the European Union can be referred to (regardless of whether the Hungarian legislators provided for the given question in accordance with the requirements of the directive).

64. HAJDÚ József – KUN Attila (eds), *Munkajog I.*, Budapest: Patrocinium, 2012. p. 79.

(b) The second general principle is that agreements which waive or restrict the rights of a person (employee) cannot be broadly construed [Subsections (1)–(2) of section 5 of the HLC].[65]

b. The Behavioural Principles of the HLC

106. (a) *Conduct expected during the execution of employment relationship.* Employment contracts must be executed as it might normally be expected in the given circumstances, unless any legal provision exists to the contrary. In exercising rights and discharging obligations, the parties involved must act in a manner consistent with the principle of good faith and fairness, they shall be required to cooperate with one another, and they shall not engage in any conduct to breach the rights or legitimate interests of the other party. [Subsections (1)–(2) of section 6 of the HLC]. New general conduct rules replaced the introductory provisions of the former Labour Code and played an important part in the legal interpretation of the HLC in force. They set down more comprehensively the general behaviour expected from each party and the requirement to act with due diligence, as well as with fair and reasonable consideration of the employee in particular cases, are both new. They also encompass employees' behaviour outside working hours and more precisely define the possible interpretation of confidentiality obligations.[66]

107. (b) *Principle of equitable assessment.* Employers should take into account the interests of workers under the principle of equitable assessment; where the mode of performance is defined by unilateral act, it should be done so as not to cause unreasonable disadvantage to the worker affected [Subsection (3) of section 6 of the HLC].[67]

108. (c) *Obligation to provide information on a mutual basis.* The parties falling within the scope of the Labour Code must inform each other concerning all facts, information and circumstances, and any changes therein, which are considered essential from the point of view of employment relationships and exercising rights and discharging obligations as defined in this Act [Subsection (4) of section 6 of the HLC].[68]

109. (d) *Requirement of proper exercise of rights.* Wrongful exercise of rights is prohibited. For the purposes of the HLC 'wrongful exercise of rights' means, in particular, any act that is intended for or leads to the injury of the legitimate interests of others, restrictions on the enforcement of their interests, harassment, or the suppression of their opinion. [section 7 of the HLC].

---

65. József HAJDÚ The basic principles of the Hungarian labour law (2015) http://acta.bibl.u-szeged.hu/45286/1/juridpol_078_394-404.pdf (26 Jul. 2023).
66. FERENCZ Jácint – GÖNDÖR Éva – GYULAVÁRI Tamás – KÁRTYÁS Gábor, *Munkajogi alapismeretek*, Budapest: ELTE Kiadó, 2013. p. 35.
67. KOZMA Anna – LŐRINCZ György – PÁL Lajos, A Munka Törvénykönyvének magyarázata, Budapest: HVG-Orac, 2020.
68. HAJDÚ József – KUN Attila (eds), *Munkajog I.*, Budapest: Patrocinium, 2012. p. 83.

110. (e) *Protection of the legitimate economic interests of the employer.* During the life of the employment relationship, workers may not engage in any conduct by which to jeopardize the legitimate economic interests of the employer, unless so authorized by the relevant legislation. Workers may not engage in any conduct during or outside their paid working hours that – stemming from the worker's job or position in the employer's hierarchy – directly and factually has the potential to damage the employer's reputation, legitimate economic interest or the intended purpose of the employment relationship. Workers may not exercise the right to express their opinion in a way where it may lead to causing serious harm or damage to the employer's reputation or legitimate economic and organizational interests [Subsections (1)–(3) of section 8 of the HLC].[69]

111. (f) *Requirement of maintaining confidentiality.* Workers must maintain confidentiality in relation to business secrets obtained in the course of their work. Moreover, workers may not disclose to unauthorized persons any data learned in connection with their activities that, if revealed, would result in detrimental consequences for the employer or other persons. The requirement of confidentiality shall not apply to any information that is declared by specific other legislation to be treated as information of public interest or public information and as such is rendered subject to disclosure requirement [Subsection (4) of section 8 of the HLC].

112. (g) *Protection of personal rights.* The personal rights of parties falling within the scope of the Labour Code must be respected. The personal right of workers may be restricted if deemed strictly necessary for reasons directly related to the intended purpose of the employment relationship and if proportionate for achieving its objective. The means and conditions for any restriction of personal rights, and the expected duration shall be communicated to the workers affected in advance. On general principle, workers may not waive their personal rights in advance. Any legal statement concerned with the personal rights of a worker must be formally valid if made in writing [Subsections (1)–(3) of section 9 of the HLC].[70,71]

113. A worker may be requested to make a statement or to disclose certain information only if it does not violate his/her personal rights, and if deemed necessary for the conclusion, fulfilment or termination of the employment relationship. An employee may be requested to take an aptitude test if one is prescribed by employment regulations, or if deemed necessary with a view to exercising rights and discharging obligations in accordance with employment regulations. Employers must

---

69. HAJDÚ, József *Véleménynyilvánítási szabadság a munkahelyen különös tekintettel a visszaélést bejelentők védelmére* In: PÁL, Lajos (szerk.) A véleménynyilvánítás szabadsága és korlátai a munkajogviszonyban: A Magyar Munkajogi Társaság 2021. június 23-i vitaülésén elhangzott előadások, hozzászólások Budapest, Magyarország: HVG-ORAC (2022) 164 p. pp. 66–81.
70. ARANY TÓTH Mariann, *A munkavállaló emberi méltóságának védelme a munkaviszonyban,* http://www.mjsz.uni-miskolc.hu/201101/10_aranytothmariann.pdf (26 Jul. 2023).
71. Adrienn LUKÁCS (2020) Protection of Employees' Right to Privacy and Right to Data Protection on Social Network Sites – with Special Regard to France and Hungary; https://www.academia.edu/104220380/Protection_of_Employees_Right_to_Privacy_and_Right_to_Data_Protection_on_Social_Network_Sites_with_Special_Regard_to_France_and_Hungary (26 Jul. 2023).

inform their workers concerning the processing of their personal data. Employers are permitted to disclose facts, data and opinions concerning a worker to third persons in the cases specified by law or upon the worker's consent.

114. An employee may only be requested to issue a declaration or to disclose data and may only be subject to a test for the assessment of his/her skills which does not violate his/her personal rights and is relevant to the establishment, maintenance or termination of employment. An employee may take an aptitude test if it does not violate his/her personal rights and which is based on rules relating to his/her employment.[72]

115. The monitoring of employees may only be extended to practices and activities related to their employment, and should not violate the human dignity of the employee. The privacy of the employee may not be monitored. The employer must inform its employees in advance of the use of any technical devices that serve to monitor the employees. In the event of the application of technical devices, the employer must determine adequate rules of data protection and data security.[73]

116. Information and data pertaining to workers may be used without their consent for statistical purposes and may be disclosed for statistical use in a manner that precludes identification of the workers to whom they pertain [Subsections (1)–(4) of section 10 of the HLC].

117. h) *Restriction of the employer's right of control.* (protection of personal rights) Employers are allowed to monitor the behaviour of workers only to the extent pertaining to the employment relationship. The employers' actions of control, and the means and methods used, may not be at the expense of human dignity. The private life of workers may not be violated. Employers must inform their workers in advance concerning the technical means used for the surveillance of workers [Subsections (1)–(2) of section 11 of the HLC].[74]

118. j) *Principle of equal treatment.* In connection with employment relationships, such as the remuneration of work, the principle of equal treatment must be strictly observed. Remedying the consequences of any breach of this requirement may not result in any violation of, or harm to, the rights of other workers. 'Wage' means any remuneration provided directly or indirectly in cash or in kind, based on

72. Adrienn LUKÁCS: *Privacy at Work: the Regulation of Camera Surveillance in Hungarian Labour Law*, Acta Universitatis George Bacovia – Juridica 6: (1) pp. 77–118.
73. Adrienn LUKÁCS: *To Post, or Not to Post – That is the Question: Employee Monitoring and Employees' Right to Data Protection,* Masaryk University Journal of Law And Technology 11: (2) pp. 185–214.
74. LAKI Mihály – NACSA Beáta – NEUMANN László, *Az új Munka Törvénykönyvének hatása a munkavállalók és a munkáltatók közötti kapcsolatokra*, Kutatási zárójelentés, Budapest: Magyar Tudományos Akadémia Közgazdaság- és Regionális Tudományi Kutatóközpont Közgazdaságtudományi Intézet, 2013, http://mek.oszk.hu/11400/11439/11439.pdf (26 Jul. 2023).

the employment relationship. The equal value of work for the purposes of the principle of equal treatment should be determined based on the nature of the work performed, its quality and quantity, working conditions, the required vocational training, physical or intellectual efforts expended, experience, responsibilities and labour market conditions [Labour Code, Subsections (1)–(3) of section 12].[75]

D. *Interpretation of Legal Declarations*

1. Types of Legal Declarations

119. According to the HLC there are six forms of legal declarations (acts):

(1) agreement;
(2) unilateral acts, statements;
(3) commitments;
(4) employer's internal policy;
(5) information;
(6) condition.

120. (1) *Agreements.* According to section 14 of the HLC, contracts concluded under the HLC constitute the outcome of an agreement resting on mutual consent of the parties, mainly employer(s) and employee(s) in individual employment relationships.[76]

121. (2) *Unilateral acts, statements.* Rights or obligations may derive from unilateral acts only in cases defined by employment regulations. Exercising the right of withdrawal as provided for in employment regulations or by agreement of the parties terminates the agreement retroactively to the date of conclusion. In the event of withdrawal, the parties will settle accounts. A unilateral act will take effect upon delivery to the recipient and – unless otherwise provided for in the HLC – it may be amended or withdrawn only upon the recipient's consent.[77]

122. (3) *Commitments.* Under unilateral commitments (hereinafter referred to as 'commitment') the carrying out of the commitments entered into may be demanded irrespective of the beneficiary's acceptance. Workers are allowed to undertake a statement of commitment only where expressly provided for by employment regulations. A commitment may be amended to the beneficiary's detriment, or may be terminated effective immediately in the event of subsequent major changes in the

75. FERENCZ Jácint – GÖNDÖR Éva – GYULAVÁRI Tamás – KÁRTYÁS Gábor, *Munkajogi alapismeretek*, Budapest: ELTE Kiadó, 2013. pp. 42–43.
76. DUDÁS Katalin – GYULAVÁRI Tamás – HORVÁTH István – Hős Nikolett – KULISITY Mária – HUNGLER Sára – KÁRTYÁS Gábor – KUN Attila – PETROVICS Zoltán – RÁCZ Réka, *Munkajog – V. átdolgozott kiadás*, Budapest: ELTE Eötvös Kiadó, 2019.
77. KISS György (ed.) *Munkajog* Ludovika Egyetemi Kiadó, Budapest, 2020.

circumstances of the person making the commitment whereby carrying out the commitment is no longer possible or it would result in unreasonable hardship. Furthermore, the provisions governing unilateral actions also apply to commitments, with the exception that the obligor cannot claim invalidity of his/her legal action, alleging that it was not served upon the beneficiary or that it was served improperly.[78]

123. (4) *Employer's internal by-laws.* Employers are able to implement the legal declarations (namely the above-mentioned agreements, unilateral acts and statements) by means of internal rules established of its own accord or by way of a procedure formulated unilaterally (hereinafter referred to as employer's internal by-laws). The employer's internal by-law is considered to be delivered if published by means considered customary for, and commonly known in, the area.[79]

124. (5) *Information.* The provisions on legal declarations (acts) will apply where the obligation to provide information is prescribed by employment regulations upon either of the parties. Unless otherwise provided for by employment regulations, information will be provided at a time and in a manner to permit the exercise of rights and the fulfilment of obligations. Information is considered provided if published by means considered customary for, and commonly known in, the area.[80]

125. (6) *Condition.* In addition, the parties may render the conclusion, amendment or termination of the agreement contingent upon certain future, uncertain events (conditions). Any condition that would alter the employment relationship to the disadvantage of workers, or that would bring about the termination of the employment relationship may not be applied. Any condition that is contradictory, impossible or unintelligible is considered invalid, in which case the agreement will be treated as if does not contain the condition in question.[81]

126. As long as a condition is pending, the parties must refrain from taking any action that would impair the other party's right that is contingent upon that condition. Neither of the parties may allege the realization or frustration of the condition if it results from the party's wrongful conduct.

2. Formality of Legal Declarations

127. In connection with the formal requirements of legal declarations, the HLC contains five principles.

---

78. CSÉFFÁN József, *A munka törvénykönyve és magyarázata*, Szeged: Szegedi Rendezvényszervező Kft., 2023.
79. KOZMA Anna – LŐRINCZ György – PÁL Lajos, *A Munka Törvénykönyvének magyarázata*, Budapest: HVG-Orac, 2020.
80. DUDÁS Katalin – GYULAVÁRI Tamás – HORVÁTH István – Hős Nikolett – KULISITY Mária – HUNGLER Sára – KÁRTYÁS Gábor – KUN Attila – PETROVICS Zoltán – RÁCZ Réka, *Munkajog – V. átdolgozott kiadás*, Budapest: ELTE Eötvös Kiadó, 2019.
81. KISS György (ed.) *Munkajog* Ludovika Egyetemi Kiadó, Budapest, 2020.

128. (a) Legal declarations in employment relations may be made without particular formal requirements (e.g., in writing, or orally, or by implicit conduct) unless otherwise provided for by employment regulations or by agreement of the parties. Upon the employee's request, legal declarations must be made in writing by the employer where this is not otherwise mandatory.

129. (b) A legal declaration is construed to have been made in writing if executed by means of an electronic document with facilities for retrieving the information contained in the legal declaration unaltered, and for identifying the person making the legal declaration and the time when it was made (hereinafter referred to as 'electronic document').

130. According to section 22, paragraph (2) of the Labour Code, a legal declaration shall be considered written if its communication is realized by an electronic document suitable for the unchanged recollection of the information contained in the legal declaration, and the identification of the declarant and the time of the declaration (further on: electronic document).[82] According to the current state of technology, it is difficult, sometimes almost impossible for the party making the legal declaration to prove the communication of electronic documents. Thus, it is risky to communicate legal declarations of a substantial legal effect (e.g., termination, withdrawal) in such a way, since according to section 24, paragraph (4) in case of dispute the party making the legal declaration has to prove that it has been duly communicated.[83]

131. For example, an employment relationship can be terminated in an electronic document (e.g., in e-mail or even text message), provided that it is suitable for the unchanged recollection of the information contained in it, and the identification of the declarant and the time of the legal declaration. Thus, the employee can terminate his/her employment relationship in a simple electronic e-mail. It is sufficient if he or she writes the following during the probation period: 'Hereby I terminate my employment relationship during the probation period with immediate effect.' Nevertheless, in the event of a dispute, he or she has to prove that the legislative requirements on electronic documents apply. The provisions of Labour Code declare these widely spread – and also being considered in public opinion as written – means of communication as written without any further requirements. There are also statements according to which notification by means of an electronic document can also be realized by e-mailing a signed and scanned document.[84]

132. Furthermore, the electronic labour law declarations carry another risk in addition to the acceptance of the e-signature by the court/authorities: the employer has to be able to prove not only the content of the declaration but also that it was

82. CSÉFFÁN József, *A munka törvénykönyve és magyarázata*, Szeged: Szegedi Rendezvényszervező Kft., 2023.
83. KARDKOVÁCS 2014, p. 86.
84. Kolos KARDKOVÁCS (ed.): Az új Munka törvénykönyvének magyarázata. (Explanation of the New Labour Code.) HVG Orac, Budapest, 2014. p. 83.

delivered to the employee, which can be problematic in case of electronic communication. The root of the problem is that an e-signature loses its legal value when printed, which means that in order to maintain its legal value, the e-signed document shall stay in electronic form, which means it shall be delivered to the recipient (e.g., the employee) by electronic means.

133. Hence, electronic delivery is a risk factor compared to 'traditional' delivery (i.e., personal delivery or postal delivery) because proving the delivery of an email or other electronic communication is more difficult than proving the delivery of a physical document, where the employee usually confirms takeover by signing the document or the postal return receipt.[85]

134. (c) Where an agreement had to be made in writing, any amendment thereto and termination thereof must also be executed in writing.

135. (d) Basically, any legal declaration made in violation of formal requirements is construed as invalid. However, the legal consequences of invalidity cannot apply to any legal declaration that has been executed upon the parties' mutual consent.

136. (e) As regards the unilateral declarations of employers, the reasons must be provided in writing in cases defined by the HLC, and workers affected must be properly informed concerning the means of enforcement of a claim and also of the time limit available, if shorter than the term of limitation. In the event of failure to provide information as to the time limit, the claim may not be enforced after a period of six months.

137. The requirement for executing legal declarations in writing is satisfied by means of an authentic instrument or a private document with full probative force if the party (representative) is illiterate or is unable to read or write.

138. The agreement must be concluded in writing, which is provided for by the employer, a copy of which must be given to the worker affected. The agreement must indicate the names of the parties and their particulars of importance from the point of view of the performance of the agreement.

139. According to section 24 of the HLC, a legal declaration made in writing is served upon delivery to the person concerned or the person authorized to receive it, or at the time when access to the electronic document is provided. The legal declaration is also considered served if the person concerned or the authorized recipient refuses to receive it or intentionally prevents delivery. Where a legal declaration is dispatched in the form of certified mail with certified delivery, it is considered served:

---

85. From Pen to Pendrive – Part V: General Rules on E-Writing in Labour Law in Hungary; https://smartlegal.hu/publication/from-pen-to-pendrive---part-v-general-rules-on-e-writing-in-labour-law-in-hungary-746 (26 Jul. 2023).

(a) if the person concerned or the authorized recipient refused to receive the consignment, or if delivery to the address provided by the person concerned failed and the consignment is returned marked addressee unavailable or address unknown, on the day when delivery was attempted;
(b) in all other cases, on the fifth working day following the day when delivery was attempted without success or following the day when the notice was posted.

140. With respect to any legal declaration that may be subject to court proceedings under the HLC, a petition may be filed to challenge the presumption of service simultaneously with filing for court action, within fifteen days from the time of receiving information concerning the presumption of service, or within six months from the actual date of service at the latest. Furthermore, the relevant provisions of the Code of Civil Procedure will apply to actions to challenge a presumption of service. If the petition to challenge the presumption of service is sustained, the time limit for filing for court action shall be considered met.

141. In case of dispute, the burden of proof for having the service of process executed properly lies with the person making the legal act.

142. Deadlines and calculation of time limits for delivering legal acts. Where a time limit is prescribed by employment regulations or by agreement of the parties for making specific legal acts or to do or not to do certain other acts, the below-mentioned relevant time limit must be calculated. A time limit is calculated from the day following the day on which the action (event) giving rise to the time limit occurred. A time limit specified in weeks will expire on the day that, by definition, corresponds to the day of initiation. The day of expiration of a deadline specified in months or years will be that day the numbering of which corresponds with the day of initiation, or the last day of the month if such day is not available in the month of expiration.

143. A time limit is considered to have elapsed at the end of the final day. A time limit is considered to have elapsed at the end of the next working day of normal working schedule, if the last day is a dedicated weekly rest day or public holiday. A time limit is considered met if the legal act is delivered by the end of the last day or certain other actions are carried out by such time. Failure to meet a deadline can be excusable if expressly permitted by the employment regulations by which it is prescribed.

144. Unless otherwise prescribed by employment regulations, a day is construed as a calendar day.[86]

86. FERENCZ Jácint – GÖNDÖR Éva – GYULAVÁRI Tamás – KÁRTYÁS Gábor, *Munkajogi alapismeretek*, Budapest: ELTE Kiadó, 2013. pp. 44–49.

E. Deviation from the Rules of the Labour Code

145. The principle of cogency pervades the whole of Hungarian Labour Law. This means that the rules of law are always binding, and agreements, stipulations, and summary dispositions contrary to these may be disregarded or substituted by corresponding provisions of the legal rule (cogent rule).

146. However, according to the jurisprudential debates, in the drafting procedure of the Labour Code (2012), the rules on the individual employment contract are – as a general rule – a 'one-sided dispositive', meaning that any deviation from the Labour Code's rules through collective agreements are to be made only in favour of the employees (favourability principle).

147. However, unlike the former system (provisions of the former HLC, 1992), collective bargaining agreements may also be able to deviate from the rules – to the disadvantage of employees. This conceptual change is supposed, and is likely, to intensify the collaboration between employers and trade unions.[87]

F. Infirmity of Legal Statements in Labour Law

148. In case of infirmity of legal statements, the HLC makes differentiation between (1) null and void statement and (2) contestable statement.

1. Null and Void

149. Any agreement that infringes upon any employment regulation, or that is entered into by way of circumvention of any employment regulation shall be null and void. Bogus agreements are null and void, and if such agreement is intended to disguise another agreement, it will be judged on the basis of the disguised agreement.

150. An agreement if annulled is considered void, unless the relevant employment regulation stipulates another legal consequence. The party concerned may allege the invalidity of an annulled contract without a time limit; the court observes the nullity of the agreement of its own motion.[88]

87. DUDÁS Katalin – GYULAVÁRI Tamás – HORVÁTH István – Hős Nikolett – KULISITY Mária – HUNGLER Sára – KÁRTYÁS Gábor – KUN Attila – PETROVICS Zoltán – RÁCZ Réka, *Munkajog – V. átdolgozott kiadás*, Budapest: ELTE Eötvös Kiadó, 2019.
88. HAJDÚ József – KUN Attila (eds), *Munkajog I.*, Budapest: Patrocinium, 2012. pp. 72–73.

2. Contestability

151. An agreement may be contestable if either party was in error regarding any material fact or circumstance at the time of its conclusion, provided that such error was caused or could have been recognized by the other party, or if both parties were under the same mistaken assumption. An agreement may be contested on the grounds of misapprehension of a legal issue if such misapprehension is deemed significant and if the advice of a legal counsel, acting within the scope of his/her competence, to the parties affected has been manifestly erroneous in terms of the contents of the relevant legislation. An agreement may be contested if it was obtained unlawfully by duress or coercion. An agreement may be avoided by a person who has been misled or persuaded unlawfully to make a legal act by duress or coercion, or by a person acting under a mistaken assumption.

152. The time limit for filing an action for contestability is thirty days, commencing upon recognition of the error or, in the case of duress or coercion, upon cessation of duress. The statute of limitations duly applies to the time limit for bringing an action for contest, with the exception that the right to contest will terminate after six months.

153. The other party can be notified in writing regarding the execution of a legal act for contestability within the above-mentioned time limit.[89]

3. Legal Consequences of Infirmity

154. Rights and obligations arising from or in connection with an infirmed agreement are treated as if they existed under a valid agreement. Unless otherwise provided for in the HLC, employers may terminate – with immediate effect – any legal relationships created on the basis of an invalid agreement, if the parties fail to abolish the cause of invalidity. Employers are liable to pay their workers severance payment covering a period otherwise due in the event of dismissal by the employer, furthermore, the rules on severance pay also apply if the employment contract is declared invalid for reasons attributable to the employer and it has to be terminated. If any part of an agreement is deemed infirmed, the relevant employment regulations will be applied instead, unless the parties would otherwise not have concluded the agreement without the invalid part. As regards the infirmity of unilateral acts, no rights and obligations arise from or in connection with such legal acts.

155. In the event that the infirmity of an agreement results in damages, the provisions on liability for damages is applied.[90]

89. DUDÁS Katalin – GYULAVÁRI Tamás – HORVÁTH István – Hős Nikolett– KULISITY Mária – HUNGLER Sára – KÁRTYÁS Gábor – KUN Attila – PETROVICS Zoltán – RÁCZ Réka, *Munkajog – V. átdolgozott kiadás*, Budapest: ELTE Eötvös Kiadó, 2019.
90. KOZMA Anna – LŐRINCZ György – PÁL Lajos, *A Munka Törvénykönyvének magyarázata*, Budapest: HVG-Orac, 2020.

§2. DEFINITIONS AND NOTIONS

I. Distinction Between Labour Law and Other Branches of Law

156. According to the opinion prevailing in the science of Hungarian labour law, labour law is that branch of the uniform Hungarian legal system which regulates the social relations connected with performing human work, i.e., the relations established between people in the work situation. Within its domain we can identify:

- individual labour relations;
- collective labour relations;
- the legal relations which organize and protect labour relations (labour administration).

157. In Hungary, labour law is an independent branch of law. Correspondingly, it is not a part of Civil Law. However, the key feature of the labour code (entered into force on 1 July 2012) is that it intends to align the regulation of the working environment with that of contractual law enshrined in the Civil Code.[91]

A. *Individual Labour Relations*

158. The individual labour relationship is a link created typically between two persons (employer and employee) in the performance of some task. Performing certain work – exerting manpower – may, however, take place for several reasons and in many different ways. Of these, only those cases are included in labour relations in which the manpower of one of the parties is placed, generally and with the intention to be of an enduring character, at the disposal of the other party. A party does this in order to assert his/her right to work and to acquire the means necessary to his/her living. The second purpose, on the other hand, is to perform his/her duties by means of the manpower at his/her disposal. According to the uniform standpoint of Hungarian jurisprudence, these labour relations form the subject of Labour Law.

159. The individual labour relationship is uniform. However, within this uniform character, different kinds of labour relations are to be found, showing certain differences in the details of regulations. These differences may be ascribed to different circumstances. With regard to the conditions of work, it may be necessary to apply solutions which are different in detail. For example, it is obvious that the question of the length of the working day or the weekly day of rest is resolved differently in the case of sailors from those working in the iron industry or even in an office or theatre. Different arrangements may likewise be necessary because of the character of the work. There will be a – for example – different wage system for a worker than for a public or civil servant. And the duties and responsibilities connected with work will have a different form in the case of a subordinate than that of

91. HAJDÚ József – KUN Attila (eds), *Munkajog I.*, Budapest: Patrocinium, 2012. p. 17.

a supervisor. Some of the new types of flexible employment relationships – telework, agency work, student work, on-call-contract, job-sharing etc. – were enacted into two independent chapters of the Labour Code. This question will be raised again in Part I in the course of dealing with individual labour relationships.

160. The present Hungarian very fundamental legal regulation of labour law has created three Acts:

- Act I of 2012 on the Labour Code;[Munka törvénykönyve].
- Act XXXIII of 1992 on the Legal Status of Civil Servants.
- Act CXCIX of 2011 on the Legal Status of Public Servants.

161. The relationship among the three Acts may be defined in the following way:

(a) The Labour Code is of general character and covers each type of employment unless otherwise provided. The HLC is mainly applicable in the competitive private sector.
(b) The Act on the Legal Status of Civil Servants covers the employees of cultural, some health care and other public service institutions financed by central and local (county, town, local government) funds. However, it does not cover those employees of such institutions who are not paid with state funds, e.g., employees of private or ecclesiastical schools, hospitals, etc. They are covered by the general rules of the Labour Code. However, unless the Act provides differently, the provisions of the Labour Code are to be applied in every respect to these employees as well. This provision unambiguously implies that the legal relationship of these employees comes within the sphere of Labour Law. Otherwise, this is the unified standpoint of the science of Labour Law.
(c) The Act on the Legal Status of Public Servants covers (a) the government service relationship of government officials and administrators in the Prime Minister's Office, ministries, ministerial offices, central offices (hereinafter referred to as central administrative authority), as well as (b) in regional and local government organs, county-level and capital administrative offices of the central administrative authority, as well as (c) in the central and regional organs of the organ appointed by the Government to maintain institutions, the police, law enforcement and official disaster management, and also (d) the government service relationship of the public administration under-secretary and deputy under-secretary of the ministry and the deputy under-secretary of the Prime Minister's Office, and (e) the public service legal relationship of public officials and administrators in the office and authoritative administrative coalition, public domain control and the office of district notary of the body of representatives of the local government, as well as (f) in the office of national minority self-governments (hereinafter referred to as office of the body of representatives).[92]

92. FERENCZ Jácint – GÖNDÖR Éva – GYULAVÁRI Tamás – KÁRTYÁS Gábor, *Munkajogi alapismeretek*, Budapest: ELTE Kiadó, 2013. pp. 17–21.

162. This situation reflects the dual character of the position of civil and public servants. On the one hand, the civil and public servant is a person who makes his/her labour available to some state organ for remuneration, and the given organ fulfils its tasks through him/her. This legal relationship shows identical elements as the other individual employment relationships. Non-ambiguity is also reflected in the framework of the science of law. According to the prevailing standpoint of the science of labour law, the employment element of civil and public servants comes within the sphere of labour law; however, according to the authors of administrative law, it should be classified under administrative law. From their standpoint, the situation of civil and public servants shows a double legal binding. From the point of view of performance of work, it belongs to labour law whereas, in respect of exercise of public powers, i.e., as to the contents of the activity displayed, civil and public servants come within the sphere of administrative law. Labour relations of the civil and public servants are regulated in an Act separate from the Labour Code. Consequently, labour relations between civil and public servants are not covered in this book.[93]

163. There are two important fundamental changes which restructured the employment relationship of two important sectors, namely health care (Healthcare Service Relationship) and public education (Status Act):

(a) *Healthcare Service Relationship.* On 14 October 2020, the Hungarian Parliament adopted Act C of 2020 on Healthcare Service Relationship which fundamentally transforms the employment relationships of only physicians at State-owned healthcare service providers. It replaced the existing public employment relationship between health professionals (mainly doctors), public providers and their controlling authorities. The Act brings the employment of health workers under strict central control by introducing a new employment status similar to that of the armed forces. The Act also provides doctors with an unprecedented 120% salary increase and criminalizes informal payments (gratitude money).[94]
(b) *Public Education Teachers Relationship.* On 6 July 2023, the Hungarian Parliament adopted Act LII of 2023 on New Career Path of Teachers. The so-called status act which introduces changes in the education law and which is expected to further limit teachers' autonomy. It will enter into force on 1 January 2024. The former civil servants status of teachers as public employees will be terminated and they will have to declare whether they wish to transfer to the status of public education employees into the new status system (public education employee), thus losing part of the protection granted by their previous civil servant status.[95]

93. HAJDÚ József – KUN Attila (eds), *Munkajog I.*, Budapest: Patrocinium, 2012. pp. 18–21.
94. Peter GAAL, Zita VELKEY, Viktoria SZERENCSES, Erin WEBB, The 2020 reform of the employment status of Hungarian health workers: Will it eliminate informal payments and separate the public and private sectors from each other? Health Policy Volume 125, Issue 7, July 2021, pp. 833–840.
95. Lawmakers Pass New Law on Teachers (2023), https://hungarymatters.hu/2023/07/05/lawmakers-pass-new-law-on-teachers/ (26 Jul. 2023).

B. Collective Labour Relations

164. Collective labour relations are legal relationships characterized by the fact that at least one side of them has a collective character (trade union, works' council, employers' organization, employees' or employers' collective, etc.). Trade union activities such as protection of interest collective negotiations and agreements, employee participation in employer's decisions, direct actions and resolution of collective conflicts, all belong here. Accordingly, Part III of the HLC deals with the legal relations connected with the activities of trade unions as representative organizations of workers and employees, as well as the role and rights of the workers' collective in the enterprise. This is the more justified because, as will be seen, the role of the trade union, at least in Hungary, includes the latter aspect, and the activity of the trade union is closely linked with that of the workers' collective. The legal problems falling within the sphere of industrial relations are, as a rule, dealt with by labour law. It is to be noted that establishing the rights of the workers' collective in the management of an enterprise falls within the scope of labour law, as does the delegation of members of the workers' collective onto the managerial board. However, the rights of members of the managerial board as such are determined by the rules concerning the organization of the enterprise and come within the scope of Company Law.[96]

C. Legal Relations Organizing and Protecting Labour Relations (Labour Administration)

165. The third branch of legal relations forming the subject of labour law is constituted by those serving to organize the labour relationship and enhance the right to work and right at work of employees/ workers. Within it, three sub-groups may be identified. The first is formed by those whose purpose is to promote the creation of legal relationships and include career advice and labour exchange (in brief: active labour market policies). The second group includes the rules of control over the application of the rules of the labour law guarantee necessary for the conditions of work (occupational safety and health legislation and labour inspection). Finally, the third sub-group includes legal relations emerging from the resolution of disputes arising from the labour relationship. Problems of delineation appear also in this regard, among them the demarcation of those legal relations falling within the system of Administrative Law and those belonging to the Law of Civil Procedure.[97]

96. LAKI Mihály – NACSA Beáta – NEUMANN LÁSZLÓ, *Az új Munka Törvénykönyvének hatása a munkavállalók és a munkáltatók közötti kapcsolatokra*, Kutatási zárójelentés, Budapest: Magyar Tudományos Akadémia Közgazdaság- és Regionális Tudományi Kutatóközpont Közgazdaságtudományi Intézet, 2013, http://mek.oszk.hu/11400/11439/11439.pdf (26 Jul. 2023).
97. HAJDÚ József – KUN Attila (eds), *Munkajog I.*, Budapest: Patrocinium, 2012. pp. 24–25.

II. Issues of Delineation

A. Scope of Delineation

166. As mentioned before, the application of manpower, that is the performance of work, may take place for different purposes and in different ways. As a result of this, the performance of work may appear in the framework of several types of legal relations. Therefore, the boundaries of these labour relations and other legal relations will be illustrated. Within this sphere, membership relations within producers' co-operatives, certain legal relations in civil law, actual work during the course of training, as well as work performed as an element of a court sentence must be dealt with in particular.

B. Legal Relations in Civil Law: Mandate and Undertaking

167. Mandates, or undertakings, are generally aimed at providing one or more defined services, products or results, that is to say, certain goods or at least a result manifested in the form of services or goods. To realize this, it is necessary to perform work. The party concerned, however, is only obliged to provide the result; he/she does not necessarily provide his/her labour power. It is also possible that he/she does not personally deliver the product. To the contrary: under a labour relationship the employee undertakes only to place his/her manpower at the disposal of the employer, not necessarily to produce any result. The uniform standpoint of jurisprudence is, therefore, that outwork does not belong in the domain of labour law. At the same time, it should be noted that the delineation between the legal relations belonging to civil law and those belonging to labour law is not always unambiguous and simple. The boundaries of both legal branches are blurred. Taking undertakings or mandates within the framework of civil law as one extreme limit, and the labour relationship within the framework of labour law as another, there are several types of legal relations the essential element of which is to perform work.

C. Vocational Training

168. The performance of work is also an element of vocational training. Its aim is, however, not to provide a source of livelihood but to acquire the practical knowledge necessary to master a trade. This occurs in secondary and higher education, where providing for vocational training is an integral part of education. The legal sources of vocational training are as follow: (1) Vocational Training Act (Act CXII of 2019), governing vocational training in and outside the school system, regulates the issue of the national list of state-recognized vocational qualifications. (2) Labour and Unemployment Act adopted in 1991 (Act IV of 1991) regulates training and retraining for the unemployed and defines the range of those who may be eligible for support and (3) Labour Code (Act I of 2012) is the basic document regulating the relationship between employers and employees. However, the uniform standpoint of labour law is that there is no labour relationship here and that education remains outside the domain of labour law.

D. Civic Duty

169. The performance of work also appears in legal relations arising from the so-called temporary obligation to work. The aim of the temporary obligation to work is, however, not to provide for the tasks of production, nor, from the perspective of the worker, to ensure a means of livelihood. The aim is to prevent some danger threatening the state or the economy i.e., the community, and to participate in its prevention. This is one of the duties affecting all citizens. This falls not within the domain of labour law but within that of Administrative Law.

E. Performance of Work as a Result of a Court Sentence

170. Performance of work may be required as a result of the enforcement imposed by a court. The aim is to educate the perpetrator of a crime. The means of this education is the performance of labour. Entering into such a legal relation does not depend on the will of the parties, for it is created by the court. The legal relationship of those sentenced to reformatory and educative work falls within the sphere of Criminal Law, not Labour Law. According to Act C of 2012 on the Criminal Code, any person sentenced to community service work is obligated to perform the work prescribed for him/her in the court ruling. The work prescribed to be performed in community service is such that the defendant is presumed to be capable of performing, taking into consideration his/her health condition and education. Unless otherwise provided for by law, the defendant performs the community service work at least on one day per week, on the weekly day of rest or on his/her day off, without any remuneration. The shortest duration of community service work shall be one day while its longest duration shall be fifty days. One day of work in community service shall constitute six hours of work.

F. Performance of Work on the Basis of Family Relations

171. Work is also performed within the framework of the family. This work is based on family relations and does not bring about a labour relationship. Its legal aspects are embraced by Family Law. If, however, this type of work performance exceeds the level usually within the framework of family relations (e.g., where a member of the family regularly works in the shop or workroom of the head of the family), this might bring about a labour relationship.

G. Bogus Self-Employment (Individual Entrepreneurs, Joint Ventures – Társas Vállalkozás)

172. Historically, the precarious form of bogus self-employed emerged during the transformation years, as a cost-saving, profit-maximizing and/or survival strategy of larger firms to outsource the 'replaceable' blue-collar workers from company payrolls. The term 'forced-entrepreneurs' (kényszervállalkozó) was coined to indicate that former employers offered incomes to workers only as service providers, and not within employment relationship. Informal sub-contracting occurs via the channels of small companies or individual entrepreneurs: typically for service-related jobs, for an invoice. There are no further statistical data or in-depth studies which would outline the share of bogus self-employed.[98]

H. Public Work

173. Public work is a special form of employment, as this legal relationship is somewhat different from primary labour market employment. It is a state-subsidized active employment programme. The subsidized period may be a maximum of 12 months in the case of the individual public work programmes, and this can be extended by a maximum of 6 additional months. The income collected under public work is higher than the amount of the social benefit but lower than the lowest wage on the primary labour market. Based on the public employment legal relationship, the public worker is entitled to social insurance and old-age pension.

174. In the case of public work operated under the control of the Ministry of Interior, the adjustment of underdeveloped regions of the country is a key consideration. One of the instruments for that is the launch of start-work model programmes in small regions and in settlements. The funds are appropriated according to the labour market situation of the individual counties, in a way that the highest amounts are allocated to regions lagging behind, and, at the same time, public employment is available to as many disadvantaged job seekers as possible. The primary objectives are to help those living in poverty and social exclusion and those entitled to employment substitution benefit, and to offer labour market services and training during the period of public work, so that the public worker should be able to find a job on the primary labour market, too, with the acquired practice. Public work is established under a public employment contract, which is different from a regular employment contract. A public employment status is a special legal status, where the rights and obligations are governed mainly by the provisions of the Labour Code with certain differences governed by the law.

98. Tamás PRUGBERGER – Andrea SZŐLLŐS *Employment Using Information Technology – Self-Employment or Employment,* European Integration Studies, Volume 17, Number 1 (2021), pp. 198–208.
http://doi.org/10.46941/2021.se1.198-208 (26 Jul. 2023).

175. A public worker can be an individual who can establish employment pursuant to the Labour Code and:

- is a job-seeker registered by the district government offices; or
- receives rehabilitation benefit;[99] or
- has applied for recognition as a refugee, protected individual or asylum seeker; or
- is a third-country citizen, obliged to stay at a location specified by law.

176. Public work is funded by the state in the form of public employment support. The form of public work support is determined by Government Decree No. 375/2010 (XII. 31) on support available for public employment[100]

177. The policy has been criticized by many observers for its low efficiency in reintegrating people into the primary labour market, its poor targeting (involving not only those in the most disadvantaged positions, from disadvantaged regions), and for the fact that it absorbed funds from other more efficient labour market tools and provided a lower income than the minimum wage. The massive extension of public works took place at the expense of other, more efficient active labour market policies such as training and mentoring. The European Commission repeatedly urged the government to reconsider the scheme, warning that it did not improve prospects for the jobless.[101]

I. School, Pensioners' and Parental Cooperatives as a Special Agency Work

1. School Cooperatives

178. Between 2012–2016 the school cooperative[102] was one type of atypical employment relationships in the LC.[103] A school cooperative[104] (employer) and its full-time student or pupil (quasi-employee) may enter into a fixed-term employment relationship so as to permit such student to perform work at a third party (customer) with a view to supplying services to such third party.[105] During the period of

99. At least 40% health detriment had been established by the rehabilitation expert body, or who is the recipient of the personal benefit payable to blind persons, or whois the recipient of disability support.
100. http://kozfoglalkoztatas.kormany.hu/download/6/eb/02000/current%20status%20of%20Public%20Work%20Scheme.pdf (26 Jul. 2023).
101. *Hungary: shrinking Public Work Scheme after reform* (2020) https://www.etui.org/covid-social-impact/hungary/hungary-shrinking-public-work-scheme-after-reform (26 Jul. 2023).
102. The first Hungarian Student Cooperative was founded in 1911.
103. Márta MOLNÁR BALOGHNÉ (2016) Az iskolaszövetkezeti munka tb-vonatkozásai, http://ado.hu/rovatok/tb-nyugdij/az-iskolaszovetkezeti-munka-tb-vonatkozasai (26 Jul. 2023).
104. In short, the school cooperative is a hidden TWA which has a competitive advantage compared with an ordinary TWA agency. The significant advantage is that they are exempt from paying social security contribution and social tax.
105. Judit WINDISCH (2016) Ki védi a diákot, ha nyáron dolgozni megy? http://hvg.hu/itthon/20160708_diakmunka_szovetkezet_veszelyek_tanacsok (26 Jul. 2023).

work performed by the employee (exclusively students), the customer would exercise and discharge the employer's rights and obligations, e.g., OSH, the employment of women, young workers and persons with reduced ability, and working time, rest period and the records of these.[106]

179. The main aim of establishing student cooperatives was for the state to bridge over the difficulties of studying and working together. By the effect of the state's role-taking, the application of student cooperatives is significantly cheaper (with 30%–50%)[107] than the 'normal' adult TWA employment. In this way, where the cooperative role-taking can be conceivable, remarkable cost savings can be achieved, especially in cities with universities.

180. Owing to the school cooperative system, youngsters are able to build their careers earlier, which can provide experience and a reference for their future full-time employment, and at the same time, they can form their needs and ability to be responsible for themselves.

181. As a significant change, all of the provisions relating to school cooperatives were repealed on 1 September 2016, as a result of which the legislation was incorporated in the text of the Act on Cooperatives. With this, the legislator intended to prevent the unfavourable outcome of the infringement procedure of the EU started on the grounds that paid vacation is not provided to employed students according to the regulation in force.[108] At the same time, the legislator inserted the basic provisions (leave, minimum wage, break, resting period etc.) of the LC into the Act on Cooperatives.[109]

2. Pensioners' Cooperative

182. The 'pensioners' cooperative' (*közérdekű nyugdíjas szövetkezet*) was introduced in Hungary in July 2017.[110] This type of cooperative is literally based on the

106. Hungary: Young people and temporary employment in Europe (2013) https://www.eurofound.europa.eu/observatories/emcc/comparative-information/national-contributions/hungary/hungary-young-people-and-temporary-employment-in-europe (26 Jul. 2023).
107. There are twofold reasons behind: (1) many times the hourly payment is lower and (2) student workers are not insured by social security.
108. Ádám KÉRI (2016) Diákmunka szeptembertől: így működhet majd az iskolaszövetkezet, http://adozona.hu/munkajog/Igy_dolgozhatnak_a_diakok_szeptembertol_mut_D5MIKK (26 Jul. 2023).
109. Labour Law Newsletter August 2016, http://www.krs.hu/sites/default/files/tudastar/krs_labour_law_newsletter_august_eng.pdf (26 Jul. 2023).
110. Since July 2017, 91 public benefit pensioner associations have been established, and these offer preferential job and tax conditions as well as flexibility. According to a survey conducted by the National Society of Public Benefit Pensioner Associations (KÖZÉSZ), the members of existing associations typically work 3–5 days a week, 4–6 hours per day and usually in the morning, but they are also open to doing night shifts. Employers also benefit from outsourcing work to pensioner associations, as payroll taxes are lower compared to the employment of a jobseeker in working age. (http://www.kormany.hu/download/e/5e/41000/Hungarian Outlook_Hungary labour market indicators continued to improve.pdf) (26 Jul. 2023).

logic of the traditional cooperatives,[111] but in practice, it is a special – highly state subsidised – form of hidden temporary work agency.[112]

183. The government's basic aim with pensioners' cooperatives was that they will employ retired persons to reduce labour shortages,[113] and keep more pensioners economically active, and provide both incomes from work and their old-age pension benefits (multiply the income sources),[114,115,116] and tax subsidy. This would help retain community contact with the elderly (active aging), as well as serving the best interests of the general public to encourage them to transfer their skills, professional knowledge and life experience to younger people. However, it should be underlined that the public and the private sector retired employees fall under different regulations.[117,118]

3. Cooperatives of Parents Staying with Young Children at Home (Parental Cooperative)

184. A cooperative for people with young children at home is a special cooperative which aim is to promote the material, social and cultural situation of people who are not grandparents and who receive childcare allowance or childcare assistance, by providing an opportunity for members to participate or re-participate in employment and to belong to the community within a flexible framework.

185. A cooperative with young children may carry out any activity not prohibited by law and which is consistent with these objectives as laid down in the law.

---

111. In the original meaning, the cooperative is firm owned, controlled, and operated by a group of users for their own benefit. Each member contributes equity capital, and shares in the control of the firm on the basis of one-member, one-vote principle (and not in proportion to his or her equity contribution). [https://www.ica.coop/en/cooperatives/what-is-a-cooperative] (26 Jul. 2023).
112. In Hungary there are two types of such bogus (quasi) cooperative-like TWAs: (1) students' cooperative (dispatching secondary school and mainly university students) and (2) pensioners' cooperative (dispatching retired persons).
113. Hungary: Co-operatives for pension age employees (2017), www.nyusz.hu (26 Jul 2023).
114. Members can receive both income from work and old-age pension benefits, and benefit from preferential taxation.
115. Historically, work besides pension (either old-age or disability) was high in Hungary. The plain reason was the low amount of the pension benefit. The 2016 national micro-census registered 126 thousand people aged 60 years or above who had paid work while receiving some type of pension benefit. This is 5.8% of the pensioner population in this age group (CSO, Central Statistical Office) (2017): 'Ezüstkor – Időskorúak Magyarországon, 2016' [Silver Age – Elderly people in Hungary, 2016]. Budapest: Központi Statisztikai Hivatal.
116. GÁL, Róbert Iván: Pensioner cooperatives combine work and retirement in Hungary, ESPN Flash Report 2018/9 p. 1.
117. While public sector pensioners cannot work after retirement to earn pension and salary from the after-retirement work, private sector workers can do it and receive both incomes.
118. HAJDÚ József *A közérdekű nyugdíjas szövetkezetekről: pro és kontra* In: Homoki-Nagy Mária, Karsai Krisztina, Fantoly Zsanett, Juhász Zsuzsanna, Szomora Zsolt, Gál Andor (szerk.) Ünnepi kötet dr. Nagy Ferenc egyetemi tanár 70. születésnapjára. 1026 p. Szeged: Szegedi Tudományegyetem Állam- és Jogtudományi Kar, 2018. pp. 369–381. (Acta Universitatis Szegediensis. Acta Juridica et Politica; Tom. 81.).

186. Only natural persons may be members of the cooperative, and a further restriction is that at least 90% of the members must be persons who are not in receipt of childcare allowance or childcare benefit as grandparents.

187. Upon the establishment of a cooperative, and upon subsequent entry into the cooperative, the establishment of membership is conditional upon the payment of a contribution in kind, which may be monetary or non-monetary, as specified in the statutes, and the relevant provisions of the Civil Code shall apply to matters not regulated in the Cooperative Act.

188. A special provision is that the cooperative shall set up a dedicated knowledge and education fund, the purpose of which is to provide members of the cooperative with a means of acquiring and expanding knowledge, skills and experience in the care and education of young children and to provide training for members. The fund may not be divided among members and must be transferred to other cooperatives or cooperative associations of persons with young children in the event of a transformation or dissolution without legal succession.

189. The cooperative member must pay a service fee for the services provided by the parental cooperative, but e/she must divide at least 85% of the annual net turnover among the members in proportion to their personal contribution.

190. External service is defined as 'a specific legal relationship in which a member of a cooperative of persons with young children at home performs his/her personal contribution in the context of an external service, and to which the rules of the Civil Code on the assignment of a person and the Labour Code and the relevant provisions of the Labour Protection Act apply accordingly.'

191. Membership shall cease when the member is no longer in receipt of either GYED or GYES.

192. The Co-operative for People with Young Children at Home creates harmony between work and childcare.[119]

§3. History of Labour Law after Socialist Period

I. Development of the Individual Labour Law

193. The regulating principle of the previous Labour Code (1992) was to establish so-called minimum standards from which the employment contract and/or the collective agreement may only depart where the law provides – and it furthermore set more favourable terms for employees.

---

119. FÜLÖP Anna (2021) Új szövetkezeti formában dolgozhatnak a kisgyermekkel otthon maradó szülők; https://ado.hu/munkaugyek/uj-szovetkezeti-formaban-dolgozhatnak-a-kisgyermekkel-otthon-marado-szulok/ (26 Jul. 2023).

194. The Act passed in 1992 was targeted towards ensuring a legal basis and framework in the employment field to help structural adjustment from a centralized, state-owned economy to a decentralized and privatized real market economy; in the political field, they also created the possibility of real freedom of association of workers and employers with a pluralistic and democratic feature.

195. This transition and the associated structural adjustment was a rather difficult process and period, especially in the social field, and was accompanied by much disappointment. What the workers hoped and expected from the transformation of politics, economy and society were: better working and living conditions; higher wages; more and better respected human rights and human dignity in the workplace; and more participation in the decision-making processes of their employers. However, many of them have had to learn new words and expressions such as: unemployment, mass redundancy, atypical workers, 'forced entrepreneurship', discrimination, flexibility, competitiveness, deregulation, etc.[120]

196. Moreover, the workers have had to know and understand many new regulations and new laws. The Labour Code of 1992 alone has been modified quite several times. The modifications of the Code were as a result of three main efforts:

(1) to make employment more flexible;
(2) to harmonize Hungarian legislations with the body of EU labour and social law; and
(3) to fight against illegal employment relationship (Employment related fraud and fictitious contract).

197. (1) Flexibilization meant, first, softening the application of the rules of 'traditional' employment relationships through the flexibilization of the contracting obligations of employers, allowing them more and more divergence from the stipulated employment contract, especially in the field of the workplace and the employee working sphere, as well as the flexibilization of working time regulations. Second, flexibilization meant greater applications of atypical and precarious forms of employment (especially fixed-term employment and the 'automatic' use of a trial period). Finally, in 2000 a new form of atypical employment was introduced in the Labour Code, i.e., temporary agency work, resulting in a less protected position for workers.[121]

198. (2) Harmonization with EU law was anticipated very strongly by trade unions because they hoped that the application of EU law would ensure protection against the negative effects of flexibilization and strengthen workers' and trade union rights. However, the harmonization process has caused, in many cases, rather more disappointment than satisfaction for them. The Government, supported by

120. A munkajog története, http://www.hrsentinel.hu/main/munkajogtortenete.html (26 Jul. 2023).
121. József HAJDÚ: *Atypical Employment Relationships in the New Hungarian Labour Code* in. Przyszlosc Prawa Pracy, Liber Amicorum Profesora Michala Sewerynskiego, ed. Zbigniew Hajn & Dagmara Skupien, Uniwersitet Lodzki, Lodz 2015. pp. 675–688.

employers, initiated the transformation of EU directives at the lowest (minimum) level and with as much derogations and exceptions as was allowed by the directives. Moreover, sometimes the whole harmonization process was utilized rather as a 'pretext' to make working conditions more flexible.[122,123]

199. However, EU labour law harmonization has brought about not only deregulation and flexibilization. In some cases, improvements have also occurred in the position of workers, especially in the field of equality and anti-discrimination, collective redundancy, information of workers and the protection of young workers. These positive results were due to the social partners' participation in the preparation of the legislation.

200. (3) Fight against illegal employment relationship (employment related fraud and fictitious contract). In the last couple of years, the widespread use of undeclared work has become a major issue in legal and political debate. Several measures have been taken to reduce the level of undeclared work. In 2001, the Labour Code extended the list of formal criteria concerning employment contracts. Most importantly, employment contracts must now be in written form and include certain elements, such as the amount of the basic wage, a job description and the location of the work.[124]

201. While illegal employment on a 'double contract' – a formal contract providing for pay at the national minimum wage and an informal (oral) contract reflecting actual pay – was widespread in the early 1990s, the late 1990s increasingly saw a new trend towards 'bogus' civil law contracts – these are contracts not governed by labour law, whereby a client commissions, for example, a lawyer or a builder for a specific task. Instead of an employment contract, contract of undertakings also concludes service contracts for 'employment-like work' with self-employed people acting as micro-enterprises, who are in fact in a position of subordinated employment ('forced entrepreneurs'). Given that employment attracts a considerable tax and social security contribution burden, and that there is a lower tax and social security payment regime for enterprises, it is the short-term interest of both employers and employees to evade employment contracts. Additionally, employers gain important flexibility advantages in using informal agreements or civil law contracts instead of employment contracts.[125]

202. Furthermore, the role of the Hungarian Employment Supervisory Authority (hereinafter: 'HESA') is of primary importance in fighting undeclared work. It can inspect bogus contract of undertakings, especially concerning compliance with employment law. When a breach of regulations is discovered, HESA can call on the

122. KECSKÉS László, *EU-jog és jogharmonizáció*, Budapest, HVG-Orac, 2011. p. 15.
123. BLUTMAN László Az Európai Unió joga a gyakorlatban – a Brexit után, Orac Kiadó, Budapest, 2020.
124. KUN Attila, 'Feketelisták' a munkaügyi hatóságok honlapjain. Fokozódó transzparencia a munkaerőpiacon?' *Munkaügyi Szemle*, Vol 51 No 3, 2007, pp. 46–49.
125. *A feketemunka elleni küzdelem eszközei és szankciórendszere* http://cegvezetes.hu/2005/09/a-feketemunka-elleni-kuzdelem-eszkozei-es-szankciorendszere/ (26 Jul. 2023).

employer to observe the legal rules governing employment relationships. In more serious cases, HLI can serve the employer with an order to stop illegal practices; it can also prohibit further employment if the breach of law is very serious or lawful practices cannot be reinstated. In cases of illegal employment of non-residents (migrant workers), HESA can fine the employer. In cases of undeclared employment of an unemployed person, it can request the suspension or even the termination of the payment of unemployment benefits to the unemployed person concerned. It can request that a fine, in case of natural person maximum HUF 1,000,000 (approx. EUR 2,667) and legal person maximum HUF 10,000,000 (approx. EUR 26,667), (Based on the Act CXXXV of 2020 on Services and Aids Intended to Promote Employment, and on the Supervision of Employment and Act CXXV of 2017 on Penalties for administrative offence) be levied on the employer. Finally, it can start 'transgression' procedures. The major practical problem for the National Labour Inspectorate is understaffing. It can inspect no more than 3% to 5% of undertakings each year, and its reach is thus fairly limited.[126]

203. One of the major components of undeclared work is tax evasion. Legal regulations authorize the National Tax and Customs Administration (hereinafter: 'NTCA', in Hungarian: Nemzeti Adó– és Vámhivatal, NAV) to investigate the nature of contracts, and if it finds that a civil contract is being used instead of an employment contract it can require the establishment of an employment contract and modify accordingly the tax obligations of the undertaking and the employee. However, this option is practically never used by NTCA.[127]

II. The Background of the Hungarian Labour Code in Force

204. The details of the 1992 Labour Code established a combination of fairly flexible regulations with some strict minimum standards. It was envisaged that sectoral and workplace-level collective bargaining by sectoral unions and workplace-level unions would ensure better terms and conditions for workers than those stipulated by the minimum standards of the labour code.

205. Nonetheless, Hungarian society and the economy changed profoundly during the nineties, which affected the regulation of the working environment. The state-owned company sector has practically ceased to exist, with the exception of large public utility companies, and a vibrant privately owned economy has sprung up. This newly created economy, however, has developed into a dual economy, comprising two very different segments.

---

126. Jelentés A munkavédelmi hatóság 2022. évi országos ellenőrzési tervének megvalósuásáról, https://www.bkmkik.hu/attachments/article/5979/230301-GFM.MV.hatosagi.ellenorzesi.terv.megvalosulasa_2022.pdf (26 Jul. 2023).

127. KUN Attila, 'Feketelisták' a munkaügyi hatóságok honlapjain. Fokozódó transzparencia a munkaerőpiacon?' *Munkaügyi Szemle*, Vol 51 No 3, 2007, pp. 46–49.

206. One segment consists of medium-sized and large companies, mostly foreign-owned, integrated into the worldwide supply networks. Within this segment, the major concern of companies is flexibility to be able to respond quickly to changes in market demands and a legal environment which enables the adaptation of best manufacturing practices.

207. The second large segment of the new private economy comprises micro and small enterprises, mostly domestically owned, where formal employment intertwines with undeclared employment.

208. The accession of Hungary to the European Union in 1 May 2004 brought about a further wave of fundamental changes in the concept and regulation of the Labour Code. This profound restructuring of the economy had a major impact on unions. Sectoral collective agreements have not played any major role in regulating terms and conditions of employment. The role of workplace collective agreements has also considerably diminished, covering only a minority of employees, mostly in larger companies.

209. The profound changes in the economy and in regulation in the wake of EU accession necessitated a partial 're-legislation' of the labour code. In 2004, the then governing left-liberal coalition government had initiated a complete re-drafting of the labour code. A new concept of regulation was hoped for, which would align the legislation of the working environment with that of contractual law, which enables a less rigid, more flexible system of regulation. According to the reasoning, a more flexible legislation would allow for a reduction of the amount of undeclared work and would also help companies to be more competitive. The preparations for the new code, however, were abandoned by the government because unions vehemently rejected the concept of the re-legislation, arguing that it aimed to weaken workers' rights.[128]

210. In 2010, however, the freshly elected right-wing government placed the re-legislation, or even replacement, of the previous labour code (1992) back on the agenda. The government aimed for a new labour code which:

(1) makes the regulation of the working environment *flexible* in order to convert Hungary into one of the most competitive economies in Europe; and
(2) cuts the traditional rights of unions to a minimal level, which would allow little more than their mere existence in workplaces.[129]

211. The key feature of the new labour code is that it intends to align the regulation of the working environment with that of contractual law enshrined in the Civil Code. Therefore, the new labour code, as a principle, allows collective agreements

---

128. KISS György (ed.) *Munkajog* Ludovika Egyetemi Kiadó, Budapest, 2020.
129. TÓTH András, *The New Hungarian Labour Code – Background, Conflicts, Compromises*, Budapest: Friedrich Ebert Foundation, 2012. p. 2.
http://www.fesbp.hu/common/pdf/Nachrichten_aus_Ungarn_june_2012.pdf (26 Jul. 2023).

– or a works agreement in cases where there are no unions – and individual labour contracts to regulate the content of work differently to what is stipulated by the law.

212. To achieve flexibility, the new labour code allows agreements to deviate to the benefit of the employer, and not only to that of the employee. (e.g., Labour Code 2012 stipulates that the basic holiday allowance is twenty days, and also states that employees are to receive additional holidays based on their age. But at the same time, it also allows for a collective agreement (works agreement) to reduce or even cut all additional holidays based on age. In practice, this means that the Labour Code 2012 only stipulates twenty days basic holiday as a minimum standard and all additional holiday may be subject to agreement.) This simple example shows that this shift towards flexibility may result in a considerable deterioration of previous minimum standards set by the labour code.[130]

213. The new Hungarian Labour Code (hereinafter: HLC) is in line with the general trend of many recent labour law reforms across Europe[131] in that it aims to allow more flexible regulation of work to help firms to regain competitiveness, while at the same time opening up the possibilities for cost cutting.[132]

214. The Hungarian regulations, however, are likely to stand out of the crowd of recent labour law amendments by constituting a comprehensive re-regulation of labour law. The stated aim of the government was to carry out revolutionary changes in Hungary. It is thus no wonder that the government wanted a wholesale turnaround in the regulation of the working environment as well. Consequently, it was conceived as a comprehensive regulation which aligns labour law with that of civil law and shifts many risks of employment to the shoulders of employees. Some unions reported that if an employer used all possibilities offered by the new code to cut wages and flexibilize work arrangements, it may save 30% of the total wage cost.[133]

III. Development of the Collective Labour Law

215. In the previous Labour Code (1992), the government aimed to adapt the German-type industrial relations system for use in Hungary. It originally wanted to see works' councils as the sole workers' organ of employee input at the workplace with the right to conclude work agreements. At the same time, the intention was to

130. LŐRINCZ György, *Az új Mt. hatálybalépése, az átmeneti rendelkezések*, Budapest: HVG ORAC, 2012. pp. 6–8.

131. *See Green Paper on Modernising Labour Law* (2006). http://europa.eu/legislation_summaries/employment_and_social_policy/eu2020/growth_and_jobs/c10312_en.htm (26 Jul. 2023).

132. BANKÓ Zoltán, BERKE Gyula, KISS György, SZŐKE Gergely László *Nagykommentár a munka törvénykönyvéhez,* Wolters Kluwer, Budapest 2019.

133. TÓTH András, *The New Hungarian Labour Code – Background, Conflicts, Compromises*, Budapest: Friedrich Ebert Foundation, 2012. pp. 9–10. http://www.fesbp.hu/common/pdf/Nachrichten_aus_Ungarn_june_2012.pdf (26 Jul. 2023).

shift collective bargaining to the sectoral level in order to set the basis for works agreements, as in Germany. Unions, however, wanted to preserve their exclusive bargaining rights at the workplace level and saw in the works' councils an artificial institution, whose main mission would be to help destroy their workplace presence. After tough negotiations, a compromise was reached: works' councils were created, but they were only granted rights to be informed and consulted about determined issues. Unions retained their exclusive bargaining rights and some entitlements to ensure their proper functioning in the workplaces. Unions were also entitled to be informed and to be consulted over issues which were deemed to be important for their bargaining activity. Therefore, somewhat confusingly, the law mandated the co-existence of workplace-level unions and works' councils which were granted partly overlapping rights.[134]

216. The legal status and role of the parties of the collective labour law has been modified in the new system. The new Labour Code regulates the relationship between the employer, the trade unions and the works' council. The regulation is based on Directive (2002/14/EC) for informing and consulting employees establishing a general framework for informing and consulting employees in the European Community. Under section 230 of the Labour Code 'In the interest of safeguarding the social and economic interests of employees and further in the interest of maintaining peace at work, the present Act regulates relations between trade unions and works' councils and employers and their interest representations. As part of this, the present Act guarantees the freedom of the trade union movement and the participation of employees in the determination of the conditions of employment and identifies the procedures for collective negotiations as well as for the prevention and resolution of labour conflicts.' The Labour Code guarantees the right of employees and employers to establish organizations with others for the representation of their interests, free from any discrimination, with a view to furthering and safeguarding their economic and social interests, under the conditions set forth in the present Act, and to join the organizations of their choice, solely subject to the rules of the given organization, or to abstain from organizations of that nature. In the new Labour Code the definitions of 'notification' and 'consultation' can also be found.[135]

217. According to the new HLC, the fact is that employers can only achieve all potential flexibilization and cost-cutting possibilities through concluding a works agreement with a works' council. Therefore, it can be observed that the new labour code drastically cuts the traditional rights and entitlements of unions. The law has curtailed the working time exemption and legal protection of union activists, which hurts the organizational strength of unions and undercuts their financial strength.[136]

---

134. FERENCZ Jácint, GYULAVÁRI Tamás, KÁRTYÁS Gábor, GÖNDÖR Éva, *Munkajogi Alapismeretek*, ELTE Eötvös Kiadó Kft., 2020.
135. http://munkastanacsok.hu/kollektiv-munkajog-korkep-a-valtozasokrol/ (26 Jul. 2023).
136. KUN Attila, 'Átrendeződés a kollektív munkajogban – szakszervezetek kontra üzemi tanácsok az új Mt. tükrében' in: *Hagyomány és érték*, Állam- és jogtudományi tanulmányok a Károli Gáspár Református Egyetem fennállásának 20. évfordulójára, Budapest: KRE ÁJK, 2013. pp. 304–315.

218. While the legislation weakens the position of unions, it elevates the rights of works' councils. The most important change is that in case of a lack of unions at the workplace, a works agreement can be concluded with the works' council. Works agreements could regulate all issues which a collective agreement could – even to the benefit of employers – with the exception of remuneration. The shift of the rights to be informed and consulted from unions to works' councils is a clear 'signal' that unions will suffer a substantial loss of entitlements and prestige.[137]

219. There is an independent part (Part Three) in the new Labour Code (2012) regulating the institutions of the collective labour law. However, the right to strike is regulated in a separate law (Act VII of 1989). The strike act served as the opening of the democratic regulation of trade union rights. Freedom of association is guaranteed as a democratic principle in the Hungarian Constitution, in which the right to strike is also expressly determined.[138]

220. The overture of pluralist and democratic trade unionism was adopted in Act II of 1989 on the Right to Association. This Act ensured the legal framework and legal possibility of organizing new trade unions, diminishing trade union monopolism and recognizing a pluralist trade unionism. The levels and the main characteristics of the system: (1) national level, (2) branch (sectoral) level, (3) enterprise level.

A. *The National Level Social Dialogue*

221. The FIDESZ Government of Hungary adopted The Declaration of National Cooperation in 2010 as part of The Programme of National Cooperation in order to acknowledge the inception of a new social contract. In order to enforce the new social contract, the Government of Hungary established the System of National Cooperation which is open to all Hungarians. The Government of Hungary offers cooperation to every member of society, to NGOs and advocacy organizations, and to economic players to find solutions to issues of national interest.

222. The Parliament adopted Act XCIII of 2011 on the National Economic and Social Council (hereinafter referred to as NESC) in recognition of the role of economic and social dialogue, in order to discuss strategies of national economy and social policy and to promote a consensus among various interest groups of society. The NESC, the widest-ranging forum of representatives of Hungarian society holds

---

137. TÓTH András, *The New Hungarian Labour Code – Background, Conflicts, Compromises*, Budapest: Friedrich Ebert Foundation, 2012. pp. 9–10. http://www.fesbp.hu/common/pdf/Nachrichten_aus_Ungarn_june_2012.pdf (26 Jul. 2023).
138. LŐRINCZ György, *Az új Mt. hatálybalépése, az átmeneti rendelkezések*, Budapest: HVG ORAC, 2012. pp. 6–7.

consultations, delivers opinions, makes proposals, discusses national strategies and comprehensive matters affecting the development of the economy and society.[139]

223. The NESC is a consultative, proposal-making and advisory body independent from Parliament and the Government. The NESC has 32 members, representing the Hungarian civil society. The Ministers or executive officers appointed by them attend the Council's plenary sessions as permanent guests with a consultative right.[140]

B. Branch (Sectoral) Level Social Dialogue

224. Sectoral level consultation and collective bargaining is not regulated but – at the same time – neither is it prohibited by the law in Hungary. The traditional level for collective bargaining level in Hungary is the enterprise, but it is also possible to bargain on a multi-enterprise basis. Sectoral-level bargaining is a rather rare phenomenon at this moment, but it is possible to extend the effect of a collective agreement, on the joint request of the contracting parties, to the entire sector (or subsector) by the decision of the Minister who is responsible for labour issues.[141]

225. At sectorial level it is possible to establish Sectorial Dialogue Committees (hereinafter referred to as SDC, in Hungarian 'ÁPB'), which are joint committees of the employee and employer organizations operating on the sectorial/subsectorial level. The establishment of these Committees, their organization, operation and rights are regulated by a separate Act (Act LXXIV of 2009). The act includes conditions (criteria) for getting into the SDC and also for exercising certain rights. SDC is primarily a bilateral consultative body; however, in case of meeting the conditions stipulated by the law, the committee also has the possibility of concluding a collective agreement. SDCs are operating in the economic sphere. In case of the public sphere the person of the employer was debatable (the state or certain institutions).

226. The traditional organizing level of workers in Hungary is also the enterprise. However, at least ten members are needed to set up a trade union. Therefore, in small (less than fifty employees) and, even more so, in micro firms, it is rather difficult, or even impossible, to organize unions because of fragmentation and the few number of workers at the same employer.

227. On the other hand, employers have not urged their own organization at the sectoral level because they rather like this non-unionized, or weakly-unionized,

139. RÁCZ Zoltán, *A gazdasági munkajog kollektív munkajogi részére vonatkozó szabályanyag az új Mt-ben*, http://www.uni-miskolc.hu/~wwwdeak/Collegium%20Doctorum%20Publikaciok/R%E1cz%20Zolt%E1n.pdf (26 Jul. 2023).

140. http://www.ngtt.hu/index_eng.html (26 Jul. 2023).

141. PETROVICS Zoltán, *Az ágazati párbeszéd bizottságok és az Ágazati Részvételt Megállapító Bizottság*, Jogélet, 2017/1. lapszám, 72–73. o. | 2017. december.

fragmented situation of workers. This situation makes easier for them the flexible use of the law or, on many occasions, the implementation or violation of the law according to their own will. The lack and weakness of sector-level industrial relations has been criticized by the EU and the Hungarian Government has been asked to support by special means (i.e., legislation and other kinds of measures) improvements to the sectoral social dialogue. In 2000, the Hungarian Government began the preparation of a project to strengthen this level (with the financial and professional support of the EU's PHARE programme). The aim of the project is the establishment of joint sectoral social dialogue committees with the mutual participation of the representatives of employers and trade unions.[142]

C. The Enterprise Level Social Dialogue

228. As indicated in the previous section, the enterprise level is the traditional collective bargaining arena in Hungary and is the best regulated level in the Labour Code. The new HLC regulates the rights of trade unions, especially the right to bargain collectively (it covers the bargaining procedure, the partners' obligation to negotiate, the entitlement to negotiations, the rules of trade union representativeness at the enterprise level, the content and the validity of the collective agreement, and the relationship between the collective agreement, the law and labour contracts.) The law in this field seems to be quite affordable, ensuring many rights for trade unions and their leaders/officials vis-à-vis employers. However, according to the complaints of the trade unions, these rights are not strong enough and they are not able to provide real protection for their members and officials against the violations of the law committed by employers. The trade union rights regulated in the Code are certainly more declarative than real, enforceable rights. In the cases of violations of the law, a judge can only state the violation committed but – in the face of the lack of real sanctions and concrete duties – it is not possible to oblige an employee to do something or to take sanctions against an employer. This is the situation which concerns, for instance, the right to information. The Labour Code provides that the trade union may request information from the employer on all issues related to the employment-related economic and social welfare interests of employees. An employer should not refuse this information or a justification of his/her actions. However, the information or data to be given by the employer is not detailed in the law; also, not disclosed is at what time, how often and in what form, etc. the employer has to provide them and what kind of issues can qualify as employment-related.[143]

229. Consequently, the fulfilment of the rules in particular cases is rather difficult. Very vulnerable points in the labour legislation are the rules concerning the

142. PETROVICS Zoltán, *Az ágazati párbeszéd bizottságok és az Ágazati Részvételt Megállapító Bizottság*, Jogélet, 2017/1. lapszám, 72–73. o. | 2017. december.
143. HAJDÚ József – KUN Attila (eds), *Munkajog II.*, Budapest: Patrocinium, 2013. pp. 151–155.

protection of workers' representatives. In spite of Hungary having ratified the relevant ILO Convention (C-135),[144] the protection of trade union officials is unsatisfactory and, even, ineffective. According to the law: Agreement from the next higher authority in the union hierarchy is required for an employer if an elected trade union official is to be transferred to another workplace on the employer's initiative, as well as for the employer's termination of a trade union official's employment by regulatory notice. (Subsection (1) of section 273 of the HLC)

230. Another difficulty for the trade unions at the enterprise level is the so-called dual channel system of worker representation. Besides the trade unions, it has been possible, since 1992, also to elect a works' council in enterprises employing more than 50 employees, or a workplace representative in establishments or more than 15 but less than 50 employees. The simultaneous presence of the two types of worker representation (trade union and works' council) at the workplace – often with the same people and, moreover, with insufficiently clear rights and scopes between them – is the source of much confusion in the protection and representation of workers and helps to weaken the position of the trade union.

231. The legislator of the new Labour Code wanted to eliminate the parallel rights of trade unions, on the one side, and of works' councils, on the other. For the purposes of the new Labour Code, a works' council is a main body of cooperation between the employer and the employees, and the body of the employee's participation in the employers' decisions.[145]

232. Furthermore, one of the significant changes of the new Labour Code was to regulate a new kind of agreement (works agreement) between the employer and the works' council. Under section 268 of the HLC, the employer and the works' council can regulate the terms and conditions of employment with the exception of the remuneration of work. One condition for this is that the employer is not subject to a collective agreement and that there is no trade union at the employer which is authorized to conclude a collective agreement. The aim of this regulation is to encourage the flexibility of employment and the protection of interests of the employee.[146]

IV. Collective Dispute Resolution: A New Alternative Dispute Resolution Service in Hungary

233. A new Alternative Dispute Resolution Service (ADR Service) was launched in 2016 under an EU-funded project managed by Hungarian social partners. The ADR Service assists employers, trade unions and employee representatives on collective labour law conflicts in order to settle collective disputes.

144. ILO Convention No. 135 on Protection and Facilities to be Afforded to Workers' Representatives in Undertakings.
145. HAJDÚ József – KUN Attila (eds), *Munkajog II.*, Budapest: Patrocinium, 2013. p. 125.
146. https://jak.ppke.hu/uploads/articles/12417/file/Road%20to%20flexibility.pdf (26 Jul. 2023).

234. The ADR Service, sponsored by the EU and available in local offices in all the seven regions of Hungary. The members of the ADR Service are labour lawyers, who have been selected by the social partners on professional criteria and listed on the project's website (jogpontok.hu). The members of the ADR Service will assist employers, trade unions and employee representatives on collective labour law conflicts in order to settle collective disputes.

235. The Labour Mediation and Arbitration Service (MKDSZ), founded in 1997, was the forerunner of this new ADR Service. However, the legal status of MKDSZ had never been clarified by law and the mandate of MKDSZ expired and was not renewed after 2010. Therefore, this new ADR Service is the continuation of the work on settling and managing collective labour conflicts between employers and employee representations, particularly trade unions.

236. The members of the Service provide the following types of support: labour law advice, mediation, conciliation and arbitration. Arbitration is compulsory in certain cases listed by the Labour Code. In all the other cases, the procedure of the ADR Service is initiated by one or both parties.

237. The parties of the conflict may include, in particular, trade unions, works councils, group of employees or employer(s). Besides large companies, the project strives for providing services for small and medium sized companies as well. At the same time, the activities of the ADR Service extend to private as well as public sector employment. It must be underlined that the ADR Service focuses exclusively on collective labour conflicts, therefore individual and/or labour law (legal) disputes are excluded from its scope.[147]

§4. Role of the Government Institutions in the Shaping and Administration of Labour and Industrial Relation Policy

I. Degree of Government Intervention

238. The fundamental tendencies of labour policy are determined by the framework of the Acts accepted by Parliament concerning the social and economic development of the country. Determination of the details of labour policy is partly within the competence of the Government, partly – according to the principles established by it – of the respective Ministers and, finally, within that of county bodies. The special tasks of realizing the labour policy fall within the domain of labour administration. The central organ of labour administration is the Ministry of Human Capacities, however, in certain specific matters other ministries also contribute.

147. HAJDÚ, József; KUN, Attila *Alternative Dispute Resolution in Disputes Relating to Labour Law in Hungary* In: Olivieri, Antonello; Fuiano, Mario Pio (szerk.) Alternative labour dispute resolutions: A Collection of Comparative Studies Bari, Olaszország: Cacucci Editore (2020) 628 p. pp. 569–596., 28 p.

Ministries

239. The scope of duties of the Ministry for Economic Developments embraces most of the fields of labour market. In this way, the Ministry deals with the legal regulation on problems of employment policy and the labour force, industrial relations, the settlement of labour disputes, wages policy, and labour safety. In addition, it supervises and controls special training schemes, as well as the instruction of workers, middle-grade specialists and supervisors outside the school system. The Ministry for Economic Development together with the Ministry of Finance governs the Public Employment Service and the Hungarian Labour Inspectorate.

240. Labour hygiene also lies within the competence of the Ministry for Economic Development. Labour hygiene includes, on the one hand, the laws and requirements connected with labour hygiene and, on the other hand, the supervision of the bodies dealing with these. Supervision of public health implies, apart from the general concern with public hygiene, the duty to oversee standards of labour hygiene, and in addition, the state medical service.

II. General Rules and Instruments of Employment Policy

241. Chapter I of the Act IV of 1991 on the promotion of employment prohibits discrimination in the course of the activity of the labour market organization. This provision includes special rights being given to those in a disadvantageous position on the labour market. The rights and obligations contained in the Act and in its implementing decrees that pertain to Hungarian nationals will also apply to the foreign nationals granted refugee status or asylum under specific other legislation and for those who have been granted immigrant or permanent resident status, and for those persons (EU and EEA citizens) with the right of free movement and residence, except for different provisions enacted by an act of Parliament or by a government decree. All persons who are entitled to take up employment in Hungary and all employers will have the right to make use of the services of the labour market organization at local government offices as regulated in the certain provisions of the Act, namely the Subsections a) and c) section 2, Article 13/A (providing information pertaining to the labour market and employment, and labour exchange), free of charge. The labour market organization will inform employees and employers on their rights and obligations and will provide assistance in fulfilling their demands. The employer must cooperate with the labour market organization in order to facilitate labour mobility and the reintegration of unemployed persons (job-seekers) in the labour market.[148]

148. József HAJDÚ *The Legal Protection of Unemployed Young People in Hungary* in. Morley Gunderson; Francesca Fazio (eds): Tackling Youth Unemployment. Newcastle: Cambridge Scholars Publishing, 2014. pp. 27–55. (ADAPT labour studies book-series.).

242. In order to realize the aims of the employment policy, the labour market organization in local government offices organizes labour exchange, promotes vocational training, and supports the expansion of employment opportunities and creation of new jobs.

A. *Careers Guidance*

243. The aim of careers guidance is to give young people institutional support in choosing a profession most suitable to their abilities taking into consideration society's future supply and demand for specialists. Careers guidance is an integral part of the educational process in primary and secondary education. It has a dual function. On the one hand, it promotes the appropriate choice of educational direction for those who wish to extend their studies. On the other hand, for those who want to go out to work, it gives advice on how to choose employment most suited to their ambitions. In either case the results of psychological and other tests are used where appropriate. Careers guidance is free. For providing careers advice on a uniform and co-ordinated basis and supporting teachers' careers guidance in the schools, a state service of occupational counselling is in operation.

B. *Private Labour Exchange Services*

244. Labour exchange (employment agency) services may be offered by any person following registration at the Ministry of Finance.

245. Apart from government employment agencies, labour exchange services (hereinafter referred to as 'private labour exchange services') may be provided by resident legal entities, business associations lacking the legal status of a legal person, their Hungarian branches and private entrepreneurs subject to the conditions prescribed by law, and if registered by the competent government employment agency. Labour exchange services concerning employment in a foreign country may be provided only in accordance with the employment-related legal regulations of the destination country.

246. Unless otherwise prescribed by the legal regulation, private labour exchange services are not permitted to charge job-seekers any fee or costs.

247. The Government set the conditions and detailed regulations on the provision of private labour exchange services and on the registration of private employment agencies. Such decree may prescribe that the agencies provide financial security if the private labour exchange services involve employment abroad or if the private employment agency charges the job-seeker a fee.

248. A person offering labour exchange services is obliged to supply statistical data required by the Ministry of Finance.[149]

III. Health and Safety at Work

A. Basic Principles

249. According to the principles of the Hungarian Fundamental Law (constitution), human beings are regarded as central, and labour law aims to ensure their defence. As a consequence of scientific and technological development, accidents are no longer necessary; there are ample opportunities to prevent them. Thus, Hungarian labour law takes the view that both in establishing and maintaining employment such conditions must be created as to eliminate the dangers in the workplace and to prevent or at least reduce accidents. Consequently, emphasis must be laid on prevention. In connection with establishing employment, labour law aims at creating situations in which health hazards are reduced as much as possible. On the other hand, during the period of employment, it aims to bring about conditions which enable the workers to maintain their health. Third, in connection with actual working, it defines those rules which the employers are obliged to carry out in order to ensure safe and healthy working conditions. In this Chapter the rules of labour safety, determined by the Act XCIII of 1993 on Labour Safety, will be discussed.

250. The Act on Labour Safety provides the following principles:

- The State, in consultation with the representative organizations of employers and employees, will determine the basic requirements of safety and health at work and establish the administrative and supervisory agencies thereof, will formulate a national policy for occupational health and safety and the working environment and the protection of working ability, and will periodically revise its implementation.
- It is the duty of employers to comply with the requirements of health and safety at work, to determine the methods of complying with the requirements of health and safety, and to provide information to every employee on the relevant rules of health and safety in a language understood by the employee.
- The employees take part in the implementation of the requirements of safety through their elected safety representatives.
- The rules of health and safety are formulated so that sufficient protection is given, not only to employees but also to persons in the vicinity or sphere of work of the enterprise, including those using a service. Work equipment is designed so that their correct use for non-scheduled work excludes as far as possible any danger of accident or damage to health.
- The State assists and supervises compliance with the rules of health and safety at work through its supervisory agencies created for this purpose.

149. HAJDÚ József, IEL Labour Law, Hungary, Wolters Kluwer, Kluwer Law Online, 2019. https://kluwerlawonline.com/Manuals/Corporate+Acquisitions+and+Mergers/705. (26 Jul. 2023).

– Employers, employees and state agencies co-operate in exercising their rights and performing their duties of labour safety.[150]

B. Content of Safety at Work

251. The rules on labour safety are divided into eight categories:

(a) general requirements for health and safety protection;
(b) provisions for investment, construction;
(c) material requirements;
(d) provision for work processes;
(e) individual conditions;
(f) rights and duties of employers and employees;
(g) workers' representation;
(h) labour safety organization.

C. General Requirements for Health and Safety Protection

252. Any workplace or facility or technology is designed, constructed, manufactured, put into operation or used, and any work equipment, material substance, energy or personal protective equipment will only be manufactured, produced, stored, moved, transported, used, sold, imported or operated in compliance with the requirements for health and safety at work as determined in the rules on labour safety or, lacking these, as can be expected at the level of science and technology. Compliance with the requirements for health and safety at work will not be redeemed, replaced or compensated by money or other means by the employer.

253. Work equipment can only be sold, imported, put into operation or used if it complies with the requirements for health and safety at work and this is demonstrated, within the framework of general quality certification, by the manufacturer or the importer or, lacking an importer, the employer who operates it.

254. Hungary ratified both ILO Conventions No. 81 (Labour Inspection) and No. 129 (Labour Inspection in Agriculture) on 4 January 1994.[151]

D. Special Occupational Safety Regulations Pertaining to Teleworking

255. The general provisions of the Labour Safety Act (Act XCIII of 1993) will apply to teleworking subject to the exceptions set out here:

---

150. EMBER Alex, *Az üzemi baleset*, Szeged: Pólay Alapítvány, 2013. pp. 72–73.
151. http://www.ilo.org/global/lang--en/index.htm (26 Jul. 2023).

By way of derogation from what is contained in the general provisions of the Act, work equipment for teleworking may also be provided by the employee subject to an agreement with the employer. Use of such equipment will be contingent upon having a preliminary inspection for occupational safety conducted by the employer in advance.

256. The work place designated for teleworking must be approved by the employer in advance for occupational safety standards. The employee will be authorized to make any changes of bearing for occupational safety purposes upon the employer's prior consent.

257. The employer must inform the employee concerning the facilities available for consultation and representation of interests with respect to safety at work, and the names of persons placed in charge of these duties and information as to where they can be reached. The labour safety representative may enter the designated place of work upon the employee's consent.

258. Apart from the inspection, the employer or his/her representative is entitled to gain admission to the property where the work is performed for carrying out the duties and procedure related to occupational safety, such as the commissioning of equipment, assessment of risks, safety inspection and the investigation of accidents.

259. The occupational safety and health board can conduct the inspection only on workdays, between 8 a.m. and 8 p.m. The occupational safety and health administration must notify the employer and the employee at least three working days in advance concerning the inspection. The employer must obtain the employee's consent for admission into the designated work place for this purpose before the commencement of the inspection.[152]

E. Material Requirements

260. Regarding material prerequisites for working in a safe and healthy environment, the Act on Labour Safety defines the following requirements:

- All employees must be provided with drinking water, facilities for changing and storing clothing, for taking meals, for resting and warming and with sanitary and washing facilities, in accordance with the nature of the work and the workplace.
- In accordance with the nature of the work and the workplace, order and cleanliness must be maintained and waste, debris and sewage treated in an appropriate way. Signalling and alarm systems must be provided at the workplace in accordance with the nature of the danger and the number of employees. Adequate space must be provided at the workplace for unhindered movement necessary for health and safety.

152. Sections 86/A-86/C. of the Act XCIII of 1993 on Labour Safety.

- In workplaces where there is a danger of persons falling or where falling objects may endanger employees or persons in the vicinity or sphere of work, protection must be provided by way of fencing or covering or another adequate method. Working platforms, scaffolds, gangways and stages must be designed, erected, placed and fastened in a way which is adequate for safe working of that nature. Storage places must be designed, constructed and arranged in accordance with the physical, chemical and biological properties and interactions of the stored materials and their environment. Power line, pipelines and sewerage systems must be adequate for the safe operation, maintenance and identification. Electrical appliances must comply with the safety requirements.
- Daylight or artificial lighting at the workplace must comply with the requirements for illumination for work of that nature. Noise, vibration, dust and chemicals, higher or lower atmospheric pressure and radiation at the workplace should not be harmful to employees or persons in the vicinity or sphere of work and should not endanger safety at work. In working premises, air must be provided in a quantity and of a quality adequate for the number of employees, the nature of work and the hazards present. If it is technically not feasible to provide the required air or climate, adequate steps should be taken to protect the health of the employees.
- In outdoor workplaces employees must be protected against adverse weather conditions by providing adequate facilities including those for warming, suitable working systems personal protective equipment and protective drinks.
- Buildings serving as workplaces must have an adequate structure and stability. Windows, roof-windows and ventilation equipment should be such that they can be safely opened, closed, adjusted or fixed. The flooring and the passages at the workplace should be adequate for the nature of the work and its cleaning requirements and for the maximum load expected; surfaces should be non-slipping, smooth, skip– and tilt-free.
- Swing-doors and swing-gates are to be made of transparent material or to have a transparent insert installed at eye level. A door for pedestrians should be installed in the direct proximity of gates primarily used for motor vehicles if no safe passage is available for pedestrians. The number, size, location and illumination of exits and emergency exits and marked escape routes shall be adequate for a quick and safe evacuation from the workplace or the dangerous area.
- In the workplaces where health and safety require no smoking, separate smoking places or smoking areas must be provided. Non-smokers shall be protected at all workplaces by providing separate smoking places, areas or rooms for smokers, or by adequate organization of the work.
- Operating documentation necessary for safe use of machinery must constitute a permanent accessory of any machinery.

F. Provisions for Work Processes

261. Work processes, technologies, machinery, materials and substances should be chosen such that they will not endanger the health and safety of employees or persons in the vicinity or sphere of work. In order to meet these requirements, the Act on Labour Safety provides the following:

- Materials or products can only be transported in places or via routes designated for transport, in compliance with the prescribed size and weight limits, and by means suitable for transport and adequate in view of the properties of the materials or products.
- In the case of dangerous work processes or technologies and in order to prevent dangers or to reduce their harmful effects, all employees concerned must be informed about the hazards, adequate personal protective equipment must be specified and provided to the employees and their use ensured. Workplaces must be equipped with adequate means for fire fighting, including fire signals and alarm systems. Measures must be taken to ensure that in case of serious and imminent danger to the health and safety of employees, work will be stopped and employees removed to a safe place immediately.
- For work processes where employees may be exposed to hazards, effective protection shall be provided. For the protection of employees and other personnel in the area, safety and health protection alarm signals shall be installed at work places where so justified by the nature of the hazards. For the occurrence of extraordinary conditions – when safety requirements for regular operation cannot be complied with – rescue plans must be prepared. All employees concerned must be informed about the parts of the rescue plan relevant for that workplace. Material, personnel and adequate organization for first aid should be provided at the workplace in accordance with the nature and location of the workplace, the hazards, the number of employees and the organization of work.[153]

G. Personnel Conditions

262. Physical characteristics of workers, a lack of suitable qualifications, or inadequate knowledge of the dangers connected with the work performed may cause accidents or illness. It is, therefore, very important to ensure individual conditions as well as material ones. Hungarian labour law attributes great importance to this. In connection with ensuring individual conditions, the question of the physical and psychological state of the workers must be mentioned.

263. The aim of regulation in this matter is to render it impossible for anyone to be employed in a job where his/her health could be impaired or where he/she might suffer an accident. (E.g., a worker with a weak physique should not be employed in a job requiring great physical efforts.) The law in certain cases establishes general prohibitions, for example determining jobs in which women, pregnant women and minors must not be employed. They also prohibit or restrict overtime employment. In certain jobs, labour law makes employment contingent upon a medical examination. The worker must also have medical examinations during employment to see whether he/she may continue in the job. The law prescribes the investigation into

153. Act XCIII of 1993 on Labour Safety.

psychological fitness in addition to that into physical fitness. In such cases (e.g., in the case of drivers), the worker or employee should be subjected to the so-called vocational selection.

264. The elimination of accident injury will not, of course, be ensured by physical examination. It is also necessary that the worker should possess suitable qualifications. Adequate qualifications are generally a prerequisite of performing work; this is why the rules relating to labour safety do not provide for them. However, jobs in which a lack of qualifications may cause accidents, not only to the worker but also to third persons outside the factory, must be deemed an exception to this rule.

265. It is important that work should not be carried out by a single person where there is threat of danger. If a particular job is done by two or more employees simultaneously, one of them should be put in charge in the interest of safety and this should be made known to the others.

266. Over and above physical fitness and qualifications, it is, however, extremely important that the worker should clearly see what dangers are connected with his/her work and how to conduct him/herself, in order to avoid them. To acquire an understanding of the regulations, workers must obtain both theoretical and practical labour safety education before starting work. Heads of sections or smaller units and others responsible for creating safe and healthy working conditions (e.g., designers, builders etc.) are obliged to pass a labour safety examination.

267. Workers in particularly sensitive risk groups must be protected in accordance with specific other legislation against the dangers which specifically affect them.

H. Rights and Duties of Employers and Employees

268. In the interest of health and safety, employers' responsibility is established. Therefore, the employer must:

- provide personnel with adequate qualifications for the professional tasks of occupational safety and give all necessary instructions to employees in due time;
- regularly check that working conditions are in compliance with the requirements and that employees know the relevant regulations and comply with them;
- provide for adequate work equipment for employees, in accordance with the working conditions and the hazards;
- in due time before the introduction of new technologies, consult with the employees and their safety representatives about the implications relevant to health and safety;
- immediately investigate any irregularity or complaint regarding health and safety at work, take the necessary measures, inform all persons concerned, and, in case of imminent danger, stop work;

- ensure that personal protective equipment in suitable hygienic conditions is available for proper use, and provide for the necessary cleaning, maintenance and replacement;
- determine and lay down in writing the conditions and procedures for providing personal protective equipment.

269. In addition, for the purpose of performing the employer's duties connected to the safe performance of work not endangering health, employers must employ and provide all necessary information related to labour safety and all material conditions to persons with specialized labour safety qualifications adjusted to the category of hazard and the number of employees.

270. Employers must ensure that employees and their safety representatives can obtain the necessary information from the occupational health service with regard to their working conditions. He/she must inform employees and their safety representatives about the person in charge of the employer's duties regarding health and safety at work.

271. On the other hand, the employee also has responsibility to follow the rules of occupational safety and health. Therefore, employees should only work in a state fit to carry out work safely and in compliance with the rules for health and safety at work. Employees must in particular:

- check that the work equipment made available to them is in a safe condition;
- use it properly and in accordance with the employer's instructions, and carry out the maintenance specified for them;
- use personal protective equipment properly, wear clothes to work which are not a hazard to safety or health;
- not turn off, remove or modify any safety equipment without being specifically so instructed;
- keep discipline, order and cleanliness at the workplace;
- learn and apply all the knowledge necessary for their safety at work;
- take part in the medical examinations as far as can be expected from them, eliminate any irregularity posing a hazard, or contact their supervisor with this request;
- immediately report any accident, injury, indisposition or sickness.

272. Employees have the right to demand from their employers: conditions for health and safety and protective measures for dangerous work, information necessary for health and safety and the possibility to obtain it, the provision of work equipment necessary for labour safety, personal protective equipment, prescribed protective drinks and washing facilities.

273. Employees should not suffer any measures prejudicial to them because of their intervention to comply with the requirements of health and safety, nor because of any complaint made in good faith about a presumed omission of an employer. They have the right to refuse work if it involves an imminent and serious danger to their life, health or safety. If an employer's instructions would lead to imminent and serious danger to other people, employees shall refuse to follow them.[154]

I. Workers' Representation in Labour Safety

274. The following worker's representation is regulated in the Hungarian Labour Safety Act: (1) labour safety representative, (2) representative body and (3) National Labour Safety Committee.

1. Labour Safety Representative

275. Labour safety representative workers have the right to elect a labour safety representative or representatives to represent their rights and interests related to occupational safety and occupational health (hereinafter referred to as 'workers' representative') according to the following:

(a) a workers' representative is elected at all employers with at least fifty workers employed in accordance with the Hungarian Labour Code. The provision of the conditions for the election and the staging of the election is the responsibility of the employer;
(b) employers with less than fifty employees – if a workers' representative is not elected – hold a consultation with the workers;
(c) at an independent establishment or division of an employer, a workers' representative may be elected if the director of the independent establishment or division is vested with some or all of the rights concerning occupational safety.

276. Workers' representatives are entitled to inspect the enforcement of occupational safety and occupational health requirements at workplaces, with particular attention to the following:

- the safe condition of workplaces, work equipment and personal safety equipment;
- the implementation of measures taken in order to protect health and to prevent accidents at work and occupational diseases;
- the preparation and preparedness of employees for occupational safety and occupational health at work.

277. Within the framework of exercising their rights defined above, labour safety representatives are entitled to:

(a) enter the workplaces in their spheres of operation during working hours and inquire among the employees working there;

154. Act XCIII of 1993 on Labour Safety.

(b) participate in the preparation of employer decisions which may affect the health and safety of employees, including the compulsory employment of specialists, the planning and arrangements for occupational safety training and the decisions on the establishment of new jobs or positions as well;
(c) request information from employers regarding any and all issues pertaining to occupational safety and health;
(d) express their opinion, and request the employer to take the necessary measures;
(e) take part in the investigation of industrial accidents and in the exploration of the circumstances of occupational diseases upon the initiative of the party entitled to conduct such investigations;
(f) petition the competent occupational safety and health administration in justified cases;
(g) express their opinion to the person conducting the regulatory inspection.

278. Based on the advance consent of employers, workers' representatives are entitled to seek the assistance of experts regarding issues related to occupational safety and occupational health, and furthermore, to conduct discussions on such issues with the occupational safety and health administrations.

279. If, within the framework of his/her obligations, an employer defines the manner of enforcement of the requirements in labour safety regulations, the consent of the labour safety representative is required for having such regulations issued.

280. Workers' representatives may not be discriminated against in connection with the exercise of their rights.

281. Labour safety representatives proceed in accordance with the provisions of labour laws pertaining to the members of works' councils (employee delegates) with regard to the disclosure of the information and facts acquired during their actions.

282. In respect of the labour law protection of labour safety representatives, the provisions pertaining to elected trade union officials are duly applied, whereby the committee is construed as the immediate higher trade union organ, or in the absence thereof, the body of employees who elected the labour safety representative.

283. A workers' representative must have legal capacity and must be employed for at least six months under contract for organized employment. These criteria will not apply in connection with the election of a workers' representative under contract at a newly established employer.

284. Workers' representatives are elected by secret and direct ballot for a term of five years. As regards the election, mandate, dismissal and recall of workers' representatives, and their area of competence, the provisions of the HLC pertaining to members of works' councils and to employee delegates are duly applied, including the possibility of the foundation of a central committee of labour safety.

285. The labour safety representatives, if there are at least three, may establish a local (plant-level) labour safety committee (hereinafter referred to as 'committee'). If a committee is established, the rights of labour safety representatives, if such rights affect all employees, must be exercised by the committee.

The employer, or its duly authorized representative, will attend the committee sessions if so requested by the committee.

286. Resources and time off. Labour safety representatives and committee members are entitled to sufficient paid time off to undertake their duties. Members of the committee are entitled to paid time off equivalent to a least 10% of their monthly working hours. Labour representatives are also entitled to 16 hours of training in the first year following their election and eight hours annually in subsequent years. This training is paid for by the employer and should be conducted during normal working time.

287. Protection against dismissal. Health and safety representatives should not be disadvantaged because of the exercise of their duties and have the same protection against dismissal as local trade union representatives or members of the works' council. This means that they can only be dismissed if the health and safety committee agrees or, if there is no committee, with the agreement of the employees who elected them.

2. Representative Body

288. Representative body. At the employers employing at least fifty workers, and where a workers' representative has been elected, a common representative body will be set up (hereinafter referred to as 'representative body'), with an equal number of delegates representing the employer and the workers.

The representatives of workers (regular and alternate members) for the representative body are delegated by secret ballot from the workers' representatives elected. The employer takes the initial step for the foundation of the representative body and provides for the conditions of the election.

289. The employer will delegate an executive employee with decision-making authority to the representative body, and a person appointed to carry out some or all of the employer's obligations concerning occupational safety (a foreman or supervisor, or an occupational safety expert engaged under contract of employment). The term of all members of the representative body (regular and alternate) is five years.

290. Employer and worker representatives will alternate in the office of the chairman of the representative body. The employer provides for the conditions of operations of the representative body.

291. In connection with its activities relating to the safety and health protection of workers at work, the representative body will:

(a) analyse the working conditions and the working environment for the safety and health of workers on a regular basis, but at least once a year, as well as the related measures that may be necessary;
(b) discuss the programme concerning safety at work and monitor its implementation;
(c) present its opinion on the drafts of internal regulations concerning safety at work.

292. Common obligation of the employers relating to the labour safety representative and labour safety committee. Employers must take measures or respond within eight days to the initiatives of workers' representatives (committees). If they disagree with an initiative, employers must explain their position in writing, with the exception of cases requiring immediate action.

293. Employers must ensure the conditions in order that workers' representatives may exercise their rights, particularly:

(a) leave of absence with average pay, as necessary for carrying out their duties, meaning at least 10% of the monthly working-time for workers' representatives and members of the representative body;
(b) the necessary equipment, such as operating, technical and material conditions, and the relevant technical specifications;
(c) the opportunity to attend, within one year of being elected, a training course of at least 16 hours during an election cycle, and the opportunity of annually taking 8 hours of training subsequently.

294. The costs involved in the execution of the above-mentioned obligation will be borne by the employer. The training referred to in point c) shall be held during regular working hours, and it may be held in an external location.

295. The local (plant-level) labour safety committee. The labour safety representatives, if there are at least three, may establish a local (plant-level) labour safety committee (hereinafter referred to as 'committee'). If a committee is established, the rights of labour safety representatives, if such rights affect all employees, will be exercised by the committee. The employer, or its duly authorized representative, will attend the committee sessions if so requested by the committee.

296. Labour safety programme. Labour safety representatives (committees) are entitled to propose to employers to have a labour safety programme prepared. If the employers defined in the decree of the minister in charge of employment and labour fail to agree, the labour safety representatives (committees) may initiate a collective labour debate as described in the HLC.[155]

155. Act XCIII of 1993 on Labour Safety.

3. National Labour Safety Committee

297. National Labour Safety Committee. National reconciliation of interests related to occupational safety and occupational health is performed by the Labour Safety Committee. It consists of the interest representation organs of employees and employers as well as of the representatives of the Government (hereinafter referred to as 'negotiating parties').

298. Within the framework of its activities relating to occupational safety and occupational health, the Labour Safety Committee shall:

(a) express its preliminary opinion on bills of legislation and drafts of other provisions and measures, as well as on the accounts (reports) and temporary programmes; its unanimous resolution or the differing opinion of the negotiating parties must be indicated in the respective presentations;
(b) take part in drawing up the programme for occupational safety and the annual schedule and timetable for the execution of the programme and in the analysis and review of the programme;
(c) negotiate and present its opinion and recommendations concerning the issues presented by the negotiating parties;
(d) adopt recommendations concerning occupational safety requirements exceeding those contained in occupational safety regulations;
(e) provide information to the general public concerning its work;
(f) make proposals, for the appropriation – by way of tender – of proceeds from the penalties imposed by the occupational safety and health administration, and will support the occupational safety information network by providing comments and information from its own database.[156]

J. Employment Supervisory Authority

299. In the interest of labour safety, suitable organization is necessary which prescribes or creates the requirements corresponding to carrying out occupational safety and health.

300. According to the Chapter II of the Act CXXXV of 2020, the central entity of the labour inspection is the Employment Supervisory Authority. The Government Offices (Kormányhivatal) of the Counties and the Capital have territorial competence for the county/capital where they are located.[157]

301. The compliance of employers with the minimum requirements laid down by legislation governing employment relationships shall be monitored by the employment supervisory authority. The authority designated by the Government by

156. Balázs DANCSECZ-Imre NAGY-Ferenc KUDÁSZ (2019) Worker participation – Hungary, https://oshwiki.osha.europa.eu/en/themes/worker-participation-hungary (26 Jul. 2023).
157. Munkavédelem, Foglalkoztatás-felügyelet (2023), http://www.ommf.gov.hu (26 Jul. 2023).

means of a decree shall function as the employment supervisory authority of general jurisdiction. The employment supervisory authority of general jurisdiction is entitled to hear all cases that do not fall under the competence of another authority designated by an act or government decree.

302. The employment supervisory authority's material and procedural scope of activity:

(a) for the qualification of the legal relationship between the employer and the employee, as well as the relationship underlying the secondment of employees for the purpose of work, and the relationship established on the basis of the actual employment;
(b) if the actual employer cannot be identified, to establish – in the absence of evidence to the contrary – the identity of the employer on the basis of presumption, where the employer is, in the following order:
  (i) the entity responsible for the coordination of activities based on the stipulations of the contract (agreement) between the parties carrying out activities at the workplace;
  (ii) the person who in fact manages the activity at the workplace;
  (iii) the entity in whose premises the work is performed.
(c) to establish the existence of an employment relationship between specific parties on the basis of paragraphs a) and b);
(d) to check the fulfilment of obligations undertaken with regard to support for employment.

303. Supervision and proceedings of the employment supervisory authority: in the proceedings of the employment supervisory authority, client means an employer who is the subject of inspection or against whom administrative proceedings have been opened, as well as an employer established in Hungary or abroad who is subject to reporting obligation under Community legislation. All inspections by the employment supervisory authority are launched ex officio; no inspection may be requested by the client.

304. The employment supervisory authority shall have the power to conduct on-site inspection at all employment locations without special permit or prior notification requirement.

Apart from the rules laid down in the Act on General Public Administration Procedures, in its official supervisory procedures the employment supervisory authority is entitled to:

(a) have access to and view the recordings of security equipment located at the site of the inspection and the data of the equipment recording entry and exit to and from the employment area, as well as to make copies thereof;
(b) establish the identity of persons affected by the inspection by means of identity check, to use their tax identification code and social security identification code (hereinafter referred to as 'social security number'), and to request information

from such persons to the extent necessary for the purposes of the inspection, as well as to interview such persons as witnesses.

305. Where an infringement is found to have been committed, the employment supervisory authority may apply the following administrative sanctions in addition to those specified in the Act on Penalizing Administrative Infractions:

(a) prohibition of further employment;
(b) administrative fine.

306. The employment supervisory authority may impose an administrative fine if it discovers an infringement within its jurisdiction, and no other sanction is prescribed by an act or government decree. A government decree may render the application of an administrative fine mandatory.

307. Where an infringement has been discovered, the employment supervisory authority orders the employer to cease the infringement and eliminate the consequences, and also to prevent further infringements, or adopts a decision establishing the fact of the infringement.

308. No administrative sanction may be applied if one year has passed since the behaviour constituting the infringement became known to the employment supervisory authority. An administrative sanction may be imposed after three years from the date of commission, if:

(a) the infringement started more than three years ago and it continues to exist at the beginning of the regulatory inspection; or
(b) the court of jurisdiction for administrative actions or the supervisory body ordered the employment supervisory authority to open new proceedings.

309. If the employer fails to comply with the notification requirement in connection with entering into an employment relationship, the employment supervisory authority establishes the existence of the employment relationship and orders the employer to comply with the notification requirement. Moreover, if the employer fails to comply with the notification requirement in connection with entering into an employment relationship, the employment supervisory authority establishes the existence of the employment relationship with retroactive effect from the thirtieth day calculated from the first day of infringement, based on regular daily working time, except if the administrative proceedings produce evidence that the unreported employment exceeded thirty days.[158]

158. HORVÁTH István – SZLADOVNYIK Krisztina: Szigorúan ellenőrzött viszonyok II. Adó Szaklap 2021/7. – Munkaügy.

K. Register of the Employment Supervisory Authority

310. For the purposes of carrying out its tasks the employment supervisory authority processes and records the following data in the IT system it has established:

(a) the employed person's:
  (i) natural identification data and citizenship;
  (ii) immigrant or permanent resident status, refugee status, subsidiary protection;
  (iii) home address, habitual residence and contact address;
  (iv) profession, employer, job title (activity);
  (v) weekly working hours;
  (vi) educational attainment, vocational skills;
  (vii) income information;
  (viii) social security number, tax identification code;
  (ix) student ID number if a member of a school cooperative;
  (x) pension registration number if a member of general interest association of pensioners.
(b) the employer's:
  (i) identification data;
  (ii) legal form;
  (iii) tax number;
  (iv) payment account number.
(c) if the employer is a natural person with no tax number, the following particulars:
  (i) natural identification data;
  (ii) home address;
  (iii) tax identification code.

311. The employment supervisory authority may disclose data to other bodies and natural persons only in a manner specified by law. The court, the public prosecutor's office, law enforcement agencies and penal institutes and the national security services are entitled to request any and all data on records with a view to discharging their duties and upon the fulfilment of applicable objectives and purposes defined by law applicable to them. The occupational safety and health authority is given access to the above-mentioned register to the extent required for carrying out inspections. The employment supervisory authority erases data from the register after fifty years from the time of receipt thereof.

L. Registries and Reporting of Accidents/Diseases at Work

312. Issues related to work permit 8 are regulated by Act XCIII of 1993 on Work Safety and the Ministry of Labour Decree 5/1993(26. XII) concerning its implementation. The labour inspector's scope is limited exclusively to the investigation, registration and processing of occupational accidents involving more than three days of work incapacity. Hungarian employers are required by law to report, investigate and register labour accidents and occupational diseases. Labour accidents involving work incapacity must be investigated promptly by the employer and the results of the investigation must be documented in a work accident report/minute.

313. The employer is obliged to immediately report severe occupational accidents to the National Labour Inspectorate or its local unit at the Government Office. The official supervision of occupational safety and health by the National Labour Inspectorate includes investigation, reporting and registration of occupational accidents, diseases and increased exposure, as well as actions aimed at preventing these situations.[159]

§5. The Sources of Hungarian Labour Law

314. Of cardinal importance among the sources of labour law is the Constitution (since 2012 it has been called Fundamental Law) of Hungary. Its significance manifests itself in two ways. On the one hand, the Fundamental Law (Constitution) lays the foundation of labour legislation. (NB: The relevant constitutional principles have already been mentioned above.) On the other hand, the Fundamental Law outlines the legal sources of labour legislation. From this point of view, it is especially important to consider the Fundamental Law which establishes that a declaration related to the basic rights and obligations of citizens can only be laid down in statutory provisions promulgated by Parliament. In accordance with the Fundamental Law, the Labour Code provides that questions connected with employment are regulated by law and/or other rules of law where the law so provides.

315. According to section 13 of the Labour Code (2012), the employment regulations (sources of law) mean (a) legislation, (b) collective agreements and (c) work agreements, and (d) the binding decisions of the conciliation committee adopted according to section 293 of the HLC.[160]

316. The purpose of framing a new HLC was the new concept of labour law based on a contractual system. The legislator's aim is to strengthen the role of the collective agreement as a contractual scope of labour law. The regulation of the relationship between the legal norm and the collective agreement has been modified. Under Act XXII of 1992 (the former LC) 'a collective agreement or an agreement between the parties may derogate from the provisions laid down in Part Three of the former Labour Code on condition that it offers more favourable terms for the employees' (section 13 Sub 3). Under these legal circumstances, it was not possible to create the regulating function of the collective agreement: Employers were not willing and trade unions were not capable of concluding a collective agreement.

159. EMBER Alex, *Az üzemi baleset*, Szeged: Pólay Alapítvány, 2013. pp. 72–73.
160. DUDÁS Katalin – GYULAVÁRI Tamás – HORVÁTH István – Hős Nikolett – KULISITY Mária – HUNGLER Sára – KÁRTYÁS Gábor – KUN Attila – PETROVICS Zoltán – RÁCZ Réka, *Munkajog – V. átdolgozott kiadás*, Budapest: ELTE Eötvös Kiadó, 2019.

317. In contrast, the new HLC regulates two types of legal norms. (1) Employees' fundamental rights and important interests are regulated by norms of ius cogens. (2) Other rights and duties of the employment relationship are regulated by norms of ius dispositivum. There are two kinds of dispositive norms, namely: It is possible to derogate in favour of the employee only; in other cases, it is possible to derogate in melius and peius as well. The legislator specified cases of the above-mentioned types of derogation in every part of the HLC.[161]

§6. International Private Labour Law

318. The current Hungarian labour law rules regulate two groups of problems in international relations: (1) The first concerns the labour relationship of foreign citizens and legal persons. (2) The other concerns the labour relations of a Hungarian citizen who works abroad or establishes a labour relationship with a foreigner.[162]

I. The Labour Relationship Established with a Foreigner

319. In regard to the labour relations of foreigners, the legal regulation affects two areas. One of these governs the conditions under which a foreign citizen can establish a labour relationship in Hungary as an employee. The second deals with the question of which rules should be applied abroad or by the foreign party concerning labour relationships established in Hungary.

320. As for the starting point, we have to state that Hungary is a Member State of the European Union, which means – according to the EU legislation, mainly Directive 2004/38/EC – that almost all non-European Union citizens (third-country nationals, TCN)[163] and only a few European Union citizens are required to be in possession of a valid work permit and work visa to be able to legally work in Hungary.

321. The HLC does not contain any special provisions for either EU or non-EU (TCN) migrant workers. A good illustration of the discrimination against regular non-EU migrant workers is the regulation of their status when it comes to losing job positions. According to Hungarian law, a non-EU migrant worker would be entitled, for example, to unemployment benefits in case of losing the job since

161. http://www.labourlawnetwork.eu/national_labour_law/legislative_developments/prm/109/v__detail/id__1661/category__15/size__1/index.html (26 Jul. 2023).
162. HAJDÚ József – KUN Attila (eds), *Munkajog I.*, Budapest: Patrocinium, 2012. p. 28.
163. Third Country National (TCN) is a term often used in the context of migration, referring to individuals who are in transit and/or applying for visas in countries that are not their country of origin (i.e., country of transit), in order to go to destination countries that is likewise not their country of origin. In the European Union, the term is often used, together with 'foreign national' and 'non-EU foreign national', to refer to individuals who are neither from the EU country in which they are currently living or staying, nor from other Member States of the EU.

he/she pays all social security contributions and taxes in Hungary including deductions to the unemployment fund.[164] But when a TCN actually loses the job, he/she also automatically loses the legal status and residence and will never get unemployment support. Such situation forces this non-EU migrant worker to leave Hungary or stay in illegality in the country. If the person wants to get employed again in Hungary, the whole authorization procedure needs to be reinitiated by the new employer.

322. In addition, even if the status of migrant workers is legalized, employers might violate certain labour regulations. Based on the Act on Supervision of Employment, the task of the Employment Supervisory Authority is the protection of employees.[165] However, migrant workers are poorly protected when it comes to wages, working time and working conditions: first, because of ineffective sanctioning of labour rules in general; second, in case of any violation of labour rules when a third country national is employed, not only the employer will be fined but also the migrant worker, who may face a loss of residence status and face expulsion.[166] The reason: he/she 'was engaged in any gainful employment in the absence of the prescribed work permit or any permit prescribed under statutory provision'.

A. *Work of EU Member States Citizens*

323. Employment of the citizens of EU Member States. Basically, EU citizens can work in any other Member State without any work permit.[167] As of 1 January 2011, citizens of the European Union / European Economic Community and Switzerland, in other words, persons entitled to freedom of movement and residence and their family members are allowed to enter into employment in Hungary without permission. The employer must submit a notification in relation to the employment of such persons to the employment office, which is competent according to the place of the employment no later than on the first working day. The obligations imposed on employment and alien regulations are in all cases incumbent upon, and the responsibility of, the employer, while the employee is responsible for obtaining the residence permit.[168]

324. Hungary opened 'in phases' its labour market to workers from Bulgaria and Romania when they joined the European Union in January 2007. The Hungarian Government has decided to open the labour market as much as possible (but) in phases. The jobs where working permits will be granted are in sectors with labour shortages, including the textiles, healthcare and construction industries.

164. Zayonchkovskaya, Z.H A. *UNESCO Series of Country Reports on the Ratification of the UN Convention on Migrants,* 2004. p. 14., p. 63. http://unesdoc.unesco.org/images/0013/001395/139533e.pdf (26 Jul. 2023).
165. Act CXXXV of 2020 on ÍServices and Aids Intended to Promote Employment, and on the Supervision of Employment.
166. Section 43 of Act II of 2007 on entry and stay of third-country nationals.
167. NB: Work permits are never required for self-employed people in the EU.
168. HAJDÚ József, IEL Labour Law, Hungary, Wolters Kluwer, Kluwer Law Online, 2019. https://kluwerlawonline.com/Manuals/Corporate+Acquisitions+and+Mergers/705 (26 Jul. 2023).

325. Hungary also opened the labour market for Croatian citizens when Croatia joined the EU in 1 July 2013.[169]

B. The Undertaking of Work by Third-Country Nationals

326. Third-country nationals may be employed in Hungary only under specific conditions. As a main rule, employment is subject to a permit, but there are exceptions that are partly connected to the activity and partly connected to the person concerned. At the same time, different rules are also relevant to the citizens of various EU countries.

327. Act IV of 1991 on the promotion of employment and on provisions for unemployed people (in the following: Act) says that third-country nationals may perform work in Hungary only with a permit – subject to the exceptions set forth in the legal regulations.[170]

328. The permit may be:

(1) individual permit; and
(2) group permit.

329. Obtaining the individual work permit. The application for a permit has to be submitted by the employer in the form specified in the annex to the legal regulation to the county (Budapest) labour unit of the Government Office.

330. An application for work permit shall be refused if:

(a) the employer has had a valid labour requirement notified for the position for which the third-country national is to be hired;
(b) after notifying the labour requirement no worker was available for the position in question, who is registered as a job-seeker according to the EmpA and its implementing decrees and who satisfies the conditions of employment prescribed by the relevant legislation or specified by the employer's labour requirement;
(c) the third-country nationals satisfy the conditions of employment prescribed by the relevant legislation and specified by the employer's labour requirement;
(d) employment of the third-country national in Hungary would exceed the limit set by the minister responsible for the employment of third-country nationals

169. http://www.workpermit.com/european_union/european_union.htm (26 Jul. 2023).
170. The implementing regulation: Government Decree 445/2013 (XI. 28.) Korm. on the Authorization of the Employment of Third-country Nationals in Hungary by a Procedure Other Than a Single Application Procedure, on Cases of Exemptions from the Authorization Requirement, on the Involvement of the Employment Centres of County (Budapest) Government Agencies in Single Application Procedures in the Capacity of Specialist Authority, on the Notification of the Employment of Third-country Nationals Who can be Employed Without a Work Permit, and on Wage Compensation.

in Hungary (hereinafter referred to as 'Minister') by means of a decree for the employment of third-country nationals in Hungary;

(e) in the position for which the third-country national is to be hired no work permits will be granted to third-country nationals taking into consideration unemployment in Hungary in terms of trends and composition;

(f) the employer does not intend to begin the employment of the third-country national applicant within one hundred and twenty days following the date when the application for the work permit is submitted;

(g) there is a worker available for the position for which the third-country national is to be hired who satisfies the qualification requirements and the employment conditions prescribed by the relevant legislation or specified by the employer, and if the employment of such worker did not materialize to reasons attributable to the employer;

(h) employment of the third-country national is likely to occur at a place other than the applicant employer;

(i) the contract for employment relationship is concluded not between the applicant employer and the applying third-country national;

(j) the sole object of the service is the assignment of the working capacity of the third-country national for an extended period of time under a private contract concluded with the foreign employer;

(k) the competent authority of the state where the third-country national's permanent residence is located applies conditions for granting work permits to Hungarian nationals which are unreasonably severe in comparison to those afforded to citizens of other countries (lack of reciprocity);

(l) there is a valid work permit in effect for the employment of the third-country national in Hungary for the duration of employment to which the application pertains;

(m) if the document the employer has submitted to verify the third-country national's vocational training or education for the purpose of employment is false or forged;

(n) if the prospective employer has been fined for any infringement of employment and occupational safety regulations within one year preceding the date of the application;

(o) if the prospective employer was ordered to pay an employment penalty or to make a mandatory contribution for illegal employment of a third-country national within one year preceding the date of the application;

(p) if, at the time when the application was submitted, there is a training programme sponsored by the National Employment Fund in progress in relation to the activity to be performed by the applying third-country national, and the programme is planned to be concluded prior to the commencement of employment of the third-country national;

(q) if the employer is apparently unable to provide the working conditions required;

(r) if there is a strike in progress at the employer at the time the application is submitted, and it affects the position to be filled by the applying third-country national;

(s) if the employer carried out collective redundancy within one year of the date of application;
(t) if the base wage (salary, remuneration) stipulated by the employer for the activities to be performed by the applying third-country national is considerably lower than the national average personal base wage. The personal base wage (salary, remuneration) stipulated for the activities to be performed by the applying third-country national shall be construed to be considerably lower than the national average personal base wage if it does not exceed 80% of the national average personal base wage.

331. Prior to submitting the application for the permit, the employer must certify that he/she possessed a valid labour force requirement for the activity to be performed by the third-country nationals. The labour force requirement must be reported to the office of the labour unit at the Government Office where the third-country nationals will be employed.

332. The labour force requirement is valid if registered by the employer:

(a) simultaneously with the submission of the application for work permit;
(b) before the time of submission of the application for work permit, within a timeframe of up to sixty days; or
(c) over sixty days before the submission of the application for work permit, provided it was renewed within a timeframe of up to sixty days.

333. The work permit of a third-country national shall specify the employer, the work place, the job or occupation – showing the FEOR code as well – for which the third-country national may be hired, including the duration of employment.

334. The work permits are issued for a maximum period of two years and may be renewed. The renewal of work permits is governed by the same rules under which the original authorization was granted.[171]

C. *Work Permit Issued for Seasonal Workers for Employment not Exceeding Ninety Days*

335. Continuous employment of a third-country national not exceeding ninety days may be authorized within the framework of seasonal employment with a seasonal work permit. If more than one seasonal work permit is issued for the employment of a particular third-country national, the duration of all such seasonal employment shown in said permits may not exceed one hundred and eighty days within a given twelve-month period. A seasonal work permit may be renewed once

---

171. GERSE Márton (2023) Külföldi munkavállalók magyarországi foglalkoztatása a gyakorlatban; https://jogaszvilag.hu/cegvilag/kulfoldi-munkavallalok-magyarorszagi-foglalkoztatasa-a-gyakorlatban/ (26 Jul. 2023).

on condition that the total duration of seasonal employment, including the extension, shall not exceed ninety days. The seasonal work permit shall be issued irrespective of current trends in the labour market.

336. An application for work permit for seasonal employment must be refused if:

(a) the third-country national's employment within the framework of seasonal work has already exhausted the one hundred and eighty-day time limit in a given twelve-month period, or it is likely to exceed such time limit with the duration of employment indicated in the application for a seasonal work permit;
(b) the duration of the third-country national's employment consecutively at different employers exceeds ninety days;
(c) employment of the third-country national in Hungary would exceed the limit set by the Minister by means of a decree for the employment of third-country nationals in Hungary;
(d) in the position for which the third-country national is to be hired no work permits will be granted to third-country nationals taking into consideration unemployment in Hungary in terms of trends and composition;
(e) the employer does not intend to begin the employment of the applicant third-country national within one hundred and twenty days following the date when the application for the work permit is submitted;
(f) the third-country national is employed by an employer other than the applicant employer, or the contract for employment relationship is concluded not between the applicant employer and the third-country national in question;
(g) within one year before the time of submission of the application for seasonal work permit, the employment supervisory authority or the tax authority (hereinafter referred to as 'competent authority') imposed a fine upon the employer for failure to comply with the obligation of notification of entering into a contract for employment relationship, including the termination or seizure thereof, or imposed a financial penalty upon the employer for the illegal employment of a third-country national; or
(h) the employer is undergoing liquidation or if no economic activity is taking place.

337. Work permits for seasonal employment may also be granted within the framework of temporary agency work (the employer is construed as temporary-work agency).

D. Hiring Third-Country Nationals Without Permit

338. Work permits must be issued irrespective of current trends in the labour market in the following cases:

(1) within the framework of international conventions;
(2) for the employment of a third-country national as key personnel;

(3) each calendar quarter, for employment in a business association under foreign majority ownership if the number of third-country nationals employed on the last day of the previous calendar quarter does not exceed 20% of the labour force in the previous calendar quarter;
(4) for the Hungarian employment of the close relatives of the staff of a diplomatic or consular mission of any foreign state, in the absence of reciprocity between the states concerned;
(5) for the employment of a third-country national who is internationally recognized in the field of education, science or art, provided that such employment exceeds ten working days per calendar year, and if invited by an institution of higher education, scientific research institute or cultural and art institutions;
(6) for the employment of a family member of a third-country national working in Hungary for at least eight years, who does not have an EU Blue Card, if they lived together in Hungary for at least five years, and if not entitled to receive a residence permit for the purpose of family reunification;
(7) for the employment of the spouse of a person with refugee status, a beneficiary of subsidiary protection, a person enjoying temporary protection, and a person who has been granted immigrant or permanent resident status, if they lived together in Hungary for at least one year;
(8) for the employment of the widow of a person with refugee status, a beneficiary of subsidiary protection, or a person enjoying temporary protection, and the widow of a person with the right of free movement and residence, if they lived together in Hungary for at least one year before the time of death;
(9) for carrying out work that involves commissioning, warranty repair, maintenance or guarantee service activities performed on the basis of a private contract with a business entity established in a third country, if it exceeds fifteen working days within a thirty-day period at any given time;
(10) for employment of a third-country national who has received authorization from the immigration authority to work in Hungary in accordance with immigration laws;
(11) for the employment of any person who has been granted refugee status, to be performed outside the premises of the refugee centre, whose employment in Hungary is supported by the refugee authority for humanitarian reasons;
(12) for employment of a third-country national by an international organization or by the diplomatic mission or consular post or other bodies of a foreign state, or their staff, if other than the regular staff and if not considered a delegated member of the state which he/she represents;
(13) for employment of a third-country national by a motion picture company that is registered by the motion picture authority according to the Act on Motion Pictures;
(14) for the employment of a third-country national when such natural person participates in hands-on training so as to obtain sufficient experience for any specific work if the duration of such work does not exceed three months in any given calendar year;
(15) for researchers who are engaging in educational activities in Hungary in addition to a research project carried out under a hosting agreement concluded with a research organization accredited according to the Government Decree on the

Accreditation of Research Organizations Hosting Researchers Who Are Third-country Nationals, and on Hosting Agreements;

(16) if the employer submits the application for renewal of work permit at the latest on or before the fifteenth day prior to the expiry of the work permit; and

(17) for the employment of a family member of a third-country national holding an EU Blue Card, to whom the provisions on family reunification apply.[172]

E. *Provisions on Exemptions from Work Permit Requirement Relating to the Employment of Third-Country Nationals in Hungary*

339. For the employment of a third-country national in Hungary within the framework of a contract for employment relationship no work permit is required:

(1) if so prescribed by international agreement, an act or government decree;

(2) for the director of a branch or representative office of a foreign-registered business association, as defined by international agreement;

(3) for the staff of diplomatic or consular missions of foreign states or the branches or offices thereof, if delegated by the state which it represents, for employment at the mission or other body, or for the employment of the close relatives of the staff of a diplomatic or consular mission of any foreign state, subject to reciprocity between the states concerned;

(4) for the staff of international inter-governmental organizations operating in the territory of Hungary under international agreement, and international organizations operating in the territory of Hungary and recognized as such by the public authorities of Hungary (hereinafter referred to as 'international organization') if working for the international organization, including their close relatives;

(5) for persons delegated by states which are parties to the agreement for setting up an international organization or a common organ not recognized as an international organization (hereinafter referred to as 'delegates') if working for the international organization or the common organ, including the close relatives of such delegates subject to reciprocity between the states which are parties to the agreement;

(6) for carrying out work that involves commissioning, warranty repair, maintenance or guarantee service activities performed on the basis of a private contract with a business entity established in a third country, if it does not exceed fifteen working days within a thirty-day period at any given time;

(7) for work performed by an employer established in a State that is a party to the Agreement on the European Economic Area, other than Hungary, within the

172. Section 9 of the Government Decree 445/2013 (XI. 28.) Korm. on the Authorization of the Employment of Third-country Nationals in Hungary by a Procedure Other Than a Single Application Procedure, on Cases of Exemptions from the Authorization Requirement, on the Involvement of the Employment Centres of County (Budapest) Government Agencies in Single Application Procedures in the Capacity of Specialist Authority, on the Notification of the Employment of Third-country Nationals Who can be Employed Without a Work Permit, and on Wage Compensation.

framework of cross-border services by way of posting, temporary assignment to a Hungarian employer for the purpose of fulfilment of a private contract;

(8) for work performed by a temporary agency worker within the framework of temporary agency work for a Hungarian employer under placement by a temporary-work agency established in a State that is a party to the Agreement on the European Economic Area, other than Hungary;

(9) for the chief executives and supervisory board members of business associations with foreign participation;

(10) for a foreign national winning a tender for post-doctorate-related employment, or the János Bolyai Research Scholarship for work performed as part of the tender or the scholarship programme;

(11) for the employment of a third-country national studying at a foreign institution of higher education as part of an apprentice training program arranged by an international student organization;

(12) for foreign nationals pursuing full-time studies at vocational schools, secondary schools, basic art schools or institutions of higher education located in the territory of Hungary, for performing work under the term of such legal relationship;

(13) education activities in education institutions in a foreign language, if performed – as verified by the minister responsible for public education or the minister in charge of vocational education – under an international education program signed by the competent ministers of the States affected;

(14) for the activities of natural persons in the service of an ecclesiastical legal entity of a listed church (ecclesiastical personnel) within the framework of a special ecclesiastical service relationship, under contract of employment or other similar relationship;

(15) for persons applying for refugee or asylum status, or for subsidiary protection, and for persons granted authorization to stay, for working in Hungary or inside the premises of the reception centre, respectively;

(16) for activities in the field of education, science or art for not more than ten working days per calendar year;

(17) for third-country nationals for activities performed under contract for some form of employment with a public-benefit trust carrying out public service functions, or with a higher education institution maintained by a public-benefit trust carrying out public service functions or any other higher education institution, if the duration of residence in Hungary in connection with that contract for employment does not exceed thirty days;

(18) for researchers for work carried out within the framework of an international agreement between Hungary and another State, provided that this is verified by a certificate issued by the Magyar Tudományos Akadémia (Hungarian Academy of Sciences);

(19) for the employment of third-country nationals attending practical training courses within the framework of the Comenius, Erasmus, Leonardo da Vinci and Grundtvig programs;

(20) for the employment of the widow of a Hungarian national, if they lived together in Hungary for at least one year before the spouse's death;

(21) for researchers for the purposes of carrying out research in Hungary under a hosting agreement concluded with a research organization accredited according to the Government Decree on the Accreditation of Research Organizations Hosting Researchers Who Are Third-country Nationals, and on Hosting Agreements;

(22) for professional athletes involved in sports activities, and for trainers for their activities to prepare the said professional athletes for sports activities;

(23) for the employment of the close relatives of the military personnel of Member States which are parties to the Convention between the Parties to the North Atlantic Treaty on the Status of their Forces, signed in London on 19 June 1951 (hereinafter referred to as 'NATO-SOFA Agreement') and promulgated by Act CXVII of 1999, stationed in the territory of Hungary and of the civilian staff described under paragraphs (a) and (b) of Point 1 of Article I of the NATO-SOFA Agreement;

(24) for the family member of a third-country sponsor provided for in section 19 of the RRTN, holding a residence permit issued for the purpose of family reunification and legally residing in Hungary for at least one year, provided that the sponsor can be employed without a work permit;

(25) for the family member of a person who has been granted refugee or subsidiary protection status, or to the parent of an unaccompanied minor recognized as a refugee, or to his/her guardian in the absence thereof, provided that he/she holds a valid residence permit for the purpose of family reunification;

(26) for the employment of a third-country national within the framework of public benefit employment, if eligible under paragraph b) of Subsection (4) of section 1 of Act CVI of 2011 on Public Benefit Employment and on the Amendment of Regulations Relating to Public Benefit Employment and Other Acts;

(27) for the employment in Hungary of a third-country national in any profession provided for in a communication of the Minister, including employment by way of temporary agency work, who is a citizen of a third country neighbouring Hungary and is residing in that neighbouring third country;

(28) if the third-country national holds a permit made out by the competent authority of the first Member State to the intra-corporate transferee and if employment in Hungary is exercised in any host entity that belongs to the company or the group of companies specified in the permit issued by the competent authority of the first Member State and employment in Hungary does not exceed ninety days within any one hundred and eighty-day period;

(29) for a third-country national applying for residence permit as a frontier worker in accordance with Article 26 of the Withdrawal Agreement;

(30) for the employment in Hungary of nationals of third-countries set out in the communication of the minister responsible for the employment of third-country nationals in Hungary, having regard to the prior resolution of the Defence Council, by a certified temporary-work agency in a position specified in the communication, including temporary agency work;

(31) for the family members provided for in the RRTN of Hungarian citizens.

340. The exemption described above will not apply to any work performed by a third-country national in excess of the limits to which the exemption pertains.[173]

F. Guest (Third-Country Nationals) Worker Residence Permit

341. On 13 June 2023, the Hungarian Parliament adopted a new law regulating the employment of foreign workers. The law introduces the concept of guest workers (third-country nationals from countries outside the EEA and from non-neighbouring countries) and establishes guidelines for their employment in Hungary.

342. Previously, Hungarian employers could hire third-country nationals who successfully applied for a combined work and residence permit (Single Permit). The new law introduces a guest worker residence permit, which can be obtained by citizens of countries that do not neighbour Hungary and countries outside the European Economic Area, as determined by a separate ministerial decree (yet to be adopted). Additionally, the decree will specify the total number of guest workers allowed each year and the maximum number of guest workers per country. The legislation also restricts the employment of guest workers to specific jobs, with the details to be regulated by the ministerial decree.

343. The law defines a limited group of employers who can hire guest workers. These include employers implementing investments of national economic importance, employers with partnership agreements within the Key Exporter Partnership Programme, and qualified temporary-work agencies.

344. An advantage of the guest worker residence permit is that no expert opinion needs to be obtained from the labour authority. This streamlines the decision-making process, enabling guest workers to start working in Hungary sooner.

345. Initially, the guest worker residence permit can be requested for two years, similar to the combined permit. However, the permit can only be extended for up to three years from its first issuance, while the 'classic' combined permit allows for periodic two-year extensions. Another downside is that guest workers' relatives may not apply for a residence permit for family reunification if they accompany the guest worker to Hungary.

346. It is important to note that the law places increased responsibility on employers regarding guest workers. If a guest worker fails to leave the European

173. Section 9 of the Government Decree 445/2013 (XI. 28.) Korm. on the Authorization of the Employment of Third-country Nationals in Hungary by a Procedure Other Than a Single Application Procedure, on Cases of Exemptions from the Authorization Requirement, on the Involvement of the Employment Centres of County (Budapest) Government Agencies in Single Application Procedures in the Capacity of Specialist Authority, on the Notification of the Employment of Third-country Nationals Who can be Employed Without a Work Permit, and on Wage Compensation.

Union when their residence permit expires, the employer is obliged to cover the costs associated with their expulsion, deportation and possible detention by immigration authorities if the guest worker cannot bear these expenses.

347. Overall, the new law on the employment of foreign workers introduces the concept of guest workers and provides regulations for their employment in Hungary. While it simplifies certain aspects of the process, it also poses limitations and responsibilities for both the workers and their employers. Experts argue that the new legislation was necessary to tackle labour shortages, particularly in the context of significant national investments. The new law will enter into force on 1 November 2023.[174]

G. EU Blue Card for Third-Country Nationals

348. The EU Blue Card[175] is a special permit that allows highly qualified third-country nationals to live and work in the European Union (excluding Member States that have opted out of the scheme) without having to obtain a work permit. The Blue Card would provide a 'one-stop shop' for non-European Union nationals with skilled work experience who wish to take employment in a European Union Member State.

349. After eighteen months of legal residence in the first Member State as an EU Blue Card holder, the person concerned may move to another Member State for the purpose of highly qualified employment and may be automatically granted an EU Blue Card in that Member State. Other caveats exist. Skilled professionals taking advantage of the Blue Card would have to earn at least 150% of the gross average salary in the country they wish to work in, or 120% for jobs for which there is a shortage of labour. It is also expected that a job offer will be required. In addition, the main applicant under the Blue Card immigration scheme would be able to bring immediate family to live with them right away. After a required time period elapses, a Blue Card holder and his family could apply for permanent residence.

350. In Hungary, the EU Blue Card is issued in accordance with the Hungarian authorization rules. A third-country national who has applied and fulfils the requirements may be issued an EU Blue Card with a duration of up to four years. However, for the first two years of legal employment as an EU Blue Card holder, access to the labour market for the person concerned will be restricted to the exercise of their initial work contract. The competent regional directorate of the Hungarian Immigration Office will request the employment authority to issue an opinion on

174. Dániel GERA: New Law on Employment of Foreign Workers in Hungary (2023), https://www.schoenherr.eu/content/new-law-on-employment-of-foreign-workers-in-hungary/ (26 Jul. 2023).

175. The Blue Card is an approved EU-wide work permit (Council Directive 2009/50/EC) allowing high-skilled non-EU citizens to work and live in any country within the EU, excluding Denmark, Ireland and the United Kingdom The term Blue Card was coined by the think tank Bruegel, inspired by the United States' Green Card and making reference to the EU flag which is blue with twelve golden stars.

whether the third-country applicant fulfils the relevant qualification requirements. Under the implementation rules, such an opinion is required for issuing an EU Blue Card.[176]

H. The Hungarian Digital Nomad Visa: White Card

351. Hungary launched, in February 2022, the 'White Card', a one-year permit for digital nomads to reside in Hungary while working for a foreign employer or clients outside of Hungary. Only third-country nationals (TCN) can apply. The applicant must have sufficient resources. DNV stay does not count for permanent residency if the DN might apply for the Hungarian permanent residence permit.

352. Contrary to how other types of Hungarian residence permits work, where the spouse and underage children can apply for family unification as soon as the main applicant has received their permit, the white card does not make the spouse and underage children of the main applicant eligible for Hungarian residency.

353. A White Card shall be withdrawn by the immigration authority if the third-country national: (1) does not fulfil the conditions for the issue of the White Card or where there are grounds for exclusion; (2) has left the territory of Hungary for a period exceeding ninety days, or (3) works for or in the interest of a Hungarian employer, engages in gainful employment or acquires a share in a Hungarian company.[177]

II. The Rules Governing Labour Relations Established by a Foreigner

A. Labour Contract

354. Formerly, the Hungarian labour law was based in essence on the territorial principle, namely on the principle of the lex loci labouris.

355. Act XXVIII of 2017 on Private International Law sets out which law be used to interpret contracts with an international element (i.e., contracts agreed by parties in different countries). According to the Rome I Regulation, Article 8(2), which supersedes Article 6(1) of the 1980 Rome Convention, says:

> To the extent that the law applicable to the individual employment contract has not been chosen by the parties, the contract shall be governed by the law of the country in which or, failing that, from which the employee habitually carries

176. Uniós kék kártya: új szabályok a magasan képzett munkavállalók segítéséért (2021) https://www.europarl.europa.eu/news/hu/headlines/eu-affairs/20210902STO11113/unios-kek-kartya-uj-szabalyok-a-magasan-kepzett-munkavallalok-segiteseert (26 Jul. 2023).
177. White Card (2023), http://www.bmbah.hu/index.php?option=com_k2&view=item&layout=item&id=1714&Itemid=2100&lang=en# (26 Jul. 2023).

> out his work in performance of the contract. The country where the work is habitually carried out shall not be deemed to have changed if he is temporarily employed in another country.

The significant change is that the applicable law is that of the country 'from which the employee habitually carries out' his/her work. It is intended to cover workers such as airline pilots who might not work 'in' any particular country, but work 'from' a country.

356. In addition, Article 7(2) of the 1980 Convention stated that 'Nothing in this Convention shall restrict the application of the rules of the law of the forum in a situation where they are mandatory irrespective of the law otherwise applicable to the contract'. Employment law is mandatory. However, Article 7(2) was not retained in the Rome I Regulation. The replacement, Article 9 defines mandatory provisions as:

> provisions the respect for which is regarded as crucial by a country for safeguarding its public interests, such as its political, social or economic organisation, to such an extent that they are applicable to any situation falling within their scope, irrespective of the law otherwise applicable to the contract under this Regulation.

It is clear that employment law is applicable in any situation to a contract falling within its scope, though some have insisted, sceptically, that employment law may not be 'crucial' in this sense, following older case law of the CJEU.[178]

357. When the labour relation is established with a foreign employer abroad who sends a worker or employee temporarily to Hungary, this does not fall within Hungarian rules (e.g., in order to equip a machine sold to a Hungarian enterprise). The application of these rules is, however, not devoid of problems. Several problems may occur.

358. If a labour contract is concluded abroad, foreign rules govern the conclusion, content, etc., of the contract. Despite this, in two cases a conflict of foreign and Hungarian law may occur. One concerns the establishment of the labour relation. In spite of the fact that the effect of Hungarian rules does not include the creation, modification and termination of labour relations, a labour relationship which conflicts with the social order of the country or with the fundamental regulation of labour relations may nevertheless not be fulfilled or implemented in Hungary.

359. Thus, child labour is forbidden in Hungary. Work may not, therefore, be implemented on the basis of a labour contract with a child under the age of 14. Equally, since it is prohibited in Hungary, a labour relationship in which remuneration, proportionate to the work, is not due to the worker or employee himself cannot be implemented. Although in such cases the labour contract cannot be regarded as

178. Yves JORENS, Cross-Border EU Employment and its Enforcement (2022), Springer, Switzerland.

invalid work may, however, not be carried out in Hungary on the basis of such a contract until the provisions which conflict with public order have been changed.

360. Another type of conflict occurs where the provisions of a labour contract collide with the Hungarian rules about carrying out the job (labour safety, working hours, etc.) This may occur, for example, when Hungarian labour-safety rules do not allow – in order to safeguard public health or prevent accidents – such work to be carried out by the person concluding the labour contract. For example, according to Hungarian rules, a woman or a person suffering from a certain disease or disability cannot be employed in certain jobs. If the worker or employee, concluding the labour contract, is such a person, the situation is similar in some respects to the case described above. In Hungary, the work can only be begun if the labour contract is brought into harmony with Hungarian rules. A second instance occurs when there are no initial obstacles to the inauguration of the work but the provisions of the labour contract conflict with Hungarian rules concerning the period or method of performing the work. For example, the labour contract may prescribe longer working hours than Hungarian rules permit. In this case, the provisions of the labour contract may not be applied but must be replaced by provisions consonant with Hungarian law.

361. According to Hungarian regulations, a labour relationship can be established by a worker or employee who has successfully completed public elementary school, who was exempt from attending school, or who is on vacation from school. In the case of a foreigner, the provisions regarding the completion of education may constitute a problem. In Hungary, the aim of the rule that education must be completed before employment is undertaken is to prevent work from impeding compulsory school education which is necessary in the interest of the general education. It may be that in the foreigner's country of domicile, the educational system is different. The point in question is whether the completion of elementary school should be investigated according to Hungarian or foreign rules. We must then start from the point that a worker or employee can only be required to do what he/she is able to do. This applies also to finishing school. In investigating legal capacity, it should only be established whether the worker or employee satisfied the compulsory schooling prescribed according to the rules of the country of domicile. Similarly, the national rules of foreigners should also be taken into consideration in respect of exemptions from attending school.[179]

B. *Labour Disputes*

362. Conflict may also occur between Hungarian and foreign law in connection with the implementation of claims arising from the individual labour relationship. If a dispute arises in regard to a labour contract concluded by a foreigner, it will be decided according to Article 8 of the Rome I Regulation. It may happen that after

179. HAJDÚ József, IEL Labour Law, Hungary, Wolters Kluwer, Kluwer Law Online, 2019. https://kluwerlawonline.com/Manuals/Corporate+Acquisitions+and+Mergers/705. (26 Jul. 2023).

termination the worker or employee goes abroad and asserts a claim arising from a labour relationship (e.g., accident compensation). In such a case, the provisions of the Rome II Regulation governing a conflict of law will apply. A similar situation may occur, if a diplomatic representative or another organ of a foreign state concludes a labour contract, not with one of its own citizens nor with a Hungarian citizen, but with a citizen of another foreign state. (Thus, e.g., the Italian embassy in Budapest employs a French cook.) It may happen that the foreign citizen returns to his/her own country and commences an action there, e.g., against the Italian embassy in Budapest. It may similarly occur that this foreign citizen makes his/her claim not before a Hungarian court but an Italian one, which is otherwise competent in Italy. In these cases, too, the rules governing conflict of international labour law, apply.

III. Collective Labour Relations

363. In case of collective labour relations, if the concluding parties select the Hungarian labour law or the principle of lex loci labouris is applied the foreign workers will be covered by Hungarian labour law. This means that in this field, too, the same rights and the same obligations apply to both a foreign worker or employee and to a foreign employer as to Hungarian workers and employees and Hungarian employers. A foreign worker or employee may, therefore, be a member of a trade union in accordance with trade union rules, may exercise the rights arising from membership, and may participate in the management of the enterprise, just as Hungarian employees do. The terms of a collective agreement also include them. The situation of an employer is similar.

364. The above-mentioned Rome I Regulation does not deal with the law governing the negotiations. Breaking negotiations could under certain circumstances give rise to non-contractual liability. This field of law is regulated by Regulation 864/2007 on the law applicable to non-contractual obligations (Rome II Regulation) as from 11 January 2009.[180]

365. Industrial Disputes. Article 9 of the Regulation specifies that, without prejudice to Article 4(2) (on the law of a common habitual residence), the law applicable to a tort in respect of the liability of a person in the capacity of a worker or an employer or the organizations representing their professional interests, for damages caused by an industrial action, pending or carried out, is the law of the country where the action is to be, or has been, taken.

366. However, the exact concept of industrial action, such as strike action or lock-out, varies from Member State to Member State and is governed by each Member States' internal rules (*The Rome II Regulation On Choice Of Law In Tort*). The special rule on industrial action in Article 9 is without prejudice to the conditions

180. Regulation (EC) No 864/2007 of the European Parliament and of the Council of 11 Jul. 2007 on the law applicable to non-contractual obligations (Rome II).

relating to the exercise of such action in accordance with national law, and without prejudice to the legal status of trade unions or of the representative organizations of workers as provided for in the law of the Member States.[181]

181. http://www.out-law.com/en/topics/dispute-resolution-and-litigation/arbitration-and-internationa l-arbitration/governing-law-and-jurisdiction-rome-ii/ (26 Jul. 2023).

Part II. The Individual Employment Relationship

Chapter 1. Definitions and Concepts of the HLC

§1. Different Categories of Employees

367. In fact, there is no expressis verbis definition of worker or employee in the HLC. Within the framework of the types of work and for reasons of simplification, the term of worker or employee respectively will be used in the private (competitive) sector. However, there is a variety of names of employees who are engaged in the public sector. It should be noted that workers and employees employed in the public service sector are uniformly called public (service) servants according to Act CXCIX of 2011, and those employed in the state-funded public institutions (e.g., kindergartens, schools, hospitals, libraries, etc.) called as civil servants according to Act XXIII of 1992. The judges, public prosecutors, military and police services are covered by separate legislations.

368. As regards the minimum wage in the labour process Hungarian labour law in the private sector indirectly distinguishes two basic groups of workers: (1) those who are unskilled workers (they are entitled to the smaller amount of minimum wage) and (2) those who are skilled workers (they are entitled to guaranteed wage minimum). The first category covers under-educated persons who mainly carry out auxiliary work (e.g., cleaners). The latter includes various types of skilled employees with at least secondary level vocational education (e.g., professionals, employees carrying out supervisory work or those performing clerical work, shorthand-typists, administrators, etc.).

369. The Labour Code (2012) regulates some special categories of employees. These categories are as follows:

(1) executive employee (vezető állású munkavállaló);
(2) home-based worker (bedolgozó);
(3) casual worker (alkalmi munkavállaló);
(4) employee under employment relationship with public employer (köztulajdonban álló munkáltatóval fennálló munkaviszony);
(5) incapacitated employee (cselekvőképtelen munkaválalló).

I. Executive Employees

370. The managing director of a company can perform his/her activities in two relationships; within the frames of either an assignment agreement according to the Hungarian Civil Code or a labour contract according to the HLC.

371. The HLC provides for special rules regarding the leading employees, and differentiates three categories of them: (1) *director of the employer* (executive employee, the employer's director: usually one person), (2) *deputy director(s)* (he/she can be any other person under direct supervision by the director and authorized – in part or in whole – to act as the director's deputy), and (3) *contractually executive employee* (employment contracts may invoke the provisions on executive employees if the employee is in a position considered to be of considerable importance from the point of view of the employer's operations, or fills a post of trust, and his/her salary reaches seven times the mandatory minimum wage, and he/she accepts this position.) The determination of the third group of executives – in contrast to the former regulation – is subject to the agreement of the parties.[182]

372. With regard to the market conditions and the nature of the organization's structure, the above approach of defining executives seems to be more reasonable and realistic, since it reflects more appropriately the increased liability linked to a higher position and greater remuneration. At the same time, the contractual freedom of the parties has been extended and the protection of managers has been reduced to the level of the guaranteed minimum.

373. It is notable that from the legal substantial point of view for these three categories of executive employees the same labour law provisions are applicable. The previous Labour Code (1992) made a distinction between the different groups of executive employees.

374. Among the detailed rules relating to executives, the change in the liability rules should also be mentioned. The civil law rules will apply to damages caused by the manager's negligence, but if the maximum amount of liability has been revoked, the executive will be fully liable for damages. Notwithstanding this, the new Labour Code maintains the special provision according to which the executive employee shall be liable for damages caused by his/her unlawful termination of his/her employment (but only in this case) up to his/her absence fee for twelve months.

375. Different regulations applicable to executive employees – as mentioned earlier – result from their respective positions in the work process. However, a different regulation is only of secondary importance because it becomes apparent only if special conditions necessitate it. The fundamental rights deriving from employment relations are also applicable to these persons.

182. BANKÓ Zoltán, BERKE Gyula, KISS György, SZŐKE Gergely László *Nagykommentár a munka törvénborn könyvéhez*, Wolters Kluwer, Budapest 2019.

376. Pursuant to the general rule of the HLC, the employment contract may derogate only to the benefit of the employee.[183] However, there is no restriction for executive employees, therefore derogation from the provisions of the act is permitted to the disadvantage of the employee, too.

377. With regard to the executive, the provisions of the HLC will apply with the following proviso contained in sections 209–211:

(a) The effects of a collective agreement will not apply to the executive employee.
(b) Executive employees work under flexible working time arrangements.
(c) Executive employees are subject to full liability for damages caused by negligence.
(d) The executive employee, if having terminated his/her employment relationship unlawfully, is liable to pay compensation in the sum of absentee pay due for twelve months.
(e) The employer is not obliged to justify either ordinary or extraordinary termination when the employment relationship is terminated by the employer.
(f) The employer may terminate the employment relationship by notice during a leave of absence taken without pay for caring for a child.
(g) There is no termination notice when the employment relationship is terminated by the employer.
(h) The right of termination without notice of an executive employee may be exercised within three years of the occurrence of the cause serving grounds therefor, or in the event of a criminal offence up to the statute of limitation.
(i) The employer shall be liable to pay up to six months' absentee pay due to the executive employee from the remuneration payable upon termination of his/her employment, if the notice of termination is delivered after the opening of bankruptcy or liquidation proceedings. Any additional sum shall be payable upon the conclusion or termination of bankruptcy proceedings, or upon the conclusion of liquidation proceedings.
(j) The executive employee may not enter into additional employment-related relationships.
(k) The executive employees:
    (i) shall not acquire shares, with the exception of the acquisition of stocks in a public limited company, in a business association which is engaged in the same or similar activities or that maintains regular economic ties with their employer;
    (ii) shall not conclude any transactions falling within the scope of the employer's activities in their own name or on their own behalf; and
    (iii) shall report if a relative has become a member of a business association which is engaged in the same or similar activities or that maintains regular

183. Section 43 of the HLC.

economic ties with the employer, or has established an employment-related relationship for an executive office with an employer engaged in such activities.[184]

II. Home-Based Worker

378. Home-based worker is a person who works at home[185] for a business firm and he/she cannot be categorized as a teleworker. According to section 198 of the HLC, home-based workers may be employed in jobs that can be performed independently, and that are remunerated exclusively on the basis of the work done [Subsection (3) of section 137]. The basic difference between telework and home-based work is the nature of the work and the method of submission of the result of the work. As for the nature, home-based work is usually simple (usually) blue-collar type work (e.g., sewing, fitting up, disassembling something, etc.), while telework is more complex (usually) white-collar work (e.g., journalist, translator, freelance expert, etc.). As for the submission of the work, the employer brings the material of the work to the home-based worker, while in the case of telework the work comes, is done and is sent back by IT equipment (computer, telephone, Internet, etc.).

379. The employment contract for home-based workers must define: (1) the work performed by the employee, (2) the place where work is carried out and (3) the method and extent of covering expenses. Basically, the home-based worker's working arrangements shall be flexible.[186]

380. Within the home-based work relationship, unless otherwise agreed, the employer's right of instruction is limited to specifying the technique and work processes to be used by the employee. In the absence of an agreement to the contrary, the employee carries out the work using his/her own means.[187]

381. In the absence of an agreement to the contrary, the employer should determine the type of inspection and the shortest period of time between the notification and commencement of the inspection if conducted in a property designated as the place of work. The inspection may not bring unreasonable hardship on the employee or on any other person who is also using the property designated as the place of work.

---

184. CSÉFFÁN József, *A munka törvénykönyve és magyarázata*, Szeged: Szegedi Rendezvényszervező Kft., 2023.
185. The employee's home or another place designated by the parties shall be construed as the place of work.
186. FERENCZ Jácint – GÖNDÖR Éva – GYULAVÁRI Tamás – KÁRTYÁS Gábor, *Munkajogi alapismeretek*, Budapest: ELTE Kiadó, 2013. p. 174.
187. N.B. It seems to be an exception from employment relationship because usually the employer provides the means and equipment necessary to work.

382. According to section 200 of the HLC, the employee is reimbursed for the expenses actually incurred in connection with the work, or – if the expenses actually incurred cannot be determined – a fixed flat-rate sum shall be paid to the employee. However, payment of remuneration and expenses shall be withheld if the work done is deemed insufficient due to reasons within the employee's control. Furthermore, payment of remuneration and expenses can be reduced if the employer is able to use the product the employee makes in part or in whole.[188]

III. Casual Worker: As a Simplified Employment Relationship

383. Casual work (simplified employment) is under twofold legal provisions; first, under sections 201–203 of the Labour Code and second, under Act LXXV of 2010 on Simplified Employment. According to the later Act, this type of work can be (1) agricultural, (2) seasonal work in tourism or (3) casual work. Here we shall deal only with the provisions of the HLC.

384. In practice, casual work usually lasts only for a few days. That is the reason why special provisions are required besides the labour law in force.

385. According to the Labour Code, casual work is called simplified employment and occasional work relationships. Section 201 of the HLC states that employers and employees who are covered by the HLC may enter into simplified employment or occasional work relationships. However, any employment contract for simplified employment or occasional work shall be considered null and void if the parties are engaged in an employment relationship at the time it was concluded.

386. It is an important guarantee that an existing employment contract may not be modified by the parties to conclude a simplified employment or occasional work relationship.

387. The most important irregulations of casual work are as follows:

(a) unlike a regular employment contract, the parties of a simplified employment relationship can set up a legal relationship by oral agreement. However, when concluding the employment contract, the parties may use the model employment contract specified by law. And the employment relationship shall be considered concluded upon fulfilment of the notification requirement specified by law. The date of the notification will be the starting date of the employment relationship;
(b) the commencement of the employment relationship is not applicable;[189]

188. KOZMA Anna – LŐRINCZ György – PÁL Lajos, *A Munka Törvénykönyvének magyarázata*, Budapest: HVG-Orac, 2020.
189. Paragraph (2) of s. 49 of the HLC.

(c) the casual worker cannot be ordered to temporarily fulfil other work assignment;[190]
(d) the legal consequences for the employee's wrongful breach of duty does not apply to the casual worker;[191]
(e) there is no need to provide a written assessment of the employee's work if the employment relationship lasted for at least one year;[192]
(f) the provisions relating to scheduled working time on Sundays or public holidays are not applicable;[193]
(g) the allocation of vacation time is not applicable;[194]
(h) the provisions of maternity leave, leave of absence without pay are not applicable;[195]
(i) the provisions of fixed-term employment relationships are not applicable;[196]
(j) the provisions relating to executive employees are not applicable to casual workers;[197]
(k) the certificates referred to in section 80 of the HLC need not be provided upon termination of the employment relationship; and
(l) the daily working time may be arranged based on an irregular work schedule regardless of any working time banking arrangement or payroll period arrangement.[198]

IV. Employee under Employment Relationship with Public Employer

388. Since 2009, separate regulations have been applicable to public employers. This is Act CXXII of 2009 on the Economical Operation of Publicly Owned Organisations. The aim of the special provisions is mainly to protect public property. This is shown by the fact that in the Labour Code disposivity is typical in general, in the case of public employers' regulations which do not allow derogations (cogency) are dominant. However, these employees aren't civil or public servants. They are still under the personal scope of the HLC.

389. The Publicly Owned Organisation means a public foundation, or a business association in which the State, a municipal government, an association of municipal governments vested with legal personality, a multi-purpose micro-region

190. Section 53 of the HLC.
191. Section 56 of the HLC.
192. Section 81 of the HLC.
193. Section 101 of the HLC.
194. Sections 122–124 of the HLC.
195. Sections 126–133 of the HLC.
196. Paragraph (4) of s. 192 of the HLC.
197. Sections 208–211 of the HLC.
198. DUDÁS Katalin – GYULAVÁRI Tamás – HORVÁTH István – Hős Nikolett– KULISITY Mária – HUNGLER Sára – KÁRTYÁS Gábor – KUN Attila – PETROVICS Zoltán – RÁCZ Réka, *Munkajog – V. átdolgozott kiadás*, Budapest: ELTE Eötvös Kiadó, 2019.

association, a development council, a minority self-government body, an association of minority self-government bodies vested with legal personality, a budgetary agency or a public foundation has majority control[199] either by itself or collectively.

390. There are some special protecting provisions, which state that in the collective agreement or in the agreement of the parties:

(a) no derogation is allowed from the duration of the notice period; and
(b) also, no derogation is allowed from provisions of severance payment.

391. In employment relationships with public employers, the full daily working time may not be reduced below the regular daily working time, unless it is deemed necessary in order to prevent any health impairment or harmful effects. In addition, working time shall not cover:

(a) break-time, with the exception of stand-by jobs; and
(b) travel time from the employee's home or place of residence to the place where work is in fact carried out and from the place of work to the employee's home or place of residence.

392. Basically the HLC's chapters on industrial relations (particularly Chapter XIX on General Provisions on Industrial Relations, Chapter XX on Works Councils and Chapter XXI on Trade Unions) are applicable.

393. The entity exercising ownership rights shall have powers to establish performance requirements for the executive employees, including the related performance-based wage and other benefits.

394. A non-competition agreement may be concluded with the executive employees for a period of up to one year, subject to approval by the entity exercising ownership rights. The entity exercising ownership rights may define the jobs in respect of which a non-competition agreement can be concluded, and may prescribe further conditions. However, the consideration stipulated in the non-competition agreement may not – for the duration of the agreement – exceed 50% of the absentee pay due for such period.[200]

199. 'Majority control' means a relationship where a person controls over 50% of the voting rights in a legal person that has dominant influence, directly, or indirectly through another legal person that has voting rights in that legal person (intermediary company). Indirect control shall be determined by multiplying the number of votes held by another legal person in that legal person (intermediary company) by the number of votes held by the holder of a participating interest in the intermediary company or companies. If the ratio of votes controlled by the holder of a participating interest in the intermediary company is greater than 50%, it shall be treated as a whole.
200. BANKÓ Zoltán, BERKE Gyula, KISS György, SZŐKE Gergely László *Nagykommentár a munka törvénykönyvéhez*, Wolters Kluwer, Budapest 2019.

V. Incapacitated Employee

395. This was a brand new section[201] in the HLC. Earlier the labour regulations in force did not allow the employment of incapacitated persons in an employment relationship. The concept of incapacity is defined in the Civil Code. Incapacity may be based on: (a) age, (b) being under conservatorship and (c) actual situation.[202]

396. There are two fundamental factors underlying this change in labour law regulations:

(a) The Convention on the Rights of Persons with Disabilities (CRPD) adopted by the UN on 13 December 2006 and the respective Optional Protocol, which Hungary was the first state in the world to ratify and to promulgate in Act XCII of 2007.[203]
(b) In its Decision No. 39/2011 (V.31) the Constitutional Court stated the breach of the constitution by failing to establish the statutory regulations of the employment relationship of incapacitated persons in the effective law.

397. According to section 212 of the HLC, the incapacitated workers may conclude employment relationships only for jobs which they are capable of handling on a stable and continuous basis in the light of their medical condition. The functions of the employee's job will be determined by definition of the related responsibilities in detail. The employee's medical examination will cover the employee's ability to handle the functions of the job.

398. The employee's work will be supervised continuously so as to ensure that the requirements of occupational safety and health are satisfied.[204]

399. The provisions of Chapter XIV on Employees' Liability for Damages will not apply to such employees. Furthermore, the provisions pertaining to young workers shall apply.

§2. Study Contract

400. In connection with help in finding or keeping employment, a study contract should be mentioned (section 229 of the HLC). The main aim of this system is to meet the employers' demands for specialists, but it also could help graduates to find employment. There is an obvious change in the new provisions. According to the HLC in force, a study contract can be concluded between an employer and an

201. Section 212 of the HLC.
202. https://www.profession.hu/cikk/a-gondoksag-alatt-allok-is-dolgozhatnak (26 Jul. 2023).
203. http://www.e-epites.hu/jogszabalyok/2007-evi-xcii-torveny-a-fogyatekossaggal-elo-szemelyek-jogairol-szolo-egyezmeny (26 Jul. 2023).
204. KOZMA Anna – LŐRINCZ György – PÁL Lajos, *A Munka Törvénykönyvének magyarázata*, Budapest: HVG-Orac, 2020.

employee. However, under the Civil Code, the employer can commit him/herself to assist a student during his/her studies and the student undertakes to pursue studies as agreed and to work for the enterprise for a defined period of time after having acquired his/her qualifications.

401. In a study contract, the employer undertakes to provide support for the duration of studies while the employee undertakes to complete the studies as agreed and to refrain from terminating his/her employment by way of notice following graduation for a period of time commensurate with the amount of support. The study contract cannot exceed five years.[205] Study contracts may only be concluded in writing. In the event the employer severely breaches the study contract, the employee can be relieved of his/her obligations set out in the study contract.[206]

402. No study contract may be concluded:

(a) for providing any benefits which are due on the basis of employment regulations, furthermore;
(b) if the employer ordered the employee to complete the studies.

403. In the case of transfer of employment upon the transfer of enterprise, the rights and obligations arising from the study contract shall be transferred to the receiving employer.

404. The employer has the right to withdraw from the study contract and may demand repayment of the support provided if the employee breaches the study contract. Breach of contract shall also cover where the employment relationship is terminated for reasons in connection with the employee's conduct in connection to the employment relationship. The obligation of repayment shall apply in proportion to the length of time that has elapsed from the term of the contract.

405. The study contract may be terminated by either of the parties effective immediately in the event of subsequent major changes in the party's circumstances whereby carrying out the commitment is no longer possible or it would result in unreasonable hardship. In the event of termination by the employee, the employer may demand repayment of the support provided. The employer's right to demand repayment of the support will apply in proportion to the length of time that has elapsed from the term of the contract. Where employment is terminated by the employer, repayment of the support may not be demanded.[207]

205. The length of time spent in employment shall be calculated according to Subsection (2) of s. 115.
206. FERENCZ Jácint – GÖNDÖR Éva – GYULAVÁRI Tamás – KÁRTYÁS Gábor, *Munkajogi alapismeretek*, Budapest: ELTE Kiadó, 2013. p. 59.
207. KOZMA Anna – LŐRINCZ György – PÁL Lajos, *A Munka Törvénykönyvének magyarázata*, Budapest: HVG-Orac, 2020.

§3. COMPETITION OF THE APPLICANTS

406. If on the basis of the rule of law, regulations pertaining to employment or the employer's decisions, a specific post is to be filled by way of a competition, then filling such a post should only take place by an employee who participated in the competition and met the conditions thereof. The content of a submitted application (competition) shall be related to a third person only with the applicant's approval.[208]

§4. THE INDIVIDUAL LABOUR CONTRACTS

407. In the contract of employment, the employer undertakes to employ a person for defined duties and for a determined payment, while the employee undertakes to be employed in the enterprise. The employee can only be requested to make a statement, fill out an information sheet, or take an aptitude test if it does not violate the employee's privacy, and may provide substantive information from the viewpoint of the establishment of employment. Employees must not be compelled to take a pregnancy test or to produce a certificate thereof unless it is prescribed by legal regulation so as to determine the employee's proficiency for the position in question.

408. There are special protective provisions for young workers who are engaged in employment relationships different from the legal relationship covered by labour law. As regards the performance of work by persons under eighteen years of age by way of means other than an employment contract, the basic protective provisions of the HLC relating to the establishment of an employment relationship shall duly apply. Furthermore, the provisions of the HLC pertaining to the employment of young workers must also be observed.

409. Section 43 of the HLC kept the previous labour law provision which similarly stated that unless otherwise provided for by law, the employment contract may derogate from the provisions of Part Two of the HLC and from employment regulations to the benefit of the employee. Such derogations will be adjudged by comparative assessment of related regulations.[209]

I. Different Categories of Labour Contracts

410. According to Hungarian labour law, contracts of employment are established for:

208. BANKÓ Zoltán, BERKE Gyula, KISS György, SZŐKE Gergely László *Nagykommentár a munka törvénykönyvéhez*, Wolters Kluwer, Budapest 2019.
209. HAJDÚ József, IEL Labour Law, Hungary, Wolters Kluwer, Kluwer Law Online, 2019. https://kluwerlawonline.com/Manuals/Corporate+Acquisitions+and+Mergers/705 (26 Jul. 2023).

(1) indefinite or definite periods of time (open-ended contract or fixed-term contract);
(2) full-time contract or part-time contract;
(3) on-call contract (call for work);
(4) job-sharing;
(5) employee sharing;
(6) telework;
(7) agency work.

A. *Indefinite or Definite Periods of Time (Fixed-Term Contract)*

411. Indefinite and definite contract. According to the HLC, the contract established for an indefinite period of time is considered typical. Thus, contracts without a definite specification of time should be considered as having been established for an indefinite period. It should be underlined that a probationary agreement (*see* later: probation period) is not considered a separate kind of contract; it is merely a condition of the above-mentioned contracts.

412. The period of fixed-term employment shall be determined according to the calendar or by other appropriate means. It can be fixed in two usual forms: (1) date-to-date basis (e.g., the fixed term contract is from 1 March 2023 to 15 November 2023), or duration (e.g., from 1 March 2023 for six months duration). If the duration of an employment relation is not determined by the calendar, the employer is obliged to inform the employee of the expected duration of employment. Where an employment relation is subject to official approval, it may only be for the duration specified in the authorization.

413. The duration of a fixed-term employment relation may not exceed five years, including the duration of an extended relation and that of another fixed-term employment relation created within six months of the termination of the previous fixed-term employment relation. By way of derogation from the above, if the particular authorization is extended, the duration of the new fixed-term employment relation may exceed five years together with the duration of the previous employment relation.

414. Where an employment relationship is subject to official authorization, it may only be concluded for the duration specified in the authorization. If the authorization is extended, the duration of the new fixed-term employment relationship may exceed five years together with the duration of the previous employment relationship.

415. A fixed-term employment relationship may be extended, or another fixed-term employment relationship may be concluded within six months from the time of termination of the previous one upon the employer's legitimate interests. The agreement may not infringe upon the employee's legitimate interest.

416. The type of contract underlying an employment relationship may not be chosen with a view to restricting or violating the provisions that provide for the protection of the employee's rightful interests. The type of contract, irrespective of the name, shall be chosen so as to best accommodate all applicable circumstances, such as the parties' prior negotiations and their statements made at the time of contracting or during the performance of work, the nature of the work to be performed, and the rights and obligations.

417. In the absence of an agreement to the contrary, all employment relations are concluded for full-time employment. In the case of part-time employment, all payments made to the employee in exchange for work, whether in money or in kind and whether directly or indirectly, must be provided in accordance with the length of time of work performed if remuneration is contingent upon the amount of working time.[210]

B. *Full-Time or Part-Time Contract*

418. Usually, a full-time job encompasses 40 hours of work per week, eight hours per day. The employer and the employee can individually agree on shorter or longer working hours. If no working time is indicated in the contract, a full-time employment is established. Part-time employment has to be indicated in the contract. Part-time employees are entitled to reimbursement of costs and paid vacation equally to full-time employees. Third-country nationals who need a work permit can only conclude contracts for the period of the work permit.[211]

419. As for part-time work, the HLC is in conformity with the legislation of the EU Directive 97/81/EC of 15 December 1997 concerning the Framework Agreement on part-time work concluded by UNICE, CEEP and the ETUC.

C. *On-Call Contract (Call for Work)*

420. According to section 193 of the HLC, part-time workers employed under an employment contract in jobs for up to six hours a day can work at times deemed necessary to best accommodate the function of their jobs. In this case, the duration of working time banking may not exceed four months. The employer will inform the employee of the time of working at least three days in advance.[212]

---

210. DUDÁS Katalin – GYULAVÁRI Tamás – HORVÁTH István – Hős Nikolett – KULISITY Mária – HUNGLER Sára – KÁRTYÁS Gábor – KUN Attila – PETROVICS Zoltán – RÁCZ Réka, *Munkajog – V. átdolgozott kiadás*, Budapest: ELTE Eötvös Kiadó, 2019.
211. CSÉFFÁN József, *A munka törvénykönyve és magyarázata*, Szeged: Szegedi Rendezvényszervező Kft., 2023.
212. DUDÁS Katalin – GYULAVÁRI Tamás – HORVÁTH István – Hős Nikolett – KULISITY Mária – HUNGLER Sára – KÁRTYÁS Gábor – KUN Attila – PETROVICS Zoltán – RÁCZ Réka, *Munkajog – V. átdolgozott kiadás*, Budapest: ELTE Eötvös Kiadó, 2019.

D. Job-Sharing

421. According to section 194 of the HLC, the employer may conclude an employment contract with several workers for carrying out the functions of a job jointly. Where any one of the employees to the contract is unavailable, another worker to the contract shall fill in and perform the functions of the job as ordered. The scheduling of work is governed by the provisions of flexible working arrangements. Wages are distributed among the employees equally, unless there is an agreement to provide otherwise.

422. The employment relationship will cease to exist when the number of employees is reduced to one. In this case, the employer is liable to pay the worker affected absentee pay covering a period that would otherwise be due in the event of dismissal by the employer; furthermore, the rules on severance pay shall also apply.[213]

E. Employee Sharing

423. According to section 195 of the HLC, several employers may conclude an employment contract with one worker for carrying out the functions of a job. The employment contract will clearly indicate the employer designated to pay the employee's wages. The liability of employers in respect of the employee's labour-related claims will be joint and several.

424. Unless otherwise agreed, the employment relationship may be terminated by either of the employers or by the employee. The employment relationship shall cease to exist when the number of employers is reduced to one.[214]

F. Telework

425. Originally (in 2012) the definition of teleworking was more peculiar: 'activities performed on a regular basis at a place other than the employer's facilities, using computers and other means of information technology, where the end product is delivered by way of electronic means'. The wording of the relevant section 196 of the HLC has been modified during the COVID-19 period. The new – less elaborated – definition is this: 'In the case of teleworking, the employee works part or all of the working time at a place separate from the employer's premises.'

426. In case of teleworking the employer, in addition to the normal information issues under section 46 of the HLC, shall inform the employee:

---

213. BANKÓ Zoltán, BERKE Gyula, KISS György, SZŐKE Gergely László *Nagykommentár a munka törvénykönyvéhez*, Wolters Kluwer, Budapest 2019.
214. HAJDÚ József *A munkakör megosztásról: tandem-munkavégzés* Miskolci Jogi Szemle: A Miskolci Egyetem Állam- és Jogtudományi Karának Folyóirata 12:(2.klsz.) pp. 154–170. (2017).

(a) concerning inspections conducted by the employer;
(b) concerning any restrictions as to the use of computing equipment or electronic devices; and
(c) concerning the department to which the employee's work is in fact connected.

427. The employer must provide all information to persons employed in teleworking as is provided to other employees. The employer must provide access to the employee for entering its premises and to communicate with other workers.[215]

428. In the employment contract, the parties agree on the employee's employment by means of teleworking. In addition to what is contained in section 46 of the HLC, the employer must inform the employee:

(a) concerning inspections conducted by the employer;
(b) concerning any restrictions as to the use of computing equipment or electronic devices; and
(c) concerning the department to which the employee's work is in fact connected.

Moreover, the employer must provide all information to persons employed in teleworking as is provided to other employees.

429. Unless there is an agreement to the contrary, the employer can determine the type of inspection and the shortest period of time between the notification and commencement of the inspection if conducted in a property designated as the place of work. The inspection may not bring unreasonable hardship on the employee or on any other person who is also using the property designated as the place of work.

430. In the absence of an agreement to the contrary, the employee's working arrangements will be flexible.[216]

G. *Agency Work (Temporary Agency Work: Hereinafter Referred to as TWA)*

431. First of all, the HLC contains the most important basic definitions relating to TWA:

(a) 'temporary agency work' means when an employee is hired out by a temporary-work agency to a user enterprise for remunerated temporary work, provided there is an employment relationship between the worker and the temporary-work agency (placement);

215. KOZMA Anna – LŐRINCZ György – PÁL Lajos, *A Munka Törvénykönyvének magyarázata*, Budapest: HVG-Orac, 2020.
216. HAJDÚ József – KUN Attila (eds), *Munkajog I.*, Budapest: Patrocinium, 2012. pp. 228–236.

(b) 'temporary-work agency' means any employer who places an employee, with whom it has an employment relationship, under contract to a user enterprise for temporary work supervised by the user enterprise;[217]
(c) 'user enterprise' means any employer under whose supervision the worker performs temporary work;
(d) 'temporary agency worker' means a worker with a contract of employment or an employment relationship with a temporary-work agency with a view to being assigned to a user enterprise to work temporarily, where employer's rights are exercised jointly by the temporary-work agency and the user enterprise (worker);
(e) 'assignment' means when the temporary agency worker is placed at the user enterprise to work temporarily;[218]
(f) qualified user enterprise/employer: an employer who is entitled to employ third-country nationals in Hungary under the conditions laid down by law.

432. The duration of assignment may not exceed five years, including any period of extended assignment and re-assignment within a period of six months from the time of termination of his/her previous employment, irrespective of whether the assignment was made by the same or by a different temporary-work agency.

433. According to section 216 of the HLC, the assignment of workers is not allowed:

(a) in the cases specified by the relevant employment regulations;
(b) with a view to replacing workers on strike;
(c) beyond the five years duration.

434. The user enterprise shall not have the right to order a temporary agency worker to work at another employer.

435. A TWA agreement is considered invalid if:

(a) it contains a clause to ban or restrict any relationship with the user enterprise following termination of the employment relationship on any grounds;
(b) it contains a clause to stipulate the payment of a fee by the employee to the temporary-work agency for the assignment, or for entering into a relationship with the user enterprise.

---

217. According to s. 215 of the HLC the following may function as temporary-work agencies:

(a) a company established in an EEA Member State that is authorized under national law to engage in the activities of temporary-work agencies; or
(b) a business association established in Hungary whose members have limited liability; or
(c) a cooperative society in respect of employees other than its members.

In addition, the agency must be registered by the government employment agency. Where a temporary-work agency is excluded from the register, the provisions on invalidity will apply with regard to employment contracts.

218. KÁRTYÁS, G. (2019). *A munkaerő-kölcsönzés hazai szabályozása az Európai Unió irányelveinek tükrében.* Pro Futuro, 9(1), 55–78, https://doi.org/10.26521/Profuturo/1/2019/3903 (26 Jul. 2023).

436. The user enterprise informs the local works' council:

(a) of the number of temporary agency workers employed and of the employment conditions;
(b) on vacant positions;
(c) at least once in a six-month period, and should keep the temporary agency workers it employs informed on a regular basis.

437. The relationship between the temporary-work agency and user enterprise is regulated under section 217 of the HLC. The agreement between the placement agency and the user enterprise will specify the material conditions of placement and the sharing of employer's rights. Employment may only be terminated by the placement agency. The agreement must be made in writing. An agreement between the temporary-work agency and the user enterprise will be null and void if:

(a) the temporary-work agency and the user enterprise are affiliated by way of ownership in part or in whole;
(b) at least one of the two employers holds some percentage of ownership in the other employer; or
(c) the two employers are connected through their ownership in a third organization.

438. The agreement between the temporary-work agency and the user enterprise may contain a clause to stipulate that non-wage benefits will be provided to the employee by the user enterprise directly.

439. The user enterprise must inform the temporary-work agency in writing:

(a) of its normal course of work;
(b) of the person exercising employer's rights;
(c) of the manner and the timeframe within which to supply the information necessary for the payment of wages;
(d) of the qualification requirements pertaining to the work in question; furthermore
(e) of all aspects that are considered significant in terms of the employment of the worker in question.

440. Unless otherwise agreed, the temporary-work agency must be required to cover all employment-related expenses, such as the employee's costs of travel and the costs of a medical examination if one is required for employment. When requested by the user enterprise, the temporary-work agency will, before the first day of employment, supply to the user enterprise:

(a) a notification the temporary-work agency has submitted to the state tax authority concerning the data of the person employed by the employer and the payer,

containing the date of commencement of the insurance relationship, as prescribed by the legislation on taxation; and
(b) a copy of the document as proof of being admitted into the register of temporary-work agencies in accordance with specific other legislation.

441. Unless there is an agreement to the contrary, the user enterprise will supply all information to the temporary-work agency by the fifth day of the month following the current month, which is required for the payment of wages, and for carrying out tax declarations, data disclosure and payment obligations relating to the employment relationship. The user enterprise must supply the above-specified information to the temporary-work agency within three working days from the last day of employment, if employment is terminated during the month.

442. As for the temporary employment relationships, the employment contract will contain a clause indicating that it was concluded for the purpose of temporary work, and will contain a description of the work and the basic wage.

443. At the time of concluding the employment contract, the temporary-work agency will inform the employee of the registration number assigned.

444. Before the assignment, the temporary-work agency must provide the employee with the following information in writing:

(a) the identification data of the user enterprise;
(b) the beginning date of the assignment;
(c) the place of work;
(d) the normal course of work at the user enterprise;
(e) the person exercising employer's rights on the user enterprise's behalf;
(f) the particulars on travel to work, room and board.

445. During the assignment, the employer's rights and obligations relating to:

(a) occupational safety and health;
(b) provide fair working conditions (Subsections (1), (3)–(5) of section 51 of HLC); and
(c) working time and rest periods, and keeping records thereof;
(d) shall accrue upon the user enterprise.

446. The principle of equal treatment. The basic working and employment conditions of temporary agency workers will be, for the duration of their assignment, at least those available to the workers employed by the user enterprise under employment relationship.

The basic working and employment conditions will, in particular, cover:

(a) the protection of pregnant women and nursing mothers; and
(b) the protection of young workers;

(c) the amount and protection of wages, including other benefits;
(d) the provisions on equal treatment.

447. As regards the payment of wages and other benefits, the provisions on equal treatment will apply as of the one hundred and eighty-fourth day of employment at the user enterprise with respect to any worker:

(a) who is engaged with a temporary-work agency in an employment relationship established for an indefinite duration, and who is receiving pay in the absence of any assignment to a user enterprise;
(b) who is recognized as a long-term absentee from the labour market as defined in Point 1 of Subsection (2) of section 1 of Act CXXIII of 2004;[219]
(c) who is working within the framework of temporary agency work at a business association under the majority control of a municipal government or public benefit organization, and a registered public benefit organization.[220]

448. The termination of employment of TWA assignment. The termination of the assignment will be construed as a reason in connection with the temporary-work agency's operation. The notice period shall be fifteen days. If termination is effected by the temporary-work agency, the employee will be exempted from work during the notice period unless otherwise agreed.

449. The employee may terminate the employment relationship without notice if the infringement is committed by the user enterprise. The employee shall submit the notice for termination of the employment relationship to the temporary-work agency.

450. The user enterprise will notify the temporary-work agency in writing concerning any infringement on the employee's part within five working days from the time of gaining knowledge. The time limit commences upon delivery of the information.

451. Liability for damages. In connection with any damage caused by the employee, the user enterprise may demand compensation from the employee in accordance with the relevant articles of the HLC. By agreement between the temporary-work agency and the user enterprise, the provisions of civil law on liability for damages caused by an employee will apply. In the application of the provisions of civil law on the employer's liability for damages caused by an employee, the user enterprise will be construed as the employer, unless there is an agreement between the temporary-work agency and the user enterprise to the contrary.

---

219. Act CXXIII of 2004 on Job Assistance Provided to Unemployed Entrants to the Labour Market, Unemployed Workers over Fifty, and to Persons Seeking Employment After Caring for a Child or Nursing a Family Member and on Employment Under Scholarship Agreement.
220. DUDÁS Katalin – GYULAVÁRI Tamás – HORVÁTH István – Hős Nikolett – KULISITY Mária – HUNGLER Sára – KÁRTYÁS Gábor – KUN Attila – PETROVICS Zoltán – RÁCZ Réka, *Munkajog – V. átdolgozott kiadás*, Budapest: ELTE Eötvös Kiadó, 2019.

452. For any damages caused to the employee while on assignment, the user enterprise and the temporary-work agency will be subject to joint and several liability.[221]

II. Probation Period

453. According to section 45 of the HLC, the probation period can be agreed upon only at the time of the contract being concluded and has to be in writing. Any later stipulation is null and void. The duration of the probation period is usually not more than three months from the date of commencement of the employment relationship. In the event that a shorter probation period has been stipulated, the parties may extend the probation period once. In either case, the duration of the probation period may not exceed three months. However, there is an exceptional provision, which can have a negative effect on the employee: the period of the probation period can be extended up to six months if it is agreed in the collective agreement, but the term of the probation period may not exceed six months as provided for in the collective agreement.

454. If employment is not terminated during the probation period, it continues according to the conditions described in the contract of employment.

455. During the probation period, it is allowed for both parties (employer or employee) to terminate immediately the employment relationship at any point and without any reason.[222]

456. Distinction between probation period and trial work. The HLC only recognises the institution of probationary periods. Although the concept of probationary (or trial) work is widespread, but it is prohibited. It is not defined in the HLC. It is often a form of undeclared work, where a job or a work process is carried out without a legal relationship and without official notification and often without payment. However, the ban on probationary work does not exclude testing at interview. Candidates can be tested during the selection procedure. Generally, testing is aimed at assessing the skills, abilities or practical experience of candidates. Depending on whether the testing concerns the assessment of theoretical or practical knowledge, it may involve solving a fictitious problem (e.g., a fictitious case or a situation) or demonstrating practical knowledge. It also follows from the above that testing can be done by performing a subtask, rather than a full, real workflow. This means that testing may not be so time-consuming. Some examples of legitimate testing: (1) to verify driving skills, a truck driver parks in a tight space; (2) to assess professional competence, the accountant describes in a fictitious case what tax and social security contributions would be deducted from the amount paid and why, and (3) to

221. HAJDÚ József – KUN Attila (eds), *Munkajog I.*, Budapest: Patrocinium, 2012. pp. 236–255.
222. CSÉFFÁN József, *A munka törvénykönyve és magyarázata*, Szeged: Szegedi Rendezvényszervező Kft., 2023.

assess situational awareness and stress tolerance, the customer service representative is asked to solve a fictitious situation on the spot.[223]

III. Form and Content of the Employment Contract

457. Section 45 of the HLC distinguishes between the questions to be settled necessarily (*mandatory contents*) and those to be settled only by mutual agreement of the contracting parties. In addition, labour law takes into consideration the *indispensable content* of the contracts.

A. *Mandatory Content*

458. The mandatory content of an employment contract has to be composed of at least three elements: (1) formal requirement: a written agreement with details of the contracting parties to establish employment, (2) a definition of the scope of work and (3) a definition as regards basic payment. Furthermore, the workplace of the employee must be defined in the employment contract. Failing this, the place where work is normally carried out will be considered the workplace.

B. *Indispensable Content*

459. In addition, the indispensable content of the employment contract consists of those rights and duties which – according to law or a collective agreement – are elements of the employment contract regardless or even in spite of the will of either party (e.g., working hours defined by law, the law concerning rest periods, etc.). The contracting parties cannot ignore these provisions, either during or after terminating employment. Agreements in contradiction with these laws are null and void. The contract shall not be null and void if it sets out more favourable terms for the employee than the collective agreement.[224]

C. *Employer's Obligation to Inform Employees in Writing*

460. During the EU legal harmonization process, the Council Directive (EU) 2019/1152 on transparent and predictable working conditions in the European Union amended the text of the HLC. It aims to improve working conditions by promoting more transparent and predictable employment while ensuring labour-market adaptability. It introduces minimum rights and updates the rules on the information

223. ANTALÓCZY Adrienn, A próbamunka tilos, de akkor mit szabad?, https://ecocreative.hu/rovid-cikkek/cikkek/a-probamunka-tilos-de-akkor-mit-szabad/ (26 Jul. 2023).
224. KOZMA Anna – LŐRINCZ György – PÁL Lajos, *A Munka Törvénykönyvének magyarázata*, Budapest: HVG-Orac, 2020.

to be provided to workers concerning their working conditions. The directive contributes to reinforcing Europe's social dimension as part of the European Pillar of Social Rights roll-out. The directive is issued in the context of Article 31 of the Charter of Fundamental Rights of the EU which says that every worker has the right to working conditions which respect the worker's health, safety and dignity, which limit the maximum number of working hours, to daily and weekly rest periods and to an annual period of paid leave. It is also a concrete follow-up of Principles 5 and 7 of the European Pillar of Social Rights. The directive applies to those who work more than three hours per week over a four-week period (i.e., more than twelve hours per month) who are bound by an employment contract or in an employment relationship as defined by national law, collective agreements or practice in force in each EU country – with consideration to the case-law of the Court of Justice of the EU. Persons covered could include workers on zero-hour contracts, such as fast-food-chain workers, workers in logistical centres, shelf-stackers in supermarkets, domestic or voucher-based workers* and platform-economy workers, such as on-demand drivers or couriers, provided they fulfil the above criteria defining a worker. Civil servants, the armed forces or members of emergency and law enforcement services may, on objective grounds, be excluded from Chapter III of the directive (Minimum requirements relating to working conditions).

461. According to the relevant provisions, there are two types of obligation of providing information:

(1) providing information to employees engaged in domestic work (work performed in Hungary);
(2) providing additional information to employees who perform work abroad.

462. (1) In the case of work to be performed domestically, according to the above-mentioned EU Directive, the employer must inform the employee in writing within fifteen days at the latest from the date of commencement of the employment relationship concerning:

(a) the daily working time;
(b) wages above the base wage, and other benefits;
(c) payroll accounting, the frequency of payment of wages, and the day of payment;
(d) the functions of the job;
(e) the number of days of leave and the procedures for allocating and determining such leave; and
(f) the rules governing the periods of notice to be observed by the employer and the employee; furthermore
(g) whether a collective agreement applies to the employer; and
(h) the person exercising employer's rights.

463. Employees must be informed of any change in the name or other major particulars of the employer, or in the above-mentioned items in writing on the day of the effective date of the change in question.

464. If the employment relationship is terminated before the seven-day period lapses, the employer must perform the obligation on the last working day.

465. In the case of work to be performed abroad for a period of more than fifteen days the employee must be informed in writing at least seven days before the date of departure of the following:

(a) the place and duration of the work abroad;
(b) the benefits in cash or in kind;
(c) the currency to be used for the payment of remuneration and other payments;
(d) the availability of a national website containing relevant information on the rights and obligations of the cross-border service provider and the posted worker; and
(e) the conditions governing the employee's repatriation.

466. In case of foreign work, all of the above-mentioned information must be conveyed to the employee before his/her departure.[225]

467. Complaints, redress, protections and dismissals. According to the EU Directive EU Member States must:

(a) ensure that workers who have not received the relevant information in due time have access to at least one of the following two measures:
    (i) submit a complaint to a competent authority and receive redress in a timely and effective manner; or
    (ii) benefit from favourable legal presumptions.
(b) ensure that workers, including those whose employment relationship has ended, have access to effective and impartial dispute resolution and a right to redress*;
(c) introduce measures to protect workers from any adverse treatment by the employer and from any adverse consequences resulting from a complaint lodged with the employer;
(d) take measures to prohibit workers from being dismissed because they have exercised the rights outlined in the directive.[226]

D. Agreement of the Parties

468. The parties can agree on other questions. Agreement may be reached concerning the start of the employment and the probation period.

225. HAJDÚ József – KUN Attila (eds), *Munkajog I.*, Budapest: Patrocinium, 2012. pp. 120–121.
226. Transparent and predictable working conditions in the EU (2019), https://eur-lex.europa.eu/legal-content/en/LSU/?uri=CELEX:32019L1152 (26 Jul. 2023).

469. The date of *commencement of the employment* relationship must be defined in the employment contract. Failing this, the day following the conclusion of the employment contract is construed as the date of commencement of the employment relationship.

470. If the employment relationship does not start immediately, the parties must follow a special obligation. During the period between the day on which the employment contract is concluded and the date of commencement of the employment relationship, the parties may not engage in any conduct to defeat the employment relationship. During the above-mentioned interim period, both parties are entitled to withdraw from the employment contract in the event of material changes taking place in his/her circumstances following the date of conclusion of the employment contract whereby carrying out the employment relationship is no longer possible or it would result in unreasonable hardship.[227]

E. *Formal Procedure*

471. Employment contracts must be concluded in writing, which must be provided for by the employer. Invalidity on the grounds of failure to set the contract in writing may only be cited by the employee within a period of thirty days from the first day on which he/she commences work. As regards the invalidity of unilateral acts, no rights and obligations will arise from or in connection with such legal acts.

F. *Void Employment Contracts*

a) Cases of void contracts

472. Contracts of employment may be partly or completely null and void. A contract of employment is completely void if:

- its establishment violates the laws concerning employment and as such is therefore prohibited (e.g., when the employee has no legal capacity or is forbidden to perform the given duty or does not have the necessary qualifications); or
- the manner of establishing the contract is irregular (e.g., lack of written records);
- there is a lack of will or decision by one of the parties (error, illegal threat).

473. A contract of employment is partly null and void if one or more of its clauses contradicts the laws of employment (e.g., stipulation of a longer probation period than is allowed).

227. HLC ss 48–49.

b) Consequences of contracts of employment being completely void

474. Rights and obligations arising from or in connection with an invalid agreement will be treated as if they existed under a valid agreement. Unless otherwise provided for in the HLC, employers may terminate – with immediate effect – any legal relationships created on the basis of an invalid agreement, if the parties fail to abolish the cause of invalidity.

475. Employers are liable to pay their workers absentee pay covering a period otherwise due in the event of dismissal by the employer, furthermore, the rules on severance pay will also apply if the employment contract is declared invalid for reasons attributable to the employer and it has to be terminated.

c) Consequences of contracts being partially void

476. If any part of an agreement is deemed invalid (partially void), the relevant employment regulations will be applied instead, unless the parties would otherwise not have concluded the agreement without the invalid part.[228]

IV. Ability to Conclude a Labour Contract

477. It is self-evident that the parties to an employment relationship are the employer and the employee. The ability to enter into employment includes two components. One of them is legal capacity, that is the possibility of being the subject of an employment contract. The other component is free will, which means that a person with legal capacity is able to enter employment according to his/her own will and decision. 'Employer' means any person having the capacity to perform legal acts who is a party to employment contracts with employees.

A. *Legal Capacity of the Employee*

478. Employment can be accepted by any natural person (only natural person) who has reached 16 years of age. Employment may be entered into by a 15-year-old who is a student completing his/her compulsory education on an adult educational programme or on an independent study programme and who is only working during school holidays.

479. In addition, young persons subject to compulsory full-time schooling and under sixteen years of age (without age limit) may only be employed for purposes of performance in artistic, sports, modelling or advertising activities upon prior authorization by the competent authority, which acts as a guardian.

228. HAJDÚ József, IEL Labour Law, Hungary, Wolters Kluwer, Kluwer Law Online, 2019. https://kluwerlawonline.com/Manuals/Corporate+Acquisitions+and+Mergers/705 (26 Jul. 2023).

480. There is a very important rule to protect young employees. According to section 4 of the HLC, the provisions pertaining to young workers must also apply mutatis mutandis to the employment of persons under the age of eighteen within a non-employment relationship, including civil law relationships, etc.

481. An employer pursuing activities carrying out the responsibility for providing care, custody, guidance or medical treatment to a person under the age of eighteen years may not enter into an employment relationship with any person:

(a) who is in the register of convicted criminals;[229]
(b) who is implicated in a criminal proceeding in relation to either of the crimes specified under the previous paragraph;
(c) who is restrained by court order from exercising his/her profession; or
(d) who is undergoing mandatory medical treatment.

482. No employment may be given to any person who was sentenced for the intentional commission of the crimes (specified under Article 44/A of the HLC):

(a) to an executable term of imprisonment:
    (i) for a period of five years from the effective time of exoneration in case of imprisonment of less than five years;
    (ii) for a period of eight years from the effective time of exoneration in case of imprisonment of five years or more.
(b) community service work or a fine, for a period of two years from the effective time of exoneration;
(c) for a suspended term of imprisonment, for a period of three years from the effective time of exoneration.

483. The person seeking employment must produce an official certificate to verify that he/she meets the above-mentioned conditions:

(a) before the employment relationship is concluded; or
(b) during the time of employment upon the employer's written request, within fifteen working days of such request, or if this is not possible for reasons beyond the employee's control, immediately when the said reason is eliminated.

484. If the employee is unable to obtain an official certificate from the body operating the penal register so as to verify his/her compliance with the conditions, or the employer learns about the grounds for exclusion by other means, the concluded contract will be null and void.

485. As for the data protection issue, in order to verify the employee's compliance with the conditions mentioned above, the employer may process the personal data of the person applying for employment, and/or of the employee contained in

229. There is an exhaustive list of the criminal actions regulated in the Hungarian Criminal Code.

the official certificate made out by the body operating the penal register for this purpose. The employer is authorized to process the personal data obtained until the time the decision in connection with entering into an employment relationship is adopted, or – if yes – until the employment is terminated.

486. In regard to the *employer*, employment may be established by any person, the state itself or any of its organs, as well as by any legal person.

B. Free Will

487. The employees' free will in practice overlaps with their legal capacity. Accordingly, every person with legal capacity may enter into employment of his/her own will and decision. However, employment may also be entered into by a person of limited legal capacity over the age of 16 without the consent of his/her legal representative.

488. In regard to the employer, only those persons may enter into an employment relationship by free will who are considered to have this ability in accordance with the Civil Code, i.e., those of at least 18 years of age or those who are married.[230]

C. The Effect of Lack of Legal Capacity or Free Will

489. A contract of employment is null and void if legal capacity or free will is lacking, either in terms of the employer or the employee.

490. There is a new provision relating to this issue in the new HLC. According to it, incapacitated workers may conclude employment relationships only for jobs which they are capable of handling on a stable and continuous basis in the light of their medical condition. There are some further conditions: (a) functions of the employee's job shall be determined by definition of the related responsibilities in detail, (b) the employee's medical examination should cover the employee's ability to handle the functions of the job and (c) the employee's work must be supervised continuously so as to ensure that the requirements of occupational safety and health are satisfied.

D. Change of Employer by Legal Succession

491. The HLC regulates the transfer of business (undertakings). According to section 36 of the HLC, the rights and obligations arising from employment

230. HAJDÚ József, IEL Labour Law, Hungary, Wolters Kluwer, Kluwer Law Online, 2019. https://kluwerlawonline.com/Manuals/Corporate+Acquisitions+and+Mergers/705 (26 Jul. 2023).

relationships, existing at the time of transfer of an economic entity (organized grouping of material or other resources) by way of a legal transaction are transferred to the transferee employer.

492. The relevant EU legislation to implement is Directive 2001/23 EC. According to Article 3 of the Directive, the transfer of undertakings means that any rights and obligations deriving from the employment at the time of the change will be transferred from the preceding employer to the succeeding employer; i.e., these rights and obligations should not be amended due to legal succession. Under Article 4(2) of the Directive, if the employment contract is terminated because the transfer involves a substantial change in working conditions to the detriment of the employee, the employer is regarded as having been responsible for termination of the contract of employment or of the employment relationship. The legislator has implemented Article 6 section 2 of the Directive for informing and consulting employees. Section 40 of the HLC regulates the termination of employment by the initiative of the employee because the transfer involves a substantial change in the employee's working conditions, which is to the detriment of the employee. Such termination is considered a termination by the initiative of the employee. In this case, the employer shall pay the employee absence pay and severance pay.[231]

493. Section 37 of the HLC states that before the time of transfer, the transferring employer must inform the receiving employer concerning the employment relationships involved, and also on the rights and obligations arising from non-competition agreements and study contracts. However, the failure to provide the information will have no bearing on the enforcement of rights arising from such covenants on the receiving employer's part.

494. Within fifteen days following the time of transfer, the receiving employer must inform in writing the workers affected concerning the transfer of employment upon the transfer of enterprise, disclosing the employer's identification data, and on changes in working conditions under Subsection (1) of section 46 of the HLC. However, if the transferring employer has no works' council – due to lacking the number of employees – and no shop steward has been elected either, the transferring or – if so agreed by the employers – the receiving employer must inform in writing the employees concerned not more than fifteen days before the date of transfer of the following:

(a) the date or proposed date of the transfer;
(b) the reason for the transfer;
(c) the legal, economic and social implications of the transfer for the employees; and
(d) any measures envisaged in relation to the employees.

231. Dr HEGYI Lívia A munkáltató személyében bekövetkező változás (munkáltatói jogutódlás), Független Szakszervezetek Demokratikus Ligája (LIGA Szakszervezetek), Budapest, 2021; https://www.jogpontok.hu/download/A_munkaltato_szemelyeben_bek%C3%B6vetkezo_valtozas.pdf (26 Jul. 2023).

495. There is an important provision which states that the transferring and the receiving employer will be jointly and severally liable in respect of obligations towards employees which arose before the date of transfer, if the employee submits the claim within one (1) year from the date of transfer.

496. According to the HLC, the employees may exercise the right of notice within thirty days from the date of transfer of employment upon the transfer of enterprise. In this case, the employee shall be entitled to period of exemption from work and severance pay due in the case of notice. These are provided by the transferee employer. The reason behind this is that the transfer of employment upon the transfer of enterprise involves a substantial change in working conditions to the detriment of the employee, and in consequence, maintaining the employment relationship would entail an unreasonable disadvantage or would be impossible. In such cases, the employee must provide the reasons for giving notice of termination.

497. If an employer violates the rights of the workers' council or the trade union, the workers' council or the trade union affected may seek remedy in court.[232]

232. CSÉFFÁN József, *A munka törvénykönyve és magyarázata*, Szeged: Szegedi Rendezvényszervező Kft., 2023.

Chapter 2. Rights and Duties of the Parties During the Employment

498. By entering into a labour relationship, the worker aims at ensuring his/her own and his/her family's maintenance by the wages he/she receives as a counter value to his/her manpower put at the disposal of the employer. The employer's aim is to ensure the manpower necessary for his/her activity against the payment of wages when establishing a labour relationship. The fundamental rights and obligations of the parties ensue from the aims: on the one side, there is the demand for employment and wages; on the other side, there is the demand for manpower being put at the employer's disposal and the appropriate work being done. In view of the personal character of a labour relationship, however, these rights and obligations have been extended both on the side of the employee and the employer, and besides the main obligations, accessory obligations were instituted (e.g., on the employee's side consideration, performance to the best of his/her abilities; on the employer's side the protection of health and physical integrity, directives furthering the fulfilment of work).

499. It can be seen, therefore, that the parties are bound by mutual obligation to co-operate. Each party must aid the other in asserting his/her rights and fulfilling his/her duties.[233]

500. It is the employer's right to claim from the worker constant, continuous and careful work, and to give instructions. If the worker does not fulfil his/her duties or carries them out badly, the enterprise may – if necessary directly – take definite steps. It is the employer's duty to provide continuous employment, adequate wages and bonuses to assure the possibility of undisturbed and safe work, to give definite instructions regarding work, to encourage more productive activity, and finally, to assure the necessary assistance to the work of the trade union. Employers are liable to compensate their employees for justified expenses incurred in connection with the fulfilment of the employment relationship. The employee's fitness for the job for which he/she is being considered must be examined free of charge before taking up work and on a regular basis during the life of the employment relationship.[234]

501. There is a provision of the HLC which ensures that in the case of the employment of persons with disabilities, appropriate steps must be taken to ensure their reasonable accommodation in the working place.

502. Furthermore, according to section 3, Article 51 of the HLC employees should be employed for work of such nature which is not considered harmful with a view to their physical condition, development or health. In the event of any change

233. DUDÁS Katalin – GYULAVÁRI Tamás – HORVÁTH István – Hős Nikolett – KULISITY Mária – HUNGLER Sára – KÁRTYÁS Gábor – KUN Attila – PETROVICS Zoltán – RÁCZ Réka, *Munkajog – V. átdolgozott kiadás*, Budapest: ELTE Eötvös Kiadó, 2019.

234. This provision is based on Directive 2000/78/EC of 27 Nov. 2000 establishing a general framework for equal treatment in employment and occupation.

in the employee's health, the employer must make adjustments in the working conditions and in the work schedule accordingly.

§1. Duties of the Employee

I. The Extent of Duties

503. The basic duty of a worker is to give continuous work as provided in the employment contract. The tasks defined in the labour contract determine the worker's activity, and the employer can require only the performance of such tasks.

504. Furthermore, the employee is obliged to:

(a) appear at the place and time specified by the employer, in a condition fit for work;
(b) be at the employer's disposal in a condition fit for work during their working time for the purpose of performing work;
(c) perform work in person, with the level of professional expertise and workmanship that can be reasonably expected, in accordance with the relevant regulations, requirements, instructions and customs;
(d) perform work in such a way that demonstrates the trust vested in him for the job in question;
(e) cooperate with their co-workers.

505. There is a new rule to fight against black work and gratitude money and the tip system.[235] According to Subsection (2) of section 52 of the HLC, the employees may not accept and may not lay claim to any remuneration from third parties in connection with their activities performed with the employment relationship without the employer's prior consent. The provision is controversial because if the employer allows such practice, the gratitude money and other extra income will be legalized, at least by the labour law. However, there is a protective provision which states that the employee's wages fixed in the employment contract or by employment regulations may not be reduced on account of the employee having received any extra remuneration from third parties, even if based upon the employer's prior consent.

506. There is a special Act on Health Care Service Employment, which strictly prohibits the *gratitude money* 'practice'. As for the history, in Hungary, the phenomenon of gratuities was considered a necessary evil due to the extremely low salaries of health care workers. Previous research has shown that 57% of doctors consider gratuities necessary because of their income.[236] In order to regulate this disordered state, a legal relationship was established in the health service, which

235. The gratitude money is well spread in the health care sector, especially in clinics and hospitals. The tip or service money is well spread in restaurants, gas stations, etc.
236. HOLLÁN Miklós – VENCZEL Tímea: A hálapénz büntetendősége a jogtudatban. (The criminality

also brought about an increase in the salaries of doctors. Healthcare workers employed by state and municipal health care providers have previously worked in a number of legal relationships, but the labour law framework was resolved in 2020 by changing the relevant legislation. In addition to the settlement of medical salaries and the abolition of gratuities, a new legal status regulation has been established. Act C of 2020 on the Legal Status of the Health Service and the government decrees implementing it contain the salary scales, the range and amount of allowances due to health care professionals, and the amount and conditions of wages to be paid by health care providers.[237] Pursuant to section 20 of Act C of 2020 on healthcare service employment, sections 290 (bribery) and 291 (acceptance of bribery) of the Criminal Code have been supplemented as of 1 January 2021 as follows: 290. § (6) 'Any person who promises or gives unlawful advantage – as defined by the Healthcare Act – to a health professional or other healthcare worker, or to a third person at the behest of such person, in connection with the provision of health services is guilty of a misdemeanor punishable by imprisonment not exceeding one year, insofar as the act did not result in a more serious criminal offense.'[238] 291. § (6) 'For the purposes of this Section, unlawful advantage as defined by the Healthcare Act shall be construed as unlawful advantage provided in connection with the provision of health services.'[239] The National Protect Service (hereinafter: NPS) has been commissioned to inspect the system. After 1 July 2021.

507. There are, however, certain exceptions. There are extraordinary cases which cannot be foreseen in the planning process, such as elemental calamities, accidents, breakdowns, material shortages, etc., which might endanger the enterprise, its activity, and the workers' life and health. It may then be absolutely necessary to assign workers temporarily to jobs not strictly within their province. It might happen that because of some unforeseen event (e.g., absence because of illness, accumulation of work, accident), the usual order of work is upset (reassignment). In such a case the worker – when justified – may be obliged temporarily to do a different type of work.[240] The employee shall be informed of the probable duration of such work. The HLC calls this the derogation from the employment contract.

508. The reassignment of an employee must not result in unreasonable harm in view of the employee's position, qualification, age, health condition or his/her other circumstances.

509. Furthermore, without the consent of the employee, he/she cannot be ordered to work in a different working place:

---

of gratitude in legal consciousness) http://real.mtak.hu/102807/3/h%C3%A1lap%C3%A9nz%20lead%207.pdf (26 Jul. 2023).

237. Emberi Erőforrások Minisztériuma: Egészséges Magyarország 2021– 2027. (Healthy Hungary 2021–2027) Egészségügyi Ágazati Stratégia. Emberi Erőforrások Minisztériuma, Budapest 2021. 114. (Ministry of Human Resources, 2021).
238. A Büntető Törvénykönyvről szóló 2012. évi C. törvény 290. § (Act C of 2012 on the Penal Code).
239. A Büntető Törvénykönyvről szóló 2012. évi C. törvény 291. § (Act C of 2012 on the Penal Code).
240. Section 53 of the HLC.

(a) from the time her pregnancy is diagnosed until the child reaches three years of age;
(b) until the child reaches sixteen years of age, if a single parent;
(c) if providing long-term care for a close relative in person; furthermore
(d) if having suffered a degree of health impairment of at least 50% as diagnosed by the body of rehabilitation experts.

510. The employee must be informed of the expected duration of reassignment. Unless otherwise stipulated in the collective agreement, the duration of work under reassignment may not exceed forty-four working days or 352 working hours in any calendar year. The duration of any number of reassignments during a calendar year must be accounted for in aggregate and proportional way.

511. An employee, if ordered temporarily to do a different type of work other than his/her original position, will be entitled to remuneration based on the actual work performed during the entire time of reassignment, which may not be less than the employee's basic wage.[241]

II. Presence at Work

512. The first condition of employment is the worker's presence in good health, at the due place and at the fixed time. If the worker does not adhere to this rule, then there is a possibility of disciplinary action.

513. The law does not precisely define fixed time. Generally, the worker should be present at work according to the employer's instructions. If there are no further instructions, this is considered the standard starting time. What is meant by an able-bodied condition is also not precise in law. In practice, the worker fulfils this duty if his/her general state – physical and mental – does not provide an obstacle to performing his/her job. In certain fields, especially where physical conditions can influence the worker's health or endanger the life and safety of others, more detailed determination is needed. Here the law establishes certain requirements, for example, a small amount of alcohol precludes a person from driving.

514. These three duties (presence at work at the due place and time, in an able-bodied condition) may be considered as preconditions of employment, duties whose fulfilment is always necessary.

515. *Exemption from work duty.* According to section 55 of the HLC, employees will be exempted from the requirement of availability and from work duty:

241. HAJDÚ József – KUN Attila (eds), *Munkajog I.*, Budapest: Patrocinium, 2012. pp. 150–153.

(a) if unfit for work (health reasons);
(b) if receiving treatment in a healthcare institution related to a human reproduction procedure, as specified in the relevant legislation; and
(c) for the duration of mandatory medical examination; furthermore
(d) for the length of time required for donating blood, for a period of at least four hours;
(e) if they are nursing (breastfeeding) mothers, for one hour twice daily, or two hours twice daily in the case of twins during the first six months of breastfeeding, and thereafter for one hour daily, or two hours daily in the case of twins until the end of the ninth month;
(f) for two working days upon the death of a relative;
(g) for the duration of classes in the case of employees pursuing elementary school studies, for the duration of training if participating in initial and continuing training by agreement of the parties;
(h) for the duration of being engaged in firefighting operations in a voluntary or workplace-related fire brigade;
(i) when called upon by the court or an authority, or for the duration of participating in proceedings in person;
(j) for any duration of absence due to personal or family reasons, or as justified by unavoidable external reasons; furthermore;
(k) up to five working days per year for the purpose of personal care for a relative who needs care for serious health reasons or for a person living in the same household as the worker; and
(l) for any duration specified by employment regulations.

516. The employer, if so required to investigate the circumstances of an employee's breach of obligations, may exempt the employee from the requirement of availability and from work duty for the period required for the inquiry, in any case for up to thirty days.[242]

III. Hours of Employment

517. A worker is expected to remain at work during working hours including overtime. He/she shall perform within the lawful working hours, the preparation and completion of the work connected to his/her position as specified in the contract of employment or the regulations pertaining to employment. If such duties can only be accomplished by working beyond the official working hours, the worker is entitled to remuneration under the regulations pertaining to overtime. In certain cases, the nature of the work may permit working outside the enterprise, as may be observed in the case of scientific research or teaching. In these cases, the law or the collective agreement only defines that period during which the employee must remain at the place of work.

242. HAJDÚ József, IEL Labour Law, Hungary, Wolters Kluwer, Kluwer Law Online, 2019. https://kluwerlawonline.com/Manuals/Corporate+Acquisitions+and+Mergers/705 (26 Jul. 2023).

518. If a worker by his/her own doing does not spend the whole day at his/her place of work, he/she violates a basic duty of employment. For this period wages are not paid and sanctions may be imposed. However, the worker does not violate his/her duty if his/her absence can be excused, as in the following cases:

(a) during rest periods (breaks, days off, holidays);
(b) if unfit for work;
(c) if receiving treatment in a healthcare institution related to a human reproduction procedure, as specified in the relevant legislation; and
(d) for the duration of mandatory medical examination; furthermore
(e) for the length of time required for donating blood, for a period of at least four hours;
(f) if they are nursing mothers, for one hour twice daily, or two hours twice daily in the case of twins during the first six months of breastfeeding, and thereafter for one hour daily or two hours daily in the case of twins until the end of the ninth month;
(g) for two working days upon the death of a relative;
(h) for the duration of classes in the case of employees pursuing elementary school studies, for the duration of training if participating in initial and continuing training by agreement of the parties;
(i) for the duration of being engaged in firefighting operations in a voluntary or workplace-related fire brigade;
(j) when called upon by the court or an authority, or for the duration of participating in proceedings in person;
(k) for any duration of absence due to personal or family reasons, or as justified by unavoidable external reasons; furthermore
(l) for any duration specified by employment regulations.[243]

519. In addition, the employer, if so required to investigate the circumstances of an employee's breach of obligations, may exempt the employee from the requirement of availability and from work duty for the period required for the inquiry, in any case for up to thirty days.

IV. Manner of Work

520. The duties defining the manner of work can be divided into two main groups. Personal duties belong to the first, the carrying out of rules and instructions to the second.

1. *Personal duties* are defined as:

(a) the full utilization of the worker's abilities;
(b) the expected expertise;
(c) diligent application.

243. Subsection (1) of s. 55 of the HLC.

521. The law does not precisely define these concepts. It refers to the level of work expected of workers of the same education, qualifications, skill and ability. There are certain legal regulations regarding qualifications. On the other hand, the employer may wish to employ workers with different types of qualifications or different levels of practical skill. A degree of guidance is given by the regulations governing piece-work: norms must only be fixed which a worker is able professionally and physically to achieve permanently with the necessary experience and adhering to the technical, health and safety regulations of the enterprise. In order to obtain the required qualification a worker, while on full pay and with costs reimbursed, may participate in a course of further training as designated by the employer and sit the prescribed examinations, unless in doing so this causes him/her disproportionate discomfort in view of his/her personal or family circumstances.

2. Carrying out of rules and instructions

522. The worker is obliged to work in accordance with the law, the instructions of his/her superiors and professional practice. Employers must notify employees as to which office or person exercises or fulfils the employers' rights and obligations (employer's rights) originating from the employment relationship. If the employer's legal competence was not exercised by the office or person authorized thereto, its actions shall be invalid, unless the employee concerned would reasonably conclude from the circumstances as to the authority of the acting person.

523. It must be emphasized that a superior can give instructions only regarding the labour relationship. In this regard, the worker is not obliged to fulfil instructions which do not concern his/her work, type of job, or employment relationship.

524. The instructions of the superior may be given verbally or in writing. However, if the ruling concerning the labour relationship prescribes a special form (e.g., written instructions), the worker is not obliged to accept instructions given in an inappropriate manner.

525. The law establishes limits to the fulfilment of instructions. According to these:

(1) Employees must refuse to carry out an instruction if it would result in direct and grave risk to the health of others or to the environment.
(2) Employees may refuse to carry out an instruction if it violates the provisions of employment regulations, or it would result in direct and grave risk to the life, physical integrity or health of the employee. The employee must warn the employer. The importance of the warning in such cases lies in exempting the worker from any financial and/or criminal liability.

526. In the event of refusal to carry out an instruction, the employee must be available nonetheless.

527. Employees may disobey the employer's instruction to the extent absolutely necessary to protect the employer from suffering losses, and the employer cannot be warned in time. The employer must be notified thereof as soon as possible.[244]

V. Place of Work

528. As it was mentioned earlier, the place of work of the employee was defined in the 1992-type employment contract under HLC (1992). Failing this principle, the place where work is normally carried out is considered the place of work. The previous labour code regulated the changing place of work.[245] The new HLC does not regulate the provision on changing place of work. However, the effective HLC does not disallow the parties to designate a larger geographical unit as the place of work. For instance, the place of work can be an entire city or county, or possibly an ever larger geographical unit. In such a case the employee may be obliged to work anywhere within the designated area.

529. The character of an enterprise (e.g., post office, delivery company, bus drivers, etc.) often demands work at a changing place of work, in which case the worker has a fixed base but works wholly or partly away from it. In such a case the place of the work is the fixed base of the employer where he/she receives the work command, for example, in case of a bus driver, the location of the bus company.

VI. Behaviour

A. The Duty to Co-operate with Fellow Workers

530. The worker in employment is not isolated; he/she is a member of a community and must behave as such. The law declares that the worker is obliged to cooperate with fellow workers. He/she must not behave in such a way as to threaten another's health or disturb another's work, or cause financial hardship.

B. The Duty of Secrecy

531. As for secrecy, during the employment-relationship, in a wide sense, the following provisions are valid:

---

244. Ferenc Jácint – GÖNDÖR Éva – GYULAVÁRI Tamás – KÁRTYÁS Gábor, *Munkajogi alapismeretek*, Budapest: ELTE Kiadó, 2013. pp. 108–109.

245. It means that the employer without any consent of the employee could change the workplace. For example, a gas station chain could order the employee to work in any of their gas station in the country. Naturally, some protective provision existed, for example, woman with small child, etc.

(1) Workers must maintain confidentiality in relation to business secrets obtained in the course of their work. Moreover, workers cannot disclose to unauthorized persons any data learned in connection with their activities that, if revealed, would result in detrimental consequences for the employer or other persons. The requirement of confidentiality does not apply to any information that is declared by specific other legislation to be treated as information of public interest or public information and as such is rendered subject to disclosure requirements.[246]

(2) Any person who is acting in the name or on behalf of the works' council or trade union is authorized to disclose any information or data acquired in the course of his/her activities solely in a manner which does not jeopardize the employer's legitimate economic interest and without violating personal rights.[247]

(3) The executive employees:
   (a) shall not acquire shares, with the exception of the acquisition of stocks in a public limited company, in a business association which is engaged in the same or similar activities or that maintains regular economic ties with their employer;
   (b) shall not conclude any transactions falling within the scope of the employer's activities in their own name or on their own behalf; and
   (c) shall report if a relative has become a member of a business association which is engaged in the same or similar activities or that maintains regular economic ties with the employer, or has established an employment-related relationship for an executive office with an employer engaged in such activities.[248]

(4) *Covenant of non-competition.* The aim of this agreement is to protect the economic and legal interest of the former employer. According to section 228 of the HLC, by agreement of the parties, the employee cannot engage in any conduct – for up to two (2) years following termination of the employment relationship – by which to infringe upon or jeopardize the rightful economic interests of the employer.[249]

532. In exchange for honouring the above-mentioned obligation, the employer will be liable to pay adequate compensation. In determining the amount of such compensation, the degree of impediment the agreement has on the employee's ability to find employment elsewhere – in the light of his education and experience – will be taken into consideration. The amount of compensation for the term of the agreement may not be less than one-third of the basic wage due for the same period.

533. The employee has the right to withdraw from the agreement if having terminated his/her employment relationship without notice.

---

246. Subsection (4) of s. 8 of the HLC.
247. Subsection (3) of s. 234 of the HLC.
248. Section 211 of the HLC.
249. Bővült a versenytilalmi megállapodások szabályozása, http://www.piacesprofit.hu/kkv_cegblog/bovult-a-versenytilalmi-megallapodasok-szabalyozasa/ (26 Jul. 2023).

534. In the case of transfer of employment upon the transfer of enterprise, the rights and obligations arising from the agreement will be transferred to the receiving employer.[250]

535. Opinion of the Administrative and Labour Law Collegium of the Curia (Hungarian Supreme Court) on the non-competition agreement (1/2019 (V.20.) KMK Vélemény). A non-competition agreement is conditional on the employer having a significant economic interest to be taken into account.

536. The HLC does not specify this conduct, but a typical case is when an employee establishes a company in competition or performs work for such a company. The non-competition agreement does not require the employee to engage in active conduct but to refrain from engaging in any conduct. In accordance with previous case law, the definition of a competitor should be based on the data of the commercial register (BH2008. 342.), but in accordance with § 3:97 of Act V of 2013 on the Civil Code (hereinafter: Civil Code), it is not of exclusive relevance. Even with the same scope of activity in the company register, it is not excluded that the employee does not jeopardise the legitimate economic interests of his former employer. Therefore, the employer must prove the breach of the non-competition agreement on the basis of the specific facts of the case in such a way that the actual damage to interests or the real threat thereof can be established beyond doubt.

537. When assessing the content of a non-competition agreement, the intention of the parties at the time of the conclusion of the contract shall prevail. During the duration of the employment relationship, the employee may not engage in any conduct that would jeopardise the legitimate economic interests of his/her employer without a separate agreement or an obligation to pay compensation. After termination of the employment relationship, such restrictions are only possible within certain limits. The parties must expressly conclude an agreement to this effect under the conditions laid down by law [Article 228 (2) of the HLC], where, according to consistent case law, it is not possible for either party to subsequently invoke circumstances that were not taken into account when the agreement was concluded (BH2001. 339). If the employee begins to perform the obligation undertaken in the agreement, i.e., does not take up employment with the company covered by the prohibition, the employer is obliged to perform for him even if the employee is not otherwise in a position to harm or jeopardise his economic interests.

538. A clause in a non-competition agreement must be suitable to protect the employer's economic interest, but must not unfairly and excessively restrict the employee's gainful activity. Therefore, in order to protect the interests of both parties, it is appropriate to specify the scope of the activity, the area of specialization and the geographical area to which the restriction applies. A prohibition covering a

250. HAJDU-DUDÁS Mária (2022) *Így óvhatja cégügyeit a konkurenciától: versenytilalmi megállapodás korlátok között* https://adozona.hu/munkajog/Igy_ovhatja_cegugyeit_a_konkurenciatol_vers_ZTN02A (26 Jul. 2023).

'foreign competitor' may also be a valid clause, provided that the geographical area is clearly defined according to the intention of the parties.

539. In the case of a non-competition agreement, the consideration is intended to compensate the employer for the restriction on the possibility of earning an income by a cash payment, i.e., to cover at least part of the cost of living for the period during which the restriction or prohibition on employment is in force. Consequently, the consideration in the non-competition agreement can only be monetary and cannot be in kind (e.g., in the form of course fees or meal contributions, BH2001. 84).

540. The non-competition agreement must contain the restriction and its value. Failure to do so is not invalidity, but a non-existent contract, since there is no consensus on the mandatory content under the law. A non-existent contract cannot be a source of law; i.e., it does not create an obligation to perform the service and a right to claim for it. This principle is also reflected in the long-established case-law of civil law (BH1997. 102., BH2003. 409.) The Civil Code provides for the rules of unjust enrichment as a legal consequence of a non-existent contract (Civil Code, Article 6:579). 31 of the HLC does not, however, allow the application of the above provision of the Civil Code in the absence of a rule to the contrary, so that no claim can be based on it in connection with the non-competition agreement. In such cases, an employer's compensation can be applied in an employment lawsuit if the employee has performed or already paid 'consideration' under the non-existent agreement. Liability for the damage caused can be established if there is evidence of the harmful conduct, the occurrence of the damage and the causal link between them. The employer's liability may be established in relation to the relationship of subordination and subordination between the parties. It must be appreciated that the non-competition agreement is essentially in the employer's interest, serves his expectations and usually determines the terms of the contract. The Hungarian Constitutional Court has also established the relationship of dependence between the parties as a characteristic of the employment relationship. '...The specificity of the employment relationship is the unequal status of the parties and the subordinate and superior nature of the legal relationship. On the other hand, the rules deriving from the employment relationship necessarily restrict the autonomy of action of the employees, and thus their conduct and opinions' [AB 14/2017 (30. VI), No. 14/2017 (21)].

541. The validity of a non-competition agreement is subject to the condition of adequate consideration and the condition that the non-competition agreement is fair and does not unfairly and unduly restrict the employee's earning potential. The amount of the benefit shall be determined by the parties, assessing the extent to which the agreement prevents the employee from entering into a new employment relationship. The lower limit of the consideration shall be at least one-third of the basic wage for the non-competition period [section 228(2) of the Labour Code]. In determining the amount, the extent to which the agreement prevents the employee from establishing a new employment relationship shall be taken into account. If the consideration stipulated in the non-competition agreement is less than one-third of the basic salary for the same period, the rules of partial nullity apply. Subject to section 29(3) of the Labour Code, if a part of the agreement is invalid, the rules applicable to the employment relationship shall apply instead, unless the parties would not have concluded the agreement without the invalid part. In the case where the party has claimed partial invalidity because the compensation, although reaching the statutory minimum, is not found to be proportionate, the 'adequacy' of the party's claim should be examined; i.e., it should be assessed whether the consideration paid is adequate to compensate for the clause restricting the employment. The Labour Code also allows for the remedying of non-apparent disproportionality between the employee's obligation and the consideration provided for its fulfilment. Section 31 of the HLC in connection with the entry into force of the Civil Code follows that the exclusion of a challenge on the grounds of a conspicuous disproportion in value follows from the fact that section 31 of the HLC does not permit the application to the employment relationship of the provisions of the Ptk. 6:98 of the Labour Code.

VII. Establishing Additional Employment Relationship

542. If the worker establishes during his/her employment with one employer additional employment or a legal relationship directed towards the performance of work, he/she must report this to the original employer. The employer, in the absence of an agreement departing therefrom, may prohibit the establishment of the legal relationship or may force the employee to terminate his/her employment if the additional legal relationship is in violation of the employer's lawful economic interests.[251]

§2. Duties of the Employer

I. Main Duties of the Employer

543. The employer can demand labour activity from the worker, but at the same time the employer has a duty to employ him/her and to assure working conditions providing safe and undisturbed work. The employer must give the appropriate instructions to the worker. Finally, the employer must promote efficiency and quality of work.

A. Provision of Work

544. In the majority of cases, the earnings of the workers are considerably influenced by the provision of the means needed for the performance of their work. This is not unrelated to the aspect of obtaining or maintaining their professional practice either. Consequently, the employer is obliged to provide the worker continuously with work within the scope of his/her job.

251. HAJDÚ József – KUN Attila (eds), *Munkajog I.*, Budapest: Patrocinium, 2012.

545. There is a special situation when the employer is unable to provide work as contracted during the scheduled working time (*downtime*); in this case, the employee is entitled to his/her absentee fee unless it is due to unavoidable external reasons.[252]

B. Provisions of Healthy and Safe Working Conditions

546. The employer must ensure for the performance of work an environment (e.g., building, machinery, equipment, material, etc.) which involves no risks for the person doing the job. If this requirement cannot be fully met, the employer is obliged to bring in appropriate safety measures (e.g., protective equipment, protective garments, etc.) to eliminate risks. In addition, the worker must be taught the healthy and safe performance of the job (training in labour safety). Prevention of the dangers accompanying certain jobs must be continuously checked and developed by utilizing the results of technological development. Besides the HLC, basically the Act XCIII of 1993 on Labour Safety and Health contains provisions on labour safety and health.

C. Assuring Adequate Working Conditions

547. The employer must ensure undisturbed working conditions. Sometimes this is called the duty of organization. Order and co-operation among workers must be assured. All circumstances must be eliminated which might disturb workers or distract their attention. This also includes the provision of a suitable place for keeping and safeguarding the workers' clothes and personal effects.

D. The Duty to Provide Direction

548. The worker must be informed about the scope and circumstances of his/her work, be instructed in a proper way, be informed of the terms of the collective agreement and organizational regulations. All the necessary instructions must be given for doing a job properly. In a similar fashion, the employer must carry out these duties when a worker is transferred to a new job or if a new technological process is introduced.

E. The Duty to Promote Efficiency and Quality

549. The employer must assist in the education of a worker and in increasing his/her professional level. He/she must advance innovation, deal with proposals aiming at the organization of more efficient and more productive work and implement accepted proposals.

252. Subsection (1) of s. 146 of the HLC.

550. The employer will pay the worker wages in accordance with the work contract and those provisions contained in the regulations pertaining to employment.

551. Employers will reimburse employees for all necessary and substantiated costs incurred in the course of fulfilling their work-related obligations, as well as for all other required expenses incurred in the employer's interests if the employer has approved it in advance. Expenses related to business trips or foreign service, or commuting to work (usually partly compensated), will be reimbursed as prescribed in separate legal regulations.

II. Enforceability

552. It was mentioned earlier that work depends on the free will of the parties. In the course of the labour relationship, the worker cannot be forced to work. Only indirect sanctions are available. These include disciplinary procedures provided for by the collective agreement, the possibility of termination of the labour relationship on the part of the employer or incurring financial responsibility on the part of the worker.

553. The worker, however, has direct means to enforce the employer's fulfilment of his/her employment duty. Judicial sanctions may also be used. Naturally, the worker can also make use of indirect sanctions, for example, he/she can break off the labour relationship immediately and can abrogate the contract.[253]

III. Infringement of Labour and Employment Obligations

A. *Infringement of Labour Duty by Worker*

554. The duty to work may be violated in two ways by the worker: (1) either the worker does not work, or (2) he/she works inadequately. The first situation may occur when the worker begins late and finishes early or when he/she does not appear in the workplace at all without any excuse. The neglect of labour duty may occur with or without culpability. The culpable neglect of one's labour obligations is called unjustified absence.

555. For the periods during which the worker's absence is unjustified, wages and other payments are not due. Sanctions as well as disciplinary measures by the employer may be imposed. According to section 56 of the HLC, in the event of any infringement of obligations arising from an employment relationship the collective agreement or – if the employer or the worker is not covered by the collective agreement – the employment contract may prescribe detrimental legal consequences consistent with the gravity of the infringement. The detrimental legal consequence

253. FERENC Jácint – GÖNDÖR Éva – GYULAVÁRI Tamás – KÁRTYÁS Gábor, *Munkajogi alapismeretek*, Budapest: ELTE Kiadó, 2013. pp. 103–106.

aforementioned may be a sanction related to the employment relationship, altering its terms and conditions for a fixed period, which shall not violate the employee's personal rights and dignity. Where the sanction is of a financial nature, it may not – on the whole – exceed the employee's monthly basic wage in effect at the time when the sanction is imposed.

556. An infringement may not be sanctioned by detrimental legal consequences if the employer has already stated it as the reason for termination of the employment relationship. The measure imposing detrimental legal consequences must be put in writing, with reasons provided.

557. Inadequate performance of one's labour obligations occurs when the worker apparently fulfils these obligations but not in the terms established by the employment contract. Examples of this would be the production of inferior articles, improper use of machines, tools, or material, or a failure to conform to safety regulations. In the case of wages paid according to piece-work, the worker loses all or a part of his/her wages for inferior articles produced. In addition, in the case of culpability, the workers may suffer disciplinary punishment.[254]

B. Electronic Surveillance at Workplace

558. Electronic surveillance is one of the measures that could help the employer to control the behaviour of the employee. In Hungary, the Privacy Act (Act CXII of 2011 on Informational Self-Determination and Freedom of Information), as a general legislation, and the HLC, as a special legislation, provides rules for electronic surveillance at the workplace. The National Agency for Data Protection and Freedom of Information monitors the practice of data and privacy protection in the workplace.

559. Under the HLC, an employer is entitled to monitor its employees in connection with their employment-related behaviour, something which certainly entails the processing of certain personal data. The HLC does not state that the employer is obliged to obtain consent from the employee, and reliance on employee consent may not be valid as per the opinion of the Article 29 Working Party. As set out in their Opinion No 15/2011, there are grounds other than consent contained in Article 7 of the EU DP Directive, which can also be used as a lawful basis for data processing. Furthermore, a CJEU ruling in joined cases C-468/10 and C-469/10 declared that Article 7(f) of the EU DP Directive – which permits processing on the grounds of legitimate interests – must be given direct effect.[255]

254. HAJDÚ József, IEL *Labour Law, Hungary*, Wolters Kluwer, Kluwer Law Online, 2019. https://kluwerlawonline.com/Manuals/Corporate+Acquisitions+and+Mergers/705.
255. LUKÁCS Adrienn (2020) Adatvédelmi jog a munkaerőpiacon, https://eta.bibl.u-szeged.hu/3589/ (26 Jul. 2023).

560. There is a data protection legislation in the EU: GDPR (General Data Protection Regulation ((EU) 2016/679)) came into force on 25 May 2018. Many existing contracts of employment will contain clauses giving consent for employers to process their employees' employment data. As a result of the GDPR, the conditions for obtaining consent to process data are stricter and it may not be possible for employers to rely on explicit consent from the employee and particularly not in the form of a blanket consent in the employment contract. Contractual provisions should now be an acknowledgment of the data processing legislation and the grounds on which employee data will be processed.

561. As mentioned, employers must be transparent and accountable in relation to the processing of their employees' data. Employers will therefore need to ensure that their Data Protection Policies are updated to reflect the new rights of employees. Other policies, such as the disciplinary and grievance procedure, employee monitoring policy and use of company devices and internet and email use policy may also be affected and need to be amended, e.g., tightening up on personal email use at work.

562. The GDPR gives greater rights to data subjects, including enhancing the existing right to make a data subject access request (DSAR) in relation to their personal data. Employers need to ensure that they have in place the necessary procedures to deal with a DSAR and the other rights available: the right of erasure, rectification and restriction, known in the press as 'the right to be forgotten'. Processes and procedures must be adapted to ensure that they can comply with these rights.

563. Not all employers are required to appoint a *data protection officer*. However, those companies which are involved in regular monitoring or large-scale processing must appoint an officer and other companies may decide to appoint one in any event. This data protection officer will have enhanced employment rights when carrying out his/her duties and employers should be clear on the terms applicable to the DPO.

564. Employers are required to notify the regulator of breaches without undue delay (within 72 hours if possible) and in certain circumstances to notify employees. Again, employers should ensure that processes are in place to respond to a breach.

565. The National Data Protection Authority has concluded that employee monitoring does not necessarily require employee consent, but certain requirements must be met:

(a) Employee monitoring is only deemed lawful if it is essential for the fulfilment of a purpose directly related to the aim of the employment.
(b) The human dignity of the employee must be respected and their private life must not be monitored.
(c) Employees must be informed in advance about the data processing.

(d) The employer must comply with the general principles set out in the Hungarian Privacy Act, including the requirement of a fair and lawful purpose for data processing.

566. The HLC provides a framework for lawful employee monitoring, but in any event, details of monitoring must be set out in a separate policy and the monitoring must also comply with principles of accountability and proportionality.

567. The HLC does not contain detailed provisions applicable to electronic surveillance devices, such as CCTV. Provisions relating to these devices are contained in the Personal and Property Protection Act (Act CXXXIII of 2005), which also establishes the lawful grounds for the use of electronic surveillance systems and obligatory retention periods. Although the rules of the Personal and Property Protection Act do not cover all aspects of electronic surveillance, the agency will take the provisions of the act into consideration until the Labour Code's provisions are adequately amended.

568. Employers are obliged to prove that their electronic surveillance systems comply with the requirements of the Privacy Act and in particular that the processing is based on a lawful purpose. CCTV surveillance must not jeopardise human dignity; therefore, cameras cannot be directed at one particular employee and cannot record his/her activity alone. Furthermore, an electronic surveillance system will be deemed unlawful if it is aimed at influencing employee behaviour in the workplace. CCTV surveillance is not allowed in locker rooms, showers, toilets, medical rooms and similar premises, or in rooms or locations where employees spend their breaks. However, these locations can be lawfully monitored after working hours when not in use by employees.

569. A camera must only aim at the designated area and only at the premises of the employer. An employer must precisely set out in its policy the purpose of installing each and every camera and the reason for monitoring for each area. It will not be enough for employers to provide employees with general information on electronic surveillance systems.

570. The general maximum retention period of personal data collected by electronic surveillance systems is three days. In exceptional cases, longer retention periods can be applied, but only if the employer is able to justify that special circumstances require a longer retention period. Only a limited number of staff may have access to personal data, and employers must also set out rules for access to data.

571. The employer must inform employees in advance about the details of the data processing. Employees must also be provided with certain particular pieces of information, including the legal grounds for data processing, the location of any CCTV cameras, the identities of any staff operating the cameras, the location where recordings are stored, the retention periods, the rights of employees and their available legal remedies.

572. The employer must be able to prove that employees have been adequately informed, for instance, by requesting employees to sign the notice. New joiners must be informed in a separate document which must be signed along with the employment contract.

573. An employer must also use visual notices in the workplace to inform employees that CCTV cameras are in operation in the area.

574. Although the agency does not keep a register on employee data, the processing of electronic surveillance data triggers a filing requirement if CCTV cameras monitor nonemployees, such as customers or suppliers.[256,257]

C. *Infringement of the Duty to Provide Employment*

575. Infringement of the duty to employ occurs if the employer does not give employment to the worker or does not fulfil his/her duties. The employer neglects its employment duties where the worker, in good health, is present and available to work, but the enterprise does not provide employment. The law distinguishes two categories:

(1) To the first category belong those instances in which an employer, for reasons such as a shortage of raw materials or energy, or the breakdown of machinery, is temporarily unable to provide employment. For such a period fixed remuneration is due to the worker, generally equal to his/her basic wage. The question of employer's culpability is irrelevant here, and the employer cannot avoid payment by reference to external causes.
(2) To the second category belong those cases where the employer, without legal cause, fails to provide employment for those appearing at work or illegally terminates a worker's employment relationship. In these cases, absence fee is due to the worker and he/she can also claim for damages. The worker may initiate a labour dispute and may ask the employer for reinstatement. (*See* details later.)

576. Improper fulfilment of the duty to employ occurs where an employer provides employment but does not ensure suitable conditions. It may be that in such a situation the worker is unable to carry out his/her job, or that the work is inadequate. For example, the employer may not have established the proper safeguards or protection, or may not have issued the necessary directions. In these cases, the worker, by initiating a labour debate, may require the employer to ensure the proper

256. GDPR kamerás megfigyelés 2023: ezek az új szabályok léptek életbe (2023); https://officina.hu/gazdasag/191-gdpr-kameras-megfigyeles-szabalyai (26 Jul. 2023).
257. LUKÁCS Adrienn *A főnök szeme mindent lát? Gondolatok a munkavállalók webkamerás ellenőrzéséről* HVG-Orac Munkajog, 2022/2. lapszám, 14–19. o. https://munkajogilap.hu/a-fonok-szeme-mindent-lat-gondolatok-a-munkavallalok-webkameras-ellenorzeserol/ (26 Jul. 2023).

conditions. If the worker is unable to do his/her work because of lack of proper conditions, he/she may refuse to work. For the period of interruption absence fee is due to him/her. Naturally, in every case, he/she may break his/her labour contract by giving warning. If the lack of proper conditions directly endangers a worker's life, health or bodily integrity, he/she may immediately terminate the employment relationship. In this case, he/she can claim for damages, such as not being able to obtain alternative employment, at once. If the worker did not work because of improper fulfilment by the employer of his/her obligations, then he/she suffers no consequences.[258]

IV. Sanctions Arising from the Neglect of Employment Duties

577. The sanctions arising from the non-fulfilment of employment duties may be divided into the following groups: (1) sanctions may be direct or indirect. A direct legal sanction enforces certain actions, such as the payment of wages. Indirect sanctions are used to induce the guilty party to behave in a lawful manner. (2) certain sanctions can be applied in cases of neglect of duty. Extraordinary sanctions are those which can be used only in certain cases of neglect. One can also differentiate financial, moral, disciplinary or even criminal sanctions. (3) distinction between sanctions against the enterprise and sanctions against the worker must be made.

A. Sanctions Against the Worker

578. The Hungarian labour law does not provide direct legal sanctions to force a worker to work. Only indirect, mainly educative sanctions may be used. In regard to a demand relating to property, direct sanctions may be used. For example, if a worker causes damage, or accepts wages paid out erroneously, the employer may compel him/her to return the wages or compensate him/her for the damage. There are also general sanctions, including termination of the employment relationship. In addition to the general sanctions, the law attaches extraordinary sanctions to the neglect of certain duties, for instance, the reduction or loss of wages for producing inferior goods, or in the case provided by the collective agreement application of detrimental legal consequences.

B. Sanctions Against the Employer

579. The worker may generally apply direct sanctions against the employer. The worker may appeal to the relevant authority designated to resolve labour disputes, who may force the enterprise to fulfil its duties. If the employer causes harm by his/her unlawful behaviour, the worker may also claim compensation.

258. HAJDÚ József, IEL Labour Law, Hungary, Wolters Kluwer, Kluwer Law Online, 2019. https://kluwerlawonline.com/Manuals/Corporate+Acquisitions+and+Mergers/705 (26 Jul. 2023).

580. Finally, the law provides that the worker may immediately terminate the labour relationship by extraordinary notice if the employer violates his/her duties. The employer may also be liable to criminal sanctions in cases where the employer seriously infringes the worker's rights or damages the worker's interests as set out in the Penal Code.

V. Interruption of Employment

581. Employment is interrupted if the worker – in accordance with certain legal regulations or the parties' agreement – for a long period is unable to fulfil his/her duties, while the employer is unable and not obliged to employ him/her. For example, an interruption of employment exists during the worker's deprivation of liberty, or unpaid leave, etc. During the period of interruption, the worker does not have any labour obligations nor does the employer have any employment obligations, and other provisions are also suspended – for example, the worker does not receive wages. The law may, however, prescribe the paying of fees or other bonuses.

582. When the period of interruption comes to an end, the worker is obliged to present him/herself at work and the employer is obliged to provide employment, in accordance with the original terms. During the period of interruption, the limits and prohibitions relating to termination of contract continue to apply. In addition, unless otherwise provided by law, the period of interruption counts as time spent in employment for purposes of calculating such benefits as vacation leave.[259]

259. BANKÓ Zoltán, BERKE Gyula, KISS György, SZŐKE Gergely László *Nagykommentár a munka törvénykönyvéhez*, Wolters Kluwer, Budapest 2019.

Chapter 3. Working Time, Annual Vacations, Holidays

§1. Working Time

I. The Concept and Definition of Working Time

583. According to the definition included in the Hungarian Labour Code, 'working time' means the duration from the commencement until the end of the period prescribed for working, that is to include any preliminary and finishing activities related to working.[260]

584. However, the working time doesn't cover:

(a) break-time, with the exception of stand-by jobs; and
(b) travel time from the employee's home or place of residence to the place where work is in fact carried out and from the place of work to the employee's home or place of residence.[261]

585. In addition, the HLC provides some basic definitions relating to working time. These are:

(1) *Working day* means a calendar day or an uninterrupted twenty-four hour period defined by the employer, if the beginning and end of the daily working time as scheduled to accommodate the employer's operations falls on different calendar days.
(2) *Working week* means a calendar week or an uninterrupted one hundred and sixty-eight hour period defined by the employer, if the beginning and end of the daily working time as scheduled to accommodate the employer's operations falls on different calendar days.

---

260. Subsection (2) of s. 86 of the HLC defines the preparatory or finishing activities. They are operations comprising a function of the worker's job by nature that is ordinarily carried out without being subject to special instructions.

261. However, the CJEU issued an important judgement: Case C-266/14 *Federación de Servicios Privados del sindicato Comisiones obreras (CC.OO.) v. Tyco Integrated Security SL*, Tyco Integrated Fire & Security Corporation Servicios SA. The EU Working Time Directive Directive (2003/88/EC of the European Parliament and of the Council) defines working time as any period during which the worker is working, at the employer's disposal and carrying out his/her activity or duties, in accordance with national laws and/or practice. Any period which is not working time is regarded as a rest period. In 2011, Tyco closed its offices in the provinces and assigned all its employees to the central office in Madrid (Spain). The technicians employed by Tyco install and maintain security equipment in homes and on industrial and commercial premises located within the geographical area assigned to them, so they have no fixed place of work. Tyco counts the time spent travelling between home and customers (i.e., the daily journeys between the homes of the workers and the premises of the first and last customers designated by Tyco) not as working time, but as a rest period.

However, the Court of Justice declared that where workers, such as those in the situation at issue, do not have a fixed or habitual place of work, the time spent by those workers travelling each day between their homes and the premises of the first and last customers designated by their employer constitutes working time within the meaning of the directive.

(3) *Daily working time* means the duration of working time fixed by the parties or specified by employment regulations for:
   (a) full-time jobs; or
   (b) part-time jobs.[262]
(4) *Scheduled daily working time* means the regular working time ordered for a working day.
(5) *Scheduled weekly working time* means the regular working time ordered for a week.[263]
(6) *Night work* means work carried out between twenty-two hours (22:00) and six hours (6:00).[264]
(7) The method of organizing the employer's work is:
   (a) *continuous (uninterrupted) work*, if the time of stoppage on a given calendar day is less than six hours or if operation is suspended only for the reasons and for the duration required by the technology employed in any calendar year and:
      (i) the employer is engaged in the provision of basic public services on a regular basis; or
      (ii) if economic or feasible operation cannot be ensured otherwise for objective and technical reasons.
   (b) *shiftwork*, if its duration reaches eighty hours in a week;
   (c) *seasonal work*, if work is to be performed in a specific season or a given time or period of the year, irrespective of the conditions under which the work is organized.[265]
(8) *Stand-by job* means where:
   (a) due to the nature of the job, no work is performed during at least one-third of the employee's regular working time based on a longer period, during which – however – the employee is at the employer's disposal; or
   (b) in light of the characteristics of the job and of the working conditions, the work performed is significantly less strenuous and less demanding than commonly required for a regular job.[266]

586. The extent of working hours is determined by two factors: (1) the *need for production* and (2) for the *protection of individuals.*

587. For producing society's material and cultural goods, specified working hours are necessary under given social conditions. Social need requires that time spent in working activity should comprise socially necessary working time.

588. The protection of the individual requires that the length of time cannot exceed the limit beyond which as a result of tiredness or other influences working

262. Section 88 of the HLC.
263. Section 88 of the HLC.
264. Section 89 of the HLC.
265. Section 90 of the HLC.
266. Section 91 of the HLC.

activity may cause danger, accident or damage to health. Similarly, sufficient leisure time is indispensable for health and mental development. The total length of working hours must be determined by balancing the requirements of production with social and individual requirements.

589. Basically, there are three methods of regulating the length of working hours. (1) First, the length of time during which the workers are obliged and authorized to work is defined. This is normal working time. (2) Second, the utilization and schedule of the working day are fixed. (3) Third, the circumstances are established in which in extraordinary cases the worker can be employed over and above normal working hours.[267]

II. Normal Working Time and Work Schedule

A. Normal Daily Working Time

590. The normal daily working time is eight hours, weekly working time is forty hours with a two-day rest period. The regulation relating to employment or the agreement between the parties may establish shorter working time than this, or longer:

- shorter: (1) in case of shortened working hours (part-time work)[268] or (2) dangerous work (e.g., radiation, divers, etc.);[269]
- longer: (1) full stand-by jobs or (2) who are close relatives of the employer or the owner[270] – up to but not exceeding twelve working hours daily or sixty working hours per week.

591. The collective agreement may contain some deviation from the provisions of the HLC. Accordingly, the collective agreements for:

(a) employees working as navigators, flight attendants and aviation engineers or engaged in the operation and control of ground equipment serving aircraft;
(b) employees working in travel-intensive jobs in domestic or international carriage of passengers and goods by road;

267. FERENC Jácint – GÖNDÖR Éva – GYULAVÁRI Tamás – KÁRTYÁS Gábor, *Munkajogi alapismeretek*, Budapest: ELTE Kiadó, 2013. pp. 117–118.

268. N.B.: It is important to point out that when the parties agree on part-time working hours in the employment contract, it is regarded as part-time working hours and not shorter working hours. However, the daily working time applicable for a specific full-time job may be reduced by agreement of the parties (part-time work). [Subsection (5) of s. 92 of the HLC.].

269. In respect of work that is highly hazardous to health or particularly dangerous, the time allowed to be spent conducting the hazardous (dangerous) activities shall be prescribed by legal regulation or by collective bargaining agreement, not to exceed six hours a day, within the working day, and other restrictions may be prescribed as well.

270. 'Owner' means any member of the business association holding more than 25% of the votes in the company's decision-making body.

(c) carriers and traffic controllers working in an urban mass transportation system;
(d) travelling workers and traffic controllers working in international carriage of passengers by rail and in domestic and international carriage of goods by rail

may contain derogations from the provisions pertaining to the limitation of daily working time.

592. In respect of healthcare employees working on-call or stand-by duty, as defined in specific other legislation pertaining to healthcare services, the collective agreement may contain special provisions.

593. The duration of overtime work performed by the employee will be included in the employee's daily or weekly working time.[271]

B. *Work Schedule*

1. General Provisions Regarding Scheduling

a. Method of Regulation

594. The work schedule is important for both workers and employer. It must be appropriate to the tasks of the employer, and at the same time must accord with the interests of the workforce. Because such needs vary so much, detailed central regulation is not possible. On the basis of the daily work time working hours may also be specified for a week or for a longer time frame. It is reasonable to agree about the general working hours in the collective agreement.

595. The *working time banking*. The employer may define the working time of an employee in terms of the 'banking' of working time or working hours as well. The essence of working time banking is that the employer has the flexibility to allocate working time within it, but the guarantee is that the average working time within the working time banking cannot exceed the legal working time. If it were more, it would be overtime.

Where working time is established within the framework of working time banking the period covered by the banking of working time will be arranged based on daily working time and the standard work pattern. In this context, the public holidays falling on working days according to the standard work pattern shall be ignored. In determining the working time, the duration of absence will be ignored, or it shall be taken into consideration as the working time defined by the schedule for the given working day. In the absence of a work schedule, the duration of leave shall be calculated based on the daily working time, whether ignored or taken into consideration.

---

271. DUDÁS Katalin – GYULAVÁRI Tamás – HORVÁTH István – Hős Nikolett – KULISITY Mária – HUNGLER Sára – KÁRTYÁS Gábor – KUN Attila – PETROVICS Zoltán – RÁCZ Réka, *Munkajog – V. átdolgozott kiadás*, Budapest: ELTE Eötvös Kiadó, 2019.

Where working time is defined within the framework of working time banking the beginning and ending date shall be specified in writing and shall be made public.

596. The maximum duration of the working time banking may be 4 months or 16 weeks. It is a new rule that the duration of the working time cycle may be 6 months or 26 weeks, in the case of employees:

- working in continuous shifts;
- working in shifts; and
- employed for seasonal work, and;
- working in stand-by jobs;
- employees working as navigators, flight attendants and aviation engineers or engaged in providing ground handling services to passengers and aircraft, and participating in or providing direct support for navigation services;
- employees working in travel-intensive jobs in the domestic or international carriage of passengers and goods by road;
- carriers and traffic controllers working in a local public transportation system for the carriage of passengers or in a scheduled intercity transportation system inside a fifty-kilometer radius;
- travelling workers and traffic controllers working in the carriage of passengers by rail and in the carriage of goods by rail;
- employees working in harbors.

597. Where justified by objective or technical reasons or reasons related to work organization, the maximum duration of working time banking fixed in the collective agreement is thirty-six months.

598. Termination of the collective agreement shall not affect work within the framework of working time banking in progress for a period of up to three months from the termination of the collective agreement.

599. The HLC sets out how to manage the situation when the employment relationship is terminated prior to the end of the working time cycle: different rules and calculation methods will apply depending on for what reasons the employment was terminated and on how many hours the employee worked.

600. According to section 95 of the HLC, the following procedure is applied when the termination of employment relationship before the expiry of working time banking arrangements. Upon the cessation of employment relationship, the employee's wages will be calculated based on the standard work pattern, the daily working time and the time actually worked.

601. The provisions on overtime work are applied if the employment relationship ends before the expiry of working time banking arrangements:

(a) upon the dissolution of the employer without succession;

(b) upon the expiration of the fixed term;
(c) upon dismissal by the employer without notice under Subsection (1) of section 79 of the HLC;
(d) upon dismissal by the employer for reasons in connection with the employer's operations;
(e) upon termination by the employee without notice, with the exception of paragraph a) of Subsection (1) of section 79;

and the employee worked more than the working time determined based on the standard work pattern and the daily working time.

602. The provisions on downtime shall apply if the employment relationship ends before the expiry of the working time banking arrangements:

(a) upon the dissolution of the employer without succession;
(b) upon the expiration of the fixed term;
(c) upon dismissal by the employer without notice under Subsection (1) of section 79;
(d) upon dismissal by the employer for reasons in connection with the employer's operations;
(e) upon termination by the employee without notice, with the exception of paragraph a) of Subsection (1) of section 79;

and the employee worked less than the working time determined based on the standard work pattern and the daily working time.

b. Principles of Scheduling

603. Basically, the rules relating to working time banking (working arrangements) are laid down by the employer. However, there are some restrictions. The restrictions in regard to working schedules are the following:

- Work must be scheduled in a way which will not endanger the worker's health and does not place a disproportionate burden on the worker in terms of his/her personal and family circumstances.
- An uninterrupted rest period of at least 11 hours should be ensured between ending work and starting work the following day. The collective agreement can reduce this but not to a period shorter than eight hours.
- As regards shift work, the allocation of shifts must be changed after a defined period unless a worker wishes otherwise.
- From the time of pregnancy until a child reaches the age of one, a woman cannot be put on night shift. (This prohibition also applies to minors.)
- If the work schedule allows for several ways of distributing work time or fixes it within a certain framework, the employer shall notify the worker of the work

schedule at least one week in advance and for a period of at least one week. In the absence of such notification, the work schedule of the most recent period shall be normative.[272]

2. Types of Schedule

a. Uniform Scheduling

604. The work of an enterprise generally requires a uniform schedule. This is also convenient for the workers because it enables them to plan ahead. Generally, working hours are distributed evenly over the prescribed working days within the period of working time. Usually, work is scheduled for five days a week, between Monday through Friday (standard work pattern). In this way, an extra day off is established every week in addition to the regular weekly day of rest. Most schedules are therefore uniform, based on an eight-hour day.

605. Unless otherwise provided by the collective agreement, the work schedule is for at least one week and must be communicated at least 168 hours in advance in a written form. If not provided, the last work schedule will remain in force. According to section 97 (5) of the HLC, the employer may alter the communicated work schedule upon the occurrence of unforeseen circumstances in its business or financial affairs, at least ninety-six hours in advance before the start of the scheduled daily working time. The employer may alter the communicated work schedule also upon the employee's request made in writing.

606. According to section 99 of the HLC, the scheduled daily working time of an employee may not be less than four hours, with the exception of part-time work.

607. The work schedule of the employee:

- the daily working time cannot exceed twelve hours;
- the weekly working time cannot exceed forty-eight hours.

608. As regards the workers employed – as a stand-by worker or close relative –, according to the work schedule:

- the daily working time of employees cannot exceed twenty-four hours;
- the weekly working time of employees cannot exceed seventy-two hours;
- if so agreed by the parties in writing. The agreement may be terminated by the employee with fifteen days' notice effective as of the last day of the calendar month, or the last day of the working time banking arrangement if applicable.

---

272. KOZMA Anna – LŐRINCZ György – PÁL Lajos, *A Munka Törvénykönyvének magyarázata*, Budapest: HVG-Orac, 2020.

609. The scheduled daily or weekly working time of employees may exceed the time limits specified above by a maximum of one additional hour, if the date of switching to winter time falls inside the employee's working hours as defined in the work schedule.

610. The scheduled daily working time of employees will include the entire duration of on-call duty, if the duration of work cannot be measured.

b. Irregular Scheduling

611. Irregular work schedule means when the working time is defined within the framework of working time banking or payroll period, working time may be determined irregularly for each day of the week or for certain days only. In certain cases, the tasks of an enterprise (e.g., in the baking industry or hotel and catering) are not evenly distributed over time. This is also true in other spheres of activity, such as in the case of costing clerks, auditors, etc. In these cases, working hours may be distributed irregularly in accordance with the nature of the work.

612. The work schedule should be for at least one week and must be made known for the employee at least 168 hours in advance in writing. If not provided, the last work schedule will remain in force.

613. The types of irregular work schedule in the HLC are the following:

- flexible working arrangement;
- multi-shifted work schedule;
- split daily working schedule.

614. Flexible working arrangement means when the employer permits – in writing – the employee to schedule at least half of his/her daily working time on the weekly average in light of the unique characteristics of the job and in the interest of autonomous work organization.

615. In a *multi-shifted work schedule* the employees succeed each other at the same work stations according to a certain pattern in a day accomplishing their regular work. Their daily work time exceeds eight hours. This daily multi-shifted work time can be permanent or shifts can succeed each other weekly.

616. Split daily working time. By agreement of the parties, the employer may schedule daily working time in up to two periods split up over the day. Between the split daily working times scheduled at least two hours of rest must be provided.

617. In the case of an *irregular work schedule*, the duration of scheduled weekly working time shall be taken into account on the average:

(a) within the time periods defined under working time banking (Subsections (1) and (2) of section 94); or

(b) where justified by objective or technical reasons or reasons related to work organization, within a twelve-month period according to the collective agreement.

c. Scheduled Working Time on Sundays or Public Holidays

618. Scheduling the working time for Sunday. A change in the new HLC is that working on Sundays is permitted if the employer provides services meeting the public's needs or services directed to a foreign country and – taking into account the nature of the services – the work performance is (also) required on such day. Another important modification applies to the unequal scheduling of working time that does not allow the employer to schedule normal working time to Sundays; however, the HLC lists several cases where it may be possible. According to the HLC, work on Sundays may be scheduled within the framework of regular working time:

- if the employer generally operates on Sundays by the nature of its business;
- in seasonal work;
- if working in continuous shifts;
- for workers working in shifts;
- in stand-by jobs;
- for part-time workers working Saturdays and Sundays only;
- in connection with the provision of basic public services or trans frontier services, where it is necessary on that day stemming from the nature of the service;
- in the case of work performed abroad; and
- at employers engaged in commercial activities covered by the Trade Act, and at providers of services auxiliary to commercial activities and providers of tourist services of a commercial nature.

619. However, if an employee working in a stand-by job is scheduled to work on Sunday within the framework of regular working time, he/she may not be scheduled to work on the preceding Saturday.

620. Scheduling the working time to a public holiday[273] will remain possible in cases defined in the currently effective rules.

621. According to section 102 of the HLC, an employer is considered to operate on public holidays by the nature of its business or a specific job is approved to operate or to be carried out on public holidays:

(a) if the service provided is required on that particular day by way of local tradition or commonly accepted social custom directly connected to the public holiday; or
(b) if provided in the interest of the prevention or mitigation of any imminent danger of accident, natural disaster or serious damage or of any danger to health, the environment or property.

273. Public holidays in the HLC are 1 January, 15 March, Good Friday, Easter Monday, 1 May, Whit Monday, 20 August, 23 October, 1 November and 25–26 December.

622. Regular working time may be scheduled for public holidays in the following cases:

- if the employer generally operates on Sundays by the nature of its business;
- in seasonal work;
- if working in continuous shifts;
- in connection with the provision of basic public services or transfrontier services, where it is necessary on that day stemming from the nature of the service; and
- in the case of work performed abroad.

623. The provisions pertaining to scheduling work on public holidays shall apply if the public holiday falls on a Sunday, or on Easter Sunday or on Whit Sunday.[274]

C. Starting and Finishing Work

624. The schedule determines the duration of the daily working hours, but cannot fix the times when they begin and end. These must be determined with regard to the tasks performed and required working conditions. They form part of the collective agreement or the decision of the employer.

625. There is a new provision in the HLC. This is the procedure upon the termination of employment relationship before the expiry of working time banking arrangements. The legislator should answer the following question: what happens if the employee works more or less than the working pattern.

626. Basically, there are two possible cases:

(a) the employment relationship terminated *before* the expiry of the working time banking frame and the employee proportionally *worked more*: the employee's wages shall be calculated based on the standard work pattern, the daily working time and the time actually worked;
(b) the employment relationship terminated *before* the expiry of the working time banking frame and the employee proportionally *worked less*: The provisions on downtime shall apply if the employment relationship ends before the expiry of working time banking arrangements.[275]

---

274. CSÉFFÁN József, *A munka törvénykönyve és magyarázata*, Szeged: Szegedi Rendezvényszervező Kft., 2023.
275. HAJDÚ József, *IEL Labour Law, Hungary*, Wolters Kluwer, Kluwer Law Online, 2019. https://kluwerlawonline.com/Manuals/Corporate+Acquisitions+and+Mergers/705 (26 Jul. 2023).

III. Extra Working Hours

A. *Types of Extra Working Hours*

627. Extraordinary events may occur which interfere with economic tasks, such as natural disasters or bottlenecks in the supply of raw materials. In such cases, extra work is needed beyond the legal limits of working hours. The employer may, in an exceptional case, oblige the employee to perform work outside the official working hours. In the event of a provision in the collective agreement or upon the employee's request, notification of extraordinary work shall be made in writing. This extra work falls into four categories:

(a) overtime, in case of work outside scheduled working hours;
(b) overtime, in case of work over and above the working time cycle; or
(c) stand-by, as well as;
(d) in the case of working on-call duty during the period from the time of arrival at the workplace until the time at which work finishes or, if the employee is required to work at various locations, the period from the time of arrival at the first workplace until the time at which work finishes at the last workplace.

628. Work performed by an employee working extra hours by consent of the employer to compensate for any authorized leave of absence will not be considered special work duty.

B. *Overtime*

1. The Concept of Overtime

629. Overtime is work carried out by the employee beyond his/her regular daily working hours. If the work time is not divided into work days in advance, then work carried out over and above the work time period qualifies as overtime. No valid departure can be made therefrom. If the employee does work to make up for a permitted absence on the basis of agreement with the employer, this is considered overtime.

630. There is a guarantee that, if so stipulated by collective agreement or so requested by the employee, special work duty shall be ordered in writing. At the employee's request overtime work should be ordered in writing.

631. Overtime work may be ordered without limitation in the interest of the prevention or mitigation of any imminent danger of accident, natural disaster or serious damage or of any danger to health or the environment.

632. Overtime work on public holidays may be ordered:

(a) if the employee can otherwise be required to work on such day; or
(b) in the case of imminent danger of accident, natural disaster or serious damage or of any danger to health or the environment.

2. Limits to Overtime Working

633. The HLC restricts working overtime as follows:

(a) It must not harm the worker's health or be a threat to his/her safety, and it must not entail a disproportionate burden in terms of personal or family circumstances.
(b) Employed women from the time of pregnancy until the baby reaches the age of one year are not allowed to work overtime.
(c) Workers employed to work under unhealthy conditions are not allowed to work overtime.
(d) An employee who is a single parent with a child under the age of one shall only be assigned to work overtime with that employee's agreement.

634. According to section 109 of the HLC, the upper limit for total overtime per calendar year can be 250 hours. It is important to note that the entire duration of stand-by work shall be included in the extraordinary working hours if the period of performing work during stand-by work cannot be measured.

635. Voluntary overtime. In addition to the yearly 250 hours, a maximum of one hundred and fifty hours of overtime work can be ordered in a given calendar year subject to agreement between the employee and the employer in writing (voluntary overtime). The employee may withdraw from the agreement at the end of the given calendar year.

636. The maximum days of overtime provisions (250 + 150= 300 hours) must be applied proportionately:

(a) if the employment relationship commenced during the year;
(b) in the case of fixed-term employment relationships; or
(c) in connection with part-time jobs.

637. Limitation of overtime work. An employee caring for his/her child as a single parent may be required to work in special work duty only with his/her consent as from the time his/her child reaches one year of age up to the time when the child reaches four years of age.

638. For working overtime, workers receive a 50% bonus plus the usual wages. On the basis of an agreement between the parties, the worker may be entitled to a lump sum instead of the above-mentioned bonus. According to the regulation pertaining to employment or to the parties' agreement, the worker may be entitled to time off instead of receiving a bonus. Time off as a form of payment for working overtime must be equal to the amount of overtime. Time off must be given in the month in which the overtime was worked. If time off cannot be given by the deadline, then payment will be due him/her. The collective agreement or the parties' agreement may provide that an employee who determines his/her own work schedule will receive neither time off nor money.[276]

3. Stand-by and On-Call Duty

639. It often happens that certain jobs must be carried out at once, as with an unexpected consignment which must be unloaded at once. In such cases, the employer must provide the required number of workers and may order the workers to be in a state of readiness, either at home, at work, or elsewhere. There are two types of such kind of overtime: (1) stand-by and (2) on-call-duty work. The common feature of these two types of overwork is that an employee may be required to stand by and remain available beyond the regular daily working hours scheduled.

640. According to points a–b) of section 91 of the HLC stand-by work means a job in which:

(a) due to the nature of the tasks belonging to the job – on the basis of a longer period – there is no work performed in at least one-third of the normal working time and the employee may spend this time resting; or
(b) the work – with special regard to the specifics of the job and the conditions of performing work – entails much less effort than general on the employee's part.

641. Standing by for a period of over four hours may be ordered:

(a) in the interest of the uninterrupted provision of basic services for the general public (e.g., health care, public transportation, electric plant work, etc.);
(b) in the interest of the prevention or mitigation of any imminent danger of accident, natural disaster or serious damage or of any danger to health or the environment; and
(c) for the proper maintenance and safe operation of technological equipment.

642. The main difference between stand-by and on-call-duty work is the place of being ready to work. In case of stand-by work the employer will decide where and until when an employee may be required to be ready to perform his/her duty

276. HAJDÚ József – KUN Attila (eds), *Munkajog I.*, Budapest: Patrocinium, 2012. pp. 183–186.

(e.g., doctor in the night in the hospital). In case of the 'on-call-duty work' the location is specified by the employee where he/she wants to stay, but he/she can be reached at any time from the place of work (e.g., bus driver in his/her home, atomic plant engineer in his/her home).

643. When on stand-by or on-call duty, the employee is obliged to remain in a condition suitable for work. At the employee's request stand-by and on-call-duty work should be ordered in writing.

644. Unless otherwise prescribed in the collective agreement, the maximum duration of on-call duty an employee may be ordered to perform in a month or in a four-week period is one hundred sixty-eight (168) hours. Where working time is defined in specific cycles instead of on a daily basis, the length of on-call duty to be performed in a month or in a four-week period shall be determined in the average of the working time cycle.

645. Unless otherwise prescribed in the collective agreement, an employee may not be ordered 'on-call-duty work' during the weekly rest day or weekly rest period if he/she has been on on-call duty on his/her weekly rest day or during his/her weekly rest period during the preceding one hundred sixty-eight hour period.

646. Stand-by and on-call duty shall be scheduled for one month ahead and the actual time must be communicated one week in advance. The employer is entitled to depart from this provision under extraordinary circumstances, during which occupational safety and health requirements must be observed. Different rules for ordering stand-by and on-call duty may be laid down in the collective agreement.

647. Because it impedes the workers' use of leisure time, besides the time limitation, the law imposes certain restrictions. Being on call must not harm the workers' health or be a threat to his/her safety and must not entail a disproportionate burden in terms of personal or family circumstances.

648. There are some special categories of workers who are better protected:

(a) workers under 18 years of age;[277]
(b) women from the time of pregnancy until the baby has reached the age of three;[278] and

---

277. *Special Provisions for Young Persons* on working time: The working time of young people (under age 18) must not exceed eight hours daily or forty hours weekly. The working time cycle of young persons shall not be longer than one week. Any young person whose working time is over four and a half hours daily shall be entitled to at least thirty minutes of break-time. The daily resting period shall be at least twelve hours for young persons. Young persons cannot be used to work night hours, for special work duty or for stand-by or on-call duty. No deviation from the above-mentioned provisions are allowed.

278. A worker with a child between the age of three to four may be on call only if he/her consents. Being on call will not be subject to any restrictions if readiness is in the interest of preventing or averting accidents, natural disasters or serious damage.

(c) workers who are employed to work under unhealthy conditions, are not allowed to be on call.

649. Remuneration for stand-by and on-call-duty work. In respect of stand-by and on-call duty, a wage corresponding to 20% and 40%, respectively, of the personal basic wage is to be paid. But in connection with stand-by work, if the work performed cannot be measured, a 50% wage supplement must be paid.

650. However, if an employee on stand-by or on-call duty is ordered to work, remuneration for such work time shall be paid in accordance with the regular overtime remuneration, or a flat-rate payment shall be determined that is to include the on-call fee and the remuneration.[279]

§2. Rest Periods

I. The Concept of Rest Period

651. A rest period is the period during which the worker is absolved from the duty to work. Working and rest time are complementary. Rest periods provide the worker with time for relaxation and rejuvenation, the opportunity to spend substantial time with the family, for entertainment, cultural pursuits, and social interaction. While the rules concerning working time fix the temporal limits of employment, the rules governing rest define the period during which the worker does not need to work. The general principles governing time off are established by law. More precise regulation is provided by the collective agreement.

652. The HLC ensures the following types of rest period:

- breaks during daily working hours;
- periods of rest between working days;
- weekly rest days;
- public holidays;
- vacation leave.

653. In addition, further rest periods are also provided by law, such as extra holidays and days off for mothers of young children and fathers bringing up children alone.

654. The HLC also provides other periods during which the worker is not obliged to work. These are not rest periods because they are not provided for the purpose of rest, so it is better to call them exceptional time off. The purpose of this time off is to fulfil useful or important personal and family needs without encroaching on resting time. These are:

279. KOZMA Anna – LŐRINCZ György – PÁL Lajos, *A Munka Törvénykönyvének magyarázata*, Budapest: HVG-Orac, 2020.

- breaks for nursing mothers and workers continuing their studies;
- exceptional paid leave;
- unpaid leave.

II. Normal Rest Periods

A. *Features of Normal Rest Periods*

655. The common characteristic features of rest periods are as follows:

- the extent and conditions are fixed by law; any agreements to the contrary are invalid;
- the worker must take up rest periods and cannot refuse them;
- when the employer orders a shortening of the rest period, the worker may refuse to obey;
- the employer must compensate the worker for damages in the event of not ensuring rest time;
- a superior offending the rules regarding rest periods is financially liable and may be disciplined.[280]

B. *Breaks*

656. Breaks during daily working hours are provided for the worker to eat and hygiene. If the daily working hours or the duration of extraordinary working hours exceed six hours, and in the case of each additional three hours of work, a break from work of at least 20 minutes and not more than one hour must be provided for the worker – while interrupting work –, of which at least 20 minutes must be provided continuously.

657. The break-time must be provided after not less than three and before not more than six hours of work. The employer can schedule the break-times in several lots. In this case, the above-mentioned 20-minute rules can be derogated from, however, the duration of the break provided within the timeframe referred to above (six hours plus an additional three hours) must be at least twenty minutes.

658. In situations in which, because of three or more shifts or continuous operation, the working time cannot be interrupted, in positions of an 'on call' nature, or in positions where meals can be enjoyed within working hours, the break will be provided during working hours. If working overtime, the worker is also entitled to a break from work after every three consecutive hours of overtime.

280. HAJDÚ József, IEL Labour Law, Hungary, Wolters Kluwer, Kluwer Law Online, 2019. https://kluwerlawonline.com/Manuals/Corporate+Acquisitions+and+Mergers/705 (26 Jul. 2023).

C. Daily Rest Period

659. The provisions regarding working hours generally provide for an adequate period of rest after a day's work has been completed. In exceptional cases – as when overtime is required – this may prove to be impossible. To prevent excessive encroachment on leisure time section 104 of the HLC provides that a minimum of eleven hours is necessary before work is resumed.

660. The HLC derogates from the main rule, saying that at least eight hours of daily rest must be provided to employees working:

(a) split shifts;
(b) continuous shifts;
(c) multiple shifts;
(d) in seasonal jobs;
(e) in on-call-duty-like jobs.

661. Moreover, the collective agreement may stipulate that, subsequent to having been on 'on-call-duty', the employee cannot be entitled to any rest time.

D. Weekly Rest Days

1. Provision for Weekly Day of Rest

662. Basically, a worker is entitled to two days off a week and one of these should fall on a Sunday. However, in the case of an irregular work schedule, the weekly rest days may be scheduled irregularly as well.

663. In such case, after six days of work, one rest day must be allocated in a given week, with the exception of employees working in continuous shifts, shift work or in seasonal jobs.

664. With the exception set out in paragraph *f)* of Subsection (1) of section 101 (part-time workers working Saturdays and Sundays only), workers can be allocated at least one weekly rest day in a given month on a Sunday.[281]

2. Provision for Weekly Rest Day

665. Each week two rest days must be scheduled (weekly rest day). Weekly rest days may be scheduled irregularly as well.

281. DUDÁS Katalin – GYULAVÁRI Tamás – HORVÁTH István – Hős Nikolett – KULISITY Mária – HUNGLER Sára – KÁRTYÁS Gábor – KUN Attila – PETROVICS Zoltán – RÁCZ Réka, *Munkajog – V. átdolgozott kiadás*, Budapest: ELTE Eötvös Kiadó, 2019.

666. In the case of an irregular work schedule, after six consecutive days of work, at least one weekly rest day shall be allocated. In the case of an irregular work schedule, for employees:

(a) working in continuous shifts;
(b) working in shifts;
(c) employed for seasonal work at least one weekly rest day shall be allocated per month.

667. With the exception of part-time employees working on Saturdays and Sundays (set out in paragraph f) of Subsection (1) of section 101), at least one weekly rest day must be allocated at least once in a given month on a Sunday.

668. There is an important judgment of the European Court of Justice in Case C-477/21 – MÁV-START on the daily rest is additional to weekly rest even when it directly precedes the latter. This is also the case when national legislation grants workers a period of weekly rest greater than that required by EU law.

669. The facts: A train driver employed by MÁV-START, the Hungarian national railway company, challenges before the Miskolc Regional Court the decision of his employer not to grant him a daily rest period of at least 11 consecutive hours (which the worker must be granted during each 24-hour period under the Working Time Directive) when that period precedes or follows a weekly rest period or a period of leave. MÁV-START claims before the court that since the collective agreement applicable to the case grants a minimum weekly rest period (of at least 42 hours) that is well in excess of that required by the Directive (24 hours), its employee is not in any way disadvantaged by its decision.

670. The Miskolc Regional Court asks the Court of Justice in particular whether, under the Directive, a daily rest period granted concurrently with a weekly rest period forms part of that weekly rest period.

671. By the judgment, the Court notes that daily and weekly rest periods constitute two autonomous rights, which pursue different objectives. Daily rest allows a worker to remove himself or herself from his or her working environment for a specific number of hours, which must not only be consecutive but must also directly follow a period of work. Weekly rest allows a worker to rest during each seven-day period. Consequently, workers must be guaranteed the actual enjoyment of each of those rights. Thus, a situation where daily rest formed part of weekly rest would render meaningless the right to daily rest, by depriving the worker of its actual enjoyment where he or she benefits from his or her right to weekly rest. In that regard, the Court finds that the Directive does not merely lay down, as a whole, a minimum period for the right to weekly rest, but is careful to expressly state that that period is additional to the period relating to the right to daily rest. It follows that the daily rest period does not form part of the weekly rest period but is additional to it, even if the daily rest period directly precedes the latter.

672. The Court also notes that the more favourable provisions laid down in Hungarian law, in comparison with the Directive, in respect of the minimum weekly rest period cannot deprive a worker of other rights which that directive confers on him or her, and in particular of the right to daily rest. Therefore, daily rest must be granted irrespective of the length of the weekly rest period provided for by the applicable national legislation.[282]

3. Cumulate Weekly Rest Days

673. Specific circumstances in certain branches of industry or jobs may necessitate giving four or more consecutive days off a fortnight. This may be desirable from the worker's point of view, as in the construction industry where workers tend to be employed far away from their homes. According to this requirement, a collective agreement may stipulate that rest days, except in the case of work hazardous to health, be allocated together, i.e., every fortnight or even monthly; however, one rest day shall coincide with a Sunday. This provision can only be departed from in regard to employers and positions of a seasonal nature, not in regard to a position that is hazardous to health.[283]

E. Public Holidays

674. The worker shall not perform work on the public holidays fixed by law. These are: 1 January, 15 March, Easter Monday, 1 May, Whitsun Monday, 20 August, 23 October, 1 November and 25–26 December. The date of some public holidays (e.g., Easter) changes; therefore, the working schedule must change accordingly.

675. The Minister responsible for employment issues must annually regulate the changes in the work schedule justified by public holidays. In the course of such changes, however, no Sunday can be declared a working day. For public holidays, a worker receives his/her average wage, except in the case of workers who are paid monthly and whose monthly salaries are inclusive of holiday pay. When a public holiday coincides with the usual day of rest, wages are not paid because no loss is entailed.

676. N.B.: Employees may be required to work on public holidays if *(a)* the employer operates in continuous shifts or if the employer operates on such days by nature of its business, *(b)* if work performed with means of information technology and informatics is necessary on such a day in order to provide service for foreign

---

282. Daily rest is additional to weekly rest even when it directly precedes the latter (2023); https://curia.europa.eu/jcms/upload/docs/application/pdf/2023-03/cp230039en.pdf (26 Jul. 2023).
283. BANKÓ Zoltán, BERKE Gyula, KISS György, SZŐKE Gergely László *Nagykommentár a munka törvénykönyvéhez*, Wolters Kluwer, Budapest 2019.

countries and *(c)* during the period of posting abroad if, pursuant to the law applicable in the country of posting, work may be required this day. No deviation from this provision is considered valid.

677. An employer or a specific job is approved to operate or to be carried out on public holidays if the service provided is required on that particular day by way of local tradition or commonly accepted social custom, or if provided in connection with the protection of human life, health, physical integrity or property.[284]

F. Vacation

1. Components of Vacation

678. Employees are entitled to paid annual leave based on the time spent at work, comprising vested vacation time and extra vacation time. A regular vacation is a resting period of more than twenty working days. Within the regular vacation (a) basic and (b) extra leave may be distinguished (section 115 of the HLC).

679. For the period of time during which an employment relationship is suspended, the employee is entitled to usually unpaid vacation time as follows:

(a) if being incapacitated to work due to illness;
(b) if receiving treatment in a healthcare institution related to a human reproduction procedure;
(c) for the duration of mandatory medical examination; furthermore
(d) for the length of time required for donating blood, for a period of at least four hours;
(e) if they are nursing mothers, for one hour twice daily, or two hours twice daily in the case of twins during the first six months of breastfeeding, and thereafter for one hour daily or two hours daily in the case of twins until the end of the ninth month;
(f) for two working days upon the death of a relative;
(g) for the duration of classes in the case of employees pursuing elementary school studies, for the duration of training if participating in initial and continuing training by agreement of the parties;
(h) for the duration of being engaged in fire-fighting operations in a voluntary or industrial fire brigade;
(i) when called upon by the court or an authority, or for the duration of participating in proceedings in person;
(j) for any duration of absence due to personal or family reasons, or as justified by unavoidable external reasons; furthermore
(k) for any duration specified by employment regulations.

---

284. HAJDÚ József – KUN Attila (eds), *Munkajog I.*, Budapest: Patrocinium, 2012. p. 182.

680. The employer, if so required to investigate the circumstances of an employee's breach of obligations, may exempt the employee from the requirement of availability and from work duty for the period required for the inquiry, in any case for up to thirty days.

2. Basic Vacation

681. According to section 116 of the HLC, the basic vacation leave is twenty working days. It increases to:

(a) 21 working days on the employee turning 25;
(b) 22 days on the employee turning 28;
(c) 23 days on the employee turning 31;
(d) 24 days on the employee turning 33;
(e) 25 days on the employee turning 35;
(f) 26 days on the employee turning 37;
(g) 27 days on the employee turning 39;
(h) 28 days on the employee turning 41;
(i) 29 days on the employee turning 43;
(j) 30 days on the employee turning 45.

682. The employee will first be entitled to more leave in the year he/she turns the age as specified in the previous paragraph.[285]

3. Additional Paid Leave

683. In certain cases the basic vacation leave is not considered adequate to restore or maintain the health and working potential of the worker, so additional leave is provided. According to the HLC, the main types of extra vacation leave are the following:

(1) having child in the household (child leave);
(2) fathers of a new-born child (fathers' vacation);
(3) young workers;
(4) underground and hazardous work;
(5) disabled workers.

684. *1.* As for *child leave*, workers are entitled to extra vacation time as follows:

(a) two working days for one child;
(b) four working days for two children;

---

285. CSÉFFÁN József, *A munka törvénykönyve és magyarázata*, Szeged: Szegedi Rendezvényszervező Kft., 2023.

(c) a total of seven working days for more than two children under sixteen years of age.

685. The above-mentioned extra vacation time will be increased for children with disabilities by two working days per child.

686. For the purposes of entitlement to extra vacation time, a child will first be taken into consideration in the year of his/her birth and for the last time in the year in which he/she reaches the age of sixteen.

687. *2.* There is a special paid extra vacation for *fathers of a new-born child.* According to Subsection (4) of section 118 of the HLC, upon the birth of his child, a father is entitled to five days of extra vacation time, or seven working days in the case of twins, until the end of the second month from the date of birth, which is allocated on the days requested by the father. Such leave will be provided also if the child is stillborn or dies.

688. *3. Young workers* are entitled to five extra days of vacation time each year. The last time such a benefit applies is in the year when the young worker reaches eighteen years of age.

689. *4.* Employees permanently working *underground* or spending at least three hours a day on a job exposed to ionizing radiation are entitled to five extra working days of vacation each year.

690. *5. Disabled workers.* Employees having suffered a degree of health impairment of at least 50% as diagnosed by the body of rehabilitation experts and blind employees are entitled to five working days of extra vacation time a year.

691. An employee, whose employment relationship was concluded or terminated during the year, is entitled to a commensurate portion of vacation time for such year. Any fraction of a day that comes to half a day shall count as a full working day.

692. It often happens that extra leave is due for more than one reason. In the absence of a provision on this in a collective agreement, an employee is entitled to extra leave running consecutively where more than one circumstance applies to him/her.

4. Calculation of Leave

693. In calculating leave, the working days according to the work schedule are taken into consideration. If the worker's employment commenced in the course of the year, he/she is entitled to a proportionate part of the leave. If the calculation of leave gives a fragment of a day, any fragment amounting to half a day will count as a full working day.

5. Taking up Leave

694. The scheduling of vacation should take into consideration both the continuity of production and the worker's personal interests. The period of leave is determined by the employer after having discussed it with the worker. However, the employer will allocate seven days of basic leave at a time that accords with the employee's request except in the first three months of the employment. The employee must indicate his/her request in this respect at least fifteen days prior to commencement of the leave.

695. Unless otherwise agreed, vacation must be allocated to contain at least fourteen consecutive days at a time.

696. With the exception set out in section 125, vacation time must not be financially compensated. There is only one exception: upon termination of the employment relationship, compensation must be provided for any vacation time not previously allocated as due.

697. According to section 123 of the HLC, as a general rule, the vacation time must be allocated in the year in which it is due. Vacation time is considered allocated during the year when it is due, provided that it begins during that year and the portion allocated in the following year does not exceed five working days.

698. However, if the employment relationship commenced on the first of October or subsequently, the employer is entitled to allocate vacation time by 31 March of the next year. If vacation time cannot be allocated as such, for reasons within the employee's control, it must be allocated within sixty days after the cause is remedied. By agreement of the parties, the employer is entitled to allocate one-third of the basic vacation time specified by the end of the year following the year when due.

699. In the event of economic reasons of particular importance or any direct and consequential reason arising in connection with its operations, the employer:

(a) may amend – postpone maximum sixty days – the date of vacation previously agreed upon, except paternity leave;
(b) may recall the employee from vacation;
(c) may allocate one-fourth of the employee's vacation time by 31 March of the following year if so stipulated in the collective agreement.

700. The employer shall state the reasons for the above measure in writing and, in the event of a postponement of leave for a maximum of sixty days, shall at the same time inform the employee of the date of the leave it proposes to grant.

701. Vacation time must be allocated according to the working days stipulated in the work schedule. If the work scheduled differs from the daily working time, in the allocation of vacation time the employee shall be relieved from work for the duration scheduled, and the vacation time allocated shall be accounted and recorded in the same number of hours. In the absence of a work schedule, the vacation shall be allocated based on the standard work pattern and on daily working time.

6. Interruption of Leave

702. Employers must reimburse the employees for any damages and/or expenses incurred in connection with the modification or interruption of vacation. In addition, the time spent by travelling from the place of stay during the vacation to the place of employment, or the return trip and the time spent working will not be included in the vacation time.

7. Records of Working Time and Rest Periods

703. According to section 134 of the HLC, employers must keep the records of:

(a) the durations of regular working time and overtime;
(b) the durations of stand-by duty;
(c) periods of leave.

704. The records aforementioned must be updated regularly and must contain facilities to identify the time of commencement and ending of any regular and overtime work and stand-by duty.

8. Wages

705. Leave can be ensured only if financial provision is guaranteed for that period. The law provides that during vacation the worker should receive his/her average wage.[286]

III. Extra Rest Periods and Time Off

A. Principles

706. The difference between rest periods and time off is that, first, rest periods occur regularly at given intervals. Extra rest periods and time off are as a result of an unexpected, extraordinary event. Second, the worker has the right to regular rest periods. In contrast with this, extra rest periods and time off are not always given as of right but depend in part on the decision of the employer. Wages are due for normal rest periods such as annual vacation, but they are not necessarily paid for

286. HAJDÚ József, IEL Labour Law, Hungary, Wolters Kluwer, Kluwer Law Online, 2019. https://kluwerlawonline.com/Manuals/Corporate+Acquisitions+and+Mergers/705 (26 Jul. 2023).

extraordinary leave or time off. Extra periods and time off due to women and mothers will be dealt with in a subsequent Chapter.

B. Sick Leave

707. A worker is entitled to fifteen working days annual sick leave for the time he/she is unable to work because of illness; not included here is inability to work as a result of an industrial accident or an occupational illness as stipulated in the social insurance regulations. If the employee is not required to work on public holidays, such days shall be treated as working days.

708. The worker's inability to work shall be certified by the doctor who treats the worker. During sick leave, the employee is entitled to 70% of his/her 'wage for absence'. In the event of employment commencing in the course of the year, the employee will be entitled to a proportionate amount of sick leave. However, if the employee has already been employed in the course of the year, this cannot be more than the as-yet unused part of the sick leave due for the calendar year. Unused sick leave cannot be carried over into the next calendar year.[287]

C. Extraordinary Paid and Unpaid Leave

1. General Characteristics

709. The purpose of extraordinary paid and unpaid leave is to provide workers with the opportunity to fulfil their personal or family needs without encroaching on their rest time. The worker does not enjoy a right to extraordinary paid leave or unpaid leave. The period of unpaid leave is fixed by the employer – after taking into consideration the reasons. Some of the needs are equally important to society as a whole (as when a worker obtains a new qualification). In such cases, the law or a collective agreement provides for the extraordinary leave for the worker.

710. Employees shall convey the request for leave of absence without pay in writing, at least fifteen days in advance. The leave of absence without pay shall end at the time the employee has indicated, or at the earliest on the thirtieth day from the date of delivery of the legal act for the termination of leave. The above-mentioned provisions will not apply to volunteer military service, as defined in section 132 of the HLC.

2. Maternity Leave

711. Women in the pregnancy period or giving birth will be entitled to twenty-four weeks of maternity leave. Such leave is scheduled so as to commence four (4)

287. HORVÁTH István, *Az új munka törvénykönyve*, Budapest: Vezinfó Kiadó és Tanácsadó Kft. 2012. pp. 153–154.

weeks prior to the expected time of birth if possible. Maternity leave is also provided to a woman who has been given custody of a child for the purpose of adoption. If the child receives treatment in an institute for premature infants, the unused portion of the maternity leave may be used after the child has been released from the institute up to the end of the first year following birth. The duration of maternity leave, except where entitlement is specifically connected to work, will be recognized as time spent at work.

712. Maternity leave ends:

(a) if the child is stillborn, six weeks subsequent to such birth;
(b) if the child dies, on the fifteenth day following death;
(c) on the day following placement of the child – according to the provisions set forth in specific other legislation – into temporary custody, temporary or permanent foster care, or in a social institution with room and board for over thirty days.

In the cases described above under points b)–c), the period of maternity leave is no less than six weeks from the date of birth.

3. Unpaid Leave for Child Raising

713. The employee is entitled to a leave of absence without pay:

(a) until the child reaches the age of 3, in order to care for the child at home;
(b) until the child reaches the age of 10, during the period of eligibility for child-care allowance, provided that the employee cares for the child at home;
(c) in order – in the event of the child's illness – to provide home care until the child reaches the age of 12.

714. The child-raising leave ends:

(a) if the child is stillborn;
(b) if the child dies, on the fifteenth day following death;
(c) on the day following placement of the child – according to the provisions set forth in specific other legislation – into temporary custody, temporary or permanent foster care, or in a social institution with room and board for over thirty days.

4. Father's Work-Time Allowance

715. Upon the birth of his child, a father will be entitled to seven days of work-time allowance, which the employer will allocate within the two-month period following the date of birth on the days requested by the father. Absentee pay will be provided for the duration of such work-time allowance. The father will be entitled to the allowance, even if the child is stillborn or dies. In accordance with the HLC 'father' means a biological or adoptive father who has parental custody. The absentee pay that is due for the duration of worktime allowance is financed from the central budget as decreed by the Government.

5. Unpaid Leave for Nursing

716. Upon the worker's request, the employer must permit unpaid leave for the purpose of nursing or providing home care of a close relative (which foreseeably may exceed thirty days). Such leave shall be for the duration of the nursing, but with a maximum of two years and provided the employee does the nursing personally. Home nursing and its justification is certified by the doctor treating the person in need of nursing (close relatives are spouse, relation of direct descent, spouse's relation of direct descent, adoptive, step– and foster child, adoptive, step– and foster parent, sibling and companion).

6. Unpaid Leave for Voluntary Military Service

717. Employees are entitled to unpaid leave for the duration of actual voluntary reserve military service. On the basis of general military service obligation, all males of Hungarian citizenship living in Hungary are obliged to conduct military service. This service obligation starts at the age of 17 and terminates at the age of 50. Those individuals are considered to be members of the reserve force who have previously conducted military service, been prepared for some position, that is they are trained for military professions. The maximum duration of reservist military services can be up to ninety days, which can be conducted in several parts of maximum thirty days each by the law. For the period of their practical military service, the volunteer reservists get the same salary as the professional and contract personnel. For the on-call-duty period when they are ready to be drafted (emergency, mobilization, etc.) they get annual on-call-duty allowance.[288]

288. HAJDÚ József – KUN Attila (eds), *Munkajog I.*, Budapest: Patrocinium, 2012. pp. 197–199.

Chapter 4. Remuneration and Benefits

§1. Wages

I. The Concept of Wages

718. According to the HLC, a worker is entitled to a wage from the employer on the basis of his/her employment. The basic wage must be at least the mandatory minimum wage. Any agreement departing therefrom will be void. In the absence of an agreement departing therefrom, the employee will be entitled to a wage corresponding to the basic wage specified in the employment contract.

719. Principle of equal pay. In respect of the remuneration of employees for the same work or for work to which equal value is attributed, the principle of equal treatment must be observed (principle of equal pay). The equal value of work for the purposes of the principle of equal treatment should be determined based on the nature of work, its quality and quantity, working conditions, vocational training, physical and intellectual efforts, experience and responsibilities.

720. Within the scope of the principle of equal pay, 'wage' shall mean any remuneration provided to the employee directly or indirectly in cash or kind, as well as social benefits, based on his/her employment. The wages of employees – whether based on the nature or category of the work or on performance – should be determined in compliance with the principle of equal treatment.

II. Evaluation of Labour

A. *The Wage System*

1. The Concept of the Wage System

721. The requirement of adequate reward for the quality and quantity of work can be fulfilled if there is a measure which considers both the quality and quantity of work and the extent of time worked. This system functions by two methods. One is the wage-rate, the other is a unit of work which can be fixed for a time period or a natural unit (piece, meter) or by specifying a level or task (e.g., there is a 10% reduction for the production of shoddy goods). Wages are determined simultaneously by these two methods. When wages are calculated according to the number of units produced, this is called task wage (piecework). When wages are calculated according to time worked without regard to the number of units produced, this is known as payment according to basic rate. According to the HLC, the wage due to the worker may be established as a time wage (wage rate), a task wage or a combination of the two. However, the basic wage must be specified on a time basis (time wage).

722. According to Subsection (3) of section 137 of the HLC, wages in the form of performance-based wages (task-based wage) exclusively may be established only if so agreed in the employment contract. This also applies where wages are paid on a time and performance basis combined, if the time rate is lower than the basic wage.[289]

2. Payment in Accordance with Time Worked

723. In the case of a wage system based on time, the sum of the wage depends on the period spent working. The wage rate is multiplied by the hours worked. A main disadvantage of such a system is that it bears no relation to the quality or quantity of work. Thus, it provides no incentive to increase efficiency and to improve the quality of output.

724. The monthly basic wage must be divided by the number of hours required in the given month according to the general working schedule, then this amount must be multiplied by the number of hours required during the period in question according to the general working schedule.

3. Task-Wage (Piecework) Rates

725. In the case of piecework systems, the wage depends directly on the amount produced. Piecework systems are advantageous in ensuring production of a given quantity and quality. They are in this respect in the interest of society and the individual workers.

726. Generally, the principle is that the piecework system should be used in every case where it offers advantages for production. Performance requirements and the task-wage factors will be determined by the employer. They must be made known in writing to the workers concerned.

727. If wages are paid on the basis of performance, performance requirements will be determined by the employer on the basis of preliminary and objective surveys and calculations covering the potential to perform 100% of such requirements during regular working hours. Performance requirements are to be established, and employee groups under the same performance requirements are to be determined in a manner consistent with the employer's operating conditions, such as the objective requirements relating to the performance of work, work organization and the technology employed.

289. DUDÁS Katalin – GYULAVÁRI Tamás – HORVÁTH István – Hős Nikolett – KULISITY Mária – HUNGLER Sára – KÁRTYÁS Gábor – KUN Attila – PETROVICS Zoltán – RÁCZ Réka, *Munkajog – V. átdolgozott kiadás*, Budapest: ELTE Eötvös Kiadó, 2019.

728. In the event of any dispute concerning performance requirements, the burden of proof to verify that the procedure did not violate the above-mentioned provisions lies with the employer.

729. In the case of full-time employees whose wages are paid on the basis of performance only, a guaranteed salary is to be paid of an amount up to the minimum wage or guaranteed wage minimum.

730. According to section 1, Article 136 of the HLC, the basic wage or the performance wage must be at least the mandatory lowest wage (minimum wage or guaranteed wage minimum) in accordance with the conditions specified; no deviation from this provision will be considered valid. The performance factors for full-time employees will be established so that the wages payable upon 100% fulfilment of the normative performance requirement and upon the completion of the entire work time shall amount to at least the mandatory minimum wage; no deviation from this provision will be considered valid.[290]

B. *Supplementary Payment*

1. The Concept of Supplementary Payment

731. When normal wage rates are fixed, special circumstances which may arise are not taken into account. Thus, provision is made for the payment of supplementary wages. These take the form of premium or bonus supplements and gratuities.

732. If the regulation pertaining to employment or the agreement between the parties prescribes the payment of a wage supplement, the worker's basic wage will be the basis for its calculation in the absence of an agreement departing therefrom.

733. Supplementary payments are generally determined by collective agreement or by agreement between the parties by the employment contract or by the employer unilaterally. In some cases, the law provides for supplementary payments in order to protect the workers' interests (some of these are treated in other Chapters, e.g., overtime supplement).

2. Night-Work Supplement

734. Employees – other than those entitled to shift supplement – will be entitled to a 15% wage supplement for night work, provided that it exceeds one hour.

735. *Night work* means work carried out between twenty-two hours and six hours.

---

290. HAJDÚ József – KUN Attila (eds), *Munkajog I.*, Budapest: Patrocinium, 2012. pp. 203–207.

3. Sunday Supplement

736. The 50% Sunday supplement is payable both for scheduled work, and also for unscheduled work in the cases already specified in the legislation (e.g., employees with working schedules involving multiple shifts).

4. Public Holidays Supplement

737. The public holidays in Hungary fixed by law and these are: 1 January, 15 March, Easter Monday, 1 May, Whitsun Monday, 20 August, 23 October, 1 November and 25–26 December. The date of some public holidays (e.g., Easter) change; therefore, the working schedule must change accordingly.

738. Employees required to work on public holidays in regular working time will be entitled to a 100% wage supplement. The same amount of wage supplement will be paid for working on Easter Sunday or Whit Sunday, or on public holidays falling on Sundays.

5. Overtime Supplement

739. In accordance with the relevant employment regulations or by agreement of the parties, employees will be entitled to a 50% wage supplement or to time off:

(a) for overtime work performed in addition to the daily working time shown in the work schedule;
(b) for work performed within the framework of working time banking; or
(c) for work performed above and beyond the payroll period.

740. The duration of time off may not be less than the overtime work ordered or the work performed and will be remunerated by a commensurate part of the basic wage.

741. Where overtime work is ordered on the scheduled weekly rest day (weekly rest period), a 100% wage supplement must be paid. The wage supplement will be 50% if the employer provides another weekly rest day (weekly rest period). When overtime work is ordered on a public holiday, the employee shall be entitled to the above-mentioned (50%) wage supplement.

742. The time off or the weekly rest day (weekly rest period) will be allocated at the latest during the month following the month when the overtime work was performed, or by the end of the banking of working time or the payroll period in the case of an irregular work schedule. In connection with work performed in derogation of the above, or over and above the relevant arrangement, the time off must be provided at the latest by the end of the next working time banking cycle. By agreement of the parties, time off should be provided at the latest by 31 December of the following year.

6. Shift-Work Supplement

743. If the beginning of the scheduled daily working time of employees changes frequently,[291] for work performed between eighteen hours and six hours a 30% wage supplement (special payment for shift work) must be paid.

7. Stand-by and On-Call-Duty Supplement

744. For stand-by duty 40%, and for on-call duty 20% wage supplement must be paid, respectively. However, in connection with stand-by work, if the work performed cannot be measured, a 50% wage supplement must be paid.

745. In the employment contract the parties:

(a) in lieu of wage supplement;
(b) in the case of stand-by and on-call duty; may stipulate a fixed monthly payment covering regular wages and wage supplements as well.[292]

III. Administration of the Wage System

A. *Fixing of Individual Wages*

746. A distinction must be made between the determination of the wage rate and a worker's individual wage. The law or the collective agreement, or the agreement between the parties contains the rules of a normative character which generally determine the wage rate in an abstract way. A worker's basic wage must be fixed in the employment contract on the basis of the wage rate.

B. *Minimum Wage System*

747. The minimum wage is determined by the law. The minimum wage is a guarantee for workers to receive a decent wage. The mandatory minimum wage and guaranteed wage minimum specified by the Government for certain groups of

291. Changes shall be considered frequent if – on a monthly basis – the beginning of the scheduled daily working time differs for at least one-third of all working days, and if the earliest and the latest start time are at least four hours apart.
292. BANKÓ Zoltán, BERKE Gyula, KISS György, SZŐKE Gergely László *Nagykommentár a munka törvénykönyvéhez*, Wolters Kluwer, Budapest 2019.

employees may differ. The amount and scope of the mandatory minimum wage and guaranteed wage minimum must, in particular, be determined based on the requirements prescribed for specific occupations, the indicators of the national labour market, the status of the national economy, and the unique requirements of certain economic sectors and geographical areas in terms of workforce. According to section 153 of the HLC, in Hungary there are two types of minimum wage: (1) compulsory minimum wage[293] and (2) guaranteed wage minimum.[294] The amount of the mandatory minimum wage and guaranteed wage minimum must be reviewed each calendar year.

748. At the least, the compulsory lowest wage (minimum wage) must be due as the basic wage or the task wage, in accordance with the conditions specified; no valid departure can be made therefrom. The performance requirement, normative for a full-time employee, will be established in such a way that, in the event of a 100% fulfilment and completion of the full working hours, the wage due will amount to at least the compulsory minimum wage. No valid departure can be made therefrom.[295]

749. A compulsory minimum wage will be established in a certain field or area if this is necessary considering the working conditions. The mandatory minimum wage specified by the Government for certain groups of employees may differ.

750. The amount and scope of the mandatory minimum wage shall, in particular, be determined based on the requirements prescribed for specific occupations, the indicators of the national labour market, the status of the national economy, and the unique requirements of certain economic sectors and geographical areas in terms of workforce.

751. The compulsory minimum wage payable to employees and the guaranteed wage minimum is established by the Government. The amount of the mandatory minimum wage shall be reviewed each calendar year.[296]

Table 1 The Rate of the Gross Compulsory Minimum Wage and Guaranteed Wage Minimum in Hungary 2010–2023

	Compulsory Minimum Wage	*Guaranteed Wage Minimum*
2010	HUF 73,500 (approx. EUR 245)	HUF 89,500 (approx. EUR 298)
2011	HUF 78,000 (approx. EUR 260)	HUF 94,000 (approx. EUR 313)
2012	HUF 93,000 (approx. EUR 310)	HUF 108,000 (approx. EUR 360)
2013	HUF 98,000 (approx. EUR 350)	HUF 114,000 (approx. EUR 400)

293. Compulsory minimum wage is a minimum wage paid for every worker, except skilled workers.
294. The guaranteed wage minimum is a minimum wage paid for skilled workers.
295. http://ado.hu/rovatok/munkaugyek/minimalber-garantalt-berminimum-2013-ban (26 Jul. 2023).
296. https://www.ksh.hu/stadat_files/mun/hu/mun0069.html (26 Jul. 2023).

	Compulsory Minimum Wage	*Guaranteed Wage Minimum*
2014	HUF 101,500 (approx. EUR 338)	HUF 118,000 (approx. EUR 394)
2015	HUF 105,000 (approx. EUR 350)	HUF 122,000 (approx. EUR 400)
2016	HUF 111,000 (approx. EUR 364)	HUF 129,000 (approx. EUR 423)
2017	HUF 127,500 (approx. EUR 350)	HUF 161,000 (approx. EUR 528)
2018	HUF 138,000 (approx. EUR 412)	HUF 180,500 (approx. EUR 583)
2019	HUF 149,000 (approx. EUR 465)	HUF 195,000 (approx. EUR 609)
2020	HUF 161,000 (approx. EUR 482)	HUF 210,600 (approx. EUR 631)
2021	HUF 167,400 (approx. EUR 458)	HUF 219,000 (approx. EUR 610)
2022	HUF 200,000 (approx. EUR 557)	HUF 260,000 (approx. EUR 724)
2023	HUF 232,000 (approx. EUR 619)	HUF 296,400 (approx. EUR 791)

Source: Author's own source.

IV. Remuneration for Periods of Inactivity

A. General Principles

752. As a rule, wages are paid only for work done. When a worker does not work, he/she is not entitled to remuneration. However, there are, of course, exceptions to this general rule. These exceptions may be divided into four groups. In the first belong rest periods. In the second are those instances when the worker does not fulfil his/her labour duties on the instructions of an outside authority. To the third group belong cases where the worker is not obliged to work according to provisions of law. In the fourth category are those cases when the worker does not work for reasons arising within the enterprise.

B. Remuneration for Rest Periods

753. Remuneration is paid for holidays, regular annual vacation and in certain cases for extraordinary leave. Workers are not paid for breaks during daily working hours.

1. The Public Holiday

754. Remuneration is paid equal to the hourly rate of the worker's absentee pay. This is to ensure that the public holiday is a genuine period of relaxation. (Those getting a monthly wage are an exception because such a wage includes remuneration due for public holidays.)

2. Annual Vacation

755. An employee is entitled to his/her absentee pay for the time of his/her annual holiday which includes both basic and extra leave.

3. Extraordinary Leave

756. Similarly, during a period of extraordinary paid leave the worker receives his/her average wage.

C. Wages for Periods Not Worked on the Directive of an Outside Authority

757. In some cases, the worker may be ordered not to work by the order of a certain external authority. As work ceases in the common interest, it is reasonable that the burden must be borne by society and that the worker receives wages for the period missed. Examples of such periods are where a worker has to be present at an election, or in court of law as a witness or has to act as a councillor. The amount, unless otherwise specified by law, is always the average wage.

D. Other Types of Absence

758. Different types of circumstances belong to this group. They have in common: absence as a result of an urgent personal or family situation, such as the death of a close relative or nursing, a social activity. The worker receives his/her absentee pay for the period of absence unless otherwise provided by law.[297]

297. HAJDÚ József, IEL Labour Law, Hungary, Wolters Kluwer, Kluwer Law Online, 2019. https://kluwerlawonline.com/Manuals/Corporate+Acquisitions+and+Mergers/705 (26 Jul. 2023).

E. Wages for Periods of Inactivity for Reasons Arising Within the Enterprise

759. Here, three categories must be distinguished: exemption from work, unlawful prevention of working activity, and closure. In these cases, if the law does not provide otherwise, basic wages are due to the worker.

1. Exemption from Work

760. Performing labour is not only the duty but also the right of the worker. So, the employer cannot exempt him/her from work except in cases determined by law or on the basis of his/her own demand.

2. Unlawful Prevention of Working Activity

761. If an employer unlawfully prevents a worker from working, the average wage must be paid throughout the entire period. The unlawful behaviour of the employer forms the basis of the duty to pay, so culpability is not the condition of the duty mentioned earlier. Unlawful circumstances may be divided into two sets: first, there are those cases where the employer is unwilling to provide work, or wrongly suspends a worker, or does not provide the necessary safety equipment so that the worker legitimately refuses to work. The second set of circumstances includes those cases where the employer infringes a worker's legal rights. In the case of employee's culpability, the employee is also entitled to compensation.

3. Temporary Closure or Standstill

762. Sometimes, for reasons internal to the employer, a worker is prevented from working. These include, for example, shortage of raw materials or fuel or breakdown of machinery. In such cases, labour law provides that his/her basic wage is due to the worker, even if there is no single individual in the enterprise who may be held liable. The employee, if he/she is unable to carry out work for a reason within the employer's scope of operation, will be entitled to his/her basic wage for the resulting lost working time (stop time). In the absence of a regulation pertaining to employment or an agreement between the parties departing therefrom, this provision shall also be normative when the employer, in an economically justified case, makes the employee temporarily work shorter time.[298]

---

298. DUDÁS Katalin – GYULAVÁRI Tamás – HORVÁTH István – Hős Nikolett – KULISITY Mária – HUNGLER Sára – KÁRTYÁS Gábor – KUN Attila – PETROVICS Zoltán – RÁCZ Réka, *Munkajog – V. átdolgozott kiadás*, Budapest: ELTE Eötvös Kiadó, 2019.

F. Wage for Absence Period

763. The wage for absence period will be paid where the regulations pertaining to employment prescribe the payment of wages in the absence of work done, without specifying the actual sum.

764. The calculation of absence payment is as follows:

(a) by default, the amount of the absence pay must be calculated on the basis of the applicable monthly basic wage and the average wage supplements, if any;
(b) in the case of employees who are paid performance-based wages and/or are eligible for wage supplements, the amount of such wages and supplements paid over the previous six months must also be considered in the course of calculating the amount of the absentee pay.

765. In simple terms: if there is no performance-based wage or wage supplement (typically in the case of employees receiving a simple monthly basic wage or hourly wage who are not eligible for wage supplements, only perhaps a fixed average supplement), only the 'fixed' amounts must be taken into account (basic wage plus average supplement). In such cases the amount of the absence pay is equal to the amount of the monthly payments proportionate to the period of absence, where the fraction of the basic wage payable for a specific period is calculated with the method described above: the monthly basic wage must be divided by the number of hours required in the given month according to the general working schedule, then this amount must be multiplied by the number of hours required during the period in question according to the general working schedule (Subsection (3) of section 136 of the HLC).

766. Subsection (2) of section 149 of the HLC offers further simplification by stating that in the case that it is not necessary to make calculations with performance-based wages and wage supplements (i.e., in the case of employees who receive simple monthly basic wages, hourly wages, and perhaps average supplements), the employer may choose to pay the time proportionate amount of the monthly basic wage, hourly wage and average supplement for the duration of the absence instead of paying an absence pay. This option means that there is no need to calculate the amount of absence pay in months when the employee is absent, and the employer should simply pay the standard monthly basic wage, hourly wage and average supplement as this amount will be equal to the amount of the absence pay.

767. The daily amount of the absence pay must be calculated on the basis of the actual date of the absence, which is defined as the start of the absence, therefore for example in the case of a leave, the absence pay must be calculated on the basis of the basic wage payable for the month in which the employee started his or her holidays, while in the case of supplements the previous six months must be taken into consideration.

768. It is important to point out that in cases when the supplements paid over the previous six months must also be considered in the course of calculating the absence pay, as of 1 August 2013, supplements paid for Sundays must also be taken into consideration, provided that over such six-month period, the employee was working at least one out of three Sundays as part of his or her regular working schedule.

769. The calculation of the absence pay is that wage supplements (shift supplements, night supplements, Sunday supplements, as well as wage supplements paid for on duty and stand-by periods) must be considered in the course of calculating the hourly amount of the absence pay by dividing the amount of wage supplements paid for the given period (i.e., the six months preceding the payment of the absence pay) by the number of hours the employee worked over this period during his/her regular, scheduled working hours.[299]

V. Legal Guarantees of Wages

A. *Types of Guarantees*

770. Legal guarantees have a dual function. They ensure, on the one hand, that the wage/salary of the worker/employee is fixed in accordance with the law. On the other hand, the law sees to it that the worker/employee receives wages/salaries based on work in full and at the specified time. Rules fixing the individual basic wage or salary, that is information about the conditions of payment, are within the scope of the first task. The second function is aided by the regulations governing the payment of wages, deductions from wages, and putting forward the law of comprisal and retaining, against the claim for wages.

B. *Fixing the Conditions of the Wages and Notification*

1. Fixing the Basic Wage

771. The basic wage of the worker has to be laid down in the contract of employment in accordance with the law. This is the basis for calculating the wage to which the worker is entitled for work carried out.

2. Notification of Conditions of Payment

772. The worker has to be notified of all conditions of payment (e.g., the wage system, the form of the wage, expected work performance), as well as of any change

299. CSÉFFÁN József, *A munka törvénykönyve és magyarázata*, Szeged: Szegedi Rendezvényszervező Kft., 2023.

in them before starting a given job. The payroll statement of wages paid must be made available in writing by the tenth day of the following month. Backdating is not admissible. The payroll statement must have facilities to allow the employee to check the authenticity of calculations, as well as the grounds and sums of deductions.

C. Withdrawal of the Claim for Wages

773. The employee must not relinquish his/her claim to his/her wage in advance. That part of the wage which is exempt from deduction will not be transferred. Regulations pertaining to employment may prohibit the transfer of a wage claim falling due in the future.

774. The worker is not entitled to a wage when, because of his/her negligence, the product does not conform to the required specifications. If, however, the scrapped product can be partly or totally utilized by the employer, the worker is entitled – in accordance with the provisions of the collective agreement or of the agreement between the parties – to a reduced wage.

D. Payment of Wages

1. Calculation and Date of Payment

775. The wage due to an employee is calculated and paid on a single occasion, in arrears, each month, unless regulations pertaining to employment or the agreement between the parties provide otherwise. If the employment lasts for less than a month, the wage is calculated and paid at the end of the employment.

776. If payday falls on a weekly rest day (weekly rest period) or a public holiday, the wages must be paid at the latest on the last preceding working day. If an employee is not at his/her place of employment for justified reasons on payday, his/her wages must be paid on the last preceding working day spent at such place, or shall be sent to his/her place of residence at the employer's expense.

777. The wage must be paid out no later than the tenth of the month following the month in question, unless the regulations pertaining to employment or the agreement between the parties provide differently. If a payment day should coincide with a rest day or a public holiday, the wage will be paid on the preceding day at the latest. If the employee, on the payment day, cannot be at his/her place of work for a justified reason, then, upon his/her request, his/her wage must be paid on the last working day prior to payment day, or be sent, at the employer's expense, to the place where he/she is staying.

778. In the case of workers whose wages are paid on the basis of performance only, if the result serving as a basis for the employee's wages, in full or in part, can only be established after a period of more than one month, it should be paid at the time as appropriate. An advance payment of wage can be paid at least monthly, amounting to half of the basic wage.

779. The employer must pay at the latest on the working day preceding the date when vacation commences:

(a) the wages due on a payday falling within the time of the vacation; and
(b) the wages payable for the time of leave.

2. Place of Payment

780. According to provisions of law, wages must be paid at the place of work. The wage should be paid during working time, except if the regulations pertaining to employment stipulate otherwise. It should be paid to the employee in person except where somebody else has been authorized to that effect or if the employee is restrained from receiving it in person as a result of a court sentence or order by some other authority.

3. Method of Payment

781. Wages must be paid in cash, or by way of transfer to the payment account the employee has indicated. If wages are paid by way of transfer to the employee's payment account, the employer must ascertain that the employee shall have access to his/her wages on payday. Payment of wages may not invoke any cost on the employees' part, except if the transfer is made to a payment account opened at a payment service provider that is established or has a branch in a state other than Hungary.

782. If employment was terminated prior to payment, the employer must forward the wages on the due day to the address indicated by the employee. The costs thereof will be borne by the employer.

4. Control

783. The possibility for the worker to check that wages have been calculated accurately must be ensured. Therefore, the employee shall be provided with a detailed written statement of his/her wage. Calculations shall be such that the employee can check not only the correctness of the calculations but also the reason and amount of any deductions.[300]

---

300. BANKÓ Zoltán, BERKE Gyula, KISS György, SZŐKE Gergely László *Nagykommentár a munka törvénykönyvéhez*, Wolters Kluwer, Budapest 2019.

VI. Deductions from Wages

A. Legal Deductions

784. Deductions may be made from wages (1) if the worker agrees (consent), or (2) if a lawful decision, such as by a court or other authority, so provides, or the law requires so (e.g., tax and social security deductions, etc.). In these cases, the worker is protected against withholding without legal cause, for he/she can clarify by certain procedure of the state administration or court whether he/she is in debt and for what amount. The deduction-free part of the wages shall not be assigned.

785. The employer may deduct any debt arising from him/her having paid the employee in advance.

786. It is forbidden to impose a wage deduction that benefits the employer, his/her representative or a mediator in exchange for the establishment or retention of the employee's employment. No set-off is permitted in relation to deduction-free wages.

B. The Upper Limits of Attachment

787. To ensure that a worker and his/her dependants have an adequate income, the law must not only provide for attachment of earnings but must also establish limits to it. Deductions from wages are subject to judicially enforced rules of law. According to these rules, two categories can be distinguished. According to the general rule, the measure of deduction is 33%. In special cases, it may reach 50% (e.g., alimony, costs arising from childbirth, or wages received in bad faith). However, the part of wages remaining after deductions cannot be less than the minimum pension determined by the rules on social insurance.

788. The upper limits of 33% and 50% have binding force. Any contract or unilateral legal declaration which raises the upper limit of attachment is null and void. The employer – without the worker's approval – cannot deduct more than 33% or 50% of wages. Deductions shall not exceed 50% of the wages, even if it would be reasonable because of priority demands. It may happen that several debts must be deducted. In such cases, the law defines the sequence in which they are deducted.[301]

C. Duties of the Employer Concerning Deductions

789. In the case of a worker's debt, as regards a third party, the employer is still responsible for deduction. If the employer ignores this, he/she as a guarantor, is responsible for prompt payment. If the worker's labour relationship comes to an

301. József HAJDÚ *Framework of the Remuneration for Work in Hungary* Szeged, Forum: Acta Juridica et Politica 7:(2) pp. 47–67 (2017).

end, the employer is obliged to make out an employer's certificate noting the worker's debts to be subtracted from his/her wages.[302]

VII. The Law Governing Retention of Wages

A. Charges Against Wages

790. A distinction must be made between deductions from wages and charges against wages. Charges made against wages are at the unfettered discretion of the employer within the framework established by law. When charges are made against a worker's wages, the regulations governing withholding apply.

B. Retention of Wages

791. Wages may be retained if the employer has a legal claim. If the claim is for money, then there is no practical difference between charges against wages and the retention of wages. The result of both legal actions is the same: the worker does not receive the full amount of the wages claimed. In determining whether retention is possible and in establishing the amount, the regulations governing withholding are applied. However, the employer shall not resort to inclusion in relation to a deduction-free wage claim, or otherwise, if that is prohibited by the regulations pertaining to employment.

C. Erroneously Paid Wages

792. Any wages paid without legal grounds may be reclaimed after sixty days if the employee should have recognized, or has him/herself caused, the unsubstantiated nature of the payment. The employer can demand the refund within the period of limitation where the worker is aware of the erroneous payment or was the cause of it. The reason for the limitation of repayment is that the worker lives on his/her wages and could get into a difficult situation if required to repay the erroneously obtained money after too long a period. If the worker has received less than his/her due because of an error, he/she may request the difference at any time within the period of limitation.

793. In the event of any delay, interest for late payment must be paid from the date of default as calculated by the central bank base rate in effect on the last day preceding the calendar half-year to which it pertains.

302. HAJDÚ József – KUN Attila (eds), *Munkajog I.*, Budapest: Patrocinium, 2012. pp. 324–325.

D. Charges the Worker Owes to the Employer

794. If the employer has a financial claim on the worker, for example, if the latter has not repaid the unused part of a sum received in advance to cover expenses when on duty outside the enterprise, the worker must be invited in writing to pay back.[303]

VIII. The Wage Guarantee Fund

795. Similarly to the Member States of the European Union Hungary operates a wage guarantee fund. The employers and employees have to pay regular contributions via compulsory insurance. The amount of the contribution employers pay bears a relationship to the number of their employees.[304]

796. In Hungary, an act on guaranteed wages was passed in 1994, well after the commencement of the political transition in 1990, via Act LXVI.[305] According to the insolvency act, employees do not get payments automatically in the case of bankruptcy or liquidation of their employer, as the principle of insurance requires for particular insurance events; it is the employer, administrator or liquidator who has to make a claim for a loan from the fund to ensure the payment of back wages. This loan must be paid back by the employer, or its legal successor, or the administrator/liquidator out of the income brought in during the bankruptcy or liquidation proceedings. This style of procedure is inconsistent with the relevant EU Directive,[306] which is based on insurance principles, and the national regulations of the Member States. Neither is it in compliance with the automatic obligations of the wage guarantee fund that the labour agencies may supervise loan requests made in insolvency cases, and that it may refuse a request if an employer has not repaid a loan sought in consequence of an earlier insolvency.

797. The liquidator, in determining the request for a loan, can take into account the amount of the entitled economic organization's back pay of wages for employees outstanding on the pay day up to a maximum of four times the amount of the monthly average national salary per employee in the second preceding year to the current year as announced by the Central Agency of Statistics.

798. The Hungarian regulation is actually a combination of the two systems: as far as resource collection is concerned, it is based on insurance elements; concerning the payment process, it is the loan elements which dominate. It is also obvious that, in line with European practice, employees' organizations are seeking to

303. HAJDÚ József, IEL Labour Law, Hungary, Wolters Kluwer, Kluwer Law Online, 2019. https://kluwerlawonline.com/Manuals/Corporate+Acquisitions+and+Mergers/705 (26 Jul. 2023).
304. Hungary: Wage guarantee in case of insolvency (2021) https://www.eurofound.europa.eu/observatories/emcc/erm/legislation/hungary-wage-guarantee-in-case-of-insolvency (26 Jul. 2023.).
305. Act LXVI of 1994 on the Wage Guarantee Fund.
306. Directive 2008/94/EC of the European Parliament and of the Council of 22 Oct. 2008 on the protection of employees in the event of the insolvency of their employer.

strengthen the insurance character of the Hungarian rules. This dual character is not completely unfortunate if we take into simultaneous consideration both the social and the economic aspects. Resources organized on an insurance basis come, on the one hand, out of the money paid by employers, managed officially as taxation and state contribution income. On the other hand, resources separate from the budget can also be brought into play. The financial resources are available and, in practice, they are sufficient to cover needs.[307]

307. HAJDÚ József – KUN Attila (eds), *Munkajog I.*, Budapest: Patrocinium, 2012. pp. 225–227.

Chapter 5. Incapacity to Work

§1. Labour Law Provisions

799. According to the HLC, an employee is entitled to fifteen working days of paid sick leave per year. After the expiry of this period, the employee is entitled to statutory sick pay provided by health insurance fund, if he/she satisfies the qualifying requirements.

800. Sick leave is provided for fifteen working days per year of the period of incapacity, and 70% of the payment for periods of absence for this period of salary is paid for this period. This period is completely financed by the employer and it is subject to personal income tax and social security contributions.

§2. Social Insurance Provisions

I. Sickness Benefit

801. Sickness insurance has two branches: services (in kind) and benefits (in cash). Persons earning income from occupational activity receive services free of charge in exchange for their paid contributions. Services under sickness insurance are determined by the relationship between the sickness and the work performed by the person carrying out the occupational activity. If there is such a relationship, i.e., there is an accident at work or an occupational disease, the benefits and services related to accidents are provided. If there is no such relationship, general sickness insurance benefits, i.e., sick pay, are available.

802. In the case of an employee who is not able to work for more than fifteen working days per year, statutory sickness benefit may be provided for up to one year by the National Health Insurance Fund of Hungary (hereinafter: 'NEAK') for those who are (i) unable to work; (ii) have an insurance relationship; and (iii) required to pay a monetary health insurance contribution. Sickness benefit is provided to insured applicants, who are incapable of work and have been registered as such by a doctor. Two-thirds of the sickness benefit is reimbursed by the employer to the NEAK.

803. If the uninterrupted insurance relationship of the employee lasted for less than one year prior to the first day of incapacity for work, statutory sick pay will only be provided for the period covered by such uninterrupted insurance relationship.

804. The amount of statutory sick pay depends on the length of the insurance period prior to the incapacity. It amounts to 60% of the daily average salary in the case of an insurance relationship of two years or more and 50% if the period of insurance is less than two years.

805. If an insured person has received statutory sick pay within one year of the first day of incapacity for work, this duration shall be deducted from the eligibility for statutory sick pay on the new grounds of incapacity.

II. Accident at Work Benefits

806. Employees suffering an accident at work, resulting in no more than 50% damage to their health, are entitled to accident medical services, financial accident pay or accident allowance.

807. When receiving accident medical services, employees suffering an accident at work are entitled to all medical services which are otherwise provided to the insured (e.g., GP services for outpatients, patient transport services, hospital care – inpatient care, operation, medicine, bandages, X-ray examinations, travel cost reimbursement, medicine and bandage prescribed by the GP). In addition, they have a right to use a wider range services provided by the health insurance system.

808. The full price of medicine, medical devices and therapeutic care is covered by the social insurance fund, even if the service concerned is not fully funded. If teeth also suffered damage, the injured is entitled to a free replacement of all teeth damaged in direct connection with the accident at work in order to restore the injured person's chewing ability.

809. Accident sickness benefit is provided to the insured and persons eligible for accident benefits, who become incapable of work as a result of an accident at work, which occurs during the term of insurance or within three days after the termination thereof (including those employed with a temporary employee's book). In such cases, social insurance benefits serve rehabilitation and support the injured person's return to work as soon as possible.

810. Accordingly, as a general rule, benefits are provided for one year, and the provided financial assistance equals the insured person's income used as a basis for calculating the health insurance contribution, i.e., 100% of income used as a basis for calculating accident sick pay, or 90% of such income in relation to road (commuting) accidents. If one year is not enough to restore the ability to work, the provision of accident sick pay may be extended after the end of this period for one additional year maximum, based on the expert opinion of the rehabilitation authority. Employees receiving accident sickness benefit may not pursue an occupational activity, because the very reason they receive 90%–100% of their earlier average income is that they are unable to carry out their work.

811. Persons who have suffered an accident at work causing over 13%, but less than 50% damage to their health are entitled to an accident allowance and, as a result, are not eligible for a rehabilitation allowance or accident-related disability pension provided by the pension insurance system. The amount of the accident allowance depends on the degree of health damage caused by the accident at work.

The basis of the accident allowance is income earned within the one-year period directly preceding the accident at work. Income used as a basis for the accident allowance is calculated according to rules applicable to pensions, with the exception that income is not reduced with the amount of tax.

812. It follows that the method used for calculating the amount of the accident allowance results in relatively higher amounts than pensions. Persons receiving an accident allowance may work, and there is no upper limit of income which would terminate eligibility for the benefit under social insurance.

813. Eligibility for an accident allowance begins from the date on which it is determined that damage to health resulting from the injury exceeds 13%. An employee receiving accident sickness benefit on this day will be entitled to an accident allowance from the day following the termination of eligibility for sickness benefit.

§3. Benefits for Persons with Changed Working Capacity (Disability Benefits)

814. The Act CXCI of 2011 on the benefits for persons with changed working capacity and amendments of certain acts entered into force on 1 January 2012. The Act has been adopted by the Parliament with the purpose of ensuring the social reintegration, employment and employment-focused rehabilitation based on remaining and improvable capacities of those with changed working capacity, and towards income substitution of the missing income.

815. In accordance with this Act, disability pensions, accident-related disability pensions, rehabilitation annuities, regular social annuities for persons with ill-health, temporary invalidity annuities and health damage annuities for miners are not awardable from 1 January 2012.

816. Persons eligible for benefits for persons with changed working capacity are those whose state of health – i.e., such state of a person's physical, mental and social well-being that occurred due to illnesses or injuries or that can be identified as permanent or terminal setbacks caused by congenital abnormalities – is assessed by the complex assessment of the rehabilitation authority at 60% or less (hereinafter referred to as 'person with changed working capacity') and who:

(a) had been insured for at least 1,095 days within 5 years before submitting the claim;
(b) has not been performing any gainful activity *neither in Hungary, nor abroad*; and
(c) does not receive any regular cash benefits – i.e., any benefits defined as regular cash benefits in the Act on Social Administration and Social Benefits; excluding benefits for war veterans and their relatives or those for wards of the nation, supplements for national commitment, nursing fees, survivors' benefits, and the

same types of such benefits disbursed by a foreign authority pursuant to international agreements on social security and EC regulations.

817. A person may be entitled to benefit for persons with changed working capacity regardless of the length of insurance period provided that:

(a) they became insured within 180 days after finishing their studies and as such, they had been insured without a break of more than 30 days before submitting the claim; or
(b) they received disability pension, accident-related disability pension, rehabilitation annuity or any pension-type benefits for persons with ill-health on 31 December 2011.

818. The above-mentioned 1,095 days shall include the period of sick pay after the termination of insurance, work accident sick pay, pregnancy-confinement benefit, child care fee, job-seeker allowance, disability pension, accident-related disability pension, rehabilitation annuity, pension-type benefits for persons with ill-health and benefits for persons with changed working capacity.

819. Depending on the motion for rehabilitation determined in the course of complex assessment by the special authority, benefits for persons with changed working capacity are:

(a) rehabilitation benefit; or
(b) disability benefit.

820. The examining authority assesses, in the course of complex assessment, whether a person with changed working capacity, who

(a) could be rehabilitated, and hereunder:
    (i) and his/her employability may be recovered by rehabilitation; or
    (ii) needs permanent work rehabilitation.
(b) to whom rehabilitation is not recommended, and thereunder:
    (i) whose employability could be recovered regarding his/her state of health, however work rehabilitation is not recommended due to other circumstances;
    (ii) who needs permanent rehabilitation regarding his/her state of health, however work rehabilitation is not recommended due to other circumstances;
    (iii) can be employed only by constant support; or
    (iv) has significant health damage and is not able to self-supply at all or only with others' help.

821. With regard to the implementation of the relevant Act, *rehabilitation* refers to a complex system of medical, social, training, employment and other activities, the aim of which is to reintegrate persons with changed working capacity to the labour market, to prepare them for employment in a suitable work place and to ensure their employments in the suitable work place concerning their working capacity.

822. A person with changed working capacity is entitled to:

- rehabilitation benefit, if he/she could be rehabilitated;
- disability benefit, in such cases where rehabilitation is not recommended if he/she could not be rehabilitated, and the time missing before reaching retirement age does not exceed 5 years.

823. Under rehabilitation benefit, a person with changed working capacity is entitled to:

- the necessary services required for the purpose of a successful rehabilitation; and
- cash benefit.

824. Any person receiving rehabilitation benefit shall cooperate with the rehabilitation authority and thus meet the requirements defined in the rehabilitation plan.

825. The rehabilitation benefit may be provided from the date of meeting eligibility criteria, with the date of submitting the claim deemed as the earliest date, to the length required for rehabilitation, but for the duration of maximum 3 years from the commencement of disbursement.

826. Regarding beneficiaries performing gainful activity, the length of the rehabilitation benefit is extended with the length of incapacity emerged during the earning activity (considering which, the eligibility to sick pay or to work accident sick pay can be acquired).

827. The payment of the rehabilitation cash benefit must be suspended in cases where the person involved performs gainful activity, participates in community employment or is not able to perform gainful activity.

828. The rehabilitation cash benefit paid for any respective period must be deducted from the benefit provided for the period commencing after the month of notice on the fulfilment of any conditions or must be reclaimed in case of termination of the rehabilitation benefit.

829. The monthly sum of the rehabilitation cash benefit amounts to:

- with regard to such eligible persons who can be rehabilitated, 35% of the average monthly income – i.e., the average monthly income deemed as thirtyfold the daily average sum of the income serving as the basic income of health care contribution in cash and as one reached in the calendar year directly before the commencement date of eligibility; if the eligible person has not acquired an income of at least 180 calendar days, thirtyfold of the daily average sum of the daily

income of 180 calendar days directly before the commencement of eligibility –, but at least 30% and the maximum of 40% of the minimum wage;
- with regard to persons who require permanent work rehabilitation, 45% of the average monthly income, but at least 40% and the maximum of 50% of the minimum wage.

830. Rehabilitation benefit must be increased according to the provisions on indexation of pensions.

831. Rehabilitation benefit will be terminated in cases when:

- upon the eligible person claim;
- the length of such person's benefit has terminated;
- receives other regular cash benefits, excluding sick pay and work accident sick pay disbursed regarding incapacity;
- has suffered from permanent deterioration in the state of health which excludes the possibility of rehabilitation;
- has reached permanent improvement in the state of health due to which they may no longer be classified as persons with changed working capacity;
- does not meet the requirements determined in the cooperation, notification or rehabilitation plan for reasons within their control;
- does not cooperate in the course of a review for reasons within their control; or
- their employment had been established without any legal statements required for the establishment of such legal relationships.

832. Within fifteen days, a person receiving such benefit must notify that:

- permanent improvement or permanent deterioration has emerged in the state of health;
- performs gainful activity; or
- if his/her gainful activity has terminated.

833. II. Disability benefit may be provided from the date of meeting the eligibility criteria, with the first day of the sixth month before the date of submitting the claim deemed as the earliest date.

834. Depending on the statements made within the course of complex assessment, the amount of disability benefit is 40, 60, 65, or 70% of the average monthly income, but at least 30, 45, 50, or 55% and the maximum of 45, 150% of the minimum wage.

835. Disability benefit should be increased according to the provisions on indexation of pensions.

836. Disability benefit must be terminated in cases where the eligible person:

- claims;
- receives other regular cash benefits, excluding sick pay and work accident sick pay disbursed regarding incapacity;
- has reached permanent improvement in the state of health due to which they do not meet eligibility criteria;
- performs gainful activity and the monthly average of his/her income regarding 3 following months respectively exceeds 150% of the minimum wage;
- his/her employment had been established without any legal statements required for the establishment of such legal relationships;
- does not fulfil the obligation to notification for reasons within their control; or
- does not cooperate in the course of a review for reasons within their control.

837. Within fifteen days, a person receiving such benefit must notify that:

- there has been a change in his circumstances relevant to eligibility criteria; or
- performs gainful activity and the monthly average of his/her income regarding 3 following months respectively exceeds 150% of the minimum wage. The amount of income shall be verified with such notification at once.[308]

838. Benefits for persons with changed working capacity can be claimed via relevant forms at the rehabilitation authority being competent of his/her residence in Hungary. If he/she is not a Hungarian resident, their claim can be lodged at the competent institution of the EU country or of the country with which Hungary has concluded a bilateral social security agreement they are residing. The procedure is exempt from duties and charges.

839. The applicant may be obliged to personal attendance at the complex assessment procedure. Provided that the applicant fails to fulfil this obligation voluntarily, the procedure will be terminated.

840. In the course of complex assessment, the examining board will examine the percentage of the applicant's state of health, the accessibility to rehabilitation and in the latter case it will determine a motion for rehabilitation.

841. Disability and rehabilitation benefits are paid by the National Health Insurance Fund of Hungary.[309]

308. József, HAJDÚ Part V. *Incapacity to Work* In: József, HAJDÚ; Attila, KUN (szerk.) Hungary: International Encyclopaedia for Social Security Law Alphen aan den Rijn, Hollandia: Kluwer Law International, (2019) pp. 131–144., 14 p.

309. HAJDÚ József *Transformation of the Hungarian Disability Pension: Possession and Legitimate Expectations of Social Security Rights, under the European Convention of Human Rights* In: Auer Ádám, BERKE Gyula, György István, Hazafi Zoltán (szerk.) Ünnepi kötet a 65 éves KISS György tiszteletére 909 p. Dialóg Campus Kiadó, Budapest, 2018. pp. 293–312.

§4. Legal Protection of People with Disabilities

842. Hungary ratified the United Nations Convention on the Rights of Persons with Disabilities in July 2007, and is working to ensure that Hungarian laws and codes comply with the Convention. In practical terms, however, wheelchair accessibility is not always available, and employment opportunities are limited.

843. The Hungarian Disability Discrimination Act is against the law for employers to discriminate against disabled people for a reason related to their disability, and employers should ensure that disabled employees are not disadvantaged by any physical feature of the workplace.

844. Any kind of discrimination can be directly reported to the Authority of Equal Treatment (EBH).

Chapter 6. Job Security

§1. Stability and Security of Employment

845. Two requirements are necessary to ensure stability and security of employment: during the period of employment conditions defined in the contract of employment should remain intact and employment should endure without threat of arbitrary dismissal. Stability and security of employment have vital significance both for the society and the individual. The employee exercises the right to work when entering into employment and through this is able to assure a living for him/herself and his/her family. Consequently, it is of vital importance to have a job which is as secure as possible. In an untroubled atmosphere, he/she is able to develop his/her abilities and creativity to the greatest extent. Nowadays, during the technological-scientific revolution the importance of this development is even more significant, since besides giving opportunities for improvement it demands permanent further education.

846. At the same time stability and security of employment mean a solid financial basis for the employee and his/her family. The realization of family aims and budget are made possible, which in turn positively affects the work of employees. Similarly, stability of employment is also in the interest of society. It makes both employment policy and well-founded social policy as well as the implementation of the respective economic purchases easier. The development of personal abilities and creativity helps the realization of the common aims of society. Besides emphasizing the importance of stability and security, it should also be mentioned that during such a permanent relation as employment there may occur phenomena which might lead to the modification or even the termination of employment. This may concern both parties. Gaining higher qualifications or personal problems, for example, may make it necessary for the employee to move, or, on the other hand, because of reorganization the enterprise may face a situation in which it must decrease the number of employees or reorganize them; the enterprise may even cease to exist.

847. Creating rules or regulations concerning the modification or termination of employment, labour law must take these components into consideration. Hungarian labour law reflects two important views here. On the one hand, it recognizes the fact that an employer should have the right to terminate the employment relationship if this becomes necessary because it is in his/her economic interest or as a result of an employee's conduct or inappropriate qualifications. On the other hand, the labour law takes notice of the fact that sociologically the position of the employer and that of the employee are not the same because the employer is far stronger. His/her existence and operation are not influenced if he/she is obliged to maintain employment despite certain difficulties or if an employee leaves. It could be extremely difficult for the employee to keep his/her job in unfavourable conditions. In addition, after termination it may be difficult to find new employment at once, especially if there are obstacles such as illness hindering this.

§2. Modification of the Contract of Employment

I. Cases of Modification

A. General Principles

848. Section 58 of the HLC establishes as a general rule that the contract of employment can only be modified bilaterally. This serves both parties. It does not force them to endure an unbearable situation if they are unable to agree upon modification. They have the possibility of unilateral termination of the employment relationship with immediate effect or with notice. In connection with this it must be stressed that in the case of the employer, the fact that a worker does not approve of a modification of the contract does not in itself imply the giving of notice. He/she may take it as such if the modification requested is based on a reasonable case, such as reorganization. However, if the modification of the contract was initiated because the employer wished to employ the worker in another job, vacated as a consequence of a death, but the worker or employee does not agree to this, notice cannot possibly be implied, for there is insufficient cause. (However, the employer can oblige the employee to perform this task provisionally.) A collective agreement must not modify the employment contract to the employee's detriment.[310]

B. Parties' Agreement

849. If on the basis of an agreement the employee is employed for a definite period of time in a way that deviates from the employment contract, his/her employment will continue in accord with the employment contract upon the expiry of this definite period, and his/her wages well be modified with due consideration to wage increases implemented in the meantime. From this section, no derogation is allowed in the agreement of the parties or in the collective agreement.

C. Modification by Law

850. In the interest of the worker, the law may prescribe obligatory modification of a contract of employment in the following cases:

(a) The employee's basic personal wages should be offered by the employer following completion of voluntary reserve military service and the cessation of unpaid leave for nursing or caring of children and adult relatives, in accordance with the average annual wage increase implemented in the meantime at the employer's for employees in the same position and with the same experience.

310. DUDÁS Katalin – GYULAVÁRI Tamás – HORVÁTH István – Hős Nikolett – KÁRTYÁS Gábor – KULISITY Mária – KUN Attila – PETROVICS Zoltán, *Munkajog*, Budapest: ELTE Eötvös Kiadó, 2012. pp. 154–159.

In the absence of such employees, the size of the actual annual wage increase implemented at the employer's should be normative.

(b) A woman, from the time of her pregnancy up to the time her child reaches one year of age and on the basis of a medical opinion pertaining to her suitability for the position, will be temporarily placed in a position appropriate to her condition from a medical viewpoint, or the working conditions in her existing position will be appropriately modified. The designation of a new position requires the employee's approval. The pregnant employee is discharged from work duty if no position appropriate for her medical condition is available. The employee must be given the base wage normally paid for the job offered, which may not be less than her base wage fixed in the employment contract. The base wage will be payable for the duration of discharge, except if the job offered is refused without good reason.

(c) The wages of a woman temporarily transferred to a different position or employed under modified working conditions without being transferred cannot be less than her previous basic wage. If the employer is unable to ensure a position suited to her medical condition, or the pregnant woman will not accept it, the woman will be relieved of work, and for this period must be paid basic wages, except if the job offered is refused without good reason.

(d) The employer must continue to employ an employee whose working ability has changed in the course of employment in a position suited to his/her condition.

(e) In the event of legal succession in the person of the employer, all employment-related rights and obligations must be transferred from the legal predecessor employer to the legal successor employer at the time of legal succession. However, in case of transfer of undertakings, the employment relationship remains unchanged.

D. Initiation of Modification by the Employee

851. The new HLC changed the procedure of this modification. Formerly, the employee had to initiate the modification. According to section 61 of the HLC, employers are to inform their workers concerning the following opportunities, indicating the jobs in which they are available:

(a) full or part-time work;
(b) teleworking; and
(c) permanent employment relationships.

852. Employers must respond to the proposition of workers for the amendment of their employment contracts within fifteen days in writing.

853. In addition, the employer must amend the employment contract based on the employee's proposition to part-time work covering half of the daily working time until the child reaches the age of three.

E. Exception from Modification

854. Employers are entitled to temporarily reassign their employees to jobs and workplaces other than what is contained in the employment contracts, or to another employer.

855. In this case, the duration of employment may not exceed a total of forty-four working days or three hundred and fifty-two scheduled hours during a calendar year. This should be applied proportionately if the employment relationship commenced during the year, or in the case of fix-term employment relationships or in connection with part-time jobs. The employee affected must be informed of the expected duration of work in derogation from the employment contract.

856. An employee may not be transferred to work at another location without the employee's consent:

(a) from the time her pregnancy is diagnosed until her child reaches three years of age;
(b) until the child reaches sixteen years of age, if a single parent; and
(c) if providing long-term care for a close relative in person; furthermore
(d) if having suffered a degree of health impairment of at least 50% as diagnosed by the body of rehabilitation experts.

857. In such cases, the employee must be entitled to the wage prescribed for the job in question, or at least to the basic wage fixed in the employment contract.

F. Procedures and Costs for Amendment

858. For modification of a contract of employment the rules at the time of its conclusion apply.

859. If modification of a contract of employment constitutes a change in the place of work of the employee, this may necessitate a move which might cause an undue burden on the worker. In the event of a move to another locality, the employer must pay the cost.[311]

§3. Termination of the Employment Relationship by the Parties

860. According to sections 63–85 of the HLC, an employment relationship may be terminated:

311. BANKÓ Zoltán, BERKE Gyula, KISS György, SZŐKE Gergely László *Nagykommentár a munka törvénykönyvéhez*, Wolters Kluwer, Budapest 2019.

(1) by mutual consent;
(2) by notice;
(3) by dismissal without notice.

861. It is an important procedural requirement that agreements and statements for the termination of an employment relationship must be made in writing.

§4. Termination of the Employment Relationship by Mutual Consent

862. The employment relationship can be terminated at any time by the bilateral agreement of the employer and the worker. In such a case the labour relationship can be terminated at the fixed time without special procedure. The agreement must be put in writing.

§5. Termination of the Employment Relationship by Unilateral Action

I. Cases of Unilateral Action

863. Termination by unilateral declaration of one party can take place either by giving notice or dismissal without notice, or with immediate effect during the probation period. A unilateral declaration operates regardless of the will of the other party. The party must put his/her statement in writing. Where termination occurs by unilateral declaration of one party, the statement, if the other party was informed, binds the declarer. The statement can be withdrawn only with the approval of the other party.[312]

II. Notice

A. The Possibility of Notice

864. The labour contract of indefinite duration may be terminated by notice, by either the worker or the employer at any time, according to section 65 of the HLC. The law, to ensure the stability and security of the employment relationship, distinguishes between the situation of a worker and that of an employer regarding the preconditions of notice. The employer may give notice when justified and when no prohibitions or restrictions to prevent notice are present. There is only one exception: the employer is not required to give reasons for terminating a permanent employment relationship if the worker affected is a pensioner.

312. HAJDÚ József, IEL Labour Law, Hungary, Wolters Kluwer, Kluwer Law Online, 2019. https://kluwerlawonline.com/Manuals/Corporate+Acquisitions+and+Mergers/705 (26 Jul. 2023).

865. In contrast with this, the worker, only in case of indefinite employment relationship, may hand in his/her notice free of any restrictions; he/she is not obliged to offer an explanation for handing in his/her notice, and cannot be obliged to do so.

866. However, the worker is required to give reasons for terminating his/her fixed-term employment relationship. The reason given for termination may only be of such a nature as would render the maintaining of the employment relationship impossible or that would cause unreasonable hardship in light of his/her circumstances.

867. The new provision in the HLC states that, if so agreed by the parties, the employment relationship may not be terminated by notice for a period of up to one year from the date of commencement of the employment relationship.[313]

B. *Justification of Notice*

868. As it was mentioned above, the employer must justify his/her notice. There is a distinction relating to reasoning the notice in the HLC between (A) open-ended contract and (B) fixed-term contract.

869. A) In case of *open-ended contract*, the justification must clearly indicate the cause of the notice. In the event of a dispute, the employer will substantiate the veracity and causality of the reason for the notice. The reason for the notice can only be a cause connected with the (1) employee's ability or (2) his/her conduct in relation to the employment, or (3) the employer's operations.

870. If the enterprise terminates the employment relationship not for the reasons mentioned above but because of personal conflict, then the law has been misused and the notice of dismissal is invalid. This view was expressed by the Curia (the name of the Supreme Court in Hungary) when it decided that an employer may dismiss a worker only where there is due cause. In giving notice, the employer must reveal his/her motivation in detail to ensure that the reasoning is clear to the worker and to any authority dealing with an appeal. Thus, it does not suffice for the employer to say: reorganization; the reasons for the necessity of the dismissal of the particular worker must be shown.

871. B) In case of *fixed-term contract*, the employer can only be permitted to terminate a fixed-term employment relationship by notice:

- if undergoing liquidation or bankruptcy proceedings; or
- for reasons related to the worker's ability; or
- if maintaining the employment relationship is no longer possible due to unavoidable external reasons.[314]

313. CSÉFFÁN József, *A munka törvénykönyve és magyarázata*, Szeged: Szegedi Rendezvényszervező Kft., 2023.
314. BANKÓ Zoltán, BERKE Gyula, KISS György, SZŐKE Gergely *László Nagykommentár a munka*

C. Prohibition and Limitation of Notice

872. The difference between prohibition and limitation is that in case of prohibition, the employer must not terminate the employment relationship by notice (absolute provision). In case of limitation, the employer may terminate the employment relationship if he/she meets the special requirement described by the HLC.

1. Prohibition of Notice

873. Section 65 of the HLC automatically limits the employer's ability to dismiss workers. In certain cases, dismissal may cause disproportionate hardship to the worker if, due to illness or other reasons, he/she has no possibility of getting another job), or would be inequitable because it prevents the worker from engaging in important social activities. Regarding this, labour law establishes limitations on dismissal by the enterprise. In certain cases, there is absolute prohibition, while in others it is relative. Dismissal in prohibited cases is invalid. Prohibition exists in cases where the worker is prevented from seeking alternative employment and thus cannot provide him/herself with a living. Such cases arise under the following circumstances:

- during pregnancy;[315]
- during maternity leave;
- during a leave of absence taken without pay for caring for a child (sections 128 and 130);[316]
- during any period of actual reserve military service; and
- in the case of women, while receiving treatment related to a human reproduction procedure, for up to six months from the beginning of such treatment.[317]

874. The prohibition of notice in case of (a) during pregnancy and (b) women receiving treatment related to human reproduction will apply only if the employee has informed the employer thereof. If the employee supplied the said information after giving notice, the employer may withdraw the notice of termination in writing within fifteen days upon receipt thereof. If the notice is withdrawn, the employee can request the labour court to reinstate the employment relationship.

---

törvénykönyvéhez, Wolters Kluwer, Budapest 2019.

315. N.B.: According to the new provision of the HLC, in case of pregnancy the prohibition clause will apply only if the worker has informed the employer thereof before the notice was given.
316. This protection will be available to the mother if unpaid leave has been taken by both parents.
317. N.B.: According to the new provision of the HLC, in case of human reproduction procedure the prohibition clause will apply only if the worker has informed the employer thereof before the notice was given.

2. Limitation of Notice

875. Reason related to the behaviour of the worker. The employer may be permitted to terminate the employment relationship of workers, other than pensioners, concluded for an indefinite duration inside the five-year period before the date when the employee reaches the age limit for old-age pension on the grounds of the workers' behaviour in relation to the employment relationship only for the reason defined in Subsection (1) of section 78. [Otherwise, section 78 of the HLC regulates the termination of employment without notice.] These grounds are the following:

- wilfully or by gross negligence commits a grave violation of any substantive obligations arising from the employment relationship; or
- otherwise engages in conduct that would render the employment relationship impossible.

876. Reason related to the worker's ability or employer's operation. The employment relationship of the workers (inside the five-year period before the date when the employee reaches the age limit for old-age pension) may be terminated in connection with workers' ability or for reasons in connection with the employer's operations if the employer has no vacant position available at the workplace which is suitable for the worker affected in terms of skills, education and/or experience required for his/her previous job, or if the worker refuses the offer made for his/her employment in that job.

877. In addition, where the employment relationship of a mother or a single father is terminated by notice, the above-mentioned prohibition and limitation provisions are applicable until the child reaches the age of three, if the employee is not taking up maternity leave or leave of absence without pay for the purpose of caring for the child.[318]

D. Period of Notice

878. A period of notice is necessary so the worker may seek other employment, or so that the employer may replace a retiring worker.

879. The notice period begins at the earliest on the day following the date when dismissal is communicated. Where employment is terminated by the employer, the notice period will begin at the earliest on the day after the last day of the following periods:

- duration of incapacity to work due to illness, not to exceed one year following expiration of the sick leave period;

318. FERENC Jácint – GÖNDÖR Éva – GYULAVÁRI Tamás – KÁRTYÁS Gábor, *Munkajogi alapismeretek*, Budapest: ELTE Kiadó, 2013. pp. 87–89.

– absence from work for the purpose of caring for a sick child;
– leave of absence without pay for providing home care for a close relative.

880. According to section 68 of the HLC, the period of notice varies from thirty days to six months. The thirty-day notice period increases with five days after three years employment, with fifteen days after five years, with twenty days after eight years, with twenty-five days after ten years, with thirty days after fifteen years, with forty days after eighteen years, with sixty days after twenty years of employment with the employer.

881. The period of notice for the termination of a fixed-term employment relationship by notice may not go beyond the fixed term.

E. Exemption from Work

882. If the employer gives notice he/she is obliged to exempt the worker from working to provide him/her with the opportunity to seeking new employment. The extent of this is half of the period of notice (part of a day is considered as a full day). The employee may take up half of the exemption period as and when he/she wishes; concerning the other half, the employer decides. However, the exemption from work duty can be allocated in not more than two parts, at the employee's discretion.

883. The worker may be exempt from working the whole period of the notice and may also be exempt from working if he/she gives notice but this is not mandatory; it depends on the judgment of the employer. During the exemption period absentee fee is due to the worker. If an employee is indefinitely relieved of his/her duties prior to the expiry of the notice period, and the circumstance precluding the payment of wages occurred subsequent to the employee being relieved of his/her duties, the wages already paid out shall not be reclaimed. The wage paid out for the duration of the exemption shall not be reclaimed either if during the notice period the employee establishes a legal relationship entailing the performance of work.

884. However, in the event of notice by the employer, if, during the notice period the employee requests the termination of his/her employment at a time prior to him/her being relieved of his/her duties, the employer may terminate the employment at the time as designated by the employee.[319]

F. Method of Giving Notice

885. A very short formal requirement of the HLC is that notice must be given in writing.

319. HAJDÚ József, IEL Labour Law, Hungary, Wolters Kluwer, Kluwer Law Online, 2019. https://kluwerlawonline.com/Manuals/Corporate+Acquisitions+and+Mergers/705 (26 Jul. 2023).

§6. Reinstatement

I. Consequences of Unlawful Termination of Employment

A. *Cases of the Unlawful Termination of Employment*

886. Termination of the employment relationship is unlawful if:

(a) in the case of notice, the reason given by the employer is not true or does not in fact constitute the reason for termination, or violates the prohibitions or limitations established by law, or the formalities of serving notice have not been observed;
(b) in the case of termination without notice, the reason given by one of the parties is not true or does not establish the termination of the employment relationship or the limitation period has not been observed;
(c) the notice or termination without reason violates the rules on exercising rights and fulfilling obligations, on the rules on prohibition of discrimination.

B. *Consequences of Unlawful Termination by the Employer*

887. The employer is liable to provide compensation for damages resulting from the wrongful termination of an employment relationship. The HLC does not mention any legal consequence of the wrongful termination by the employee.

888. Compensation for loss of income from employment payable to the employee may not exceed twelve months' absentee pay.

889. In addition to the above-mentioned amount, the employee is entitled to severance pay as well, if:

(a) his/her employment relationship was wrongfully terminated; or
(b) he/she did not receive any severance pay at the time his/her employment relationship was terminated.

890. In addition to the above-mentioned legal consequence, at the employee's request, the court will reinstate the employment relationship:

(a) if it was terminated in violation of the principle of equal treatment;
(b) if it was terminated during the prohibition of notice period;
(c) if the employment relationship of trade union leader was terminated wrongfully;
(d) if the employee served as an employees' representative at the time his/her employment relationship was terminated;
(e) if the employee successfully challenged the termination of the employment relationship by mutual consent or his/her own legal act therefor.

C. Consequences of Unlawful Termination by the Employee

891. The employee, if having terminated his/her employment relationship unlawfully, will be liable to pay compensation in the sum of absentee pay due for the notice period when the employment relationship is terminated by the employer.

892. The employee, if having terminated his fixed-term employment relationship unlawfully, will be liable to pay compensation in the sum of absentee pay due for the time remaining from the fixed period, up to three months' absentee pay at most.

893. Employers will be entitled to demand payment for damages if such are in excess of the amount described above. These sums in total may not exceed the employee's absentee pay due for twelve months.

894. The provisions on wrongful termination of employment shall apply if the employee fails to leave his post according to regulations.[320]

§7. Termination Without Notice (Just Cause)

895. An employer or employee may terminate an employment relationship without notice (just cause) if the other party:

- wilfully or by gross negligence commits a grave violation of any substantive obligations arising from the employment relationship; or
- otherwise engages in conduct that would render the employment relationship impossible.

896. The right of termination without notice may be exercised within a period of fifteen days of gaining knowledge of the grounds therefor, in any case within not more than one year of the occurrence of such grounds, or in the event of a criminal offence up to the statute of limitation. If the right of termination without notice is exercised by a body, the date of gaining knowledge shall be the date when the body, acting as the body exercising employer's rights, is informed regarding the grounds for termination without notice.[321]

897. The right of termination without notice may be exercised, without giving reasons:

- by either party during the probation period;
- by the employer in connection with fixed-term employment relationships.

320. BANKÓ Zoltán, BERKE Gyula, KISS György, SZŐKE Gergely László *Nagykommentár a munka törvénykönyvéhez*, Wolters Kluwer, Budapest 2019.
321. MIHOLICS Tivadar, *A munkaviszony megszüntetése III.* http://munkajog.hu/rovatok/munkahely/a-munkaviszony-megszuntetese-iii (26 Jul. 2023.).

898. In the case of termination of fixed-term employment relationship without notice, the employee will be entitled to absentee pay due for twelve months, or if the time remaining from the fixed period is less than one year, for the remaining time period.[322]

§8. Mass (Collective) Redundancy

I. Conditions of Mass Redundancy

899. A mass redundancy means when an employer, due to reasons in connection with its operations and based on the average statistical work force for the preceding six-month period or for the number of months, if the employer was established less than six (6) months[323] before, intends to terminate the employment relationship:

- of at least 10 persons, when employing more than 20 and fewer than 100 employees;
- of 10% of employees, when employing 100 or more, but fewer than 300 employees;
- of at least 30 persons, when employing 300 or more employees with a 30-day notice by regular dismissal.[324]

900. If the employer has more than one business location, the above-mentioned provisions are separately applied for each place of business. However, the number of workers employed at various locations, but within the jurisdiction of the same county (Capital) will be calculated on the aggregate. The employee should be accounted at the location where he/she works in the position registered at the time when the decision on collective redundancy was adopted.

901. Where the projected collective redundancy concerns members of the crew of a seagoing vessel, the employer must notify the competent authority of the State of the flag which the vessel flies.[325]

902. Employees eligible for or receiving old age pension, and employees employed in subsequent employment relationships will not be included in the number of employees affected by work force reduction.

322. KOZMA Anna – LŐRINCZ György – PÁL Lajos, *A Munka Törvénykönyvének magyarázata*, Budapest: HVG-Orac, 2020.
323. For employers in operation for less than six months, the average statistical number of employees is determined for the period applicable.
324. A csoportos létszámcsökkentés szabályai (2022), https://www.origo.hu/jog/20220630-origo-jog-das-jogszerviz-munkajog-csoportos-letszamcsokkentes-szabalyai.html (26 Jul. 2023.).
325. DOBOSI Kinga (2023) *Létszámleépítés és a felmondás indokolása*, https://ado.hu/munkaugyek/letszamleepites-es-a-felmondas-indokolasa/ (26 Jul. 2023).

II. Consultation with Works' Council

903. Prior to the decision for large-scale dismissals, employers must initiate discussions with the works' council. At least seven days before the discussions, the employer must inform the works' council in writing regarding:

- the reasons for the projected collective redundancies;
- the number of workers to be made redundant broken down by categories; or
- the number of workers employed during the period;
- the period over which the projected redundancies are to be effected, and the timetable for their implementation;
- the criteria proposed for the selection of the workers to be made redundant; and
- the conditions for and the extent of benefits provided in connection with the termination of employment relationships, other than what is prescribed in employment regulations.

904. The employer's obligation of consultation will apply until the conclusion of an agreement, or failing this for a period of fifteen days after the beginning of negotiations.

905. In order to reach an agreement, the negotiations must, at least, cover:

- the possible ways and means of avoiding collective redundancies;
- the principles of redundancies;
- the means of mitigating the consequences; and
- the reduction of the number of employees affected.

906. The agreement concluded in the course of negotiations must be made out in writing, a copy of which shall be sent to the government employment agency. This agreement may lay down the guidelines for the employer to select the workers affected by the termination of employment relationships.

III. The Content of Decision

907. The decision for the implementation of collective redundancies must specify:

- the number of workers affected, broken down by job categories; and
- the date of commencement and conclusion and the timeframe of collective redundancy, or the timetable for implementing the said redundancies.

908. Collective redundancies shall be effected in thirty-day periods. To this end, the timetable indicated in the employer's decision shall be taken into account.

909. The number of workers will be calculated on the aggregate, if within thirty days from the date of disclosure of the legal act for the termination of the last employment relationship or from the date of reaching an agreement the employer communicates another statement or concludes an agreement for the termination of employment in a given period.

IV. Notification

910. The employer must notify the government employment agency of its intention regarding collective redundancies, and of the details and aspects of mass redundancy. One copy of the above-mentioned notification should be given to the works' council.

911. The employer must notify in writing the government employment agency of its decision regarding collective redundancies at least thirty days prior to delivering the notice of dismissal. This aforementioned notification must contain:

- the identification data;
- the position; and
- the qualification of the employees to be made redundant.

912. The employer must notify in writing the workers affected of its decision regarding collective redundancies at least thirty days prior to delivering the notice of dismissal or the dismissal without notice. The notice of dismissal or the dismissal without notice may be delivered after thirty days following the time of notification. The notification must be sent to the works' council and the government employment agency as well. If the employer breaches the requirement of the abovementioned notification, a dismissal will be considered unlawful.[326]

§9. Severance Pay

913. An employee is entitled to severance pay if (1) his/her employment ceases in consequence of ordinary notice by the employer or (2) his/her cessation without legal successor or (3) if the employer taking over the economic entity under the legal transaction on the strength of law is not covered by the HLC.

914. However, there are some exceptions: (1) if the employee has become eligible for old-age pension, or (2) upon expiry of a secondary occupation or upon the termination of a subsequent employment relationship or (3) if the employee is dismissed for reasons in connection with his/her behaviour in relation to the employment relationship or on grounds other than health reasons.

915. Severance pay is due to an employee after at least three years with the same employer. In terms of entitlement for severance pay, any period of at least thirty

326. HORVÁTH István, *Az új munka törvénykönyve*, Budapest: Vezinfó Kiadó és Tanácsadó Kft. 2012. pp. 152–156.

consecutive days for which the employee did not receive any wages will not be taken into consideration, with the exception of:

- maternity leave and any leave of absence without pay for nursing or caring for a child;
- any leave of absence without pay taken for the purpose of actual reserve military service for a period of not more than three months.

916. Severance pay amounts to one month absentee pay in the case of at least three years' service, two months in the case of at least five years, three months in the case of at least ten years, four months in the case of at least fifteen years, five months in the case of at least twenty years, six months in the case of at least twenty-five years.

917. The amount of severance pay must be increased by one-three (according to the time spent in employment relationship) month's absentee pay, if the employment relationship is terminated inside the five-year period before the date when the employee reaches the age limit for old-age pension.[327]

§10. Special Protection for Members of Interest Representative Bodies

918. Trade union officials. In case of transfer and/or ordinary dismissal, according to the HLC, only the official(s) of the trade union is protected by law. In such a case, a written agreement from the next higher authority in the union hierarchy is required for an employer if an elected trade union official is to be transferred to another workplace on the employer's initiative, as well as for the employer's termination of a trade union official's employment by regulatory notice. (Subsection (1) of section 273 of the HLC)

919. Chairperson of works council. The new labour code reduced works council and trade union rights, accordingly only the chairperson of the works council has protection against dismissal and all other members are no longer protected. The chairperson of the works council can only be dismissed or transferred with the consent of the works council.

The protection against dismissal of Hungarian European works council representatives is now unclear. According to Article 10-3 of the EWC Directive they 'shall, in the exercise of their functions, enjoy protection and guarantees similar to those provided for employees' representatives by the national legislation .... in force in their country of employment'. Since simple members of a Hungarian works council

327. CSÉFFÁN József, *A munka törvénykönyve és magyarázata*, Szeged: Szegedi Rendezvényszervező Kft., 2023.

no longer have any protection against dismissal, Hungarian EWC members are consequently also no longer protected – unless they are the chairperson of a Hungarian works council.[328]

920. Health and safety representatives should not be disadvantaged because of the exercise of their duties and have the same protection against dismissal as local union representatives or members of the works council. This means that they can only be dismissed if the health and safety committee agrees or, if there is no committee, with the agreement of the employees who elected them.

§11. Termination of the Employment Relationship Beyond the Control of the Parties

921. Termination of the labour relationship owing to circumstances beyond the control of the parties takes place:

(a) upon death of the worker;
(b) upon the employer ceasing to exist without a legal successor;
(c) upon expiration of the fixed term of the contract;
(d) upon the transfer of employer's legal status from Labour Code to the Act on Public Servant or Civil Servant.

922. a) The employment relationship terminates with immediate effect in the event of a worker's death. Naturally, unpaid wages and other benefits of the worker are due to his/her heirs.

923. However, the death of the employer (in case of natural person) does not mean termination of the labour relationship. The labour relationship is not attached to a person on the employer's side. The legal successor who does not pursue the activity of the previous employer or who does so but finds the labour relationship superfluous or unsatisfactory may, of course, discontinue it because of this, corresponding to the provisions of law discussed above. Similarly, the right of notice also applies to the worker or employee. However, if the employer is not an individual, in the absence of a legal successor, the employment relationship must be wound up ex lege. In this case, the employee is entitled to a sum equal to his/her average wages payable for the period of exemption from work specified for regular dismissal by the employer, unless the employee is not entitled to any wages for the period of exemption from work under regular dismissal.

924. b) If the employment relationship ceases without legal successor of the employer, the employee will be paid the sum equal to his/her absentee fee due for the period of exemption from work during the notice period if dismissed by the

328. http://www.ewc-news.com/en022013.htm (26 Jul. 2023).

employer, unless the employee is not entitled to any wages for the period of exemption from work under ordinary dismissal.

925. c) The employment relationship of a fixed-term contract terminates upon expiration of the term for which the labour relationship was established. No special report or arrangement is needed. Those circumstances which limit or prohibit dismissal do not prevent the termination of the employment relationship for a fixed term.

926. d) Transfer of employers status from Labour Code to the Act on Public Servant or Civil Servant. Where an employer that falls within the scope of the Labour Code changes because the employer is transferred in whole or in part (strategic business unit, specific material or non-material assets, or specific duties and competencies) – by decision of the founder or the employer – to an employer that falls within the scope of the Act on the legal status of public servants or the Act on the legal status of civil servants, the strategic business unit that is transferred and the employment relation of the employees it employs terminates at the time of transfer.

927. In the case of above-mentioned transfer the transferring employer must, no later than fifteen days prior to the date of transfer, inform the employees concerning (a) the date or planned date of transfer and (b) the reasons of the transfer.[329]

§12. Duties of the Employer in Regard to Termination of the Employment Relationship

928. The employee, upon termination (cessation) of employment, will relinquish his/her position as ordered and settle accounts with the employer. The employer must sufficiently provide for the conditions of job transfer and accounting.

929. Upon termination of the employment relationship by notice, the employee will be paid his work wages and other emoluments from the last day of work, in any case on the fifth working day after the termination of employment relationship, and will be supplied the statements and certificates prescribed by employment regulations and other relevant legislation.

930. At the employee's request, the employer will – at the time of termination (cessation) of the employment relationship, in any case within one year from that time – provide a written assessment of the employee's work if the employment relationship lasted for at least one year. However, if the assessment contains any false facts, the employee may bring action before the court to have such facts abolished or revised.[330]

329. HAJDÚ, József – KUN, Attila (eds), *Munkajog II.*, Budapest: Patrocinium, 2013. pp. 17–21.
330. HAJDÚ, József – KUN, Attila (eds), *Munkajog II.*, Budapest: Patrocinium, 2013. pp. 44–45.

Chapter 7. Protection of Certain Categories of Workers

§1. The Protection of Working Women

I. The Scope of Protection

931. The particular protection of working women is necessitated by various circumstances. These are mainly of a physiological character and more or less unchangeable, but partly also of a subjective nature.

932. First, we should mention primarily here the different statuses of women, owing to which it can be dangerous for their life, health, and physical condition to perform certain kinds of work.

933. Second, there are women's maternal functions. These similarly prevent women from doing certain work, managing certain activities, and they make it imperative for women to take leave for shorter or longer periods. They also mean that mothers, in connection with raising their children, are burdened to a greater extent outside the place of work.

934. Third, there is the additional burden of childcare and housework for women. Basically, almost every child-care and family benefits are provided on equal basis for woman and man. However, in the practice mainly the women who are staying at home with child(ren). Other problem is to harmonize family life and working life (workplace).

935. Fourth, in the framework of labour relations, too, identical treatment is not always assured even in cases of identical training and jobs. Women have fewer chances of promotion than men, as evidenced particularly by the small proportion of women in high-level jobs even in fields where the large majority of employees are women. In eliminating the disadvantages caused by these circumstances, labour law and equal treatment legislation has a great role to play. The provisions of the Hungarian labour law express attitudes to women in three respects: (a) they declare the equality of women before the law, (b) they eliminate the dangers at work arising from physical stature and pregnancy, and finally, (c) they establish certain benefits and allowances to promote the equalization of the more disadvantageous position of women.

II. Equality of Rights of Working Women

936. Already in treating the fundamental principles of labour law, it has been established that according to the Fundamental Law (Constitution) women and men in Hungary enjoy equal rights. Correspondingly, in the Fundamental Law it is prohibited to discriminate between citizens on grounds of their sex. Taking these provisions into consideration, section 12 of the HLC declares that in connection with employment relations the principle of equal treatment must be strictly observed. Of course, the prohibition against discrimination applies only to unjustified distinctions between men and women, as when they are of equal qualifications. When qualifications differ, clearly distinctions may be made.

III. Rules Concerning the Establishment, Modification and Termination of the Employment Relationship

A. *Prohibitions*

937. Women, particularly owing to their physique and maternal functions may be in a disadvantageous position as opposed to men, even under identical labour conditions. For the actual equal rights of women, it is necessary, therefore, to make further provisions which take into consideration these differences, assuring in this way the increased protection of wage-earning women. Pregnant women and mothers of young children are to be preferred for employment, all things being equal. This rule refers to pregnant women and mothers of young children who have suitable qualifications for the job to be filled. From this point of view the concept of a 'mother with a young child/children' has not yet been clarified by the law. According to the opinion of the Labour Division of the Curia, a mother with a young child is generally a mother who looks after or maintains a child under school age. This benefit is due only to the mother herself.

938. As a general rule, women may not be employed for work that might involve adverse physical consequences for them. Thus, work assignments that may not be performed by women, or may only be performed under the insurance of specified working conditions, or on the basis of a preliminary medical examination, are determined by rule of law.

939. No woman may be transferred to a job on the prohibited list during her period of employment, nor temporarily be employed in such a position. In addition to this, further protection is provided by law to pregnant women. After pregnancy is established, a woman may not be employed in any sphere of activity – determined by law – which is harmful to her health. She must, therefore, be transferred temporarily – with no reduction of earnings – to another post. From the beginning of the fourth month of her pregnancy until the child reaches the age of three, a woman cannot be obliged without her consent to perform her work in another community.

B. *Duty to Transfer*

940. In addition to the case mentioned in the previous paragraph, a woman must be transferred temporarily, at her own request and on the basis of a medical certificate, to a job corresponding to her state of health, or the working conditions in her existing position must be appropriately modified from the beginning of her pregnancy until her baby is one year old. According to the Labour Division of the

Curia, a transfer may be requested not only on grounds of an existing medical condition; it is sufficient if – according to medical opinion – the work performed in the original job could exert a harmful effect on the pregnant woman, even if only subjectively, taking into consideration her individual characteristics. The new sphere of activity or place of work cannot be fixed unilaterally by the employer but in agreement with the woman. According to the standpoint of the Labour Division of the Curia, the enterprise is obliged to exert considerable effort, offering more than an alternative job and modifying the labour relationship in other respects, taking into consideration the circumstances connected with pregnancy or maternity, in order to provide a new job that is acceptable to the pregnant woman. In addition, the earnings of the transferred woman cannot be lower than her previous average earnings.

C. Prohibition and Limitation of Notice

941. In regard to terminating a labour contract, the following prohibitions and limitations are determined by legal regulation:

The employer may not terminate the employment relationship by notice:

(a) during pregnancy;
(b) during maternity leave;
(c) during a leave of absence taken without pay for caring for a child;
(d) in the case of women, while receiving treatment related to a human reproduction procedure, for up to six months from the beginning of such treatment.

The above-mentioned points *a)* and *d)* shall apply only if the worker has informed the employer thereof before the notice was given.

D. Rules Concerning Working Hours and Rest Time

942. In addition to the general rules concerning working hours, women are protected, according to the HLC, by the following prohibitions and limitations connected with working hours and extra work:

(a) A woman should not be obliged to work night shifts from the beginning of her pregnancy until her child reaches the age of one.
(b) A working woman should not be obliged to work overtime or be 'on-call-duty' from the beginning of her pregnancy until the child reaches the age of one. Finally, a mother with a child of less than four years of age may be ordered to work overtime or to be 'on call' only with her consent.

943. In connection with the regular annual vacation section 118 of the HLC provides that the wife or the husband – on the basis of their decision – should be entitled to an annual supplementary leave of two to seven days depending on the number of children. This supplementary leave is also due to a single parent.

944. Pregnant women are entitled to 24 weeks' maternity leave. This shall be allocated in such a way that four weeks are preferably taken up prior to the expected time of birth. If the child is being looked after in a centre/unit for premature babies, the unused part of maternity leave may be used after the child has been released from the centre: however, not after the end of the first year after the birth. During maternity leave, women are entitled to health care according to the rules relating to social insurance and depending on their average earnings.

945. Nursing mothers are entitled to unpaid leave for one hour twice daily, or two hours twice daily in the case of twins during the first six months of breastfeeding, and thereafter for one hour daily, or two hours daily in the case of twins until the end of the ninth month.

E. *Unpaid Leave*

946. Upon the employee's request, the employer shall permit unpaid leave:

(a) for the purpose of looking after a child after the expiration of maternity leave up to the time at which the child reaches three years of age, or the age of ten in the case of a chronically ill or seriously disabled child; and
(b) in the case of the child's illness and for the purpose of nursing it at home, for the duration of the illness up to the time at which the child reaches the age of ten.

F. *Posting of the Pregnant and Child-Raiser Woman*

947. A woman shall not be obliged to carry out work at another location without her consent as of the time of her pregnancy up to the time when her child reaches three years of age. This provision shall apply mutatis mutandis to men if the man is a single parent.[331]

§2. YOUNG WORKERS

I. Definition

948. Hungarian labour law contains three concepts, partly overlapping one another. These are: the young person, and the child. In labour law, a young/minor is

331. HAJDÚ József, IEL Labour Law, Hungary, Wolters Kluwer, Kluwer Law Online, 2019. https://kluwerlawonline.com/Manuals/Corporate+Acquisitions+and+Mergers/705 (26 Jul. 2023).

a person who has completed his/her 14th year but has not yet turned 18. Regulations take as their starting point the premise that the bodies of these young persons are still developing. They respond more strongly to increased effort, to the possible damage caused by work, endangering to a greater extent their life, health and safety. In addition, those of this age are – because of their lesser maturity and lack of experience – much more susceptible to corruption. The increased protection is necessitated by the dangers threatening both physical and spiritual development.[332]

949. The concept of the young person has a sociological basis. It is considerably wider than that of the minor and it has no generally defined precise age limit. The Hungarian Fundamental Law speaks generally of the protection of young people. In general, the term young people is taken to embrace schoolchildren, students, and those who have begun to make an independent life for themselves. Certain legal provisions do make reference to specific age groups but these are only important in particular instances. In practice, the lower limit is generally the beginning of the school age, i.e., at the age of six years, and the upper limit is drawn in the vicinity of 25–30 years of age. This is, however, a very flexible limit.

950. Not only is the concept of young people wider than that of minors the scope of protection is also considerably broader. The consideration here is that the appropriate education of young people must be ensured because this is crucial for their future lives and for the entire society as well. In the course of this process, the all-round development of their physical and mental faculties should be made possible, as well as the consolidation of their moral convictions and ideology. After finishing their studies, the finding of employment should take place as smoothly as possible, with employment corresponding as far as possible to ability and education. Settling into work should be undisturbed, and young people should obtain the opportunity as early as possible to evolve and further develop their creative capacities. They should become equal members of the collective of employees, being active in the internal life of the place of work and in developing a democratic climate of opinion. Establishing a family ought to be promoted and the bearing of the financial burdens connected with this must be contributed to. Finally, young people must have the possibility of protecting their own interests, and shaping their independent youth organization so that this organization may always make its voice heard, both in the place of work and outside it, and intervene in the interest of its members.

951. The third concept is that of the child. The child is seen in terms of family bonds, that is to say, from a legal point of view it is a concept of family law. Apart from this, the term 'child' is often used in legal regulations to denote a period of life. Both versions are to be found in the sphere of labour law. One of these is connected with employment. In labour law childhood endures until reaching working age. Working age begins, according to law, at the age of 16. A child of less than 16 years of age basically is not permitted to work. In this sense, there is no concept of

332. BANKÓ Zoltán, 'Gondolatok a fiatalok munkajogi védelméről' *Jogtudományi Közlöny* Vol 53 No 7-8, 1998.

child labour in Hungarian labour law. The other usage, however, refers to family bonds. This is connected with determining the rights and benefits due to employees with children.

952. In the Hungarian legal system, the special protection of young people – in regard to labour relations – is dealt with in the HLC. Three groups of legal regulations falling within the sphere of labour law may be distinguished. First, there are the regulations regarding entering into employment. Second, there are the regulations which ensure the protection of young people during the existence of the employment relationship, in connection with rights and duties arising from relation. The third group consists of the rules connected with the protection of the interests of young people, and especially with their participation in the life of the enterprise.

II. Employment

953. In connection with entering into employment, labour law establishes certain conditions and limitations. It also ensures equal opportunities for young people. Finally, labour law makes provisions regarding the finding of employment. In respect to the first, the Hungarian labour law – to protect the physical and intellectual development of young people – lays down two general conditions: a young person must have reached school-leaving age. These questions have been dealt with above. In addition, there are minor limitations upon the capacity of a young person to enter into a contract. In the case of a person under the age of 16, the consent of his/her legal guardian is essential to the acceptance of the job. This is the case in order that the parent or guardian may prevent the young person from undertaking, without due consideration, a job which might be unsuitable and may even be harmful, or in order that the parent can persuade him/her to continue with his studies for the purpose of obtaining appropriate qualifications.[333]

954. Being of a certain definite age is, at any rate, only one element of the protection of young people in connection with employment. The work itself may conceal some dangers. Taking this into consideration, it is established in the HLC that as a general rule the juvenile must not be employed in a sphere of work that, with respect to his/her state of development, could result in harmful consequences to him/her. In order to realize this provision, there are four general methods:

- In certain jobs further age limitations are applied. Thus, for instance, the provisions for labour safety permit the operation of machines only after a person has reached the age of 16.
- It may be forbidden to employ juveniles in certain jobs as enumerated in the legal regulations, in which, owing to conditions within a given enterprise, the performance of such a job may be injurious to the health of the juvenile.

333. *A fiatalok munkahelyi védelme*, https://osha.europa.eu/hu/publications/factsheets/64 (26 Jul. 2023.).

- In the cases determined by the regulations, the minor seeking employment requiring physical exertion requires a medical examination.
- A labour contract with a minor for employment in a legally prohibited job is always null and void.

955. As mentioned above, the protection of young people is served not only by prohibiting jobs detrimental to their health but also by ensuring that during employment treatment identical with that of adults is ensured to them. For this, labour law prohibits any discrimination between employees on the basis of age. In respect of equal treatment, one of the most crucial areas is the adjustment of wage-rates.

956. The requirement of equality is, of course, not violated if certain jobs are not offered to young people because they are below the legal age limit. Similarly, there is no violation of the provisions for equal treatment in the field of wages if – with respect to the principle of remuneration according to quantity and quality of work performed – there are differences.[334]

957. Because they have less experience, finding suitable employment for young people will generally present more difficulties than for adults. It is, therefore, not sufficient to take negative steps, designed to prevent them from working in dangerous jobs. To ensure opportunities essentially equal to those of adults, it is also necessary to take steps to promote employment and facilitate their adaptation to employment. Thus Act IV of 1991 on employment policy promotes the employment of young people in jobs suitable for their educational level and natural talents, to offer work corresponding to their qualifications, to enable young people to adapt themselves to the community and to their place of work. In addition to this general duty, labour law promotes employment of young people by means of career counselling and the system of study contracts.

III. Protection During the Period of Employment

958. In the case of young people, it is not sufficient to pay particular attention to finding employment. This attention ought to be maintained throughout the whole of the employment relationship. In Hungarian labour law, two types of provisions are made: (1) protection of health and physical safety of young people and (2) the establishment of certain benefits and allowances to promote the educational development of the young employee, and help him/her overcome initial financial difficulties.

959. The HLC lays down particular legal provisions for cases in which the performance of work can be harmful to health, physical safety or development. Thus:

334. Council Directive 94/33/EC of 22 Jun. 1994 on the protection of young people at work.

(a) The prohibition existing in connection with minors entering into employment apply throughout the course of the employment relationship. Therefore, a minor cannot be transferred or temporarily attached to a job for which he/she may not enter a labour contract.
(b) Minors should not be employed for night work. This prohibition has a wider scope than that of the International Labour Organisation for it refers not only to trade and industry but to all employment.
(c) Minors must not work overtime nor may they be kept on call. This prohibition applies even in situations where the enterprise is requiring overtime to prevent or deal with accidents or natural disasters.
(d) Minors, for the sake of protecting their health and development, are entitled to additional leave. This amounts to five working days, annually.[335]

§3. Protection of Disabled Persons of Reduced or Altered Working Capacity

I. The Nature of Protection

960. In addition to international norms and the Hungarian Fundamental Law, the protection of disabled persons falls under two main sources of provisions: (a) labour law and (b) social security law.

961. a) Labour law provisions: According to section 212 of the HLC, the labour law directly protects the disabled workers. This is a new provision in the HLC. According to labour law provisions, incapacitated workers may conclude employment relationships only for jobs which they are capable to handle on a stable and continuous basis in the light of their medical condition.

962. The functions of the employee's job will be determined by definition of the related responsibilities in detail. The employee's medical examination will cover the employee's ability to handle the functions of the job. The employee's work must be supervised continuously so as to ensure that the requirements of occupational safety and health are satisfied.

963. As for special protection, the HLC states that the provisions of Chapter XIV (employees' liability for damages) will not apply to disabled employees, but the provisions pertaining to young workers must apply.[336]

964. b) Social security provisions: The employment rate of disabled people remarkably improved to 50.2%. However, it is still below the EU average of 51.3% and much below the average of national non-disabled persons. Almost 14% of the

335. HANTI Erzsébet, *Az Európai Uniós munkaügyi irányelvek és érvényesítésük a hazai kollektív tárgyalásos gyakorlatban Kézikönyv*, Budapest: Vasas-Köz Nyomda, 2003. pp. 82–86.
336. EMBER Alex, *Az üzemi baleset*, Szeged: Pólay Alapítvány, 2013. pp. 59–64.

active age population (aged 15–64) in Hungary suffer from some sickness or disability which reduces their capacity to work. Aside from the 154,000 working persons registered with so-called reduced work capacity, an estimate used by representatives of ministries responsible for disability issues at various public events, there is no data on the total number of disabled public workers, their transitions to open market jobs, or evidence about the impact of benefit reforms.

965. The role of financial incentives to strengthen the recruitment attitude of private employers has also been confirmed recently by a survey in 2019. It was found,[337] that 62% of companies having at least a staff of 10 employed disabled persons, and its main motive was access to the relief of rehabilitation contribution (67%).27 This is also in line with the assessment of possible incentives for employers who do not yet have such a staff; 34% of them would consider it if the creation of suitable working environment was to be financially supported for them.[338]

966. Since 2005, the system of rehabilitation subsidies was gradually revised partly to increase the social integration of disabled people and partly to curb growing public expenditures, most of which went on subsidising sheltered employment. According to the new system, only accredited employers equipped to provide employment rehabilitation qualify for wage subsidies. However, though formally meeting the accreditation criteria, most firms do not provide services that would support transfer to unsubsidised jobs in the regular labour market. A large share of subsidies goes to sheltered employment where disabled workers are employed in segregated workshops. By contrast, the few NGOs that offer rehabilitation services are quite successful at getting disabled people back to work: the reemployment chance of their clients is 30 to 50 times higher compared to disabled workers in a sheltered workshop, controlling for age, education and work capacity.[339]

967. The rehabilitation of persons of reduced working capacity is based on the view that disability is relative. This is expressed by the legal rule which refers to persons not with reduced but with altered working capacity. If a waiter injures a leg he/she will be unable to continue his/her original job but, probably, he/she will be able to work in a different job. At the same time, if an accountant injures a leg, he/she will still be able to perform his/her normal duties. Consequently, in each case a job must be sought in which the effects of the disability are felt only to a small extent or not at all. If a job is found, those prerequisites must be created which make it possible for the worker to resume work. This procedure, i.e., the rehabilitation of the disabled, needs the co-operation of several disciplines as well as practical efforts. Medicine and medical assistance play a basic role in this procedure since

337. Employment of disadvantaged or disabled workers in Hungary, Economic and Enterprise Research, Budapest, December 2019, pp. 1–4. https://gvi.hu/research-details/597/employment-of-disadvantaged-or-disabled-workers-in-hungary. (26 Jul. 2023).
338. Tamás GYULAVÁRI-Éva Gellérné LUKÁCS-Anita Kaderják-Kata Nagy (2021) European Semester 2020–2021, country fiche on disability equality-Hungary.
339. http://www.onyf.hu/?module=news_archive&action=list&fname=ONYF_LEFT_MENU_UGYINTEZES_REHABILITACIO&rand=657473def511e650dd7f2d6073b637f5 (26 Jul. 2023).

they determine those conditions in which the disabled may be employed most properly. Creating these necessary conditions then often means technical and organizational work and may require the retraining of the worker. Lastly, Hungarian labour law defines the responsibility of the enterprise or state organ concerning proper employment and the rules of procedure. The concept of providing employment for those who are disabled by industrial accident or occupational disease or other causes emerged after the Second World War when legal regulation took shape. Its essence was that employers were obliged to employ a certain proportion of disabled persons.[340]

II. Essential Change in the Rehabilitation System

968. The Hungarian system of disability benefits and its institutions were changed by Act CXCI of 2011 on Benefits Provided for Persons with Changed Working Capacity and the Amendment of Certain Pieces of Legislation. At the end of 2011, the Parliament decided upon a new Act on the benefits for persons with changed working capacity. The new Act has the purpose of ensuring social reintegration, employment and employment – focused rehabilitation based on remaining and improvable capacities of those with changed working capacity.

969. Moreover, the Act regulates income substitution of the missing income. The focus is on remaining working capacities and the aim is to lead persons with changed working capacity back to the labour market.

970. According to the new rules, the former disability pension (rokkantsági nyugdíj), accident-related disability pension (baleseti rokkantsági nyugdíj), rehabilitation annuity (rehabilitációs járadék), regular social annuity for persons with ill-health (rendszeres szociális járadék), temporary invalidity annuity (átmeneti járadék) and health damage annuity for miners (bányász dolgozók egészségkárosodási járadéka) cannot be awarded from 1 January 2012 further on. In their place, new benefits are awarded through a newly established complex assessment method.

971. Pursuant to the new Act, the Rehabilitation Specialized Authorities of the capital/county government authorities have been established as of 1 July 2012. One of the primary tasks of the new Specialized Authority is to promote the employment of persons with changed working capacity who are in a disadvantageous position on the labour market, and of persons who are permanently outside the labour market, and to equalize their competitiveness on the labour market.

972. The official employment of persons with changed working capacity is also necessary because employers with more than 25 employees shall pay rehabilitation contributions in the interest of assisting in the rehabilitation of workers with some

340. http://ec.europa.eu/employment_social/empl_portal/SSRinEU/Your%20social%20security%20rights%20in%20Hungary_en.pdf (26 Jul. 2023).

degree of incapacity and if the number of such incapacitated workers in the employer's employment is below 5% of the total labour force.

973. The rate of the rehabilitation contribution is nine times the statutory minimum amount of the basic salary for full-time employees on the first day of the year in question, per person, per year. On 1 January 2023, the compulsory minimum basic wage for a monthly wage is HUF 232,000, of which nine times HUF 2,088,000 (EUR 5,583). The annual amount of the employer's rehabilitation contribution is the product of the number of employees missing from the compulsory employment level and the rehabilitation contribution.[341,342]

III. New Forms of Support to Promote the Employment of Persons with Changed Working Capacity

Wages and costs support for protected workplaces

974. It is special form of sheltered or supported employment of persons with changed working capacity in protected workplaces. Any employer can apply for accreditation if, among others, the monthly statistical number of employees with changed working capacity is at least 30 persons, or their proportion is at least 25%.[343]

975. As from January 2013, support for wages and costs paid through applications has been introduced, only for accredited employers, which can be paid to the employers for transit and permanent employment.

976. On the accreditation of employers of disabled workers, and the granting of budgetary aid for the employment of workers with reduced working capacity (XI. 16.) of the Government Decree 327/2012 (hereinafter: Government Decree) forms of aid:

(a) grants for the rehabilitation employment of workers with reduced working capacity individual aid for the employment of disabled workers in the employment of disabled persons;
(b) a one-off grant linked to an individual allowance;

341. For example, an employer who employs a labour force of 100 persons has to employ five persons with changed working capacity in order to be exempt from paying the contribution. If he/she employs, for example, only three persons, he/she has to pay 2 x HUF 2,088,000 every year in respect of the missing two persons.
342. Rehabilitációs hozzájárulás, 2023; http://www.nav.gov.hu (26 Jul. 2023.).
343. Tájékoztató a Rehabilitációs kártyáról (2017). https://szgyf.gov.hu/phocadownload/foglalkozasi_rehabilitacios_informaciok/Tajekoztato_a_Rehabilitacios_kartyarol.pdf (26 Jul. 2023).

(c) for the conversion of workplaces for rehabilitation purposes or the creation of new rehabilitation workplaces job creation aid for the creation of new jobs.[344]

977. Among the costs incurred during employment, support can be provided for maximum 75% of the wages and the social contribution tax, or maximum 100% in the case of activities performed in the form of association, foundation, or in the case of non-profit business associations for non-economic-entrepreneurial activities.

978. They were employed especially in jobs with less stringent physical requirements, such as doorkeeper, night watchman, delivery man. Implementing this rule often meant formal work only, for it was considered a kind of social assistance rather than satisfying the employers' manpower needs. A recent legal ruling sets forth the following principles:

IV. The Scope of Protection

979. Persons eligible for benefits for persons with changed working capacity are those:

(a) whose state of health is assessed at 60% or less; and
(b) who had been insured for at least 1,095 days within five years before submitting the claim;
(c) who are not performing any gainful activity; and
(d) who do not receive any regular cash benefits.

980. The benefit for persons with changed working capacity consists of two separate provisions:

(1) the person is entitled to rehabilitation benefit, if he/she can be rehabilitated. The rehabilitation benefit may be provided for the period required for rehabilitation, within the limit of 3 years from the start of the benefit;
(2) a person with changed working capacity is entitled to disability benefit if rehabilitation is not recommended; or he/she cannot be rehabilitated, or the person reaches the retirement age within five (5) years.

V. Benefits for Persons with Changed Working Capacity

981. The benefits for persons with changed working capacity are health insurance benefits. Earlier these benefits fell under the scope of the pension insurance scheme.

344. https://www.kormanyhivatal.hu/download/7/4f/48000/%C3%9Atmutat%C3%B3%202023%20%C3%A9vi%20t%C3%A1mogat%C3%A1s%20elsz%C3%A1mol%C3%A1s%C3%A1hoz.pdf (26 Jul. 2023).

The amount is based on the average monthly income, and its minimum is set to certain percentages of the minimum wage:

(1) Rehabilitation benefit:
  (a) persons for whom rehabilitation is possible within an expected time frame:
    (i) Amount: 35% of the average monthly income.
    (ii) Minimum: 30% of the minimum wage.
    (iii) Ceiling: 40% of the minimum wage.
  (b) persons who need permanent rehabilitation:
    (i) Amount: 45% of the average monthly income.
    (ii) Minimum: 40% of the minimum wage.
    (iii) Ceiling: 50% of the minimum wage.
(2) Disability benefit varies according to the decision on the health status and the possibility of rehabilitation:
  (a) Amount: 40–70% of the average monthly income.
  (b) Minimum: 30–55% of the minimum wage.
  (c) Ceiling: 45% or 150% of the minimum wage.

VI. Assessment of Eligibility

982. The eligibility is assessed by the rehabilitation authority, which conducts a multidisciplinary examination (so-called complex assessment) on the state of health and the possibility of the rehabilitation of the claimant.

983. From 1 January 2012, benefits for persons with changed working capacity can be claimed free of charge via the relevant printed or electronic application forms at the newly established rehabilitation bodies of the county government office of the claimant's place of residence.

984. The applicant may be obliged to report to the rehabilitation body for the complex assessment. Failure to do so may result in termination of the procedure. In the course of the complex assessment, the rehabilitation body will examine the applicant's state of health and whether he/she qualifies for rehabilitation.

In the latter case it shall issue a decision on rehabilitation. Disability and rehabilitation benefits are paid by the Pension Payment Directorate.[345]

VII. Prohibition of Dismissal

985. According to Subsection (7) of section 66 of the Hungarian Labour Code, the employer may terminate by notice the employment relationship of a worker who is receiving rehabilitation treatment or rehabilitation benefits due to the worker's capacity related to medical reasons if the worker can no longer be employed in his/

345. http://ec.europa.eu/employment_social/empl_portal/SSRinEU/Your%20social%20security%20rights%20in%20Hungary_en.pdf (26 Jul. 2023).

her original position and no other job is available that is considered appropriate for his/her medical condition, or if the employee refuses to accept a job offered by the employer without good reason.

986. It is important to mention the Case No. IV/2415/2022. of the Hungarian Constitutional Court on unlawful termination of employment for retired employee who receives rehabilitation benefit. The Constitutional Court has declared Article 294(1)(g)(gg) of Act I of 2012 on the Labour Code (Labour Code) in force until 31 December 2022 to be unconstitutional. The contested provision provides that the applicant is a retired worker in receipt of rehabilitation benefits. In the case in the main proceedings, the applicant's employment was terminated without justification by reason of the contested provision. The applicant submits that the contested provision does not facilitate but hinders the establishment of an employment relationship for persons in receipt of rehabilitation benefits and makes it easier for employers to terminate the employment relationship, thus infringing the provisions of the Fundamental Law guaranteeing the right to work and equal treatment. In its decision, the Constitutional Court explained that after 1 January 2012, disability pensions ceased to exist, and instead disabled persons became entitled to benefits for persons with reduced capacity for work (rehabilitation or disability benefits) before reaching the retirement age, and to old-age pensions after reaching this age.

987. Both rehabilitation benefits and invalidity benefits may be combined with gainful employment, but under the contested provision, a person who worked while receiving invalidity benefits (and who was only younger than the retirement age under the relevant rules) was considered to be a pensioner. Thus, a worker who had not yet reached retirement age and was in receipt of invalidity benefits was not subject to the general rules on dismissal and severance pay, but to those applicable to pensioners, with fewer employment law guarantees (as in the case of the applicant). The legislator therefore treated persons in different situations (over and under retirement age) in the same way and provided reduced employment law guarantees for both categories of persons.

988. The unjustified withdrawal of labour law guarantees from persons receiving disability benefits constitutes offensive discrimination based on their health condition or disability, and the Constitutional Court declared the previously in force provision to be unconstitutional and ordered its application to be prohibited.[346]

346. AB határozat jogszabályi rendelkezés alaptörvény-ellenességének megállapításáról (2023) https://www.alkotmanybirosag.hu/a-legfrissebb-dontesek/ab-hatarozat-jogszabalyi-rendelkezes-alaptorveny-ellenessegenek-megallapitasarol/ (26 Jul. 2023).

Chapter 8. Covenants of Non-competition

989. With the termination of a labour relationship, all relations between a worker and the enterprise cease. Thus, the enterprise basically cannot make a stipulation for the period after termination which would prevent the worker from finding employment. However, there is a legal possibility to protect the economic interest of the employer. This provision is the non-competition clause (agreement). The aim of this agreement is to protect the economic and legal interest of the former employer. The HLC provides that based on the agreement by the employer and the employee, an employee may – for a period of a maximum of two years after termination of the employment – not engage in any conduct which jeopardizes or intervenes with the employer's rightful business interests. The employer must pay appropriate consideration in exchange for the non-competition undertaking. When it comes to determining the amount of appropriate compensation, one must examine particularly the extent to which the non-competition agreement prevents the employee from getting a new job and also take into account his/her qualification and experience. The amount of appropriate compensation may not be less than one-third of the employee's basic wage, payable for a period equal to the length of the non-competition period.

990. The non-competition agreement shall be made in writing. The employee has the right to withdraw from the agreement if having terminated his/her employment according to the provisions of the „termination without notice (*See*: section 78(1) of the HLC).

991. In the case of transfer of employment upon the transfer of enterprise, the rights and obligations arising from the agreement shall be transferred to the receiving employer.

992. If any contractual penalty is stipulated, sections 6:186–6:189 of the Civil Code shall be governing.

993. In addition to the maximum period of a non-competition undertaking and the amount of appropriate compensation, the new HLC also brought about an additional novelty. Namely, the employee may rescind (i.e., unilaterally terminate with retroactive effect) the non-competition undertaking if he/she terminates his/her employment with immediate effect by way of extraordinary termination notice. Under Hungarian labour law, an employer or employee may terminate an employment relationship by extraordinary termination notice in the event that the other party:

(a) wilfully, or by gross negligence, commits a grave violation of a substantive obligation arising from the employment relationship; or
(b) otherwise engages in conduct rendering the maintenance of the employment relationship impossible.

Of course, the parties are free to grant rescission rights to each other in other cases too.

994. The new HLC makes it clear that in the event there is a legal succession on the employer's side, the rights and obligations of the employer concluding the non-competition agreement will pass on to the new employer. Including such a provision in the HLC was necessary because judicial practice has not been authoritative as to whether the rights and obligations laid down in a non-competition agreement would pass on to a new employer that happens to be a legal successor of the former employer.

995. It is also worth noting that the new HLC does not stipulate that the non-competition agreement is subject to the provisions of the Civil Code. Therefore, such an agreement may not be challenged on grounds of the considerations being considerably disproportional. However, if the compensation paid as consideration for the non-competition undertaking is not appropriate, the agreement may be partially invalid. In this case, courts may either require the employer to pay to the employee an appropriate compensation in exchange for the non-competition undertaking, or declare that the entire agreement is null and void.

996. It is also worth noting that, under the new HLC, the employment agreements of executive employees[347] may deviate from the provisions governing employment relationships that are laid down in the new HLC, with the one exception being that they cannot deviate from the provision which provides that collective labour agreements are not applicable to executive employees. If a non-competition agreement is not regarded as part of the employment agreement, but rather as a separate agreement, the conclusion will most probably be that no deviation is allowed from the provisions governing non-competition agreements. If, however, the non-competition agreement is regarded as being part of the employment agreement, deviation is allowed. It seems that the question of whether the parties may deviate from the provisions of the HLC governing non-competition agreements will need to be interpreted and decided by the court.

997. Typically, trade secret as a condition is not examined. The reason for this is that trade secrets could not be the subject of the agreement not to compete, because an independent act (Act of prohibition of unfair market practices and restriction of economic competition) regulates that the employee should protect and not disclose the trade secrets after the termination of the employment relationship. If the employee in the covenant not to compete takes upon him/herself to protect trade secrets, it would mean stopping from an unlawful activity.

998. The burden of proof determined by the general provisions of the Code of Civil Procedure: facts required for the adjudging of a case must be proved by the party who is interested in their acceptance.

347. Managing directors and those employees working under the direct control of the managing director who may partially or fully substitute the managing director.

999. The rights and obligations of the agreement not to compete are only binding for the contractual parties: employer and employee. It does/should not contain provisions for an unknown third party, the new employer. The new employer is responsible for the damage that he/she causes to the old employer, for example, when getting the customers' list by fraud according to the rules of the Civil Code and the Act of Prohibition of unfair market practices and restriction of economic competition. This kind of lawsuit falls within the competence of the civil law and not the labour/employment law courts. If there is no covenant not to compete, the employee's responsibility still exists according to these rules and not the HLC.[348]

348. CSÉFFÁN József, *A munka törvénykönyve és magyarázata*, Szeged: Szegedi Rendezvényszervező Kft., 2023.

Chapter 9. Inventions by Employees

§1. Types of Inventions

1000. In Hungary, sections 9-17 of the Act XXXIII of 1995 on the Protection of Inventions by Patents (the 'Patent Act') is the key piece of legislation in respect of inventions created in employment relationships. According to the right of the inventor to both the invention and the patent granted thereto, inventions created by an inventor employed at a company fall into one of three categories:

(a) Service inventions – these are inventions made in the course of the employee's work duties In this case, the right to the invention and its patent belongs to the employer.
(b) Employees' inventions – these are inventions created by an inventor with no direct or indirect duty to work in the relevant technical, but that fall within the scope of the employer's activities. In such cases the rights to the invention and the patent belong to the inventor, although the employer is entitled to use the invention upon payment of a licence fee. The employer's right of use is non-exclusive and the employer may not grant a licence of use itself.
(c) Free inventions – these are inventions created by an inventor with no direct or indirect duty to work in the relevant technical field, and which fall outside the scope of the employer's activities.

1001. The most frequent and relevant of these three groups is that of service inventions. In such cases, both the inventor and the employer must follow certain steps. The inventor must notify the employer of the invention and the employer must then respond within a given timeframe stating whether it wishes to acquire the rights to the invention and will process it as a service invention. All administrative duties and costs connected with preparing and filing a regular patent application and any subsequent foreign applications based on such inventions should be borne by the employer. The employer will own the rights to the invention and will have unlimited freedom to:

- keep the invention secret and use it as non-public know-how;
- obtain domestic and foreign IP rights and grant licences; and
- otherwise use the rights without limitation.[349]

§2. Reporting and Management Requirements

1002. The inventor is required to report the service invention to the employer immediately following its creation. The employer has ninety days following receipt

349. TEPFENHÁRT Dóra (2022) *A szolgálati találmányok szabályozásának vitás pontjai* https://www.danubia.com/hu/szabadalom/a-szolgalati-talalmanyok-szabalyozasanak-vitas-pontjai/ (26 Jul. 2023).

of such notification to make a declaration signalling his intention to claim the service invention. Absent this declaration in the prescribed time period, the inventor employee may freely dispose of the rights in the service invention. The same is true if the employer consents to such an outcome.

1003. In the event the employer chooses to claim the service invention, he/she is obliged to file a patent application within a reasonable time following receipt of notification regarding the existence of the invention. The Patent Act imposes an additional duty on the employer to act with the level of care generally expected in acquiring a patent. Moreover, if the employer omits or commits an act that would result in the rejection of the patent application, the employer must offer a free assignment of the patent claim to the inventor.

1004. If the employer considers the invention to be utilized as a trade secret, he/she will not file a patent application or withdraw it if it has already been submitted and has not been publicized. Under these circumstances, the employer must acknowledge that absent its trade secret characterization, the service invention would otherwise be eligible for patent protection. The employee must be notified of this decision and in case of dispute, the burden of proof is on the employer to demonstrate that the invention was ineligible for patent protection.

§3. Remuneration of the Inventor

1005. There are two possibilities for the remuneration of inventors: (i) payment through a license analogy or (ii) a lump sum amount. The inventor's right to remuneration arises upon the utilization of the invention. As outlined in greater detail below, the concept of utilization is broadly interpreted. The Patent Act includes a number of provisions in connection with the statutory claim of remuneration that is due to inventors.

1006. The following rules apply unless a remuneration agreement is concluded between the inventor and the employer that departs from these mandatory rules:

- Time span of the remuneration claim: the general rule provides for the presumed entire term of patent protection, i.e., twenty years (plus the term of the supplemental patent certificate in the case of medicines), even if the patent is terminated earlier through any act or omission of the employer.
- Types of utilization by the employer on the basis of which the inventor employee is entitled to remuneration: production, use of process, and/or licensing, and/or assignment of the patent, and/or any omission of utilization in order to create or maintain an advantageous market position.
- The inventor is entitled to remuneration separately in respect of each and every type of utilization including the granting of any licenses or assignments without consideration.
- The remuneration claim may be enforced against the employer. In the case of licensing or assignment of the patent, the licensee or assignee may assume the

obligation to pay remuneration without prior consent from the employee. In the absence of a remuneration agreement, the claim may always be enforced against the employer (in case of multiple employers, against the employer utilizing the service invention).

- The remuneration of the inventor must be governed by a remuneration agreement.

1007. As mentioned above, the application of the statutory provisions can be avoided through the use of well-drafted invention regulations (i.e., by-laws) and remuneration agreements.

I. Remuneration on the Basis of the License Analogy

1008. In the event the employer itself utilizes the service invention, the remuneration provided to the employee shall be proportionate to the fee that would be paid by the employer as a licensee pursuant to a patent licensing agreement, in view of the licensing practice in the given technological field and in accordance with the subject matter of the invention.

1009. If the service invention becomes the subject of a license or an assignment, the royalty paid must be proportional to the proceeds of a license or assignment, or to the transfer or economic benefit/advantage resulting from a free license or free assignment.

1010. Remuneration will be deemed proportional where due regard is paid to the employer's contribution to the creation of the invention as well as to the obligations of the inventor in the employment relationship. Further guidance in the form of jurisprudence is yet to come with respect to proportionality as well as license analogy.

II. Lump Sum Payments

1011. As previously mentioned, the Patent Act allows for possible departures from the statutory remuneration provisions. In fact, the Act expressly allows for lump sum remuneration agreements.

1012. As noted above, two possible avenues are allowed: (i) a remuneration of a fixed amount paid per invention and if necessary, determined specifically by the type of utilization (own exploitation, license, assignment); or (ii) a lump sum replacing all remuneration payable for all types of utilization of all future inventions of the employee.

1013. A remuneration agreement qualifies as a civil law contract despite the fact that it is concluded in the context of an employment relationship, and this is reinforced by the Patent Act itself. Although feasible under the express terms of the statute, the second option is more fragile as the enforcement of a claim by the inventor before the courts given a substantial change in circumstances can be more easily verified in the case of a general lump sum agreement designed to satisfy all future claims. Further, there is no published case law on whether the inventor may challenge the agreement based on the legal cause of flagrant disproportion between the services rendered and the consideration paid for services, of error or deceit.

1014. Companies often address remuneration issues by the way of internal invention regulations (i.e., by-laws). Such invention regulations are in fact regarded as a general term of the (employment) contract to which all rules laid down by the Hungarian Civil Code are applicable. However, in the event a works' council or other similar representative organization duly accepts such a regulation, it qualifies as an individual agreement binding upon the employee pursuant to the employment contract, although under the HLC, the works' council only has a right of consultation.

§4. Potential Claims

1015. In Hungary, there is not a significant level of disputes in connection with employers' ownership claims. Disputes tend to occur in cases where it does not obviously result from the nature of the employment relationship that the elaboration of a given solution in the domain of the invention is the employee's obligation. This may arise, for example, where an employee develops an invention or solution in connection with and during the course of employment that falls within the sphere of activities of the employer. These disputes, however, can be minimized through the consistent use of appropriate contractual practices.

1016. The enforceability of claims in connection with remuneration agreements may actually turn out to be limited if the regulation of the invention is not a unilateral act of the employer but rather the result of a consensus. Subject to certain limits, such regulation may restrict the ability to challenge the agreement based on the legal cause of flagrant disproportion between the services rendered and the consideration paid for services, of error or deceit.

1017. Additionally, the legal cause to challenge an agreement crystallizes only following its execution, meaning that the difference between the remuneration provided and actual revenues from sales becomes disproportionate at a later stage. In view of this fact, the chance of a 'classic' challenge based on invalidity for reasons listed above is slim in any case. At present, there is no published judicial practice to provide guidance regarding the drafting of remuneration agreements or enforceability of claims.

1018. In sum, the employer in Hungary may become the rightful holder of a patent that is granted in respect of an invention created by its employee by fulfilling his/her labour responsibilities. The inventor of a service invention has a statutory right to remuneration in case of utilization even in the absence of a remuneration contract; remuneration must be calculated using the license analogy or a lump sum payment.

1019. If the parties conclude a remuneration agreement and/or they use agreed-upon general terms and conditions of remuneration agreements (in the form of internal by-laws), they can take advantage of the permissive possibilities offered by the remuneration rules, including the possibility to conclude a lump sum agreement. If the internal by-laws are accepted by consensus and separate remuneration agreements are concluded in accordance with the bylaws, the risk of enforcement of a claim by a service inventor diminishes.

1020. Clearly drafted employment agreements and internal regulations governing remuneration issues are vital in the area of service inventions. While jurisprudence covering service inventions and remuneration agreements is still forthcoming in Hungary, consistently drafted employment and remuneration agreements, including invention by-laws, will ensure successful employment relationships and a competitive business.[350]

350. Hungarian Intellectual Property Office (2023), https://www.sztnh.gov.hu/en/about-the-hungarian-intellectual-property-office (26 Jul. 2023).

Chapter 10. Liability

§1. Liability for Violation of Rights and Duties Arising from the Employment Relationship

1021. Liability for culpable breach of rights and duties in employment arises in the case of wrongful conduct committed in the framework of employment by one of the parties concerned. Its purpose is to educate the parties to respect and fulfil the rights and duties arising from employment.

1022. The concept of liability in labour law implies sanctions against those breaking the law. This injurious conduct takes place in the framework of permanent legal relations. However, liability is not the only means of education; there are also other legal and extra-legal social means at our disposal. This circumstance makes its effect felt in labour law in more than one respect. It manifests itself in connection with the injurious conduct committed by the employee in the following: on the one hand, the legal regulation establishes a differentiated system of sanctions, making it possible to take into consideration the situation within the collective, and it considerably restricts the extent of material liability. On the other hand, it leaves it to the discretion of the one who is entitled to claim liability whether he/she wishes to use this means of individual and collective prevention. Finally, it has repeatedly been expressed in judicial practice that in applying sanctions one of the essential points of view to be considered is the internal situation and the level of order and discipline in the enterprise. In the case of an injury suffered by a worker, this manifests itself in that the employer, as a general rule, is held liable irrespective of culpability and emphasizes that the enterprise should organize the work and co-operation within its scope of activity in such a way as to prevent misconduct or accident.

1023. Liability in labour law arises only upon the infringement of a given right. However, it does not arise automatically. A declaration in this respect and intervention of the injured party is also necessary.[351,352]

I. The Limits of Liability

1024. One aim of providing for liability is to influence the violator of law. But this can only be successful if in future the offender party is able to avoid similar conduct, i.e., if he/she is really capable of different behaviour. It also follows that the institution of liability can only be used for protecting the interests defended by law when there exists such a possibility of reform. This implies certain limits of the

351. HAJDÚ József, 'A munkavállalói általános kártérítési felelősség szabályozása az új Mt.-ben: tények és kihívások' in. KUN Attila (ed.). *Az új munka törvénykönyve dilemmái* Acta Caroliensia Scientiarium Iuridico-Politicarum V. Budapest: KRE, 2013. pp. 112–129.
352. Hungary – Country Commercial Guide (2022) https://www.trade.gov/country-commercial-guides/hungary-protecting-intellectual-property (26 Jul. 2023).

effectiveness of liability. This does not mean that in a given case there is no action possible against the offender outside this sphere, for example, there is an obligation to compensate damage or losses. This, however, does not fall within the concept of liability but is dealt with by the laws governing compensation.

1025. The possibility of influencing the offender is assumed by law in two cases. One exists when he/she saw or could have seen that he/she deviated from the social requirements made upon him/her. This is liability based on fault. The other exists when the law does not examine whether the party concerned was capable of foresight but in the particular circumstances assumes that a calling to account will have the desired effect. Cases of liability without fault belong in this category.

1026. The influencing character of the system of culpability is direct. Namely, in the course of calling to account and the application of sanctions, the fault committed is revealed and the damage is shown to have resulted from the misconduct of the perpetrator. In a system disregarding culpability, only the result is shown, and the sanction inflicted is to encourage the perpetrator to investigate the circumstances of the loss and to draw the necessary lessons from them. Here, therefore, education goes on in an indirect way. Therefore, if there is a possibility of satisfactorily establishing culpability, then direct methods are to be preferred. Liability based on culpability is the fundamental form in the event of infringement of law by the employee. But in the event of injurious conduct by the enterprise, it is only applied as an auxiliary solution.

II. Liability and the Duty of Co-operation

1027. In the course of the employment relation co-operation between the parties concerned is essential, as was noted above. Both parties are, therefore, obliged to do everything possible so that the other party may fulfil his/her duties and practise his/her rights. This also implies that each party should assist in mitigating the consequences of the breach of duty – in this case, of causing damage – by the other party. In establishing liability, the conduct of the injured party must also be considered. In so far as it was relevant to the injury committed, or to its extent, it is to be evaluated in determining sanctions, as a factor alleviating the extent of the sanction or excluding it entirely. This evaluation takes place in various ways, depending on the type of liability.

III. Types of Liability in Hungarian Labour Law

1028. Liability in labour law is of two kinds: (1) compensatory and (2) disciplinary. The essential differences between them can be summarized as follows:

(a) Disciplinary liability has a single aim: to influence the negligent party by imposing sanctions. Material liability, on the other hand, serves two aims: partly to repair the damage caused by the injury, partly – as in the former case – to influence.
(b) Compensation may be a consequence of the injurious conduct of either the employer or of the employee where injury caused damage to the other party. Disciplinary liability, however, is only based on a breach of duty by the employee. However, it is not limited to damaging conduct. In such a case, the employee may initiate a labour dispute to enforce abandonment of the injurious conduct or fulfilment of the obligation.
(c) Disciplinary liability exists only in cases of culpability; compensatory liability may exist without culpability, as well.
(d) Disciplinary liability provides for several types of sanctions. Compensatory liability provides for only one type, namely compensation for damages caused. Within this, however, there is some differentiation.

1029. The two kinds of liability do not exclude one another. As a result of the same injurious conduct – as established by the Labour Section of the Curia – both may apply simultaneously.

1030. The HLC does not regulate directly the concept of 'disciplinary liability'. Indirectly, it provides for the possibility for the collective agreement to establish detrimental legal consequences against an employee violating his/her duties arising from the employment relationship. In reality, this is a sort of disciplinary liability. (However, the public sector employment legislation (e.g., public and civil servants, etc.) do contain the institution of disciplinary liability.)[353]

A. *Compensatory Liability*

1. Concept and Limits of Compensatory Liability

1031. Compensatory liability is a special form of liability which applies to cases of violation of the law causing damage. It entails compensation for the damages caused. In connection with this, it is to be noted that the lack of fulfilment of the duties arising from the labour contract or inadequate or delayed fulfilment enables the employer to require satisfactory fulfilment or, possibly, to apply immediate termination of the labour relationship.

1032. This does not fall within the sphere of compensatory liability. In addition, in cases like this, the injured party can also make a claim for compensation if – as a result of non-fulfilment or unsatisfactory fulfilment of duty – he/she also suffered some financial disadvantage.

353. HAJDÚ József, IEL Labour Law, Hungary, Wolters Kluwer, Kluwer Law Online, 2019. https://kluwerlawonline.com/Manuals/Corporate+Acquisitions+and+Mergers/705 (26 Jul. 2023).

1033. In labour law liability can only arise between the subjects of the labour relationship. If, therefore, in the course of an activity exercised in the framework of a labour relationship a third party suffers damage as an outsider, his/her claim of compensation does not come within the sphere of compensatory liability for damages caused in the framework of a labour relationship. However, if the employer is forced to pay damages to a third party, then he/she may seek compensation from the employee who was at fault, according to the precepts of labour law.

1034. As compensatory liability of the employer or the employee only refers to damages caused within the framework of labour relations, the provisions of labour law cannot apply to damages caused after the expiration of an employment relationship. It may, however, occur that damages were caused during the existence of the labour relationship but were only discovered after its termination. In such cases, the rules of labour law are applied because from this point of view the date of the activity causing damages is decisive.

2. Conditions of Compensatory Liability

a. The Principles of Liability

1035. It was mentioned above that in cases of liability based on culpability the influencing aims are manifested more directly. Departure from this principle is only justified where it would not jeopardize the effectiveness of the fundamental aim of material liability: compensation. Culpability, therefore, plays no longer an essential role if compensation would be jeopardized. This course is adopted by law in the case of a deficiency occurring in items which the employee has received on trust with an obligation to return or render account, as well as in cases of compensatory liability of the employer.

b. Liability Based on Culpability

1036. Culpability implies that in a given case the perpetrator did not conduct him/herself as society expects although he/she knew or should have known what the proper conduct was. Culpability is, therefore, a subjective concept; it expresses the relation between the perpetrator and the injurious conduct or consequences. In forming a judgment on this a comparison is made between a conscious situation characterized by concrete injurious conduct with a prescribed standard, namely a social requirement. This, however, is not of the same extent in every case. In the work of society, it is not abstract human beings who participate but workers, engineers, book-keepers, judges, etc. In addition, they do not act in a vacuum but exert influence on one another. From this, it also follows that in speaking of social requirements one should not take as the point of departure citizens in general, but individuals of definite vocations or spheres of activity living under similar circumstances. The standard will be the average conduct within a given group to which the conduct in a concrete case is to be compared.

c. Liability Without Culpability

1037. The basic principle of the system of liability without culpability is that in certain cases it is objectively possible to avoid damage. Therefore, in applying compensatory liability the aim is to ensure that the person causing the damage will act in the future in such a way as to eliminate or at least reduce damage. This basic principle also determines the limits of the system of liability. Liability is only applicable in so far as there is genuinely an objective possibility of avoiding damage. The consequences of this are clear at two levels. One of these is the level of lawmaking. It is not proper to establish compensatory liability in cases where there is no opportunity to avoid damages. The other level is the occurrence of actual damage. The basis of a calling to account is that damage is objectively avoidable. The person considered liable should have an opportunity to exonerate him/herself from liability on the grounds that, in the given case, damage was unavoidable.

1038. Relief from liability has two aspects. Firstly, it must be shown that the cause of damage was not the responsibility of the person considered liable and in fact prevented the fulfilment of the duty arising from the labour relationship. The other criterion is that the damage was unavoidable. If the activity of a person was not unpreventable, then the cause of damage will not be this person but the one who has failed to prevent it. Thus, a person causing damage will be relieved of liability if he/she proves that it resulted from an unpreventable external cause.

1039. In judging the existence of avoidability or unavoidability, one starts from the view that an event may be unavoidable because, at the present-day level of science and technology, either there is no possibility of preventing it from taking place or despite the possibility, owing to the unexpected occurrence of it, it was nevertheless impossible to utilise this possibility.

3. Consideration of the Conduct of the Injured Party

1040. It often occurs that the conduct of the injured party also contributes to the damage. In connection with this there are two cases. One is the situation in which the damage was caused only by the conduct of the injured party. The other is that in which the conduct of the injured party was only one factor in causing the damage. The latter embraces the so-called mitigation of damages. Here, additional damages were caused by the injured party who failed to take certain preventative measures. Thus, the culpability and innocence of the injured party may occur simultaneously.

1041. The contribution of the injured party to damage means he/she is also a partial cause of damage. This contribution is taken into consideration only if, in the given case, the prevention or reduction of damages was to be expected. This is generally so if the injured party foresaw or could have foreseen the consequences of his/her conduct, that is to say, if he/she is culpable. But to take into consideration the contributory conduct of the enterprise no culpability is demanded by law. If both the causer of damage and the contributing injured party are culpable, the proportion of contribution to damage will be determined by the ratio of both culpabilities. In the absence of homogeneous comparable conduct, culpability shall be considered in itself and the measure of sharing damages shall be determined on this basis.[354]

4. Compensation

a. Extent of the Liability

1042. The principle of full compensation of damages is decisive in labour law. A departure from this only takes place in the sphere of the liability of employees.

b. Damage

1043. Damage implies some disadvantage, manifested by the injured party. The disadvantages in the case of material nature as well as in the case of a non-pecuniary nature can be taken into consideration.

a) Material damage

1044. Material damages may be divided into two main groups. One of these is the loss of goods as a result of the damaging conduct. The other is the loss of money-making or income in the future, i.e., unrealized profits or income.

1045. Cases belonging to the sphere of resulting damages are similarly divided into two groups. The first includes the actual losses of goods occurring as a result of the damaging conduct; the other includes the costs and expenses incurred. The latter are not the primary, immediate consequences of damage; they are generally of an ancillary nature. Many of them are serving the purpose of making possible the reduction of the consequences of damaging. In connection with this, another difference is to be pointed out as well. Damages generally occur independently of the will of the injured party. Expenses, however, though they are similarly the consequence of damage, occur in most cases only if they are desired by the injured party.

1046. The profit or income lost refers to the increment in property from which the damaged person was deprived as a result of the loss suffered. This is established if it may be seriously supposed that, if the damage had not occurred, there would have been an increase in the property of the injured party, the money value of which increase can be assessed in an exact way. If, however, the enterprise is damaged, it generally cannot request compensation for unrealized profits.

1047. Damages are reduced by every income increment received by the injured party in connection with the damage or with regard to it. There are essentially two cases to be clarified here. To the first belong the services or amounts received from insurance; to the other, the amounts acquired which were saved, or acquired in

354. NÁDAS György, 'A kárfelelősség szabályainak változásairól' in. KUN Attila (ed.), *Az új munka törvénykönyve dilemmái* Acta Caroliensia Scientiarium Iuridico-Politicarum V. Budapest: KRE. 2013. pp. 104–111.

another way, owing to the damages suffered by the injured party. Insurance here includes social insurance, as well as life or accident insurance or that against damage. In the case of social insurance and insurance against damage the person suffering damage can only claim damages exceeding the benefits received, while in the case of life and accident or pension insurance, in assessing the amount of damage the benefits received on the basis of the insurance cannot be taken into consideration, except for that paid by the insurance agency with an express, definite purpose (e.g., medical expenses).

1048. There fall within the sphere of savings, profits in connection with utilising the goods etc., remaining after damage, as well as the situation in which when the person who suffered loss, as a consequence of this, is rid of some expenses which were usual until then. There also fall within this sphere situations in which a person, in consequence of injury, is able to enjoy certain income by utilizing his/her labour power or some of his/her goods. For instance, an illegally dismissed employee, utilizing his/her released manpower, undertakes work. Savings and income arise partly independently of the will of the injured party, partly, however – as with expenses and costs – depending upon the will of the person suffering loss. If, however, savings or profit become possible, this cannot be made dependent exclusively on the will of the person who suffered damage whether he/she uses this possibility or not. It follows from the principle of reducing and preventing damages that if they can be reduced by any savings or in another way, the person who has suffered damage is obliged to use such possibility. If he/she does not do this – although he/she could have done – the amount is attributed to him/her according to the rules of the contribution of the injured party.

In assessing the amount of damage, the point of departure is generally the amount for which the damaged item can be procured again or repaired by the person who has suffered the damage.

1049. In principle, punitive damages are prohibited under the Hungarian Civil Code, hence the HLC as well. Where one person has suffered harm from a wrongful act of another, compensatory and contract damages are generally the amount of money needed to restore the damaged party to the condition that existed before the wrongful act or contractual breach occurred. Fines and sanctions are generally amounts of money paid to a government body when rules are broken. By contrast, punitive damages are awards of money to punish a party and to deter others from similar outrageous or reckless conduct by setting an example. Punitive damages are awarded in addition to compensatory damages and are often described as quasi-criminal punishment. Punitive damages can also be described as exemplary damages. However, as in other European countries, punitive elements are considered when it is deemed Personal Rights have been infringed, and in connection with generally accepted penalty clauses in contract law (§246 Civil Code).[355]

355. http://www.biztositasiszemle.hu/files/201206/punitive_damage_in_europe.pdf (26 Jul. 2023).

b) Non-material damage

1050. According to the HLC, the injured person (employee) can also be compensated for non-pecuniary damage which is not of a financial nature.[356]

1051. In the spirit of full reparation, the employer is also obliged to compensate the employee for non-material damage, without limitation (RO1998. 612.). Non-material compensation is payable if the employee's personal rights are infringed as a result of the injury and he/she suffers actual further disadvantage or loss of interest (e.g., his/her daily quality of life is adversely affected). The purpose of non-material compensation is to compensate for the non-material injury suffered by providing a financial benefit of approximately equivalent value.

1052. The practice considers the decision of the Constitutional Court No. 34/1992 (VI. 1.) as the guiding principle in the assessment of non-material damages. In the light of this, non-material compensation is a general instrument for the protection of personality, but in labour law practice it is mostly used in connection with various types of health impairment (e.g., loss of sight, paralysis, severe brain injury, amputation of fingers, visual impairment due to psychological trauma and depression). In addition, in employment law practice, non-material damages may be awarded in particular for violations of the following rights of the person: the right to health, physical integrity, life, family, equal treatment, honour, dignity, reputation, protection of personal data, freedom of expression, etc.

1053. Calculation of non-pecuniary damage: The determination of the amount of non-material damages is a matter of judicial discretion in the absence of an objective yardstick and a 'flat-rate list' (BH 1998, No. 99). Judicial practice is not to apply a damage apportionment, but to determine the amount of compensation for non-material damage by considering all the circumstances of the case (BH2006, 96; MK 30; EBH 2001, 572). However, the court is bound by the claim, and therefore cannot award a higher amount than the non-material damages specified in the claim, even if it would otherwise find it justified.

1054. In the case of non-material damages, the amount of compensation necessary to mitigate or compensate for the damage suffered by the victim must be in proportion to the damage suffered. Therefore, the same injury may have different consequences because of differences in individual, specific circumstances. Non-material damages may be awarded either as a lump sum or as an annuity. Non-material damages may be awarded in addition to general damages.

1055. Non-material damage is linked to the person of the injured party and, accordingly, a claim for non-material damages can only be brought by the person

356. HAJDÚ József, IEL Labour Law, Hungary, Wolters Kluwer, Kluwer Law Online, 2019. https://kluwerlawonline.com/Manuals/Corporate+Acquisitions+and+Mergers/705 (26 Jul. 2023).

whose personal rights have been infringed. The claim can only be enforced personally (no transfer or inheritance is possible).[357]

B. Disciplinary Liability

1056. Section 56 of the HLC describes the quasi-disciplinary liability measures. In the event of any infringement of obligations arising from an employment relationship the collective agreement or – if the employer or the worker is not covered by the collective agreement – the employment contract may prescribe detrimental legal consequences consistent with the gravity of the infringement.

1057. The detrimental legal consequence aforementioned may be a sanction related to the employment relationship, altering its terms and conditions for a fixed period, which will not violate the employee's personal rights and dignity. Where the sanction is of a financial nature, it may not – on the whole – exceed the employee's monthly base wage in effect at the time when the sanction is imposed. An infringement may not be sanctioned by detrimental legal consequences if the employer has already stated it as the reason for termination of the employment relationship. The measure imposing detrimental legal consequences shall be put in writing, with reasons provided.

1058. Prior to the new HLC, disciplinary action could only be taken if it was appropriate under the terms of a collective agreement. Now, it is advisable to include a disciplinary procedure in the employment contract. In the absence of a relevant collective agreement, the employment contract can stipulate what disciplinary sanctions will apply.

§2. LIABILITY OF THE EMPLOYER

I. Compensatory Liability of the Employer

1059. Based on the previous Labour Code, the Labour Court developed extensive employer liability for damage suffered by employees. It was a clear goal of the new HLC to narrow such extensive liability of employers.

1060. According to sections 166–178 of the HLC, the employer is to bear full liability, irrespective of intention or neglect, for damage caused to the employee within the scope of his/her employment. Where the worker is employed by another employer, the liability of the employers will be joint and several.

357. A munkáltató kártérítési felelőssége; http://projektjeink.birosag.hu/sites/default/files/allomanyok/e-learning/munkatrv/munkajog1/lecke7_lap21.html (26 Jul. 2023).

1061. The employee can be relieved of liability if able to prove:

(a) that the damage occurred in consequence of unforeseen circumstances beyond his/her control, and there had been no reasonable cause to take action for preventing or mitigating the damage; or
(b) that the damage was caused solely by the unavoidable conduct of the aggrieved party.

1062. Concerning the unavoidable cause, judicial practice is based on the examination of objective possibilities. Two facts must be examined. First, it must be determined whether existing scientific and technological techniques or equipment could have prevented the damage or not. (It is not important whether or not the employer knew of these possibilities; their existence is considered decisive.) The fact that it may be difficult to obtain the necessary means of prevention does not excuse the employer. On the other hand, it must be ascertained whether the possibilities assured by scientific and technological development provided ample time for prevention or not. Activities aimed at preventing damage may not be formal since they must eliminate dangerous effects as far as possible (e.g., it is not sufficient to hang out a sign saying 'Entry prohibited' in places where the possibility of accidents is high).

1063. The employer must compensate the employee for all his/her losses in full. No compensation is required if the employer is able to verify that the occurrence of such loss could not have been anticipated.

1064. However, the court, under special and equitable circumstances, may grant partial exemption from liability to the employer held liable for damages, upon weighing the financial standing of the parties, the gravity of the infringement and the consequences of providing compensation.[358]

A. *Contribution of the Worker*

1065. No liability will apply to the portion of the damage resulting from the employee's wrongful conduct or that was incurred due to the employee's failure to perform his/her obligations in relation to the mitigation of damage.

1066. Attention must be drawn to the view represented by the Labour Department of the Curia according to which, in judging whether or not damage was caused by an act of an employee, the unfavourable effects and special conditions of the work must be taken into consideration. Even if an accident was the result of inattention, carelessness, neglecting technological and safety regulations on the part of the employee, this does not necessarily mean that these were the only causes; while performing his/her duties a worker is influenced by many other factors connected with the activity of the employer which may result in inattention. Similarly, if the

358. BERKE Gyula – KISS György (eds), *Kommentár a munka törvénykönyvéhez*, Budapest: Complex – Wolters Kluwer, 2012. pp. 461–464.

employer knows of violations of regulations, the worker alone cannot be blamed for the accident. It must also be considered whether an indisposition or sickness of a worker are linked with the particular working conditions or with any kind of excess strain (e.g., too much overtime).

B. Types of Damage

1067. The employer is obliged to compensate for all damages caused to the worker. The following are included here:

(1) lost earnings
(2) loss of goods;
(3) any expenses in connection with the damage;
(4) non-pecuniary damages.

1. Lost Earnings

1068. Income lost within the framework of employment may include the following:

- lost wages, which are determined both in cash and in kind;
- the cash value of those regular services to which the employee is entitled on the basis of the employment over and above the wage if prior to the occurrence of the damages caused he/she regularly availed him/herself of these;
- other regular earnings lost outside of employment as a result of the grievance;
- earnings the employee asserts as a result of extraordinary work performance despite major handicaps arising from the grievance shall also be compensated.

1069. The amount of lost wages is calculated according to the regulations of the HLC pertaining to the calculation of average earnings. If there has been a general wage increase within the period that is normative for the calculation of average earnings, then, in the case of an employee employed under a performance wage, his/her lost wages would be calculated only from the time of the wage increase if this is more favourable for the employee.

1070. The value of provisions 'in kind' must be determined on the basis of the retail price at the time compensation is determined.

2. Material Damage (Loss of Goods)

1071. The sum for material damage is calculated on the basis of the retail price with consideration for wear and tear. If the damage caused to an item can be repaired without loss of value, then the repair cost will be taken into consideration when assessing the damage.

3. Expenses

1072. The responsibility of the employer for compensation also includes the obligation to cover all the employee's expenses both in connection with the damage and redressing the consequences. In this field, the Labour Department of the Curia is also concerned with the employee's interests. Three typical examples may be mentioned here:

(a) Expenses in connection with medical treatment. Since medical treatment for most part is free of charge on the basis of the social insurance this includes expenses incurred in visiting the insured person in hospital, the supply of food during nursing at home, and payment for such nursing. In the latter case, payment is due even if nursing is done by a member of the family (e.g., wife) not otherwise employed. Those medical expenses requiring payment, such as a second pair of orthopaedic shoes, also belong to this section. Taking into consideration the importance of restoration to health, these expenses are also assured in cases where the accident (occupational or other disease) resulted partly through the fault of the employee himself/herself.
(b) Extra expenses incurred as a result of the accident (occupational or other disease) in the employee's everyday life: payment for nursing, extra hearing and lighting, and costs in connection with accommodation. In this latter case, judicial practice accepts increased rent if the injured person cannot remain in a room together with other members of family, as well as cost connected with the installation of a bathroom if the worker needs special washing facilities as a consequence of the accident. Extra travel expenses may also be mentioned here. In this respect, the Labour Division of the Curia will approve expenses for the purchase of an individual car in the case of an employee's mobility having become greatly restricted. The employee might be in need of constant nursing or may require domestic help. According to the Curia, he/she is entitled to this assistance even if the work is done by a member of the family.
(c) Another group consists of expenses arising from the proceedings connected with the employee's demands (e.g., correspondence, travel, legal fees).

4. Non-pecuniary Damage

1073. The employee is also to be compensated for non-pecuniary damages arising from the conduct of employers.

1074. In the spirit of full reparation, the employer is also obliged to compensate the employee for non-material damage, without limitation (RO1998. 612.). Non-material compensation is payable if the employee's personal rights are infringed as a result of the injury and he/she suffers actual further disadvantage or loss of interest (e.g., his/her daily quality of life is adversely affected). The purpose of non-material compensation is to compensate for the non-material injury suffered by providing a financial benefit of approximately equivalent value.

1075. The practice considers the decision of the Constitutional Court No. 34/1992 (VI. 1.) as the guiding principle in the assessment of non-material damages. In the light of this, non-material compensation is a general instrument for the protection of personality, but in labour law practice it is mostly used in connection with various types of health impairment (e.g., loss of sight, paralysis, severe brain injury, amputation of fingers, visual impairment due to psychological trauma and depression). In addition, in employment law practice, non-material damages may be awarded in particular for violations of the following rights of the person: the right to health, physical integrity, life, family, equal treatment, honour, dignity, reputation, protection of personal data, freedom of expression, etc.

1076. Calculation of non-pecuniary damage. The determination of the amount of non-material damages is a matter of judicial discretion in the absence of an objective yardstick and a 'flat-rate list' (BH 1998, No. 99). Judicial practice is not to apply a damage apportionment, but to determine the amount of compensation for non-material damage by considering all the circumstances of the case (BH2006, 96; MK 30; EBH 2001, 572). However, the court is bound by the claim, and therefore cannot award a higher amount than the non-material damages specified in the claim, even if it would otherwise find it justified.

1077. In the case of non-material damages, the amount of compensation necessary to mitigate or compensate for the damage suffered by the victim must be in proportion to the damage suffered. Therefore, the same injury may have different consequences because of differences in individual, specific circumstances. Non-material damages may be awarded either as a lump sum or as an annuity. Non-material damages may be awarded in addition to general damages.

1078. Non-material damage is linked to the person of the injured party and, accordingly, a claim for non-material damages can only be brought by the person whose personal rights have been infringed. The claim can only be enforced personally (no transfer or inheritance is possible).[359]

1079. Curia (Hungarian Supreme Court) case Mfv.I.10.526/2018. The applicant was employed by the defendant as a permanent employee from 1 September 1981. On 13 January 2003, the defendant terminated the plaintiff's employment by giving her notice of termination. The defendant was entitled to terminate the employment relationship during the period of the notice under the HLC 90(1)(a) of the notice of dismissal, the defendant declared the notice of dismissal invalid.

1080. As a result of problems at work, the applicant developed an anxiety-depressive state and a mood disorder, which caused her anxiety and agitation, for which she had been undergoing treatment since 28 April 2002. The psychiatric illness, which began in the spring of 2002, continued in a fluctuating manner until the date of the medical expert's opinion of November 2002. In the action for unlawful

359. Dr. TÁLNÉ DR. MOLNÁR Erika (2018) A munkáltató kártérítési felelőssége összegszerűségének kérdései a bírói gyakorlat tükrében, Munkajog, 2018/4. pp. 52–58.

termination of employment and its consequences, the applicant sought, *inter alia*, an order that the defendant pay compensation for non-material damage in the amount of HUF 25,000,000. The defendant sought the dismissal of the action. By judgment of the Court of First Instance, the defendant was ordered to pay the applicant the sum of HUF 1,500,000 by way of compensation for non-material damage and default interest on that sum from 27 January 2004 until the date of payment. The court dismissed the action as in excess of that amount.

1081. The court of second instance partially altered the judgment of the Court of First Instance in the appealed part, increased the amount of the non-material damages to HUF 5,000,000, with the defendant being liable to pay default interest from 27 January 2004. In its application for review, the applicant sought primarily the annulment of the judgment of the court of second instance and a decision in accordance with the law, increasing the amount of the non-material damages to HUF 25,000,000. In the alternative, it sought partial annulment of the judgments of first and second instance and an order that the court of second instance should conduct a new trial and issue a new judgment. The defendant's counterclaim for review sought to maintain the final judgment in force. The request for review is unfounded. The appellant claims, without any basis, that the court of second instance excluded from evidence the medical documents annexed by the appellant. On the contrary, it can be noted that the court examined all the findings contained in the expert's opinion, including the evidence submitted by the applicant. In its application for review, the applicant itself did not specifically indicate which evidence, the medical expert opinion which it had submitted, had not been assessed by the courts before it and what different findings or conclusions they could have reached. It was the applicant's mental illness which was to be assessed in the context of the award of compensation for non-material damage (HLC (1992– old Labour Code), section 177(2)), which, according to the expert opinion, was showing an improving trend or at least a maintained condition. In its judgment, the Court of Appeal stated, without any error of law, that the fact of unlawful dismissal is not in itself sufficient to establish a claim for non-material compensation. It was for the claimant to prove that the employer's action had caused the personal injury giving rise to the non-material damage.

1082. Medical experts' opinions stated that the applicant's mental illness was not fatal, as he developed a mental disorder after the event in the case, which prevented him from working and resulted in a loss of capacity to work. However, the claimant made unfounded allegations that he would have been healthy and fit for work without the employer's action, which he could not prove, and that natural illnesses also played a role in his 71% reduction in fitness for work. The Court of Appeal also ruled correctly on the amount of the compensation for non-material damage. In its decision 34/1992 (VI. 01.) AB, the Constitutional Court stated, *inter alia*, that the function of monetary compensation for non-material damage is to provide for the approximate compensation of the damage suffered by providing a pecuniary benefit which is approximately equivalent to the damage suffered. The amount of non-pecuniary compensation is determined by the courts on the basis of the specific features of the case and the personal circumstances of the injured party.[360]

C. Survivors' Claims

1083. The employer must also compensate the employee's close relatives for their damages and justified expenses arising in connection with the damages caused. If the employee dies as a result of injuries sustained or disease inflicted, his/her dependent relatives may, in addition to the above, claim compensation to substitute for the provision of a sum that ensures the meeting of his/her needs, at the level maintained prior to the grievance it is necessary to be taking into account his/her actual or expected wage and income.

1084. An employer is also liable for reimbursing the relatives of employees for any damages incurred in connection with the incidence of damage. In the event of the employee's death in connection with the incidence of damage, the dependent relative of such employee may demand compensation in substitution for the lost support, in the amount required to ensure his/her previous living standards, also taking into account of his/her factual or presumably achievable wages or income.

1085. Compensation may be provided in the form of regular payments as well. Regular payments can, on a general principle, be awarded if the compensation is intended to be used for the support of the employee or his/her relative eligible thereto, or as a supplement to such support.

D. Calculation of Compensation

1086. In calculating the amount of compensation, the following should be deducted from the amount of compensation:

(a) benefits provided under the social security system or by a voluntary mutual insurance fund;
(b) the income in fact earned by the employee, or which could have been earned in the given situation within reason;
(c) the profit earned by the employee (his/her relatives) through the utilization of the damaged property;
(d) the benefit gained by the beneficiary as a result of expenses saved as consequence of the occurrence of the damage.

360. Nem vagyoni kártérítés megfizetése tárgyában hozott határozatot a Kúria illetékes tanácsa (2019) https://kuria-birosag.hu/hu/sajto/nem-vagyoni-karterites-megfizetese-targyaban-hozott-hatarozatot-kuria-illetekes-tanacsa (26 Jul. 2023).

1087. If the extent of the damage or a part of it cannot be precisely calculated, the employer must pay a sum in general compensation, which would appropriately and fully compensate the aggrieved financially. General compensation may also be established in the form of an allowance.

1088. The sum of compensation established for an employee who is a minor shall be reviewed upon him/her turning 18 years of age or after one year of having completed his/her studies pursued in the interest of acquiring vocational qualifications. Compensation due to him/her for the time subsequent to that must be determined in accordance with the changes that have occurred in his/her ability to work and his/her qualifications.[361]

E. Changes after the Determination of Compensation

1089. If subsequent to the establishment of compensation, a substantive change in the circumstances of the aggrieved employee occurs, both the aggrieved and the employer and, in the event of compensation provided on the basis of liability insurance, the insurance company may request modification of the specified compensation.

1090. In determining the extent of the wage increase serving as the basis for modifying compensation, the actual average annual wage increase of employees working in the employer's department where the aggrieved was working at the time the grievance occurred and in a position identical to that of the aggrieved must be normative. In the absence of employees in identical positions, the actual average annual wage increase in the department should be taken into consideration as the basis for the modification. In the event of the department mentioned above having ceased to exist, employees of the employer in positions identical to that of the aggrieved or, in the absence of such employees, the extent of the actual average annual wage increase at the employer's must be normative in modifying compensation.[362]

II. The Employers' Liability for Custody

1091. Employers are subject to liability in accordance with sections 166–167 of the HLC for damages caused to objects and things of the employees brought along to the place of employment.

1092. Employers may require things brought to the workplace to be deposited in a safe place or to have them reported. Articles which are not essential for the commute to and from work, or for the work itself may be carried into the workplace

361. EMBER Alex, *Az üzemi baleset*, Szeged: Pólay Alapítvány, 2013. pp. 25–27.
362. HAJDÚ, József – KUN, Attila (eds), *Munkajog II.*, Budapest: Patrocinium, 2013. pp. 71–75.

upon the employer's consent. In the event of breaching these rules, the employer will be held liable for damages only if caused wilfully.[363]

§3. Compensatory Liability of the Employee

1093. The compensatory liability of employees, according to sections 179–191 of the HLC is divided into two great groups: A. liability based on culpability, and B. without culpability. Within the second group, further sub-categories can be made: (1) general liability for safeguarding goods and (2) liability for inventory deficits.

I. Liability Based on Culpability

A. *General Principles*

1094. Employees are subject to liability for damages caused by any breach of their obligations from the employment relationship stemming from their failure to act as it might normally be expected in the given circumstances.

B. *Contribution of the Employer*

1095. It was established above that generally it is only justified in cases of culpability to take into consideration the contribution of the injured person. In regard to the contribution of the employer the situation is different. The burden of proof to verify the facts, the occurrence of loss, as well as the causal link, lies with the employer.

C. *Extent of Liability*

1096. In the field of compensatory liability of employees, a deviation from the principle of compensation for full damages can be observed. The employee is wholly liable (cover the full extent of losses) for damage only in the case of damage caused intentionally or through grave negligence.

1097. In the case of unintentional damage liability (minor negligence) is generally restricted. The reasons for restricting liability can be classified into two groups. Those falling into the first group are of a general nature, while the second group consists of reasons arising from the special circumstances of the employment relationship.

363. FERENC Jácint – GÖNDÖR Éva – GYULAVÁRI Tamás – KÁRTYÁS Gábor, *Munkajogi alapismeretek*, Budapest: ELTE Kiadó, 2013. p. 157.

1098. In the first group, it must first be reaffirmed that the basis of an employee's living is his/her wage. Burdening it with compensation of a considerable amount makes life more difficult for the employee and his/her family. It would perhaps result not in educating the perpetrator of damage but in precisely the opposite. Compensation, therefore, which is unduly high as compared with the earning capacity of the employee cannot have a due influencing and preventive effect. It should also be taken into consideration in this regard that today the possibility of causing considerable damages is much increased. As a result of the development of technology, the working process has become considerably accelerated; at the same time, the worker works with machines and materials of high value. Under such conditions, owing to momentary inattention – which may happen to anyone – very grave damage may ensue. In productive work, the possibility of such incidents is very high.

1099. In addition to these general causes – affecting almost all citizens – there are also particular causes. The employment relationship is generally a permanent bond in the course of which the employee performs his/her work, usually within a collective. Here, there is an opportunity to become acquainted with the employee very thoroughly. Apart from this, within the scope of this enduring relationship, several educational means are at one's disposal for influencing the employee. In connection with this, not only legal but also various extra-legal means could be included and – last but not least – the influencing effect of the collective. By applying these prudently, due influence may be exerted on the employee, even if using less strict methods in the province of compensatory liability. In the second place, one must take into consideration the fact that wages have not only the function of ensuring the living of the employee but also provide considerable incentive. If wages are reduced to provide compensation over a long period, then wages would considerably lose their incentive function. In the third place, one must take into consideration the fact that damage is caused by the employee to employer's property. It is society which suffers or perhaps a sub-system of society. Yet the employer can endure partial compensation of the loss more easily if this appears to be proper with a view to influence to prevent further damage.

1100. The wide-ranging limitation of the sphere of liability with regard to the material liability of employees is justified by all these points taken together. This limitation is of a relative character, that is, it restricts the scope of liability not in relation to the damage but to the wages of the employee causing it. Thus, if the amount of damages is within this limit, the legal limitation does not apply.

1101. In the sphere of liability for damages through being culpable two groups may be identified:

(a) in the event of damages caused through minor negligence, the amount of compensation payable by the employee may not exceed four months' absentee pay;
(b) in the event of damages inflicted intentionally or by grave negligence the employee will make full compensation.

1102. No liability will apply with respect to any damage that is considered unforeseeable or that resulted from the employee's wrongful conduct, or that was incurred due to the employee's failure to perform his/her obligations to mitigate the damage. Compensation for damages will, furthermore, be governed by the provisions of the Hungarian Civil Code.[364]

II. Compensatory Liability Without Culpability

A. *Scope of Liability*

1103. Liability without culpability exists for things acquired with a receipt, with accountability or the obligation to return them. Items may be turned over to an employee for various purposes – selling, processing, custody, etc. – with such a stipulation. The common criterion in each case is that what is taken is to be returned at a given date or, if it no longer exists, the employee shall render an account of its allocation.

1104. Liability without culpability is divided into two groups. These are:

(a) general liability for safeguarding goods; and
(b) the liability for inventory deficits of employees working in warehouses, commercial or catering trade units, etc.

B. *General Liability for Safeguarding Goods*

1105. An employee, irrespective of culpability, will make full compensation for the damages in the event of a loss of items he/she received with the obligation to return or account for them and which he/she constantly keeps in his/her custody or uses or manages exclusively. A precondition of the employee's liability is that he/she took over the item (tool, product, commodity, material, etc.) on the basis of a list or receipt. A cashier or handler of assets will, even without this, be liable for money, securities and other assets handled by him/her. The employer must prove the existence of the preconditions as well as the occurrence and size of the loss.

1106. The employee is exonerated from his/her responsibility if he/she can prove that the loss was the result of an unavoidable external cause or that the employer had not ensured the conditions for safeguarding.

1107. If damage has been caused because of a fault in a protective item, the employee's liability will be judged in accordance with the regulations laid down for culpable liability, but in such a case the employee will bear the obligation to prove his/her innocence.

---

364. EMBER Alex, *Az üzemi baleset*, Szeged: Pólay Alapítvány, 2013. pp. 25–27.

1108. The employee will not compensate for that part of the damage which occurred as a consequence of the employer's action.

1109. There is a special group of employees (cashiers, handlers of money and valuables) who are liable for the money, securities and other valuables they handle, regardless of having the list or acknowledgement receipt.

1110. The burden of proof to verify the above-mentioned liability conditions and the damage lies with the employer.[365]

C. *Joint Liability of Employees*

1111. According to section 180 of the HLC, liability for damages is borne by the employees involved consistent with the degree of their culpability, or – if this cannot be determined – in proportion to their respective involvement.

1112. Employees may jointly liable for damages if the degree of culpability or involvement cannot be verified.

1113. As regards any loss in property given to several employees for safeguarding, liability will be borne by such employees in proportion to their wages.

1114. Liability for damages caused wilfully by several persons shall be joint and several.

III. Liability for Inventory Deficits

1115. First of all, two definitions should be made: (a) inventory shortage: 'marketing loss' and (b) inventory period:

(a) *Inventory shortage.* Any shortage in the material and/or goods (inventory) or commodity properly deposited and received, for the purpose of resale, supply or management, caused by unknown reasons and in excess of natural quantitative degradation and permissible losses (hereinafter referred to collectively as 'marketing loss') are construed as inventory shortage.
(b) *Inventory period* means the time span between two consecutive inventory controls.

1116. An employee subject to an agreement on inventory liability will be liable for all shortages regardless of whether or not it results from any misconduct. Any shortage in the material and/or goods (inventory) or commodity properly deposited and received, for the purpose of resale, marketing or management, caused by

365. HAJDÚ, József – KUN, Attila (eds), *Munkajog II.*, Budapest: Patrocinium, 2013. p. 78.

unknown reasons and in excess of natural quantitative degradation and permissible losses (hereinafter jointly referred to as 'marketing loss') will be construed as inventory shortage.

1117. The following is construed preconditions for inventory liability:

(a) conclusion of an inventory liability agreement for the inventory period;
(b) proper delivery and receipt of inventory stocks;
(c) inventory shortage determined by a procedure to include all stocks on inventory and conducted according to inventory regulations; and
(d) working at the given workplace covering at least half of the inventory period.

1118. As a formal requirement, the inventory liability agreement must be in written form. The agreement must define the specific inventory stocks for which the employee is responsible.

1119. The employer is responsible to establish:

(a) the scope of materials and/or goods for which marketing loss can be claimed in view of the characteristics and size of the material or of the conditions of warehousing or storage;
(b) the permissible amount of marketing loss;
(c) the method and rules of delivering and receiving inventory stocks;
(d) the procedure for determining inventory shortage or inventory liability;
(e) the employer's liabilities for the safe storage of inventory stocks.

1120. The employee will be informed in writing regarding the above-mentioned conditions prior to the conclusion of an inventory liability agreement and/or before the inventory period.

1121. Group inventory liability agreement. It may be concluded if an inventory is administered by more than one employee. Such agreement will define the positions where an inventory count is to be taken when filled by a new employee.

1122. There is a special provision relating to an employee who is not subject to liability for inventory shortages, but he/she also has access to the inventory stocks. His/her liability will – furthermore – be contingent upon the prior written consent of the employee responsible for inventory shortages for employment in the given job or workplace.

1123. Termination of inventory liability. The inventory liability agreement will be terminated when the employee no longer handles the stocks due to changes in his/her position. The employee will have the right to cancel in writing – without explanation – the inventory liability agreement effective as of the last day of the inventory period. In the case of a group inventory liability agreement, the agreement will be considered cancelled only in respect of the employee who made the legal act.

A. Inventory Liability Proceedings

1124. When taking inventory, the presence of the employee, or his/her representative if the employee is not available, or the employees specified in the procedural rules in respect of collective liability, should be provided for. If the employee fails to attend or delegate a representative, the employer will appoint an unbiased representative with expertise in the field in question.

1125. The employee affected by the procedures must be notified regarding the inventory count and its outcome. The employee may make his/her opinion known during the procedure, and – unless the employee failed to attend in spite of being duly notified – should be heard.

1126. Employers may submit their claims for compensation for inventory shortages during the sixty-day limitation period following the conclusion of inventory control. In the event of criminal procedure, the time limit is thirty days and it will commence on the day following the date when the final or definitive decision of the court bringing the criminal proceedings to a conclusion, or the resolution adopted by the public prosecutor's office or the investigating authority, that is not subject to further remedy, is delivered.

B. The Amount of the Inventory Liability

1127. Unless otherwise provided for in the agreement for inventory liability, the employee who permanently handles the inventory stocks by him/herself will be liable for the full amount of shortages.

1128. The employee subject to liability for inventory shortages may only be accountable for up to six months' absentee pay if an employee who is not subject to liability for inventory shortages also has access to the inventory stocks.

1129. In respect of an agreement for group inventory liability, the amount of compensation for damages may not exceed the aggregate amount of six months' absentee pay of the employees included in the agreement. An agreement for group inventory liability may specify the sharing of responsibility among the employees concerned; joint and several liability, however, may not be stipulated. If the sharing of responsibility is not specified in the collective agreement for inventory liability, the employees will bear liability according to the percentage of their respective absentee pay.

1130. When establishing responsibility and/or the amount of damages, all circumstances of the case must be taken into consideration, such as in particular, the ones having an effect on the employee's liability, and which may have influenced the safe and proper administration of inventories, such as the fulfilment of employer's obligations concerning security and the duration of the absence of the employee, if any.[366]

366. CSÉFFÁN József, *A munka törvénykönyve és magyarázata*, Szeged: Szegedi Rendezvényszervező Kft., 2023.

Chapter 11. Settlement of Disputes

§1. Grievance Procedures

1131. According to international standards (ILO), the Hungarian labour law distinguishes between individual and collective labour disputes. The first one may arise from a labour contract made between an employee and an employer and/or from the labour relationship established on the basis thereof.[367] The latter one may arise between the trade union representing the employees' interests, or some elected employees body and the employer. A collective labour dispute may also come into being because the existence or the lawfulness of an action of an individual labour dispute has come into dispute. In the sphere of collective labour disputes one can distinguish – as regards the subject-matter of the dispute – between legal disputes and extra-legal disputes, the so-called interest disputes. Within the scope of the first belong those cases in which the existence or non-existence of a right of one of the parties is disputed, or in which violation, non-performance or non-satisfactory performance has given rise to the dispute. The latter ones comprise of cases where the dispute arises in the interest of protection or enforcement of the interest of one or the other party – which is not secured by law.[368]

I. Principles

1132. In connection with a definition of the system relating to deciding labour disputes, the science of Hungarian labour law takes as a starting point the fact that the law has to promote quick and unimpeded realization of rights and obligations resulting from both individual and collective labour relations. Therefore, in the course of legal regulation a system has to be defined which promotes disputes or conflicts coming to the surface, and ensures quick and fair decisions. Accordingly, a system of deciding labour disputes must be based on the following principles:

(a) The possibility of unimpeded enforcement of a claim arising out of or connected with an individual or some collective labour relation must be ensured.
(b) There shall be an attempt at solving a dispute with the participation of the parties by way of reconciliation procedures.
(c) In any case, if a legal dispute arises, all the interested parties have to be assured that they can go to law in connection therewith. From this point of view, it makes no difference whether or not the dispute has arisen within the framework of an individual or collective labour relationship.
(d) The system of bodies deciding labour disputes must be defined so that they can be near the places where disputes arise. This facilitates a quick settlement of the dispute. Moreover, a basic advantage is that the bodies deciding the dispute can acquaint themselves better with the circumstances which led to the dispute.

367. KISS György (ed.) *Munkajog* Ludovika Egyetemi Kiadó, Budapest, 2020.
368. HAJDÚ József, IEL Labour Law, Hungary, Wolters Kluwer, Kluwer Law Online, 2019. https://kluwerlawonline.com/Manuals/Corporate+Acquisitions+and+Mergers/705 (26 Jul. 2023).

(e) The rules of procedure must be established so that they allow quick decisions of disputes.
(f) Trade unions have to be assured that they can intervene in the course of labour disputes in the interest of the employees.[369]

II. Individual Labour Law Disputes

A. *The Concept of Individual Labour Law Disputes*

1133. According to subsection (1) of section 285 of the HLC, an employee, employer, the trade union and the works' council may initiate a legal dispute under the provisions of the Code against an action of the employer which is in violation of the regulations pertaining to employment. Unless otherwise stipulated in the Code, the employer may similarly initiate a legal labour dispute against the employee towards the assertion of his/her claim related to employment.

1134. By way of derogation from the above-mentioned subsection (1) of section 285, employers may enforce their claims from workers arising from the employment relationship, if less than three times the mandatory minimum wage, by means of a payment notice. The payment notice must be made out in writing.

1135. Discretionary decision. An employment-related legal action may be filed against a decision adopted by the employer within its right of discretion if the employer has violated the provisions pertaining to such decisions.

1136. The term of limitation for labour-law claims will be three years. The term of limitation for claims for compensation for damages caused by a criminal offence will be five years, or longer, as consistent with the statute of limitations for such criminal liability. The lapse of a claim must be recognized ex officio. Furthermore, periods of limitation will be governed by the relevant civil law provisions, where the term of limitation for the claims of employees may not be reduced by the parties.

B. *The Procedure*

1137. In the case of individual labour disputes, competence lies with the Administrative and Labour Court.

1138. The parties should seek conciliation prior to going to court. In the course of conciliation, any accord reached by the parties qualifies as an agreement; this has to be put in writing. A clause ordering the participation of a conciliator in employment-related legal disputes may be included in the collective agreement or

369. HAJDÚ, József – KUN, Attila (eds), *Munkajog II.*, Budapest: Patrocinium, 2013. p. 151.

in the employment contract for the purpose of attempting to reach an agreement. Negotiations will be initiated with the conciliator in compliance with the provisions of the HLC. The conciliator must put the agreement in writing.

1139. If the above-mentioned conciliation (section 288 of the HLC), as stipulated in the collective agreement or in the parties' agreement, produced no results, a court action may be filed within the term of limitation.

1140. There are some exceptions to these provisions, which state that a lawsuit may be filed within thirty days of the notification of the action, in connection with:

(a) an amendment of the employment contract implemented by the unilateral decision of the employer;
(b) unlawful termination of the employment contract, including termination based on mutual consent;
(c) the legal consequences applied on account of breach of obligation by the employee;
(d) payment notice and a resolution for awarding damages, including compensation for inventory shortages.

1141. An action can be brought within the above-mentioned time limit (thirty day), in connection with:

(a) termination without notice by the employee; and
(b) wrongful termination of the employment relationship by the employee.

1142. In the case of challenging the termination of the employment relationship by mutual consent, an action may be brought within thirty days from the date when the challenge was declared declined. The challenge will be declined if the other party fails to respond within fifteen days from the date of delivery, or refuses to accept it.

1143. The deadline for bringing an action must be met if the statement of claim is dispatched on or before the last day of the deadline. A party that misses the deadline will have the option to file an application for continuation. Claims may not be pursued after six months.

1144. If conciliation is stipulated in the collective agreement or in the parties' agreement, this will have no effect on the above-mentioned shorter time limits (thirty days).

1145. The employer, the works' council or the trade union may bring an action within five days in the event of any violation of the provisions on information or consultation. In such cases, the court will hear within fifteen days in non-contentious proceedings. The decision of the court may be appealed within five days from the date of delivery of the decision. The court of the second instance must deliver its decision within fifteen days.[370]

§2. Role of the Courts

I. Courts of General Jurisdiction

1146. In Hungary, legal practice takes place in a unified system of jurisdiction, which has four levels: (1) local-level courts, (2) district courts, (3) courts of appeal and (4) the Curia).[371]

A. *Local Courts*

1147. In Hungary first instance courts are divided into 111 local and district courts as general jurisdictions, these courts are located in the major towns (105) of Hungary and in Budapest (6). Local courts are competent to hear civil, commercial and criminal cases as first instance courts. As a general rule, the local competency of courts conforms to the area of public administration. The name of the local court generally coincides with the location of its seat. The local court will proceed as single judge or in chamber (one professional judge and two assessors). Assessors will also take part in the adjudication of other cases and in the manner defined by Act. The rights and obligations of assessors are identical in adjudication with those of professional judges, but only a professional judge may proceed as a single judge or as the president of a chamber.

B. *District (County) Courts and the Metropolitan Court of Budapest*

1148. According to the administrative division of Hungary, 20 county courts (19 counties and Budapest) are competent to hear as first instance courts the cases established by an Act, and review appeals lodged against the decisions of local courts in the second instance. Only the district courts are competent to hear all conflicts involving an amount over EUR 20,000, etc. Chambers of a county court are established differently from first instance courts. The chamber of district courts is composed by one professional judge and two assessors or two professional judges and three assessors (depending on the complexity of the cases). As a second instance court the county court will review appeals in chamber composed by three professional judges.

370. KISS György (ed.) *Munkajog* Ludovika Egyetemi Kiadó, Budapest, 2020.
371. Bírói szervezeti rendszer, http://www.kormany.hu/hu/mo/az-igazsagszolgaltatas-rendszere/biroi-szervezeti-rendszer (26 Jul. 2023.).

C. Regional Courts of Appeal

1149. In Hungary, five regional courts of appeal are seated in Budapest, Debrecen, Győr, Pécs and Szeged. These courts have competence to render judgement on legal remedy submitted against the decision of local or county courts. The Court of Appeal re-examines the facts of the case and reaches its own conclusions. In most cases it is possible to contest the decision by appealing for cassation to the Curia.

D. The Curia

1150. The supreme judicial body of Hungary is the Curia. Its seat is in Budapest. The Curia adjudges the legal remedies submitted against the decisions of the county courts or the regional courts in the cases set forth by an Act; adjudges petitions for review; adopts obligatory uniformity decisions applicable to the courts.[372]

II. Courts with Special Jurisdiction over Labour Matters

1151. Administrative and labour courts ceased to exist on 31 March 2020. As of 1 April 2020, the administrative courts of first instance will be the Regional Courts of Budapest, the Budapest Environs, Debrecen, Győr, Miskolc, Pécs, Szeged and Veszprém. The Capital (Budapest) Tribunal had exclusive jurisdiction over cases which until 31 March 2020 were within the exclusive jurisdiction of the Capital (Budapest) Közigazgatási és Munkaügyi Bíróság (Administrative and Labour Court of the Capital), as well as over most of the cases which were previously within the exclusive jurisdiction of the Capital (Budapest) Tribunal. The administrative court cases are subject to appeal and review by the Curia. In certain court cases, the Curia has exclusive jurisdiction. Also, as of 1 April 2020, labour court cases are heard by the competent tribunals at first instance, by the courts of second instance and by the Curia in review proceedings.

1152. As of 1 January 2018, labour lawsuits will only include those arising from employment relationships under the Act I of 2012 on the Labour Code, civil servants, with the exceptions provided for in the Act, civil service, public employment and employment contracts under the Sports Act, employment claims arising from vocational training employment contracts concluded in the course of vocational training, student employment contracts under the National Higher Education Act and employment contracts with social cooperatives and employment cooperatives.

These include, for example, actions relating to wages and other employment-related benefits, actions relating to the termination of employment (actions for the unlawful termination of employment, etc.), actions for damages against the employer or the employee, or actions relating to collective agreements or works agreements.

372. A mai bírósági rendszer (2023), http://www.lb.hu/hu/mai-birosagi-rendszer (26 Jul. 2023.).

1153. An employment action must be brought by means of a statement of claim. In an employment action, if the employee is acting without a legal representative, he/she can only submit their claim on a form, he/she cannot draft it themselves. In an employment action, the parties are not obliged to be represented by a lawyer. If they wish to have assistance in completing the form, they may present their claim orally at the court of their place of residence, domicile or place of work or at the court having jurisdiction for the case, during the opening hours fixed by the President of the court for that purpose by law, and the court will record your claim on the form provided for that purpose.

1154. Certain types of disputes defined as labour disputes before 1 January 2018 (e.g., civil service disputes, social security, proceedings relating to the provision and support of a public employment agency) will be dealt with under the rules of the Code of Administrative Procedure from 1 January 2018. As of 1 April 2020, these cases will be heard by eight courts (the Budapest Metropolitan Court, the Budapest District Court, the Debrecen Court, the Győr Court, the Miskolc Court, the Pécs Court, the Szeged Court and the Veszprém Court), which will have regional jurisdiction.

Part III. Collective Labour Relations

Chapter 1. Trade Union Freedom

§1. Introduction to the Concept of Collective Labour Relations

1155. In Hungary, the development of collective labour relations was of little interest due to the existing socialist planned economy. The development, however, accelerated after the introduction of the economic reform of 1968 (e.g., conclusion of the collective agreement of workers' participation in the decision-making of an enterprise). Owing to the changing political, state and economic system of the country and the beginning of the creation of converging conditions for the development of a market economy, a decisive change presented itself demonstrated by the promulgation of two Acts (on collective agreements and on strikes) in 1989. The next step was the promulgation of the Labour Code in 1992. The Code provided for and summarized the rules on the collective labour relations. Section 14 of the Code expressed 'With a view to protecting employees' social welfare and economic interests as well as maintaining peace in labour relations, this law regulates the relations between employees, employers and the organizations that represent their respective interests. Within this framework, it guaranteed the freedom of organization and employees' participation in shaping working conditions; it determined the system of collective talks as well as the procedures for preventing and resolving labour conflicts.' Part III of the new Labour Code regulated the most important institutions of collective labour law.[373]

1156. Regulation of collective labour law: The legal status and role of the parties of the collective labour law has been modified in the new system. The HLC regulates the relationship between the employer, the trade unions and the works' council. The regulation is based on Directive (2002/14/EC) for informing and consulting employees establishing a general framework for informing and consulting employees in the European Community. Under section 230 of the HLC 'In the interest of safeguarding the social and economic interests of employees and further in the interest of maintaining peace at work, the present Act regulates relations between trade unions and works' councils and employers and their interest representations. As part of this, the present Act guarantees the freedom of the trade union movement and the participation of employees in the determination of the conditions

373. TÓTH Ferenc, A munkaügyi kapcsolatok rendszere, Budapest: Zsigmond Király Főiskola, 2003. pp. 10–15.

of employment and identifies the procedures for collective negotiations as well as for the prevention and resolution of labour conflicts.'[374] The HLC guarantees the right of employees and employers to establish organizations with others for the representation of their interests, free from any discrimination, with a view to furthering and safeguarding their economic and social interests, under the conditions set forth in the present Act, and to join the organizations of their choice, solely subject to the rules of the given organization, or to abstain from organizations of that nature. In the new HLC, the definitions of 'notification' and 'consultation' can also be found.

1157. The legislator wanted to eliminate the parallel rights of trade unions, on the one side, and of works' councils, on the other. Trade unions and works' councils have the same rights against the employer. Different legal consequences are among these entitlements. Therefore, a trade union and/or works' council could paralyse the employer's operations.

1158. For the purposes of the new HLC, a works' council is the body of cooperation between the employer and the employees, and the body of the employee's participation in the employers' decisions.[375,376]

1159. As for terminology, it is to be noted that the notion of 'industrial relations' is often used in labour practice. 'Collective labour relations' is used in Hungary; however, they have a very similar meaning to 'industrial relations'.

1160. It must also be underlined that the detailed regulations concerning representation of workers' interests relating to occupational safety,[377] and for the reconciliation of interests related to occupational safety are laid down in the Act on Labour Safety.[378]

1161. Hungarian laws regulate four forms of employees' representation:

- First, trade unions are autonomous legal entities, typically confrontational organizations of employee representation.
- Second, works councils assure the participation of employees in management, without a separate organization or legal personality. Contrary to their German counterparts, their codetermination right is limited to company welfare issues.

374. KISS György (ed.) Munkajog Ludovika Egyetemi Kiadó, Budapest, 2020.
375. The HLC makes a difference between information sharing and consultation: (a) 'information' means transmission of information specified by law as related to industrial relations or employment relationships in order to enable the recipients to acquaint themselves with the subject matter and to examine it, and to formulate an opinion to prepare for consultations, while (b) 'consultation' means the establishment of dialogue and exchange of views between the employer and the works council or trade union.
376. The European Works Council legislation in transition, Forum in. Acta Juridica et Politica, Szeged 2013. pp. 119–145.
377. HAJDÚ József, IEL Labour Law, Hungary, Wolters Kluwer, Kluwer Law Online, 2019. https://kluwerlawonline.com/Manuals/Corporate+Acquisitions+and+Mergers/705 (26 Jul. 2023).
378. EMBER Alex, Az üzemi baleset, Szeged: Pólay Alapítvány, 2013. pp. 25–27.

Works councils (or public employee's council) are to be elected in all establishments, where the number of employees exceeds 50.
- Third, representatives of employees on the supervisory board of a company constitute a special form of employees' participation, but this is only possible if the company has more than 200 full-time employees, unless the works council waives its right to nominate such representative(s).
- Fourth, representation in health and safety matters is a special form of employees' participation to contribute to work safety. Their election is compulsory at establishments with more than 20 employees.[379]

§2. General Principles

1162. Employees and employers have the right to form, together with others, without any form of discrimination whatsoever, an organization that represents their interests and is directed towards the promotion of their economic and social interests. They have the right to join an organization of their choice, depending exclusively on the regulations of the given organization or to avoid such organizations.

1163. The interest-representing organizations are entitled to establish federations or associations or to join such, including international federations.

1164. Within the framework of Part III of the Labour Code on collective labour relations, the following subjects are regulated:

- employees' right to participate in the employer's decision-making and the works' council;
- trade unions;
- collective negotiations and collective agreements.

1165. The rules on strikes are provided in a separate Act (No. VII of 1989).[380,381]

1166. According to the general rules of the HLC, the employer, the works' council and the trade union must inform each other in writing concerning their authorized representatives and officers.

1167. Consultation should take place with a view to reaching an agreement, in such fashion as consistent with the objective thereof and ensuring:

379. Industrial relations in Hungary: background summary (update March 2019); https://www.etui.org/covid-social-impact/hungary/industrial-relations-in-hungary-background-summary-update-march-2019 (26 Jul. 2023).
380. RADNAY József, 'A magyar sztrájk-törvény', Magyar Jog Vol. 37 No. 12, 1990. pp. 993–1006.
381. Strikes in Hungary: background summary (update March 2019), https://www.etui.org/covid-social-impact/hungary/strikes-in-hungary-background-summary-update-march-2019 (26 Jul. 2023).

(a) that the parties are properly represented;
(b) the direct exchange of views and establishment of dialogue;
(c) substantive discussions.

1168. The employer may not carry out the proposed action during the time of consultation, or for up to seven days from the first day of consultation, unless a longer time limit is agreed upon. In the absence of an agreement the employer will terminate consultation when the said time limit expires.

1169. However, the employer is not obliged to communicate information or undertake consultation when the nature of that information or consultation covers facts, information, know-how or data that, if disclosed, would harm the employer's legitimate economic interest or its functioning.

1170. The representatives acting in the name and on behalf of works' councils or trade unions are not authorized to disclose any facts, information, know-how or data which, in the legitimate economic interest of the employer or in the protection of its functioning, has expressly been provided to them in confidence or to be treated as business secrets, in any way or form, and are not authorized to use them in any other way in connection with any activity in which this person is involved for reasons other than the objectives specified in this Act.

1171. Any person who is acting in the name or on behalf of the works' council or trade union swill be authorized to disclose any information or data acquired in the course of his/her activities solely in a manner which does not jeopardize the employer's legitimate economic interest and without violating personal rights.[382]

§3. Freedom to Establish and Join Unions

I. Constitutional Provisions

1172. The Hungarian Fundamental Law (Constitution) guarantees all citizens the right to establish trade unions and guarantees the freedom of association and organization. It follows from this that no kind of state approval, permission or registration is needed for the creation and functioning of trade unions. The organs of the state administration are not entitled to exercise any kind of supervision over the trade unions. The Act concerning the operation and supervision of associations states explicitly that it does not apply to trade unions. The state cannot dissolve trade unions; thus the state ensures the complete autonomy of trade unions.

1173. Trade union autonomy includes the right of unions to possess property in order to perform their functions, to conclude legal transactions and to assume rights

382. HAJDÚ József, IEL Labour Law, Hungary, Wolters Kluwer, Kluwer Law Online, 2019. https://kluwerlawonline.com/Manuals/Corporate+Acquisitions+and+Mergers/705 (26 Jul. 2023).

and obligations under the laws of property for this explicit purpose. In connection with their social activities, rules referring to legal entities which might impede the functions of trade unions are not valid.

II. The Autonomy of Trade Unions

1174. Because the state provides for the complete autonomy of trade unions, it follows that the state cannot intervene in the internal life of the unions and in relations between the union and its members. It means that the law cannot contain any provisions in this respect. This is a field beyond the domain of legislation. Trade unions establish in their statutes the rules and regulations governing their own functions. The Supreme Court of Hungary has held that 'the courts must recognize the validity of trade union statutes'. In drawing up these statutes, the unions are entitled to regulate their activities, organization, management, and the rights and obligations of their members. The only limitation in this respect is that the statutes cannot contravene the provisions of the Fundamental Law (Constitution).[383]

1175. The statutes have a normative character, but the rules they lay down are not rules in law. They belong to the sphere of social norms outside the law. It will be clear from the aforesaid that the state does not put, either directly or indirectly, legal means at the disposal of the trade union or of its members in order that they might be able to formulate rights or obligations against each other on the basis of trade union norms.

1176. In the internal life of the trade unions, social, not legal, means are used to ensure the enforcement of their statutes and the resultant measures. A member can assert his/her influence, submit proposals and observations, and request the fulfilment of rights through the internal machinery (meetings, congresses, etc.) of the trade union. In the same manner, the union can only take steps against members of the union through those methods laid down in the union statutes; the only measures by which members can be compelled to fulfil the obligations resulting from membership are those sanctions which are laid down in the statutes and are valid in the internal life of the trade union.

1177. It should be underlined that trade union sanctions can have no effect on the member's relationships outside the trade union, especially on his/her employment relation. It follows that the rights and obligations of members defined in the statutes are not rights and obligations in a legal sense; and secondly, that the measures and decisions taken by individual trade union bodies cannot be set aside or controlled by state organs. If a measure or decision is contrary to union statutes or

383. HAJDÚ József: Az Alaptörvény munkajogi tartalmú cikkeiről In: Balogh Elemér (szerk.) Számadás az Alaptörvényről: Tanulmányok a Szegedi Tudományegyetem Állam- és Jogtudományi Kara oktatóinak tollából. Budapest: Magyar Közlöny Lap- és Könyvkiadó, 2016. pp. 64–79. (12 Aug. 2013.).

is otherwise incorrect, it can only be annulled within the framework of union autonomy; this means that the body authorized by the statutes can take steps in order to have it cancelled.

1178. The giving of autonomy to an organizational body implies that within the sphere of its autonomy, it can take decisions freely in the manner obligatory within its own organization; but, of course, these measures do not have this character outside the sphere of the organization.

1179. Membership in a trade union is completely voluntary both as regards admission and withdrawal. No social or economic pressure is exerted to compel citizens to become members of trade unions or to resign from them. The legal guarantee of this principle is represented by that provision of the Fundamental Law, mentioned above, which concerns the freedom of organization. This is supplemented by the trade union statutes which emphasize, on the one hand, the voluntary character of membership, and on the other hand, the fact that in questions of trade union membership no distinction may be made in respect of nationality, party allegiance, ideology, sex, occupation, or employment.

1180. Another guarantee of the voluntary principle, although a negative one, is the fact that the law does not – either in the field of labour relations or in any other sphere – make any connection between the rights and obligations of citizens and trade union membership. The law makes no distinction between trade union members and workers not belonging to organizations. From this it follows that persons who resign membership or who are excluded from it do not suffer any legal prejudice. According to section 271 of the HLC, an employer cannot demand from an employee a statement concerning his/her trade union affiliation. Employment of an employee may not be rendered contingent upon his/her membership in any trade union, on whether or not the employee terminates his/her previous trade union membership, or on whether or not he/she agrees to join a trade union of the employer's choice. It is forbidden to terminate the employee's employment, to put the employee into a disadvantageous situation in any other way, or to cause him/her damage on account of his/her trade union affiliation or trade union activities. It is forbidden to make any entitlement or benefit dependent on affiliation with some trade union or on avoidance of such.

1181. The Hungarian trade union movement has a pluralistic character.

1182. The following rights ensue from the trade union's autonomy:

- to establish organizations inside a company and to involve their members in their operation;
- to inform their members of their rights and obligations concerning their material, social, cultural as well as living and working conditions, to represent them in actions against the employer on matters concerning collective labour relations and employment, and to represent them before state authorities;

- to represent its members, on the basis of authorization, before a court or any other authority or office on matters concerning their living and working conditions;
- to conclude a collective agreement in accordance with the regulations determined under the HLC.

1183. An employer may not deny entry of a person acting on behalf of a trade union who is not employed by the employer into the employer's premises, if any member of the trade union in question is employed by the employer. The trade union must notify the employer accordingly in advance. This person will abide by the regulations pertaining to the employer's order of business during his/her proceedings.[384]

1184. Trade unions in Hungary are organized in a range of ways: there are trade unions organized by sectors, regions, occupations and company sites.[385]

384. HAJDÚ József, IEL Labour Law, Hungary, Wolters Kluwer, Kluwer Law Online, 2019. https://kluwerlawonline.com/Manuals/Corporate+Acquisitions+and+Mergers/705 (26 Jul. 2023).
385. Industrial relations in Hungary: background summary (update March 2019); https://www.etui.org/covid-social-impact/hungary/industrial-relations-in-hungary-background-summary-update-march-2019 (26 Jul. 2023).

Chapter 2. Trade Unions and Employers' Associations

§1. Trade Unions Confederations

1185. Trade unions confederation have the right to social dialogue and negotiations with employers' organizations about framework agreements for education, labour, working and social conditions, and they have the right to information and consultation within the tripartite bodies of the national conciliation.

1186. Sectoral trade unions have the right to collective bargaining at branch level and to sectoral social dialogue. Trade unions at company level have the right to negotiate collective agreements and – with the exception of military personnel and police officers – the right to strike. Even though it was necessary to make a number of smaller legal changes when implementing the acquis communautaire into the Hungarian legal system, there were no major changes necessary in labour legislation. Company level is by far the most common level of collective bargaining. Main issues of bargaining are wages (often as an annually agreed appendix of the valid framework agreement), working time, health and safety.

1187. A fundamental change was made with the introduction of the HLC (2012). This new Labour Code is much more flexible concerning individual workers' rights than the earlier one, but in general keeps the system of two-channel interest representation. One change is that the role of work councils is strengthened to the detriment of company trade unions' power. However, the new Labour Code is not described in detail here because most of the changes affect individual working rights and duties, while this article will concentrate on a description of (collective) industrial relations and social dialogue.

1188. Trade union federations and confederations regard themselves as the head of more or less independent companies' unions, although there are some exceptions like the Metal Workers' Union (VASAS). The relative strength of the company level as compared to the sectoral level is reflected by the fact that company union organizations have their own budget. Employers deduct the membership fee directly from wages and transfer it to the company union.

1189. Trade union membership in Hungary is around 9% of the workforce on average. Union density is much higher in the public sector and the state-owned companies (20%), than in the private sector (5%). It is estimated that there are around 330,000 trade union members in Hungary, according to the data provided by the 2015 Labour Force Survey of the Central Statistical Office. While in 1992, two years after the political changes, the Tax Authority registered 2.7 million trade union members in a labour market of about 4 million workers, in 2001, it reported only 650,000. Trade union membership declined sharply in the first half of the 1990s, due to political developments and changes in the structure of the economy and workforce. One key development was the collapse, bankruptcy or foreign takeover of huge state-owned industrial companies where trade union membership used to be very high. Since the second half of the 1990s, membership numbers have been slowly decreasing, resulting in a gradual erosion of trade unions. The erosion of trade unions is explained by several factors, including the expansion of small and middle-sized companies in the industry, green-field plants of multinational companies with anti-union management, spreading the precarious form of employment (most importantly temporary agency work), financial and organizational problems etc. The highest rate of trade union membership is currently in the energy, transport, education and healthcare sectors.[386]

1190. There are five trade union confederations: Trade Union Association of Intellectuals (ÉSZT), Democratic League of Independent Trade Unions (LIGA), Hungarian Trade Union Association (MASZSZ), National Alliance of Workers Councils (MOSZ) and Co-operative Forum of Trade Unions (SZEF). Cleavages between the confederations along their (open or covert) political affiliation often hinder their united action. According to the search engine of the webpage of the Registry Court, currently there are 995 active, registered trade unions.

1191. Beyond these national level associations, there are a large number of independent trade unions at workplace level, which play an important role in company-level bargaining. The most prominent example, maybe the strongest company union in the country, is Independent Trade Union of Audi Hungária which staged a successful one-week wage strike at the Audi plant in January 2019.[387]

§2. Employers' Associations

1192. There are five employers' confederations, the more significant organizations are Confederation of Hungarian Employers and Industrialists (MGYOSZ) and National Association of Entrepreneurs and Employers (VOSZ). All of them have a seat in the VKF (The Permanent Consultation Body of the Competitive Sector and the Government).

1193. Prior to 2011, the National Council for Interest Representation (OET) was the national forum of representing employers and employees in consultation and negotiation with the government. OET was replaced by the National Economic and Societal Council (NGTT) where, in addition to social partners, various NGOs, civil organizations and representatives of other interest groups are present. However, no government representative is a member of the forum.

1194. Since 2011 in the business sector, a new tripartite committee, the Standing Consultative Forum for the Competitive Sector and the Government (VKF) has been operating, where participation is subject to government invitation. A similar

386. Industrial relations in Hungary: background summary (update March 2019); https://www.etui.org/covid-social-impact/hungary/industrial-relations-in-hungary-background-summary-update-march-2019 (26 Jul. 2023).
387. Industrial relations in Hungary: background summary (update March 2019); https://www.etui.org/covid-social-impact/hungary/industrial-relations-in-hungary-background-summary-update-march-2019 (26 Jul. 2023).

forum for the government owned company sector was set up in 2018. Formally, the tripartite forums of the public sector remained intact after 2010. In spite of the very existence of old and new forums, recent years have witnessed the lack of meaningful social dialogue. However, major legislative changes passed without social partners having any say in it.

1195. There are all kinds of memberships of VKF possible (individual membership, companies, regions, sectors federation, etc.). The banking sector is a typical example of this diversified environment.

1196. Employers' organizations often are not clear whether they are professional lobby organizations or employers' organizations negotiating and concluding collective agreements.

1197. Employers' organizations are facing a decrease in members, as the 2012 labour law offers businesses no incentives to join a social partner organization. There are some attempts at reorganization within some organizations, but there have been no significant consequences of this yet.

1198. The most important employers' organizations are:

- Confederation of Hungarian Employers and Industrialists (Munkaadók és Gyáriparosok Országos Szövetsége, MGYOSZ).[388]
- National Association of Entrepreneurs and Employers (Vállalkozók és Munkáltatók Országos Szövetsége, VOSZ).[389]
- National Federation of Consumer Cooperatives (Általános Fogyasztási Szövetkezetek Országos Szövetsége, ÁFEOSZ).[390]

388. The origin of the Organization goes back to 1902 (GYOSZ). In 1998 the two biggest federations the Federation of Industrialists and the Hungarian Employer's Association merged, creating the largest employers representative organization (MGYOSZ). The Confederation counts among his members around fifty sectoral professional associations and sixteen regional employers' associations. The Confederation represents the interest of thousands of companies, employing 1.2 million employees.
389. The National Association of Entrepreneurs and Employers (VOSZ) was founded in 1989 before the political transition in Hungary. It was the first non-governmental, politically neutral, nation-wide representation of employer's interests in Hungary. It represents companies in all sectors of business. Economic and business climate of Hungary necessitated its foundation in the period of development of market economy. Members are mostly SMEs. VOSZ has 12.000 directly registered members. Their proportion of contribution to the Gross National Product is 31% and the total number of employees working in these enterprises represents 28% of active wage earners of the national economy. VOSZ has forty-two cooperation agreements with different associations. Actually VOSZ counts 45,000 enterprises as its members.
390. The Federation was formed in 1990 as successor of SZÖVOSZ (the Federation of Hungarian Cooperatives). Its main goal – as employer organization – is to represent the interests of the more than 1,000 enterprises belonging to the Coop-group. By doing so, AFEOSZ-COOP Federation comments on the various draft legislation related to economics, finances and labour. They pay specific attention to the economic conditions of commercial activities in small towns and rural areas.

- Hungarian Association of Craftsmen's Corporations (Ipartestületek Országos Szövetsége, IPOSZ).[391]
- National Association of Strategic and Public Utility Companies (Stratégiai és Közszolgáltató Társaságok Országos Szövetsége, STRATOSZ).[392]

1199. NB: the more significant organizations are Confederation of Hungarian Employers and Industrialists (MGYOSZ) and National Association of Entrepreneurs and Employers (VOSZ).

1200. There were no major changes among employers' organizations concerning membership and collective agreements in past years.

1201. The Hungarian government negotiates strategic agreements with large companies, mainly with multinational companies in the manufacturing sectors. These agreements guarantee cooperation and mutual support in favour of Hungary and the welfare of the companies. Employers' organizations are not involved.

1202. As the main level of collective agreements is at company level, it often happens that a company that is a member of an employers' organization has no collective agreement at all.[393]

---

391. IPOSZ is the largest national employer and professional organization of Hungarian micro and small-sized enterprises, and crafts since 1884. IPOSZ is a national umbrella organization of 279 legally independent craftsmen's corporations operating on a voluntary basis, including 220 regional craftsmen's corporations, 39 national professional craftsmen's corporations and 20 county associations. It includes in total of 50,000 individual entrepreneurs and business companies, 200,000 employees, 6,000 apprentices, and 110,000 assisting family members.
392. STRATOS was formed (registered by the court) in 1994 under the name 'National Association of Strategic and Public Utility Companies' for the purpose of the national representation of the economic interests of strategic important public service companies (telecommunication, road and railway traffic, energy, water management, the media, etc.). The establishment of STRATOS became timely and necessary because companies playing a decisive role in the country's economic life had no suitable representation in the then operating Committee for the Reconciliation of Interests (CRI). Due to the social circumstances of its establishment, STRATOS was formed as an association with national competence, without local (county) organizations, and its operation was solely financed by the members. In the years following establishment, the number of member companies well exceeded a hundred and the number of their employees came near to 750 thousand. The Association, comprising in addition to numerous smaller companies the biggest Hungarian companies, became practically the strongest employers' association representing infrastructure.
393. KRÉN, I. (2013), Hungary – labour relations and social dialogue: annual review 2013, Regional Project on Labour Relations and Social Dialogue, Friedrich-Ebert-Stiftung, Warsaw, available at http://library.fes.de/pdf-files/bueros/warschau/10436.pdf (26 Jul. 2023).

Chapter 3. Institutionalized Relations Between Employers and Employees

§1. In the Enterprise and at Plant Level

1203. The participation of workers in employers' decision-making is based on two principles. One is the protection of workers' interests; the other is the extension and development of democracy in the workplace. The right of participation ensures the employees a second instrument over and above the trade union. The trade union – usually – represents the collective and individual interest of employees against the employer or employers' organization, and on the basis of negotiations with them participates in the determination of rights and duties arising from employment relations by concluding the collective agreement. This relation is characterized by the contradiction in interests. Workers participating in the employer's decision-making also contribute to the protection of their interests. They can intervene in questions of creating collective and safe working conditions, of production, economy, the distribution of income, etc. The methods by which means and materials at the disposal of the employer are deployed, including the organization of work and the use of income directly influence the conditions of employees. In this respect, one should bear in mind not only the conditions of performing work, the more or less satisfactory way of safeguarding safety, but also how better or poorer organization of work and regularity or inconsistency in the supply of materials affect the formation of workers' earnings. And, in the final analysis, as a result of inadequate functioning of the employer's factory, etc., it may even ensue that an employee loses his/her place of work. The greater the opportunity for the employee to take part in the decision of the enterprise, the more he/she can prevent them from endangering his/her interests. In this respect, therefore, participation in the management of the enterprise within the framework of labour relations has created an instrument of safeguarding employees.[394]

1204. Section 235 of the HLC provides the right of employees' participation. This right is exercised in the name of the workforce by the shop steward, the works' council, central works' council, or the corporate-level works' council.

394. HAJDÚ József, European Works Council Hungary, The Netherlands: Kluwer Law International BV, 2012. pp. 37–40.

Table 2 Workplace Representation in Hungary

	Main Channels of Employee Representation in Hungary			
	Works' Council (WC)	*Trade Union (TU)*	*Health and Safety Committee (HSC)*	*Supervisory Board*
1 Most important body	X	X		
2 Alternative body			X	X
Notes	Regulated by law, with additional workplace agreement on functioning of the WC In private establishments and public sector establishments with more than 49 employees. In establishments with more than 19 and fewer than 49 employees, there is a workers' representative (üzemi megbízott)	Regulated by law, but voluntary – can be established at workplace level, if more than 10 employees agree	Regulated by law It is not in any case a committee, but one or more health and safety representatives, mainly nominated by the union (if there is one) or by the works' council	Regulated by law Workers' representatives are delegated to the establishment's supervisory board, if the establishment has more than 200 employees

Source: http://www.eurofound.europa.eu/eiro/country/hungary_4.htm (26 July 2023).

I. Shop Stewards

1205. A shop steward (üzemi megbízott) is elected if, during the half-year prior to the date when the election committee was established, the average number of employees at the employer or at the employer's independent establishment[395] or division (hereinafter referred to as 'fixed establishment'), is higher than fifteen, but less than fifty, respectively. The provisions pertaining to works' councils will also apply to shop stewards. There is one important exception: the shop steward cannot conclude works agreement.[396]

II. The Works' Councils

1206. A shop steward, or a works' council will be elected if, during the half-year prior to the date when the election committee was established, the average number of employees at the employer or at the employer's independent establishment[397] or division (hereinafter referred to as 'fixed establishment'), is higher than fifteen (shop steward) or fifty (works' council), respectively. Works' councils are elected for terms of five years. The justified expenses incurred in connection with the election and operation of the works' council will be borne by the employer.[398]

A. *Election Procedure of Works' Council*

1207. Eligibility to vote. A list of the employees eligible to vote and those who have the right to stand as candidates will be established by the election committee (*see* later) and published at least fifty days before the election. The employer must supply the information necessary for such a list at the request of the election committee within five days.

1208. Nomination of works' council candidate. A candidate may be nominated by at least 10% of the employees eligible to vote or by at least fifty employees eligible to vote, or by the local trade union branch represented at the employer. Nomination of candidates is valid if the number of candidates reaches the number of members that can be elected to the works' council. In the event that the nomination proceedings are considered invalid, the nomination period will be extended by up to fifteen days.

---

395. A fixed establishment of the employer is considered independent if the head of the establishment is vested with competence in respect of the works council's rights of participation.
396. CSÉFFÁN József, A munka törvénykönyve és magyarázata, Szeged: Szegedi Rendezvényszervező Kft., 2023.
397. A fixed establishment of the employer is considered independent if the head of the establishment is vested with competence in respect of the works council's rights of participation.
398. BANKÓ Zoltán, BERKE Gyula, KISS György, SZŐKE Gergely László Nagykommentár a munka törvénykönyvéhez, Wolters Kluwer, Budapest 2019.

1209. Precondition of election. Members of the works' council will be elected by secret ballot and popular vote. Eligible employees have one vote.

1210. Election committee. The preparation and execution of elections, and laying down the detailed rules of elections is the responsibility of the election committee. The election committee must set up by the works' council[399] from among the employees eligible to vote at least sixty days prior to the election. The election committee should have at least three members. Any person who holds a seat in the works' council may not serve in the election committee. Members of the election committee will be exempted from work for the duration necessary to discharge their duties, and will be entitled to absentee pay for the period of such absence.

1211. The election committee will register the candidates at least thirty days prior to the election and shall publish this information.

1212. The election committee will publish the list of candidates at least five days prior to the election.

1213. The results of the ballot will be announced by the election committee. The election committee will draw up a report on the election, which shall, in particular, contain the following:

(a) the number of those eligible to vote;
(b) the number of those participating in the ballot;
(c) the number of votes validly cast, and those declared void;
(d) the number of votes cast for each candidate;
(e) the name of the elected works' council members and alternate members;
(f) disputes, if any, related to the election, and the decision thereon.

1214. The election committee is obliged to publish the election report without delay.

1215. Starting the mandate. The mandate of the works' council will begin on the working day following the day of receipt of the election report.

1216. Annulment of the vote. A vote must be annulled if:

(a) it was not cast according to regulations;
(b) it cannot be established for whom the vote was cast;
(c) the number of candidates for whom votes are cast is greater than the number of members eligible for election.

1217. The elected members of works' council. The persons receiving the highest number of votes, or at least 30% of the valid votes will be construed as having

399. In the absence of a works council, the election committee will be created by the employees.

been elected members of the workers' council. In the event of a tie vote, the length of the employment relationship with the employer should be taken into consideration.

1218. The nominees having received 30% of the votes are declared elected members of the works' council. A new election must be held within a period of thirty days to fill the remaining positions. For the new election, new candidates may also be nominated up to the fifteenth day prior to the election.

1219. The second election will be declared valid if more than one-third of those eligible to vote have participated. The nominees receiving the highest number of votes, or at least 30% of the valid votes will be declared elected members of the works' council.

1220. The alternate members of works' council. Persons receiving at least 20% of the valid votes will be regarded as alternate members of the works' council.

1221. Persons receiving at least 15% of the valid votes shall be regarded as alternate members of the works' council.

1222. Validity of the election. A works' council election is declared valid if more than half of those eligible to vote have participated. To this end, an employee eligible to vote will not be counted – provided that he/she did not participate in the election – who, at the time of the election, was:

(a) incapacitated to work due to illness;
(b) on leave of absence without pay.

1223. In the event of an invalid ballot, the election must be repeated within a period of ninety days. The new election may not be held inside a period of thirty days.

1224. The second election can be declared valid if more than one-third of those eligible to vote have participated. The nominee receiving the highest number of votes, or at least 30% of the valid votes, will be declared an elected member of the works' council. If the repeated election is declared invalid, a new works' council ballot should be held after one year at the earliest.

1225. An election will be declared invalid if the number of candidates did not receive 30% of the votes cast.

1226. If the repeated election is declared invalid, a new works' council ballot should be held after one year at the earliest.

1227. Legal remedy. Employees, employers and local trade union branches represented at the employer may bring a court action in connection with nominations, the procedure and the outcome of elections. The court will annul the results of the election if it finds any material infringement of the relevant procedural regulations. An infringement can be considered material if it did have an impact on the outcome of the elections. This should be substantiated in the action.[400]

B. *Termination of the Mandate of Works' Council Members*

1228. The mandate of a works' council member will be terminated in the following cases:

(a) an employee has no legal capacity and has not been employed by the employer – other than newly formed employers – for a period of at least six months, and works at the given fixed establishment;
(b) upon dissolution of the works' council;
(c) persons exercising employers' rights;
(d) relatives of the employer's executive officers;
(e) members of the election committee;
(f) upon resignation;
(g) upon dismissal.

1229. A ballot must be held with regard to the dismissal of a works' council member if so proposed in writing by at least 30% of the employees eligible to vote. The ballot can be declared valid upon the participation of more than half the employees eligible to vote. More than two-thirds of the valid votes will be required for dismissal.

1230. A motion for dismissal may not be filed for the second time within a period of one year. In such case, the provisions pertaining to the election procedure should be duly applied for the dismissal of a works' council member.

1231. Upon termination of the mandate of a works' council member, an alternate member should be appointed according to the ranking by the number of votes received.[401]

C. *Operation of Works' Councils*

1232. The works' council will convene within fifteen days following its election, and will elect a chairman from among its members at its inaugural session. Members should attend the works' council meetings in person. The works' council's operating regulations will be laid down based on its order of business.

400. KOZMA Anna – LŐRINCZ György – PÁL Lajos, A Munka Törvénykönyvének magyarázata, Budapest: HVG-Orac, 2020.
401. DUDÁS Katalin – GYULAVÁRI Tamás – HORVÁTH István – Hős Nikolett – KÁRTYÁS Gábor – KULISITY Mária – KUN Attila – PETROVICS Zoltán, Munkajog, Budapest: ELTE Eötvös Kiadó, 2012. 474.

1233. Reduction of working time. With a view to discharging their duties, the chairman of the works' council will be entitled to working time reduction amounting to 15% of his/her monthly working time, while members of the works' council will be entitled to 10%. Claiming any working time reduction should be notified at least five days in advance, except if claimed under unforeseen and overriding reasons of urgency, or under exceptional circumstances. Absentee pay shall be provided for the duration of working time reduction.

1234. The works' council's consent is required for terminating the employment relationship of the chairman of the works' council by notice, or for posting or secondment by the employer, if this later action is affecting the chairman of the works' council. The chairman of the works' council is entitled to protection for the duration of his/her term in office and for a period of six months thereafter, provided that the chairman held the office for at least twelve months.

1235. The works' council should make known its opinion in writing with respect to the employer's above-mentioned action within eight days of receipt of the employer's written notice. If the works' council does not agree with the proposed action, the statement should include the reasons therefor. Failure by the works' council to convey its opinion to the employer within the above-specified time limit will be construed as agreement with the proposed action.

1236. Employers must provide for – by way of the means fixed in the works agreement – the opportunity for works' councils to publish information related to their activities.[402]

D. Levels of Works' Councils

1. Central Works Councils

1237. A central works' council may be set up by several works' councils. Members to the central works' council can be delegated by the works' councils from among their members. The central works' council may not have more than fifteen members. Furthermore, the provisions on works' councils will apply to the central works' council as well.[403]

2. Corporate-Level Works' Councils

1238. Central works' councils or, failing this, works' councils may set up a corporate-level works' council at a recognized or de facto group of companies. Members to such works' council will be delegated by the central works' councils or

402. FERENC Jácint – GÖNDÖR Éva – GYULAVÁRI Tamás – KÁRTYÁS Gábor, Munkajogi alapismeretek, Budapest: ELTE Kiadó, 2013. p. 189.
403. HAJDÚ, József – KUN, Attila (eds), Munkajog II., Budapest: Patrocinium, 2013. p. 139.

the works' councils from among their members. The corporate-level works' council may not have more than fifteen members. The rules of cooperation shall be laid down within the group of companies by the works' council having the right to adopt decisions relating to employees and by the corporate-level works' council. Furthermore, the provisions on works' councils will apply to the corporate-level works' council as well.

E. Powers and Responsibilities of Works' Councils

1239. Works' councils, in general, will monitor compliance with the provisions of employment regulations. To the extent required for their responsibilities, works' councils are entitled to request information and to initiate negotiations, with the reason indicated, which the employer may not refuse.

1. The Rights of the Works' Council

1240. The right of the works' council can be: A. notification, B. co-decision and C. consultation.[404]

1241. A. Right to notification. According to section 262 of the HLC, the employer should notify the works' council semi-annually regarding:

(a) the issues affecting the employer's economic standing;
(b) changes in wages, liquidity related to the payment of wages, the characteristic features of employment, utilization of working time, and the characteristics of working conditions;
(c) the number of workers in employment and the description of the jobs they perform.

The works' council shall inform the employees concerning its activities semi-annually.

1242. B. Right to co-decision. The employer and the works' council will collectively decide concerning the appropriation of welfare funds. This right of works' council is very limited. Therefore, Hungarian works' councils are lack the codetermination rights which make German works' councils so powerful and thus enable them to conduct real bargaining with employers.

1243. C. Right to consultation. Employers should consult the works' council fifteen days prior to passing a decision in respect of any plans for actions and adopting regulations affecting a large number of employees.

404. HAJDÚ József, European Works Council Hungary, The Netherlands: Kluwer Law International BV, 2012. p. 42.

1244. The cases of consultation are as follows:

(a) proposals for the employer's reorganization, transformation, the conversion of a strategic business unit into an independent organization;
(b) introducing production and investment programmes, new technologies, or upgrading existing ones;
(c) processing and protection of personal data of employees;
(d) implementation of technical means for the surveillance of workers;
(e) measures for compliance with occupational safety and health requirements, and for the prevention of accidents at work and occupational diseases;
(f) the introduction and/or amendment of new work organization methods and performance requirements;
(g) plans relating to training and education;
(h) appropriation of job assistance related subsidies;
(i) drawing up proposals for the rehabilitation of workers with health impairment and persons with reduced ability to work;
(j) laying down working arrangements;
(k) setting the principles for the remuneration of work;
(l) measures for the protection of the environment relating to the employer's operations;
(m) measures implemented with a view to enforcing the principle of equal treatment and for the promotion of equal opportunities;
(n) coordinating family life and work;
(o) other measures specified by employment regulations.[405]

2. The Transfer of Employment

1245. In the case of transfer of employment upon the transfer of enterprise, the transferring and the receiving employer will, within fifteen days before the effective date of transfer, inform the works' council concerning:

(a) the schedule or proposed date of transfer;
(b) the reasons;
(c) the legal, economic and social consequences affecting the employees.

1246. Within the above-mentioned time limit, the transferring and the receiving employer must – with a view to the conclusion of an agreement – enter into negotiations with the works' council concerning other proposed actions affecting employees.

405. BANKÓ Zoltán, BERKE Gyula, KISS György, SZŐKE Gergely László Nagykommentár a munka törvénykönyvéhez, Wolters Kluwer, Budapest 2019.

1247. The above-specified negotiations will cover the principles of the actions, the ways and means of avoiding detrimental consequences as well as the means for mitigating such consequences.

1248. The transferring and the receiving employer shall meet the obligation of information and negotiation if the decision underlying the transfer of employment upon the transfer of enterprise had been adopted by the body or person exercising control over the employer. The employer shall not be excused regarding their failure to satisfy the obligation to supply information and hold talks on the grounds that the controlling organization or person had failed to inform the employer concerning its decision.

3. The Position of Works' Council in Case of Strike

1249. Works' councils must remain unbiased in relation to a strike organized against employers, and they may not organize, support or obstruct strikes. The mandate of works' council members participating in a strike will be suspended for the duration of the strike.[406]

F. Works Agreement

1250. Works agreement (üzemi megállapodás) is a new-old instrument in the Hungarian labour law. It was introduced formerly and soon abolished in the previous (1992) Labour Code. The works agreement is one of the most important changes in the new HLC (2012). According to this change, works' councils now have the right to conclude works agreements with the employer in cases where there is no collective agreement in force and no union organization present at the workplace which is entitled to negotiate a collective agreement. The works agreement may regulate terms and conditions of employment as a collective agreement, with one important caveat: it cannot regulate wages and remuneration.[407]

G. Dissolution of Works' Councils

1251. The works' council shall be dissolved:

(a) if the employer is terminated without succession;
(b) if the corporate (branch) is not independent anymore;
(c) if its mandate expires;
(d) upon resignation;

406. HAJDÚ, József – KUN, Attila (eds), Munkajog II., Budapest: Patrocinium, 2013. pp. 144–145.
407. DUDÁS Katalin – GYULAVÁRI Tamás – HORVÁTH István – Hős Nikolett – KULISITY Mária – HUNGLER Sára – KÁRTYÁS Gábor – KUN Attila – PETROVICS Zoltán – RÁCZ Réka, Munkajog – V. átdolgozott kiadás, Budapest: ELTE Eötvös Kiadó, 2019.

(e) if it is dismissed;
(f) if its membership decreases by more than one-third;
(g) if the number of employees drops below fifty or decreases by at least two-thirds;
(h) if the results of the election were annulled by the court; and
(i) in all other cases prescribed by law.

1252. A ballot must be held with regard to the dismissal of a works' council, if so proposed in writing by at least 30% of the employees eligible to vote. The ballot is declared valid upon the participation of more than half the employees eligible to vote. More than two-thirds of the valid votes will be required for dismissal. A motion for dismissal may not be filed for the second time within a period of one year. The provisions pertaining to the election procedure shall also apply to the dismissal of a works' council.

1253. The mandate of a works' council, if dissolved on the grounds specified in the paragraphs b)–c) and f)–g) of section 252, will remain in force until the new works' council is elected, or for up to three months from the time of dissolution.

III. Health and Safety Representation

1254. Elected health and safety representatives are the main way that the interests of employees are represented in the area of health and safety in Hungary. However, in larger employers, there is also a joint health and safety committee, made up of representatives of both sides.

A. Basic Approach at Workplace Level

1255. The employer has a duty to ensure the existence of healthy and safe working conditions. However, employee health and safety representatives should cooperate with the employer in order to achieve this.

1256. The main structures representing employees in the area of health and safety are health and safety representatives (munkavédelmi képviselő), who can come together in their own employee-only health and safety committee (munkahelyi munkavédelmi bizottság), and, in larger employers, the joint health and safety committee (paritásos munkavédelmi testület) made up of representatives of both employees and the employer.

B. Numbers and Structure

1257. There is an obligation to have health and safety representatives in all organizations with 50 or more employees. In smaller organizations, health and safety representatives must be elected if the local union organization, the works council or a majority of employees want this. If there are no health and safety representatives, the employer should inform and consult the employees directly on health and safety issues.

1258. Where there are three or more health and safety representatives, they can set up an employee-only health and safety committee, which the employer must attend if requested. This committee has the same rights as the health and safety representatives and is different from the joint health and safety committee.

1259. In organizations with 50 or more employees and where there are health and safety representatives, the employer should set up a joint health and safety committee with an equal number of representatives of the employer and the employees. The legislation states that the committee chair should alternate between a representative of the employees and the employers, but it leaves other matters, such as the number of the members, the rules of procedure and the precise activities of the committee, to be agreed between the employer and the employees' representatives. Health and safety specialists employed by the company should also participate regularly in this joint committee.

C. *Tasks and Rights*

1260. The health and safety representatives or members of the employee-only health and safety committee have the right to monitor compliance with the appropriate health and safety obligations, and in particular to monitor:

(a) whether workplaces, work equipment and personal protective equipment are in safe condition;
(b) whether measures to safeguard health and prevent accidents have been carried out;
(c) whether employees have been trained and prepared to enable them to work safely.

1261. In particular, health and safety representatives or members of the employee-only health and safety committee may:

(a) enter the workplaces they cover during working hours and obtain information from employees working there;
(b) participate in the preparation of decisions by the employer that might have repercussions on employees' health and safety;
(c) request information from the employer concerning any issues related to healthy and safe working conditions;
(d) express opinions and make proposals to the employer;
(e) participate in accident investigations of occupational accidents and, where appropriate, in the investigation of the causes of occupational diseases;
(f) refer justified cases to the health and safety inspectorate.

1262. They can also discuss health and safety issues with the labour inspectorate and, subject to the employer's agreement, ask for experts for advice.

1263. The employer must respond to any request for information or proposal for action within eight days. If the employer decides not to provide the information or agree to the proposal, this refusal must be explained in writing.

1264. The health and safety representatives can also propose that the employer draws up a health and safety programme. If the employer refuses to do this and is of a certain size (this varies according to the nature of the hazards in the company), the health and safety representatives can initiate a collective labour dispute, which involves the intervention of a mediator.

1265. Internal health and safety rules can only be issued with the agreement of the health and safety representatives or the employee-only health and safety committee.

The joint health and safety committee should:

(a) assess the health and safety situation in the company and measures that could be taken to improve it at least once a year;
(b) discuss the company's health and safety programme and monitor its implementation; and
(c) comment on any internal health and safety regulations.

1266. The joint health and safety committee should not affect the operation of the health and safety representatives.

D. *Frequency of Meetings*

1267. The legislation does not lay down rules on the frequency of meetings other than stating that the joint health and safety committee should review the health and safety situation at least annually.

E. *Election and Term of Office*

1268. Where there are 50 or more employees, an election by secret ballot must be organized to choose one or more health and safety representatives. In organizations with fewer than 50 employees, an election to choose a safety representative must be organized if this is requested by the local union or by the works council or by the majority of the employees. Candidates must have at least six months' service, although this does not apply in newly established companies.

1269. The term of office is five years. Members of the joint health and safety committee (both full members and substitutes) are chosen by secret ballot of the health and safety representatives from among themselves. They also serve for five years.

F. Resources and Time Off

1270. Health and safety representatives and committee members are entitled to sufficient paid time off to undertake their duties. Members of the joint health and safety committee are entitled to paid time off equivalent to a least 10% of their monthly working hours.

1271. Health and safety representatives are also entitled to 16 hours of training in the first year following their election and eight hours annually in subsequent years. This training is paid for by the employer and should be conducted during normal working time.

G. Protection Against Dismissal

1272. Health and safety representatives should not be disadvantaged because of the exercise of their duties and have the same protection against dismissal as local union representatives or members of the works council. This means that they can only be dismissed if the health and safety committee agrees or, if there is no committee, with the agreement of the employees who elected them.

IV. Trade Union

A. The Concept of Trade Union

1273. According to section 270 of the new HLC, the rights afforded by the HLC to trade unions will be due to the local trade union branch[408] represented at the employer.

1274. The HLC states that each employees' organization whose primary function is the development and protection of employees' interests concerning employment shall be considered a trade union.[409] This means, it is not necessary to use in

408. Local trade union branch represented at the employer means: a trade union which, according to its statutes, operates an organization authorized for representation or has an officer at the employer.
409. BANKÓ Zoltán, BERKE Gyula, KISS György, SZŐKE Gergely László Nagykommentár a munka törvénykönyvéhez, Wolters Kluwer, Budapest 2019.

the name of the organization the term 'trade union' (e.g., the name of one of the Hungarian trade unions is the National Confederation of Workers' Councils).[410,411]

B. The Right to Information

1275. An essential right of the trade union is to request information from the employer on all issues related to the employees' employment-related economic and social welfare interests. The employer cannot refuse to provide such information or a justification of his/her actions.

1276. However, all information the employer has expressly disclosed as a trade secret to a person acting in the name of the trade union or for it and on its behalf under power of attorney may not be disclosed to third persons, may not be published and may not be used in any other way in connection with any activity in which this person is involved for reasons other than the objectives specified in the HLC.

1277. Any person who is acting in the name of the trade union or for it and on its behalf under power of attorney will be authorized to publish any information or data acquired in the course of operations solely in a manner which does not jeopardize the employer's justified business interests and without violating the employees' personal rights.

1278. The trade union, moreover, is entitled to make its position with regard to the employer's decision known to the employer and, furthermore, to initiate consultations in connection with this.

1279. Trade unions are entitled to represent their members – under authorization – before the court, the relevant authority and other organs with a view to protecting their economic interests and social welfare.

1280. Trade unions have the right to use the employer's premises after or during working hours, as agreed with the employer, for the purposes of interest representation activities.

1281. Employers cannot claim any compensation for withholding and transferring membership dues to the trade union.[412]

410. Szakszervezet/ Az új Munka törvénykönyve XXI. Fejezet, http://munkastanacsok.hu/szakszervezet-munka-torvenykonyve-xxi-fejezet/ (26 Jul. 2023.).
411. CZUGLERNÉ IVÁNY Judit, MÉLYPATAKI Gábor (2021) Érdekképviseletek a munkajogban, https://ijoten.hu/szocikk/erdekkepviseletek-a-munkajogban (26 Jul. 2023).
412. A Munka törvénykönyve XXI. fejezet: szakszervezeti jogok, https://munkastanacsok.hu/blog-grid3/erdekegyeztetes/munkahelyi-szint/szakszervezet-munka-torvenykonyve-xxi-fejezet/ (26 Jul. 2023).

C. *The Right to an Inspection*

1282. The trade union is entitled to verify compliance with the regulations pertaining to working conditions. Before an inspection takes place, it must inform the competent authority (e.g., labour safety inspector). In relation to the inspection, the trade union may request information from the authorities concerned about the implementation of regulations pertaining to employment, and the necessary information and data must be placed at its disposal. On the basis of the result of the inspection, it may draw the attention of the authorities in charge of implementation to the mistakes and omissions observed in the course of the inspection and if the authorities do not take the necessary measures in time, the union may institute appropriate procedures. The authority carrying out the procedure shall inform the union of the outcome.[413]

D. *The Employer's Obligations*

1. Consultation and Information

1283. The employer should ensure that trade unions have the opportunity to publicize information and appeals regarded as necessary, as well as data related to its activities in a manner customary with the employer or in another appropriate way.

1284. In the event of legal succession in the person of the employer, if no works' council exists in the workplace, the employer's legal predecessor and legal successor will notify the trade unions regarding the reason for legal succession, on the legal economic and social consequences of such affecting the employees and will in due time initiate talks concerning other proposed actions which affect the employees prior to legal succession or at least before such would affect the employment relations or work conditions of the employees.

2. Promotion of Union Activities

1285. Trade unions – with the employer's agreement – can use the employer's premises after or during working hours for the purpose of union activities.

1286. With a view to discharging their trade union functions of interest representation, employees will be entitled to working time reduction, and the trade union officials (they are employees designated according to Subsections (3)–(4) of section 273 of the HLC) will be exempted from work for the duration of consultation with the employer.

413. DUDÁS Katalin – GYULAVÁRI Tamás – HORVÁTH István – Hős Nikolett – KULISITY Mária – HUNGLER Sára – KÁRTYÁS Gábor – KUN Attila – PETROVICS Zoltán – RÁCZ Réka, Munkajog – V. átdolgozott kiadás, Budapest: ELTE Eötvös Kiadó, 2019.

1287. The total amount of working time reduction in a given calendar year will be one hour monthly for every two trade union member employed by the employer. The amount of working time reduction available will be determined based on the number of trade union members registered on the first of January.

1288. Working time reduction will be provided to the employee designated by the trade union. The trade union will notify the employer of its intention to claim working time reduction at least five days in advance, except if claimed under unforeseen and overriding reasons of urgency, or under exceptional circumstances.

1289. Working time reduction can be claimed by the end of the given year. Basically, working time reduction will not be financially compensated by the employer. However, absentee pay will be provided for the duration of working time reduction and for the duration of consultation with the employer.

1290. In the case of an employer wishing to transfer an elected trade union official to another place of work, or wishing to terminate his/her employment by notice, he/she must request the appropriate higher ranking trade union organization's consent in advance. In the case of an extraordinary notice, or applying legal consequences provided for in a collective agreement, or transfer to another post, the employer must inform the appropriate trade union official in advance.

1291. Trade union officials will be entitled to the above-mentioned protection for the duration of their term in office and for a period of six months thereafter, provided that the officials held the office for at least twelve months.

1292. The number of officials the trade union is entitled to designate from among the union officials employed at a fixed establishment that is considered independent according to Subsection (2) of section 236 of the HLC, if the average statistical number of employees – on the first day of the calendar year – employed during the previous calendar year is:

(a) less than five hundred, it will be one;
(b) between five hundred and one thousand, it will be two;
(c) between one thousand and two thousand, it will be three;
(d) between two thousand and four thousand, it will be four;
(e) more than four thousand, it will be five.

1293. Apart from the union officials referred above hereof, the protection will also be afforded to one other union official designated by the supreme body of the local trade union branch represented at the employer.

1294. Trade unions are entitled to replace the union official if the employment relationship or trade union office of such union official has been terminated.

1295. The trade union will make known its opinion in writing with respect to the employer's action within eight days of receipt of the employer's written notice.

If the trade union does not agree with the proposed action, the statement will include the reasons therefor. Failure by the trade union to convey its opinion within the above-specified time limit will be construed as agreement with the proposed action.[414]

§2. At National and Industry Level

I. Tripartite Consultations: National Economic and Social Council (NESC)

1296. The most important aim of the National Economic and Social Council (hereinafter: NESC) – a body that replaces earlier forums for employers, unions and the government (Interest-Coordinating Council) – is to create Europe's most competitive economic environment in Hungary by 2014.

1297. The legal basis of the establishment of the NESC is that the Hungarian Government adopted The Declaration of National Cooperation in 2010 as part of The Programme of National Cooperation in order to acknowledge the inception of a new social contract. In order to enforce the new social contract the Government of Hungary established the System of National Cooperation which is open to all Hungarians.[415]

1298. The Government of Hungary offers cooperation to every member of society, to NGOs and advocacy organizations, and to economic players to find solutions to issues of national interest.[416]

1299. The Parliament adopted Act XCIII of 2011 on the National Economic and Social Council in recognition of the role of economic and social dialogue, in order to discuss strategies of national economy and social policy and to promote a consensus among various interest groups of society.[417]

1300. The NESC is a combination of the former National Interest Conciliation Council (in Hungarian: OÉT), the Economic and Social Council (hereinafter: ESC) and the Economic Interest Coordination Forum (hereinafter: 'EICF'), all of which before operated in parallel. The government wanted to replace that 'obsolete and inefficient' tripartite consultation system.

414. HAJDÚ József, IEL Labour Law, Hungary, Wolters Kluwer, Kluwer Law Online, 2019. https://kluwerlawonline.com/Manuals/Corporate+Acquisitions+and+Mergers/705 (26 Jul. 2023).
415. Létrejön a Nemzeti Gazdasági és Társadalmi Tanács az OÉT helyett, http://hvg.hu/gazdasag/20110704_ngtt_alakul_oet_vege (26 Jul. 2023.).
416. LAKI Mihály – NACSA Beáta – NEUMANN László, Az új Munka Törvénykönyvének hatása a munkavállalók és a munkáltatók közötti kapcsolatokra, Kutatási zárójelentés, Budapest: Magyar Tudományos Akadémia Közgazdaság- és Regionális Tudományi Kutatóközpont Közgazdaságtudományi Intézet, 2013, http://mek.oszk.hu/11400/11439/11439.pdf (26 Jul. 2023.).
417. http://www.ngtt.hu/index_eng.html (26 Jul. 2023).

1301. The NESC is a consultative, proposal-making and advisory body independent from Parliament and the Government. The NESC's members representing the Hungarian civil society, creating the following sides:

(1) Side of Representatives of Economy: advocacy groups and organizations of employers, national business chambers.
(2) Side of Employees: advocacy groups and organizations of employees.
(3) Side of NGOs: NGOs active in the field of national policy.
(4) Side of Representatives of Sciences: Hungarian representatives of academia.
(5) Side of Churches.

1302. It is important to underline that the NESC will no longer include state representatives. Therefore, the NGTT is not a tripartite body any more. However, at the council's plenary sessions ministers or executive officers appointed by them will attend the Council's plenary sessions as permanent guests with a consultative right. In addition, the President or Vice President of the Hungarian Competition Authority and the Central Statistical Office shall attend the Council's plenary sessions as guests with a consultative right.

1303. The rotating President of the NESC is elected from the representatives of the sides. The rotating Presidency is based on the rotation of the sides. The mandate of NESC members is valid for four years.

1304. One of the main declared tasks for the council is to find ways to reduce the debt of the state and families and how to create more jobs.

1305. As compared to the previous system, the most important change is that the NESC holds consultations, makes proposals and advise, but will not take any decisions.

II. Sectorial Level Consultation

1306. In Hungary at sectorial level, it is possible to establish Sectorial Dialogue Committees[418] (hereinafter referred to as SDC, in Hungarian 'ÁPB'), which are joint committees of the employee and employer organizations operating on the sectorial/sub-sectorial level. The establishment of these Committees, their organization, operation and rights are regulated by a separate Act (Act LXXIV of 2009). The act includes conditions (criteria) for getting into the SDC and also for exercising certain rights. SDC is primarily a bilateral consultative body; however, in case

418. During summer 2009 and based on a ruling of the Hungarian Constitutional Court questioning the codetermination rights granted to sectoral social dialogue structures, the Hungarian Parliament adopted the Act LXXIV on sectoral social dialogue committees (Ágazati Párbeszéd Bizottságok, ÁPB) – revising the powers of these structures and setting representation criteria for the organizations involved. The new system came into force in October 2009.

of meeting the conditions stipulated by the law, the committee also has the possibility of concluding a collective agreement. SDCs are operating in the economic sphere. In case of the public sphere the person of the employer was debatable (the state or certain institutions).

Chapter 4. Collective Bargaining and Collective Agreements

§1. Levels of Collective Bargaining

1307. Collective bargaining primarily takes place at company/organizational level, despite considerable efforts by both unions and previous governments to encourage industry level bargaining. Around one-third of employees are covered by collective bargaining of any sort.

1308. Despite efforts by the unions and the previous governments to strengthen bargaining at industry level, the main level of bargaining is company/organization level, although it is losing out to a situation where no bargaining takes place at all. Until 2010 national level discussions between unions, employers and government were also very important in setting the framework for bargaining and making recommendations to lower-level negotiators.[419]

1309. Figures from the official Industrial Relations Information System (Munkaügyi Kapcsolatok Információs Rendszer)[420] show that in May 2022, there were 5,238 collective agreements registered.

1310. The vast majority of the agreements are for a single employer. Almost two-thirds of these agreements are for employers in the public sector, although, in terms of the numbers of employees covered, the proportions are reversed. The prevailing attitude of employers is a reluctance to join employers' organizations or to authorize them to conclude industry agreements.

1311. The OECD sources (2015) indicate that the trade union density in the private sector is 5%–10%, employer's organization density 40%–50%; collective bargaining coverage rate 20%–30%.[421]

1312. Until 2011, unions were able to influence bargaining developments through a tripartite body called the National Interest Reconciliation Council (in Hungarian: OÉT). This was reconstituted by the then socialist-led government in 2002 after being largely dismantled by the previous right-wing government. It provided a forum in which the three parties could agree on the national minimum wage for the coming year and set a minimum rate for skilled workers. It also had an important role in making recommendations on the proposed level of pay increases to lower-level bargainers, although these recommendations were not binding. However, in 2011, the government decided to replace the OÉT with a new body, the National Economic and Social Council (NESC). This includes a wider range of

419. GERSE Márton (2019) Kollektív szerződés a munkajogban, https://ado.hu/munkaugyek/kollektiv-szerzodes-a-munkajogban/ (26 Jul. 2023).

420. Kollektív Szerződések Elektronikus Nyilvántartókönyve, http://mkir.gov.hu/ksznyilv.htm (26 Jul. 2023).

421. Collective Bargaining in OECD and accession countries, Hungary (2015), https://www.oecd.org/employment/emp/collective-bargaining-Hungary.pdf (26 Jul. 2023).

organizations, including chambers of commerce, civic organizations and churches, and it will no longer be able to set minimum rates. The change was strongly criticized by the unions.

1313. The situation changed again in February 2012, when a new tripartite body, the Standing Consultative Forum (VFK) was set up to discuss employment issues. However, only three union confederations, LIGA, MOSZ and MSZOSZ have joined this new body, and its role is more limited than the former OÉT.[422]

§2. The Negotiating Parties

1314. Negotiations at both company and industry level are between employers or employers' associations and the unions in most cases. However, in this area, as in others, the Labour Code, which came into effect in 2012, has introduced changes. Works' councils (which cannot organize strikes and have a very limited ability to influence employers – *see* the section on workplace representation – can now negotiate agreements with the employer, where there is no union at the workplace and it is not covered by a collective agreement. The one important exception is that these agreements cannot cover pay. This is virtually a return to the position under an earlier right-wing government when works' councils were given negotiating rights at company level, where there were no unions present – something that was reversed by the socialist government in 2002.

1315. Between 1992 and 2012, union rights to negotiate – their representativeness – depended on their support in works' council elections. A union needed to get 10% of the votes in the works' council elections to be entitled to negotiate. Local agreements could be signed by a coalition of unions in the workplace, provided that together they had the support of at least 50% of the workforce – a measure which encouraged the creation of local union coalitions. If a single union had more than 65% support, it could sign the agreements alone. However, here again the Labour Code has made changes. Now trade unions can only conclude collective agreements at company level if their membership exceeds 10% of those employed at the company. The same 10% rule also applies to industry level agreements, where unions must have 10% of those employed in the industry to be able to reach an agreement.[423]

1316. Collective agreements setting a range of issues normally last for two years, although they are often for an unlimited period. However, pay increases at company level are often annual.

422. HAJDÚ József, IEL Labour Law, Hungary, Wolters Kluwer, Kluwer Law Online, 2019. https://kluwerlawonline.com/Manuals/Corporate+Acquisitions+and+Mergers/705 (26 Jul. 2023).
423. HAJDÚ, József – KUN, Attila (eds), Munkajog II., Budapest: Patrocinium, 2013. pp. 121–122.

§3. The Content of Bargaining

1317. Agreements typically cover pay, working conditions and procedural issues. However, since 2001, negotiations have concentrated on working time and work organization because legislative changes have made it possible to have greater flexibility in working time arrangements, provided that it is negotiated.

1318. In the public sector, the new Labour Code has introduced significant restrictions on what can be negotiated. In many areas, it is impossible for a collective agreement to include terms which improve on the minimum set out by law.[424]

§4. The Concept and Content of the Collective Agreement

I. The Concept of the Collective Agreement

1319. This Chapter contains the rules of the HLC on collective agreements. A collective agreement is an agreement concluded on the basis of the collective negotiations between on the one hand a trade union[425] or trade union confederation[426] and on the other hand an employer or employers' organization. The trade unions with entitlement to conclude a collective agreement may do so collectively.

1320. An employer may enter into one collective agreement. Where a collective agreement is concluded by more than one employer, an employer may conclude the collective agreement, of which the employer will also be a party, under authorization given in such collective agreement. The collective agreement concluded by several employers should be construed to have a broader scope.

1321. Any trade union (trade-union confederation) that meets the above-mentioned requirements after the collective agreement is concluded will be able to request an amendment of the collective agreement, and to participate in the negotiations relating to the amendment in an advisory capacity.

---

424. ETUI, Worker-participation Hungary, https://www.worker-participation.eu/national-industrial-relations/countries/hungary (26 Jul. 2023).

425. A trade union is entitled to conclude a collective agreement if its membership of workers at the employer reaches 10%:

   (a) of all workers employed by the employer;

   (b) of the number of workers covered by the collective agreement concluded by the employers' interest group.

   For counting, the average statistical number of employees for the half-year period before the date of conclusion of the contract should be taken into consideration.

426. A trade-union confederation is entitled to conclude a collective agreement if at least one of its local trade union branch members meets the above-mentioned requirements for trade union and if so authorized by its members.

1322. According to the general opinion of Hungarian labour law science, collective agreements form a source of labour law. If the HLC mentions a regulation pertaining to employment, this must denote both the statutory provision and the collective agreement.

1323. As it was discussed earlier, the HLC (2012) makes it possible for employers to sign works agreement with the works' council instead of concluding collective agreements with the trade unions. Employers expect that this will be more favourable for their flexible needs; therefore, a large number of companies have not renewed collective agreements since the new HLC was published.

II. The Content of the Collective Agreement

1324. The parties may determine two kinds of rules in the collective agreement: on one hand, there are the rights and obligations arising from employment, and on the other hand, the mode of exercising and fulfilling these, the order of the procedure related thereto and on the other hand, the relations between the parties concluding the collective agreement.

1325. Basically, the collective agreement cannot stipulate rules contrary to the rules of law. However, in the absence of an agreement to the contrary, in the collective agreement derogations are allowed from the provisions of Part Two and Part Three of the HLC.

The collective agreement:

(a) may not contain derogations from Chapters XIX (Industrial Relations General Provisions) and XX (Works Councils); and
(b) may not contain any restrictions concerning the provisions contained in sections 271–272 of HLC.

1326. A collective agreement of limited effect may derogate from one with a broader scope – unless otherwise provided therein – insofar as it contains more favourable regulations for the employees. Derogations for the benefit of employees will be adjudged by a comparative assessment of related regulations.

1327. The collective agreements may only be concluded in writing.[427]

III. Types of Collective Agreements

1328. The Hungarian labour law distinguishes between three types of collective agreements:

427. KOZMA Anna – LŐRINCZ György – PÁL Lajos, A Munka Törvénykönyvének magyarázata, Budapest: HVG-Orac, 2020.

– at branch level;
– by several employers together;
– by one employer (company level).

1329. As for the coverage rate of collective agreements, in Hungary there are only a few sector-wide collective agreements. A further very limited range (approx. 2%) of workers are covered by multi-employer agreements. The main significant level of collective bargaining is the company level.

Table 3 Levels of Collective Bargaining

	Levels of Collective Bargaining		
	National Level (Intersectoral)	*Sectoral Level*	*Company Level*
Principal or dominant level	X National Interest Reconciliation Council (OÉT) until September 2011		X
Important but not dominant level			
Existing level	Ad hoc and incidentally	X	

Source: http://www.eurofound.europa.eu/eiro/country/hungary_4.htm (26 July 2023).

IV. Conclusion of the Collective Agreement

A. *The Parties to a Branch Collective Agreement*

1330. The parties to the collective agreement at branch level are the trade union and the employers' organization. They shall be independent of each other in representation of their respective interests. The organization representing the employer's interests requires authorization to act by its members.

1331. Since 2003, the Sectoral Social Dialogue Committee (hereinafter: 'SSDC') can conclude collective agreements on sectoral, sub-sectoral and branch level. In one SSDC, only one collective agreement can be concluded for a sector, sub-sector or branch. The interest representation organization is entitled to conclude a collective agreement in the SSDC only if its rules and regulations or its supreme decision-making body authorizes it to do so. The employer may authorize only one employer interest representation organization to conclude a collective agreement.

1332. All the interest representation organizations taking part in the SSDC are entitled to conclude a collective agreement jointly in the SSDC.

1333. The collective agreement – unless specified otherwise – will take effect on the 15th day following the conclusion of the agreement. The employer interest representation organization is obliged to make the collective agreement known by the employees employed by its members.

1334. The scope of the collective agreement concluded in the SSDC will cover the employer interest representation organization which concluded the collective agreement and the employees employed by it.

1335. The scope of the collective agreement concluded in the SSDC will cover the employers who join the employer interest representation organization subsequently and the employees employed by them only if the employer interest representation organization joining the SSDC after the conclusion of the collective agreement declares that it also intends to join the collective agreement concluded in the SSDC.

1336. If the collective agreement was concluded by several sectorial trade unions in the SSDC and any of these trade unions cancels it, the collective agreement will cease to have effect if the collective agreement could not have been concluded without the participation of this trade union. Pursuant to this regulation, the trade union which has a representation at one of the employers of the employer interest representation organization which joined the collective agreement subsequently will not have the right of cancellation. In case of cancellation, the effect of the collective agreement will cease after the expiry of the period of cancellation of six months.

B. *The Parties to a Collective Agreement at Employer's Level*

1337. At the employer's level, only one collective agreement may be concluded. (Of course, if there are different professions represented by different trade unions, independent collective agreements may be concluded for each profession, e.g., in the case of an Airline Company: e.g., one collective agreement for pilots, another for navigators.)[428]

§5. The Negotiations

1338. Neither party can reject a proposal for negotiations aimed at concluding a collective agreement where the proposal was made by a party entitled to conclude a collective agreement. Such conditions also apply to negotiations directed towards an amendment of a collective agreement. The employer has to propose annually, in addition to providing the necessary data, to the trade unions concerning the settlement on the regulations pertaining to remuneration for work in the collective agreement.

428. HAJDÚ, József – KUN, Attila (eds), Munkajog II., Budapest: Patrocinium, 2013. pp. 125–126.

1339. All the trade unions represented at the employer's and irrespective of their representativity may attend the talks aimed at concluding the collective agreement.

1340. In the case of a dispute related to entitlement to conclude a collective agreement, the Administrative and Labour Court decides in non-legal proceedings upon the request of the organization concerned.

§6. Validity of the Collective Agreement

I. Scope of Collective Agreement

1341. The collective agreement, in the absence of an agreement departing thereof, enters into effect upon publication.

1342. The effect of a collective agreement will apply to any employer who:

(a) is a party to the collective agreement; or
(b) is a member of the employers' interest group that concluded the collective agreement.

1343. The effect of the provisions of the collective agreement governing the means of communication of the parties will apply to the undersigning parties of the collective agreement.

1344. The effect of the provisions of the collective agreement governing employment relationships will apply to all the workers (non-unionized workers as well) employed by the employer.

II. Denunciation of a Collective Agreement

1345. A collective agreement can be denounced after six months of signing it, providing three months' notice is given. Any of the parties can terminate it if the agreement or any other agreement does not specify otherwise. In the case of a multi-employer collective agreement, the agreement will be terminated only for the party that initiates the denunciation. If a new trade union wins the right to bargain, it can also denounce the existing collective agreement.

III. Termination of a Collective Agreement

1346. If one of the parties terminates its activity without a successor, the collective agreement will be terminated. An exception is in the case of a multi-employer collective agreement, where the collective agreement still applies for the rest of the parties.

1347. Upon dissolution of an employer, an employers' interest group or a trade union (trade-union confederation) without succession, the collective agreement will be terminated as well.

1348. As regards a collective agreement that was concluded by more than one employer or by more than one employers' interest group, the collective agreement will cease to apply only to the employer or employers' interest group terminated without succession.

1349. As regards a collective agreement that was concluded by more than one trade union, the collective agreement will cease to apply upon the dissolution of all such trade unions without succession.

1350. The collective agreement will cease to have effect if the trade union (trade-union confederation) that is a party to the collective agreement is not entitled to conclude a collective agreement any more.

1351. A fixed-term collective agreement shall cease to exist upon the expiry of the fixed term.

§7. Extension of the Collective Agreement

1352. Upon the joint request of the contracting parties, the effect of the collective agreement may be extended to the entire sector or a part of it by the Minister in charge. The decision must be publicized in the Official Gazette of the Ministry. In the absence of any provision in the collective agreement departing from this, publication will qualify as the date of entry into force.

1353. Collective agreements can be extended by law in the case of sectoral collective agreements.[429] In Hungary, there are two levels of collective bargaining and collective agreements. One is the sector level: sectoral agreements can be negotiated and signed by representative employer associations on the one side and trade unions on the other side. Since 2003, the so-called sectoral social dialogue committees (SSDC) have been established. To establish such an SSDC or to participate in it, representativeness must be proven. These committees have the right to negotiate collective agreements and other agreements for the sector concerned, but only a few sectoral collective agreements have been concluded so far: in the agriculture, hotel, catering, tourism, bakery, chemistry and electricity sectors. The sectoral agreements are registered at the ministry concerned. Some of the agreements are extended to

429. BERKE Gyula: A kollektív szerződés a magyar magánjogi gondolkodásban. Pécsi Munkajogi Közlemények, 2014, különszám, pp. 58–59.

the whole branch; others are only valid for the companies affiliated to the employers' association. Extended collective agreements are found in the catering, electric energy, bakery and construction sectors.[430]

1354. Any trade union, employers' organization or employer operating in the sector affected by a collective agreement may turn to the Administrative and Labour Court to oppose the Minister's resolution.

§8. Information on the Collective Agreement

1355. The employer is obliged to render assistance in the employees acquainting themselves with the collective agreement. The employer should forward a copy of the collective agreement to each employee, whose duty it is to carry out its provisions, as well as to trade union's workplace representatives.

§9. Notification and Registration Requirement

1356. The parties to the collective agreement must jointly send it to the Minister in charge for registration within thirty days following the date of conclusion and will supply the related data and information required (hereinafter referred to collectively as 'notification requirement').

1357. In accordance with the instructions contained above, the parties also convey a notification if the collective agreement is:

(a) amended;
(b) terminated;
(c) cancelled.

1358. The Minister in charge is responsible to register the concluded collective agreements.

§10. Transfer of Employment upon the Transfer of Enterprise and the Collective Agreement

1359. In the case of transfer of employment upon the transfer of enterprise, the receiving employer is required to maintain the working conditions specified in the collective agreement covering the employment relationship existing at the time of transfer for a period of one year after the date of transfer. This obligation will not apply to the employer if the collective agreement expires within one year after the

430. L. FULTON (2013) Worker Representation in Europe. Labour Research Department and ETUI. Produced with the assistance of the SEEurope Network, online publication available at, http://www.worker-participation.eu/National-Industrial-Relations (26 Jul. 2023).

date of transfer, or if the employment relationship is covered by a collective agreement after the date of transfer.[431]

431. CSÉFFÁN József, A munka törvénykönyve és magyarázata, Szeged: Szegedi Rendezvényszervező Kft., 2023.

Chapter 5. Strikes, Lock-Outs and Other Legal Forms of Industrial Actions

1360. The Fundamental Law of Hungary lays down the right of any citizen to strike. Act VII of 1989 provides for the conditions for exercising this basic right.[432]

§1. The Aim of a Strike

1361. According to the above-mentioned legislation, every worker in Hungary has the right to strike. This is not attached to trade union membership. According to Article 1 of the Act, a worker's legal due is his/her right to strike – under the conditions determined in this Law – in order to secure his/her economic and social interests. However, it is the legal due of trade unions to initiate a solidarity strike.[433]

1362. Participation in a strike is voluntary; nobody can be forced to participate in it or to stay away from a strike. No coercive measures aimed at stopping a strike shall be used against workers participating in a lawful strike.

1363. Earlier, the obligation of the employer and employees to cooperate within the frame of employment relations was mentioned. This obligation is reflected in the Act on strikes. The Act provides for employers and employees to cooperate in exercising their right to strike. Violation of the right to strike is forbidden.[434]

§2. Legality of a Strike

I. The Precondition of a Strike

1364. According to the Hungarian legislation, a strike can be initiated if:

(a) reconciliation procedures on the debated issue did not bring about any results within seven days; or
(b) reconciliation procedures did not take place for reasons the initiator of the strike cannot be blamed for.

1365. In the case of a solidarity strike, a previous conciliation can be omitted. If it cannot be determined who is the employer concerned in the strike demands, the Minister in charge within five days appoints its representative to participate in the

432. Zsuzsa RINDT (2012) Amended strike law one year on, https://www.eurofound.europa.eu/publications/article/2012/amended-strike-law-one-year-on (26 Jul. 2023).
433. BERKI Erzsébet: A sztrájkok hazai gyakorlata. In: Halmos Csaba (szerk): Sztrájkjog Magyarországon. Budapest, Complex, 2010. pp. 145–155.
434. RADNAY József, 'A magyar sztrájk-törvény', Magyar Jog Vol. 37 No. 12, 1990. pp. 993–1006.

reconciliation procedures. If the strike concerns more than one employer, the employers, on request, are obliged to appoint their representatives.[435]

1366. A strike can be organized once, even during the period of conciliation procedures taking place, but it cannot be for longer than two hours.

II. Prohibition and Limitations of a Strike

1367. A strike in Hungary is illegal if:

(a) it is not initiated to defend the workers' social and economic interests;
(b) it has omitted the reconciliation procedures;
(c) the aim of the strike is anti-constitutional;
(d) it is organized in opposition to any individual measure or default of the employer whereas the decision on changing it comes within the jurisdiction of the Courts;
(e) it is organized during the effective period of the collective agreement in order to change the arrangements fixed in the collective agreement;
(f) it would directly and seriously threaten human life, health, security and the environment or hinder the prevention of elementary damage.

1368. No strike can be organized at institutions of the judiciary, military forces and the police organizations. The right to strike can be exercised in the organs of state administration according to specific rules laid down in an agreement between the Government and the trade unions concerned.

1369. If working for an employer whose products or services meet society's basic requirements, i.e., especially in the field of public transport and telecommunication, the supply of electricity, water, gas and other forms of energy, the right to strike can only be exercised if it does not restrain the performance of yet satisfactory services. This condition must be determined prior to the strike.[436]

III. Conditions of Minimum Service

1370. Hungary's strike law was amended in December 2010 after a long debate among political parties and after a series of strikes in 2009 and January 2010, in particular at a number of public companies in the public transport sector.

435. Strikes in Hungary: background summary (2019), https://www.etui.org/covid-social-impact/hungary/strikes-in-hungary-background-summary-update-march-2019 (26 Jul. 2023).
436. BERKI Erzsébet, 'Kísérlet néhány, a sztrájkokkal kapcsolatos illúzió eloszlatására', Munkaügyi Szemle Vol. 54, No. 1, 2010. pp. 42–51.

1371. The employers wanted a more detailed definition of the 'minimum services' that should be guaranteed by potential strikers, and a requirement that they set out clearly when a proposed strike will start and finish.

1372. As it stood, industrial action legislation required the parties involved to cooperate on the terms and conditions of minimum services that should be put in place during strikes for utilities such as electricity, gas, water supply, public transport and communication. 'Minimum services' were not, however, clearly defined. Where the parties could agree, a minimum service was provided; if not, there were limited or no services.

1373. Under the modification of the Strike Act (*see* in Act CLXXVIII of 2010), industrial action such as strikes will only be lawful if employers and trade unions agree in advance on the minimum level of services to be provided. Should they fail to agree, the Court in charge will have the final say.[437]

1374. The level of service deemed sufficient and the related requirements may be defined by an act of Parliament. If not governed by an act of Parliament, the level of service deemed sufficient and the related requirements shall be agreed upon previously, during the pre-strike negotiations.

1375. In this case, the strike may be carried out if the parties concluded the agreement, or failing this, if the level of service deemed sufficient and the related requirements had been determined by final decision of the court hearing labour disputes, acting on the request of either of the parties.

1376. An interested party can request the Administrative and Labour Court to decide on the question of legality or illegality of a strike. The Court decides within five days, in non-legal proceedings, and if needed after hearing the parties. Appealing against the decision is possible. The court of the second instance adopts a decision within five working days.[438]

§3. Reconciliation Procedure

1377. The parties are obliged to participate in reconciliation procedures within seven days, except if these can be omitted according to the provisions of the Act. Owing to the obligation of cooperation, the parties are obliged to continue conciliation to settle the issue debated during the period of strike and they have to provide for the protection of person and property.

---

437. Zsuzsa RINDT (2012) Amended strike law one year on, https://www.eurofound.europa.eu/publications/article/2012/amended-strike-law-one-year-on (26 Jul. 2023).
438. BERKI Erzsébet, 'Az elégséges szolgáltatás problémája', Pécsi Munkajogi Közlemények Vol. 2 No. 1, 2009.

§4. THE LEGAL POSITION OF THE WORKER

1378. Initiating a strike and participation in a strike cannot be considered as disregarding the obligation arising from employment; no measures can be applied against an employee as a consequence of him/her striking. The same rights originating from employment are due to workers who participate in a lawful strike. However, unless agreed otherwise, a worker is not entitled to pay or other benefits from employment for those working hours missed as a consequence of the strike.[439]

439. HAJDÚ József, IEL Labour Law, Hungary, Wolters Kluwer, Kluwer Law Online, 2019. https://kluwerlawonline.com/Manuals/Corporate+Acquisitions+and+Mergers/705 (26 Jul. 2023).

Chapter 6. Settlement of Industrial Disputes and Protection of Vital Needs

§1. The Concept of Collective Labour Disputes

1379. Disputes qualify as collective labour disputes if they arise in connection with collective labour relations between the employer and trade union or works' council or employers' organization.

1380. One can distinguish – as mentioned above – between two categories of the collective labour disputes. On the one hand, there are disputes arising as a result of a conflict of interests (non-legal disputes); on the other hand, there are disputes arising from the violation or non-performance of rights or obligations, or disputes on the existence or non-existence of certain rights or obligations (collective legal law disputes).

1381. The HLC (sections 291–292) determines two kinds of conciliation procedures for solving collective labour disputes: (A) conciliation [committee] (N.B.: the works agreement or the collective agreement may contain provisions for a standing committee as well) and (B) arbitration.

§2. Conciliation Committee

1382. The conciliation committee will be composed of an equal number of members delegated by the employer and the works' council or trade union, and an independent chairman.

1383. The chairman will consult with the members delegated by both parties on an ongoing basis, and will draw up an executive summary upon conclusion of the conciliation process which contains the argument of the members and the outcome of the procedure. The justified expenses incurred in connection with the committee's proceedings will be borne by the employer.

1384. The employer and the works' council or the trade union may agree in writing in advance to abide by the decision of the committee, in which case the committee's decision will be considered to be binding. In the case of a tie vote, the chairperson's vote will be decisive.

§3. Arbitration

1385. The disputes arising in connection with:

(a) the justified expenses incurred in connection with the election and operation of the works' council; and
(b) appropriation of welfare funds will be decided by an arbitrator.

1386. The decision of the arbitrator is binding upon the parties. In the absence of agreement between the parties, the arbitrator will be chosen by random selection from among the persons nominated by the parties.

1387. During the proceedings of the committee or the arbitrator, the parties shall not engage in any conduct aiming to frustrate the agreement or the implementation of the decision.

§4. Labour Mediation and Arbitration Service

1388. To promote an effective and quick resolution of industrial disputes of interests, the state and the social partners agreed to establish the Labour Mediation and Arbitration Service (in Hungarian: Munkaügyi Közvetítői és Döntőbírói Szolgálat, MKDSZ) in 1996. The role of the MKDSZ was to facilitate the peaceful resolution of collective interest related industrial (non-legal) disputes between employer(s) and employees' representatives by providing third party mediation and arbitration. The MKDSZ, however, has been barred to provide third-party participation in individual legal disputes and in collective disputes over statutory rights, namely in legal disputes. The MKDSZ was an independent organization. The arbitrators and mediators were elected every five years by the national tripartite body. The functioning of the MKDSZ was covered by the state. MKDSZ has two full-time employees: a director and a secretary. The secretary performed the administrative and management activities.[440]

1389. Life after the MKDSZ: new ADR service launched in Hungary – MTVSZ (Labour Advisory and Dispute Settlement Service). As it was already mentioned, to promote collective bargaining in general, and an effective and quick resolution of industrial disputes of interests more concretely, the state and the social partners had established the MKDSZ in 1996, but its operation ended in 2015. In place of the MKDSZ, a new independent, modernized, more flexible, decentralized alternative dispute resolution service (Munkaügyi Tanácsadó és Vitarendező Szolgálat, MTVSZ) was created in 2016 in order to promote an effective, peaceful and quick resolution of industrial disputes of interests. Services of MTVSZ are available for all trade unions, works' councils and employers (and employers' associations).[441] The members of the Service are experienced, independent, specialized labour lawyers who are selected by the social partners along professional criteria (based on merit and expertise).[442] The MTVSZ also maintains a separate open list of other experts, mediators.

---

440. LUX Judit, Alternatív vitarendezés régen és most, Munkaügyi Szemle 2019/május, https://www.munkaugyiszemle.hu/alternativ-vitarendezes-regen-es-most (26 Jul. 2023).
441. RÁCZ Zoltán (2015): Quo uadis, MKDSZ? Az alternatív vitarendezés helyzete a munkajog területén Publicationes Universitatis Miskolcinensis Sectio Juridica et Politica, Tomus XXXIII, Miskolci Egyetem, Miskolc.
442. BANKÓ, Zoltán; KUN, Attila; Szabó, Imre Szilárd (2019): A munkaügyi tanácsadó és vitarendező szolgálat; In: Glavanits Judit (ed.): A gazdasági jogalkotás aktuális kérdései, Budapest; Pécs: Dialóg Campus Kiadó, 141–152.

1390. The services of the MTVSZ are free of charge and widespread, including consultancy, conciliation, negotiation, mediation and arbitration (it is to be noted that arbitration is still compulsory in certain – very limited – cases listed by the Labour Code). MTVSZ aims to promote collective bargaining and peaceful industrial relations and it also aims to function as a prominent 'think-thank' in collective bargaining and in collective labour law. The legal background of the MTVSZ is the Government Decree 320/2014. (XII. 13.). The Central Hungary region of the MTVSZ is operated by the government, while in the six other regions of the country, MTVSZ is operated by an independent consortium of social partners (including the National Federation of Workers' Councils and Confederation of Unions of Professionals, together with four employer organizations of the SME sector).[443]

1391. Besides large companies, the MTVSZ aims to provide services also for small- and medium-sized companies (SMEs). At the same time, the activities of the ADR Service by MTVSZ extend to private as well as public sector employment (however, most of the cases are from the private sector). It should be noted that the ADR Service focusses exclusively on collective (industrial) labour conflicts, therefore individual and/or labour law (rights-based) disputes, and legal advice[444] in general are excluded from its scope.

1392. The main goals of MTVSZ are the following: to improve the functioning of collective labour relations in Hungary, to help the parties to conclude mutually beneficial collective agreements, to support the parties' communication, to prevent industrial and labour disputes, to resolve such disputes. In sum, MTVSZ is a countrywide, unified, professionally independent support system for the prevention and resolution of collective labour disputes.

1393. The majority of the cases brought before the MTVSZ are about consultancy on collective labour law issues, but it is not uncommon that – in the spirit of interchangeability of procedures and trust-building – after the advice, the Service (and the given member of the Service) can also serve in further proceedings (conciliation, mediation). In terms of their subject matter, cases are varied, covering a wide range of conflicts of interests along the lines of collective labour law.[445]

1394. It is important to underline that, fully in line with the original mission of the MTVSZ, most of the procedures (cases) are related to the support, review and interpretation of collective bargaining agreements (and works agreements). In many cases, the counselling procedures are aimed at understanding legal interpretations and the concrete practical, interest-driven realization of the possibilities provided by the law, in which cases the 'legal thinking' of the members proved to be extremely useful and effective (in contrast, the former MKDSZ was not focused on labour law

443. LUX Judit Mi is az az MTVSZ, Munkaügyi Szemle, 2021. május, https://www.munkaugyiszemle.hu/mi-az-az-mtvsz (26 Jul. 2023).
444. MTVSZ is competent only in interest-disputes (in a broad sense), but no legal advice is provided.
445. BERKE Gyula – BANKÓ Zoltán – SZABÓ Imre Szilárd (2017): Prevenció. A tanácsadás lehetősége a Munkaügyi Tanácsadó és Vitarendező Szolgálat keretében. HVG- ORAC, Budapest.

expertise, as it was more oriented on the method of mediation). In general, it can be said that the parties are often not precisely aware of the relevant legislation (or the room for manoeuvre provided by the law for bargaining), so often the legal exploration and situation-assessment alone can promote the resolution of disputed situations and the conclusion of an agreement. Thus, it was not primarily genuine dispute settlement (such as mediation) that flourished during this period, but rather the involvement of the professional members of the MTVSZ into the management of professional insecurities. It is important for the Service to try to match the real needs of industrial relations' players, and it seems that this is mostly consultancy. It is important to emphasize that members of the Service (mostly university professors and attorneys) shall act in a specific, independent role within the Service (not thinking, for example, as a private 'lawyer'), advocating for the amicable settlement of requests received (counselling, etc.) rather than primarily seeking redress.

1395. In addition to collective bargaining matters, diversified issues of 'labour relations' in the broadest sense were touched upon by the procedures, such as (but not limited to): the establishment and development of training systems; changes in working conditions in connection with transfer of undertakings; dress codes; the consequences of sham, bogus legal relationships; issues related to the election of a works' councils; the possibility and organization of overtime work in certain professions; the procedure for the formation of occupational health and safety (OHS) representation bodies; specific controversies surrounding the right to strike, etc.

1396. On the one hand, the main strengths of the MTVSZ are the following. First, the regional embeddedness and proximity of the Service and the apparent professional reputation, independency and labour law expertise of the members of the Service seems to be a huge added value. Second, the (informal, but apparent) linkage of MTVSZ to local universities' labour law departments helps to build a close and stable relationship with local industrial relations' players and contributes to the local visibility and recognition of the Service and boosts the 'channelling' and 'involvement' of cases, as well as ensuring independence, credibility and professionalism. Third, the operational structure of MTVSZ is embedded into the fabric of social partnership – 'outsourced' by the state. The fact that the MTVSZ is not part of the state administration but an autonomous body rooted in social partnership has advantages (e.g., self-organization, flexibility, full professional independence, responsiveness etc.) as well as disadvantages (e.g., lack of background administrative support, the need for constant internal coordination between consortium partners, earmarked and limited funding, etc.). Fourth, the Service is able to flexibly handle a substantially full range of collective disputes arising in the field of collective labour law and industrial relations with its services. Fifth, MTVSZ aims (and also seems) to become the central focal point, professional 'think-tank' and 'networking' platform in the field of industrial relations (with its conferences, forums, publications, trainings, extensive professional networks, constructive partnerships with other organizations active in industrial relations, etc.).

1397. On the other hand, the main weaknesses and challenges of the MTVSZ are the following. First, the reputation of the Service is to be surely strengthened (as a relatively new entity, without much resources for PR, popularization is a challenge). Second, the lack of legal personality of the Service and the lack of its explicit recognition ('institutionalization') in labour law (e.g., the Labour Code does not mention MTVSZ) is not helpful. As we have already mentioned, the wording of the HLC is very laconic about the matter of labour disputes and it does not offer effective 'channelling' mechanisms towards ADR (e.g., a wider range of cases of compulsory arbitration / mediation and their normative 'connection' to the Service could be justified, desirable and helpful). Third, MTVSZ has a relatively fragmented structure and coordination among the numerous consortium partners (social partners), regional units is not an easy task, rendering it difficult to form a uniform image, appearance, quick response, administration, and 'identification' of the Service by lay people, etc. Fourth, the shallow practical contours of the concept of 'conflict of interest' (and its frequent confusion and combination with legal disputes) 46 often makes it difficult to delineate the potential scope of authority of the Service. Fifth, the project-based logic of the MTVSZ creates an unfavourable atmosphere of ambiguity and temporariness, making long-term planning extremely difficult.

MTVSZ certainly aims to fill a gap in the sense that institutional promotion of collective bargaining in Hungary is rather weak and inadequate. Furthermore, the generally flexible, employer-friendly nature of labour law offers not much motivation for employers to bargain collectively.[446,447]

§5. Collective Legal Labour Disputes

1398. Legal labour disputes of a collective nature can be classified into several groups:

(a) a legal dispute concerning the activities of trade unions can take place on whether an employer or some state organ violates the rights of the trade union or works' council as defined in the HLC;
(b) a legal dispute can arise in connection with collective negotiations and/or a collective agreement or works agreement on the question:
   - whether a given negotiating party, either the works' council, trade union or the employer's representative is entitled to negotiate (e.g., whether it qualifies as an organ representing interests, or whether it is representative in the given case);
   - whether the collective agreement is valid as to its contents or, from a formal point of view, whether it subsists or not;

446. KUN, Attila (2019): Hungary: Collective Bargaining in Labour Law Regimes. In: LIUKKUNEN Ulla (ed.), Collective Bargaining in Labour Law Regimes, Cham: Springer International Publishing, pp. 333--356 Ch. 12. (2019) (Ius Comparation – Global Studies in Comparative Law 2214-6881; 32).
447. HAJDÚ, József; KUN, Attila Alternative Dispute Resolution in Disputes Relating to Labour Law in Hungary In: Olivieri, Antonello; Fuiano, Mario Pio (eds) Alternative labour dispute resolutions: A Collection of Comparative Studies Bari, Olaszország: Cacucci Editore (2020) 628 pp. 569–596.

   - whether termination of the collective agreement by notice conforms to the legal rules;

(c) a legal dispute concerning the right of an employee to participate can arise if:
   - the rules prescribed for the works' council are violated;
   - the employee finds that he/she has prejudicially been left out of the list of the electors against the rules, or he/she has been unlawfully prevented from participating in the election;
   - the employer violates any rights ensured to the works' council, either by not ensuring the necessary conditions of the contract of employment as prescribed by the legal rules, or by not performing in questions falling within the competence of the works' council, such as the obligation to obtain joint decisions, consent, requesting an opinion or information as laid down in these cases.

(d) in connection with exercising the right to strike, a legal dispute can arise on questions of:
   - whether the strike serves the purpose as defined in the relevant legal rule, that is the protection and/or the enforcement of employees' economic and social rights, and especially whether it might qualify as a political strike;
   - whether the strike is organized by an entity entitled thereto (this right, according to the legal rule, is only ascribed to trade unions or to groups of employees) and whether it is organized on a voluntary basis;
   - whether or not, in the given climate or branch, the strike is prohibited or whether or not it jeopardizes the functioning of important public utilities.

1399. The decision falls finally within the competence of the Administrative and Labour Court. In some cases, the Code lays down that conciliation procedures need to be initiated in advance. However, there is no general rule in this field. According to the authors' opinion, the party who wants to go to court is obliged to initiate conciliation procedures. (In the case of individual labour disputes, the Code provides for compulsory conciliation procedures.)[448]

448. FERENC Jácint – GÖNDÖR Éva – GYULAVÁRI Tamás – KÁRTYÁS Gábor, Munkajogi alapismeretek, Budapest: ELTE Kiadó, 2013. pp. 204–206.

Selected Bibliography

ANTALÓCZY Adrienn, A próbamunka tilos, de akkor mit szabad? https://ecocreative.hu/rovid-cikkek/cikkek/a-probamunka-tilos-de-akkor-mit-szabad/.

ARANY TÓTH Mariann, A munkavállaló emberi méltóságának védelme a munkaviszonyban, http://www.mjsz.uni-miskolc.hu/201101/10_aranytothmariann.pdf.

ÁRVA Zsuzsanna, Nagykommentár Magyarország Alaptörvényéhez, Budapest, Wolters Kluwer, 2022.

BANKÓ Zoltán, BERKE Gyula, KISS György, SZŐKE Gergely László Nagykommentár a munka törvénykönyvéhez, Wolters Kluwer, Budapest 2019.

BANKÓ, Zoltán; KUN, Attila; SZABÓ, Imre Szilárd (2019): A munkaügyi tanácsadó és vitarendező szolgálat; In: Glavanits Judit (ed.): A gazdasági jogalkotás aktuális kérdései, Budapest; Pécs: Dialóg Campus Kiadó.

BERKE Gyula – BANKÓ Zoltán – SZABÓ Imre Szilárd (2017): Prevenció. A tanácsadás lehetősége a Munkaügyi Tanácsadó és Vitarendező Szolgálat keretében. HVG– ORAC, Budapest.

BERKI Erzsébet: A sztrájkok hazai gyakorlata. In: Halmos Csaba (szerk): Sztrájkjog Magyarországon. Budapest, Complex, 2010.

BERKI Erzsébet, 'Kísérlet néhány, a sztrájkokkal kapcsolatos illúzió eloszlatására', Munkaügyi Szemle Vol. 54, No. 1, 2010.

BLUTMAN László Az Európai Unió joga a gyakorlatban – a Brexit után, Orac Kiadó, Budapest, 2020.

Levente CSENGERY (2020) The Equal Treatment Authority Will Be Abolished from 1 January 2021; https://ceelegalmatters.com/hungary/15413-the-equal-treatment-authority-will-be-abolished-from-1-january-2021.

CSÉFFÁN József, A munka törvénykönyve és magyarázata, Szeged: Szegedi Rendezvényszervező Kft., 2023.

CZUGLERNÉ IVÁNY Judit, MÉLYPATAKI Gábor (2021) Érdekképviseletek a munkajogban, https://ijoten.hu/szocikk/erdekkepviseletek-a-munkajogban.

DOBOSI Kinga (2023) Létszámleépítés és a felmondás indokolása, https://ado.hu/munkaugyek/letszamleepites-es-a-felmondas-indokolasa/.

DUDÁS Katalin – GYULAVÁRI Tamás – HORVÁTH István – HŐS Nikolett– KULISITY Mária – HUNGLER Sára – KÁRTYÁS Gábor – KUN Attila – PETROVICS Zoltán – RÁCZ Réka, Munkajog – V. átdolgozott kiadás, Budapest: ELTE Eötvös Kiadó, 2019.

EMBER Alex, Az üzemi baleset, Szeged: Pólay Alapítvány, 2013.

Selected Bibliography

FERENCZ Jácint – GÖNDÖR Éva – GYULAVÁRI Tamás – KÁRTYÁS Gábor, Munkajogi alapismeretek, Budapest: ELTE Kiadó, 2013.
FERENCZ Jácint, GYULAVÁRI Tamás, KÁRTYÁS Gábor, GÖNDÖR Éva, Munkajogi Alapismeretek, ELTE Eötvös Kiadó Kft., 2020.
L. FULTON (2013) Worker representation in Europe. Labour Research Department and ETUI. Produced with the assistance of the SEEurope Network, online publication available at http://www.worker-participation.eu/National-Industrial-Relations.
FÜLÖP Anna (2021) Új szövetkezeti formában dolgozhatnak a kisgyermekkel otthon maradó szülők; https://ado.hu/munkaugyek/uj-szovetkezeti-formaban-dolgozhatnak-a-kisgyermekkel-otthon-marado-szulok/.
GÁL, Róbert Iván: Pensioner cooperatives combine work and retirement in Hungary, ESPN Flash Report 2018/9.
Dániel GERA: New Law on Employment of Foreign Workers in Hungary (2023) https://www.schoenherr.eu/content/new-law-on-employment-of-foreign-workers-in-hungary/.
GERSE Márton (2019) Kollektív szerződés a munkajogban https://ado.hu/munkaugyek/kollektiv-szerzodes-a-munkajogban/.
GERSE Márton (2023) Külföldi munkavállalók magyarországi foglalkoztatása a gyakorlatban; https://jogaszvilag.hu/cegvilag/kulfoldi-munkavallalok-magyarorszagi-foglalkoztatasa-a-gyakorlatban/.
Tamás GYULAVÁRI-Éva GELLÉRNÉ LUKÁCS-Anita KADERJÁK-Kata NAGY (2021) European Semester 2020–2021, country fiche on disability equality-Hungary.
HAJDU-DUDÁS Mária (2022) Így óvhatja cégügyeit a konkurenciától: versenytilalmi megállapodás korlátok között https://adozona.hu/munkajog/Igy_ovhatja_cegugyeit_a_konkurenciatol_vers_ZTN02A.
HAJDÚ József – KUN Attila (eds.), Munkajog I-II., Budapest: Patrocinium, 2012.
József HAJDÚ The European Works Council legislation in transition, Forum in. Acta Juridica et Politica, Szeged 2013.
József HAJDÚ The Legal Protection of Unemployed Young People in Hungary in. Morley Gunderson; Francesca Fazio (eds.): Tackling Youth Unemployment. Newcastle: Cambridge Scholars Publishing, 2014. pp. 27–55. (ADAPT labour studies book-series.).
József HAJDÚ: Atypical Employment Relationships in the New Hungarian Labour Code in. Przyszlosc Prawa Pracy, Liber Amicorum Profesora Michala Sewerynskiego, ed. Zbigniew Hajn & Dagmara Skupien, Uniwersitet Lodzki, Lodz 2015.
József HAJDÚ The basic principles of the Hungarian labour law (2015) http://acta.bibl.u-szeged.hu/45286/1/juridpol_078_394-404.pdf.
József HAJDÚ The right to Social Security in the Hungarian Fundamental Law in. The right to Social Security in the Constitutions of the World: Broadening the moral and legal space for social justice; Alexandre Egorov and Marcin Wujczyk (eds), International Labour Organization, 2016.
HAJDÚ József: Az Alaptörvény munkajogi tartalmú cikkeiről In: Balogh Elemér (szerk.) Számadás az Alaptörvényről: Tanulmányok a Szegedi Tudományegyetem Állam– és Jogtudományi Kara oktatóinak tollából. Budapest: Magyar Közlöny Lap– és Könyvkiadó, 2016.

HAJDÚ József A közérdekű nyugdíjas szövetkezetekről: pro és kontra In: Homoki-Nagy Mária, Karsai Krisztina, Fantoly Zsanett, Juhász Zsuzsanna, Szomora Zsolt, Gál Andor (szerk.) Ünnepi kötet dr. Nagy Ferenc egyetemi tanár 70. születésnapjára. 1026 p. Szeged: Szegedi Tudományegyetem Állam– és Jogtudományi Kar, 2018. pp. 369–381. (Acta Universitatis Szegediensis. Acta Juridica et Politica; Tom. 81.).

HAJDÚ József Transformation of the Hungarian Disability Pension: Possession and Legitimate Expectations of Social Security Rights, under the European Convention of Human Rights In: Auer Ádám, Berke Gyula, György István, Hazafi Zoltán (szerk.) Ünnepi kötet a 65 éves Kiss György tiszteletére 909 p. Dialóg Campus Kiadó, Budapest, 2018.

József, HAJDÚ Part V. Incapacity to Work In: József, Hajdú; Attila, Kun (szerk.) Hungary: International Encyclopaedia for Social Security Law Alphen aan den Rijn, Hollandia: Kluwer Law International, 2019.

HAJDÚ József, IEL Labour Law, Hungary, Wolters Kluwer, Kluwer Law Online, 2019.

HAJDÚ, József; KUN, Attila Alternative Dispute Resolution in Disputes Relating to Labour Law in Hungary In: Olivieri, Antonello; Fuiano, Mario Pio (eds.) Alternative labour dispute resolutions: A Collection of Comparative Studies Bari, Olaszország: Cacucci Editore, 2020.

HAJDÚ, József Véleménynyilvánítási szabadság a munkahelyen különös tekintettel a visszaélést bejelentők védelmére In: Pál, Lajos (szerk.) A véleménynyilvánítás szabadsága és korlátai a munkajogviszonyban: A Magyar Munkajogi Társaság 2021. június 23-i vitaülésén elhangzott előadások, hozzászólások Budapest, Magyarország: HVG-ORAC, 2022.

HAJDÚ, József Right to Work and Partial Unemployment Based on the Reflection of the ECSR on COVID-19 In: Ristivojević, Branislav (szerk.) Harmonizacija srpskog i mađarskog prava sa pravom Evropske unije = A szerb és a magyar jog harmonizációja az Európai Unió jogával = Harmonisation of Serbian and Hungarian Law with the European Union Law Újvidék, Szerbia: Újvidéki Jogtudományi Kar, Kiadói Központ (2022).

HALMAI, Gábor – TÓTH Gábor Attila, Emberi jogok, Budapest: Osiris Kiadó, 2008.

HANTI Erzsébet, Az Európai Uniós munkaügyi irányelvek és érvényesítésük a hazai kollektív tárgyalásos gyakorlatban Kézikönyv, Budapest: Vasas-Köz Nyomda, 2003.

HEGYI Lívia A munkáltató személyében bekövetkező változás (munkáltatói jogutódlás), Független Szakszervezetek Demokratikus Ligája (LIGA Szakszervezetek), Budapest, 2021;

https://www.jogpontok.hu/download/A_munkaltato_szemelyeben_bek%C3%B6vetkezo_valtozas.pdf.

HORVÁTH István, Az új munka törvénykönyve, Budapest: Vezinfó Kiadó és Tanácsadó Kft. 2012.

HORVÁTH István – Szladovnyik Krisztina: Szigorúan ellenőrzött viszonyok II. Adó Szaklap 2021/7.

Yves JORENS, Cross-Border EU Employment and its Enforcement (2022), Springer, Switzerland.

JUHÁSZ Gábor: A gazdasági és szociális jogok védelme az Alkotmányban és az Alaptörvényben, Fundamentum 2012. évi 1. szám.

KECSKÉS László, EU-jog és jogharmonizáció, Budapest, HVG-Orac, 2011.

Ádám KÉRI (2016) Diákmunka szeptembertől: így működhet majd az iskolaszövetkezet, http://adozona.hu/munkajog/Igy_dolgozhatnak_a_diakok_szeptembertol_mut_D5MIKK.

KISS Barnabás, Alkotmányjogi alapismeretek, Szeged: Pólay Elemér Alapítvány, 2012.

KISS György, Az Európai Unió munkajoga, Budapest: Osiris Kiadó, 2003.

KISS György (ed.) Munkajog Ludovika Egyetemi Kiadó, Budapest, 2020.

KOLOS KARDKOVÁCS (ed.): Az új Munka törvénykönyvének magyarázata. (Explanation of the New Labour Code.) HVG Orac, Budapest, 2014.

KOZMA Anna – LŐRINCZ György – PÁL Lajos, A Munka Törvénykönyvének magyarázata, Budapest: HVG-Orac, 2020.

KUN Attila, 'Feketelisták' a munkaügyi hatóságok honlapjain. Fokozódó transzparencia a munkaerőpiacon?' Munkaügyi Szemle, Vol 51 No 3, 2007.

KUN Attila, 'Átrendeződés a kollektív munkajogban – szakszervezetek kontra üzemi tanácsok az új Mt. tükrében' in: Hagyomány és érték, Állam– és jogtudományi tanulmányok a Károli Gáspár Református Egyetem fennállásának 20. évfordulójára, Budapest: KRE ÁJK, 2013. pp. 304–315.

Tóth András, The New Hungarian Labour Code – Background, Conflicts, Compromises, Budapest: Friedrich Ebert Foundation, 2012.

KUN, Attila (2019): Hungary: Collective Bargaining in Labour Law Regimes. In: LIUKKUNEN Ulla (ed.), Collective Bargaining in Labour Law Regimes, Cham: Springer International Publishing, pp. 333–356 Chapter 12. (2019) (lus Comparation – Global Studies in Comparative Law 2214–6881; 32).

KRÉN, I. (2013), Hungary – labour relations and social dialogue: annual review 2013, Regional Project on Labour Relations and Social Dialogue, Friedrich-Ebert-Stiftung, Warsaw, available at http://library.fes.de/pdf-files/bueros/warschau/10436.pdf.

LAKI Mihály – NACSA Beáta – NEUMANN László, Az új Munka Törvénykönyvének hatása a munkavállalók és a munkáltatók közötti kapcsolatokra, Kutatási zárójelentés, Budapest: Magyar Tudományos Akadémia Közgazdaság– és Regionális Tudományi Kutatóközpont Közgazdaság-tudományi Intézet, 2013,

http://mek.oszk.hu/11400/11439/11439.pdf.

LEHOCZKYNÉ KOLLONAY, Csilla, 'Kezdeti lépések a foglalkoztatási diszkrimináció bírósági gyakorlatában' Fundamentum, Vol 2 No 4, 1998.

LŐRINCZ György, Az új Mt. hatálybalépése, az átmeneti rendelkezések, Budapest: HVG ORAC, 2012.

LUKÁCS Adrienn (2020) Adatvédelmi jog a munkaerőpiacon, https://eta.bibl.u-szeged.hu/3589/.

Adrienn LUKÁCS (2020) Protection of Employees' Right to Privacy and Right to Data Protection on Social Network Sites – with Special Regard to France and Hungary; https://www.academia.edu/104220380/Protection_of_Employees_Right_to_Privacy_and_Right_to_Data_Protection_on_Social_Network_Sites_with_Special_Regard_to_France_and_Hungary.

Adrienn LUKÁCS: Privacy at Work: the Regulation of Camera Surveillance in Hungarian Labour Law, Acta Universitatis George Bacovia – Juridica 6: (1).

Adrienn LUKÁCS: To Post, or Not to Post – That is the Question: Employee Monitoring and Employees' Right to Data Protection, Masaryk University Journal of Law And Technology 11: (2).

LUKÁCS Adrienn A főnök szeme mindent lát? Gondolatok a munkavállalók webkamerás ellenőrzéséről HVG-Orac Munkajog, 2022/2. lapszám, 14–19. o. https://munkajogilap.hu/a-fonok-szeme-mindent-lat-gondolatok-a-munkavallalok-webkameras-ellenorzeserol/.

LUX Judit, Alternatív vitarendezés régen és most, Munkaügyi Szemle 2019/május, https://www.munkaugyiszemle.hu/alternativ-vitarendezes-regen-es-most.

LUX Judit Mi is az MTVSZ, Munkaügyi Szemle, 2021. május, https://www.munkaugyiszemle.hu/mi-az-az-mtvsz.

MIHOLICS Tivadar, A munkaviszony megszüntetése III. http://munkajog.hu/rovatok/munkahely/a-munkaviszony-megszuntetese-iii.

Márta MOLNÁR BALOGHNÉ (2016) Az iskolaszövetkezeti munka tb-vonatkozásai http://ado.hu/rovatok/tb-nyugdij/az-iskolaszovetkezeti-munka-tb-vonatkozasai.

NÁDAS György, 'A kárfelelősség szabályainak változásairól' in. Kun Attila (ed.), Az új munka törvénykönyve dilemmái Acta Caroliensia Scientiarium Iuridico-Politicarum V. Budapest: KRE. 2013.

András PATYI-Balázs SCHANDA-András Zs. VARGA (eds) The Basic (Fundamental) Law of Hungary, A Commentary of the New Hungarian Constitution Clarus Press, 2015.

PETROVICS Zoltán, Az ágazati párbeszéd bizottságok és az Ágazati Részvételt Megállapító Bizottság, Jogélet, 2017/1. lapszám, 72–73. o. | 2017. December.

POZSÁR-SZENTMIKLÓSY Zoltán – SOMODY Bernadette, Alkotmányos alapok, Budapest: HVG-ORAC, 2012.

Tamás PRUGBERGER – Andrea SZŐLLŐS Employment Using Information Technology – Self-Employment or Employment, European Integration Studies, Volume 17, Number 1, 2021.

RÁCZ Zoltán, A gazdasági munkajog kollektív munkajogi részére vonatkozó szabályanyag az új Mt-ben http://www.uni-miskolc.hu/~wwwdeak/Collegium%20Doctorum%20Publikaciok/R%E1cz%20Zolt%E1n.pdf.

RÁCZ Zoltán (2015): Quo uadis, MKDSZ? Az alternatív vitarendezés helyzete a munkajog területén Publicationes Universitatis Miskolcinensis Sectio Juridica et Politica, Tomus XXXIII, Miskolci Egyetem, Miskolc.

RADNAY József, 'A magyar sztrájk-törvény', Magyar Jog Vol. 37 No. 12, 1990.

Zsuzsa RINDT (2012) Amended strike law one year on, https://www.eurofound.europa.eu/publications/article/2012/amended-strike-law-one-year-on.

SZABÓ, Lajos Tamás (2020) The Effect Of Public Work Programme In Hungary on Private Sector Wages, MNB Working Papers No. 7; https://www.mnb.hu/letoltes/mnb-wp-2020-7-final.pdf.

TÁLNÉ DR. MOLNÁR Erika (2018) A munkáltató kártérítési felelőssége összegszerűségének kérdései a bírói gyakorlat tükrében, Munkajog, 2018/4. pp. 52–58.

TÓTH Ferenc, A munkaügyi kapcsolatok rendszere, Budapest: Zsigmond Király Főiskola, 2003.

Selected Bibliography

TEPFENHÁRT Dóra (2022) A szolgálati találmányok szabályozásának vitás pontjai https://www.danubia.com/hu/szabadalom/a-szolgalati-talalmanyok-szabalyozasanak-vitas-pontjai/.

TÓTH András, The New Hungarian Labour Code – Background, Conflicts, Compromises, Budapest: Friedrich Ebert Foundation, 2012.

TÓTH Ferenc, A munkaügyi kapcsolatok rendszere, Budapest: Zsigmond Király Főiskola, 2003.

TRÓCSÁNYI László, 'Magyarország alaptörvényének létrejötte és az alaptörvény vitatott rendelkezései' Kommentár Vol 6 No 4, 2011.

TRÓCSÁNYI László – SCHANDA Balázs: Bevezetés az alkotmányjogba, Budapest: HVG-ORAC, 2012.

Judit WINDISCH (2016) Ki védi a diákot, ha nyáron dolgozni megy? http://hvg.hu/itthon/20160708_diakmunka_szovetkezet_veszelyek_tanacsok.

Index

The numbers here refer to paragraph numbers.

Index

Index

Index

www.ingramcontent.com/pod-product-compliance
Lightning Source LLC
Chambersburg PA
CBHW071422230926
51846CB00001B/109
* 9 7 8 9 4 0 3 5 2 3 2 8 6 *